The Bloomsbury Companion to Metaphysics

Bloomsbury Companions

The *Bloomsbury Companions* series is a major series of single volume companions to key research fields in the humanities aimed at postgraduate students, scholars and libraries. Each companion offers a comprehensive reference resource giving an overview of key topics, research areas, new directions and a manageable guide to beginning or developing research in the field. A distinctive feature of the series is that each companion provides practical guidance on advanced study and research in the field, including research methods and subject-specific resources.

Titles currently available in the series:

Aesthetics, edited by Anna Christina Ribeiro
Analytic Philosophy, edited by Barry Dainton and Howard Robinson
Aristotle, edited by Claudia Baracchi
Continental Philosophy, edited by John Ó Maoilearca and Beth Lord
Epistemology, edited by Andrew Cullison
Ethics, edited by Christian Miller
Existentialism, edited by Jack Reynolds, Felicity Joseph and Ashley Woodward
Hegel, edited by Allegra de Laurentiis and Jeffrey Edwards
Heidegger, edited by Francois Raffoul and Eric Sean Nelson
Hobbes, edited by S.A. Lloyd
Hume, edited by Alan Bailey and Dan O'Brien
Kant, edited by Gary Banham, Dennis Schulting and Nigel Hems
Leibniz, edited by Brandon C. Look
Locke, edited by S.-J. Savonious-Wroth, Paul Schuurman and Jonathan Walmsley
Philosophy of Language, edited by Manuel García-Carpintero and Max Kölbel
Philosophy of Mind, edited by James Garvey
Philosophy of Science, edited by Steven French and Juha Saatsi
Plato, edited by Gerald A. Press
Pragmatism, edited by Sami Pihlström
Socrates, edited by John Bussanich and Nicholas D. Smith
Spinoza, edited by Wiep van Bunge

The Bloomsbury Companion
to Metaphysics

Edited by
Neil A. Manson and Robert W. Barnard

Bloomsbury Academic
An imprint of Bloomsbury Publishing Plc

B L O O M S B U R Y
LONDON · NEW DELHI · NEW YORK · SYDNEY

Bloomsbury Academic

An imprint of Bloomsbury Publishing Plc

50 Bedford Square	1385 Broadway
London	New York
WC1B 3DP	NY 10018
UK	USA

www.bloomsbury.com

BLOOMSBURY and the Diana logo are trademarks of Bloomsbury Publishing Plc

First published in paperback 2015

First published as *The Continuum Companion to Metaphysics* 2012

© Neil A. Manson, Robert W. Barnard and Contributors 2015

Neil A. Manson and Robert W. Barnard have asserted their right under the Copyright, Designs and Patents Act, 1988, to be identified as the Editors of this work.

British Library Cataloguing-in-Publication Data
A catalogue record for this book is available from the British Library.

ISBN: PB: 978-1-4725-8585-1
ePDF: 978-1-4725-8586-8
ePub: 978-1-4725-8587-5

Library of Congress Cataloging-in-Publication Data
A catalog record for this book is available from the Library of Congress.

Typeset by Deanta Global Publishing Services, Chennai, India
Printed and bound in Great Britain

Contents

Contributors

Robert W. Barnard
Associate Professor
Department of Philosophy and
   Religion
University of Mississippi
University, MS, US

Stephan Blatti
Assistant Professor of Philosophy
Department of Philosophy
University of Memphis
Memphis, TN, US

Roy T. Cook
Associate Professor
Department of Philosophy
University of Minnesota
Minneapolis, MN, US

Matthew Davidson
Associate Professor
Department of Philosophy
California State University
San Bernardino, CA, US

Nikk Effingham
Lecturer
Department of Philosophy
University of Birmingham
Edgbaston, Birmingham, UK

David B. Hershenov
Professor
Department of Philosophy
State University of New York
Buffalo, NY, US

Neil A. Manson
Associate Professor
Department of Philosophy and
   Religion
The University of Mississippi
University, MS, US

Graham Oppy
Professor
Department of Philosophy
Monash University
Melbourne, VIC, AU

Thomas W. Polger
Associate Professor
Department of Philosophy
University of Cincinnati
Cincinnati, OH, US

Tony Roy
Professor
Department of Philosophy
California State University
San Bernardino, CA, US

Amie L. Thomasson
Professor
Department of Philosophy
University of Miami
Miami, FL, US

Kevin Timpe
Associate Professor
Department of Philosophy
Northwest Nazarene University
Nampa, ID, US

D. Gene Witmer
Associate Professor
Department of Philosophy
University of Florida
Gainesville, FL, US

Introduction

Robert W. Barnard

Metaphysics is a curious discipline, if it counts as a single discipline at all. It is hard to point to anything narrower than the nature of reality as the special subject of metaphysics. Within philosophy, ethics and epistemology are more unified and coherent; each focuses on a handful of easily recognized central themes. Logic is narrower still. This situation is complicated by the fact that there is a commonly held picture of "metaphysics" that is different from that of the philosophers. Witness that in many popular bookstores, the "Metaphysics" shelf might include some philosophy books, but will almost certainly include tomes on the powers of crystals, the nature and role of angels, the foibles or achievements of ancient astronauts, and perhaps some works on eastern religion. The bedtime story told to young philosophers is that *The Metaphysics* was what the editors of Aristotle's work had left over and put on the shelf next to his works on nature ("meta-" means "beyond" or "after"). So, from the beginning, metaphysics has been the catch-all category for leftover, mysterious, supernatural, and sometimes off-the-wall speculations. But if you are reading this volume, you probably already know that this is not what most philosophers mean by metaphysics.

The history of philosophy can help us narrow our interest; it has collected a more or less specific set of questions under the heading of metaphysics. In some cases these questions seem scientific or quasi-scientific—for example, how consciousness is related to the brain. More often, these questions are about the ultimate nature of things, including not just how things are, but how they might or must be and how they relate to one another. The centrality of such questions can be illustrated with a thumbnail sketch of the history of metaphysics.

The very first western philosophers were easily recognized as metaphysicians. Thales of Miletus is best known for his attempt to explain the experienced world by assuming that reality consisted of nothing more than various states of water—how the world is and how it might be with respect to water. Parmenides denied the reality of change; reality was a big lump of being. Democritus held that reality comprised various minute and un-cuttable bits (atoms) that were falling through the void, but regularly combined to form familiar complex macroscopic objects. Plato and Aristotle too were both a part of this tradition of trying to offer an account of the nature of reality.

Much of medieval philosophy adapted the arguments of the ancients in an attempt to offer an account of a reality that included God. As a result, metaphysics needed to be able to offer accounts of God's nature and the nature of creation, and even arguments for why the universe must include God. Though not an innovation, in such a domain the categories of possibility, necessity, and impossibility play an important theoretical role, as does the notion of identity. Is God limited? Is God one or many? Could there be an infinite regress of causes? Here, theories often turned on what the universe could possibly be like, not how it actually was.

Worrying about how things might be leads one to worry that they might not be as they seem. So, the fascination of philosophers in the modern period with epistemology is a complement to the metaphysician's fascination with the nature of reality and with what is possible. While the modern period is usually thought of as dominated by epistemic concerns, it was Descartes who first made explicit the problem of the relationship between the mind and the body. Leibniz postulated the domain of possible worlds to explain the rational choices of God; he also populated the universe with monads—independently existing minds operating in perfect harmony with one another—in an attempt to avoid the mind–body problem. Likewise, the problems of personal identity and the persistence of objects through time—notably articulated by Locke—assume their modern form in the critiques of substance and causality offered by Berkeley and Hume. Kant showed the connection between how experience is conceptualized and what entities might or must exist, but also defined a theoretical domain in which God and human freedom alike were understood to be separate from the realm of nature and science.

One by-product of Kant's critical philosophy was that it privileged the mind in a sufficiently strong way that it suggested a way for the universe to be essentially mental. Following Hegel, many came to think just that. And for many, it is the rejection of Hegelian idealism that marks the beginnings of twentieth-century Anglophone analytic philosophy. The early analytic philosophers tended toward unapologetic mind-independent realism about the Good (Moore) and about classes, numbers, colors, properties, and relations (Russell).

In the years leading up to the Second World War, the promise of the physical sciences overtook the work of the metaphysicians. The excessively speculative metaphysical theorizing of the idealists led to logical positivism and to a period where metaphysics was actively suppressed. But after the war, metaphysics has been resurgent and largely focused on resolving the old metaphysical questions in a domain broadly defined by the natural sciences, much as the medievals had been cornered by the demands of theism.

Many undergraduates come to philosophy with only some grasp of this history, but with imaginations excited by the works of figures such as Plato, Descartes, Hume, Kant, and Mill. Almost every central question in philosophy is on the table once one has studied these figures. But much of contemporary philosophy is not primarily concerned with historical texts, even if they are concerned with many of the same questions and puzzles. As a result, there is a looming gap between what an undergraduate philosophy student reads and what graduate students must work on. This book is intended as a bridge of sorts spanning the gap between the familiar figures of the history of philosophy and the more technical and specialized approaches favored by today's philosophers. In fact, the authors of the chapters in this volume were asked to lay out the concepts, ideas, and methods they wish that their students had already mastered on day one of an ideal graduate seminar.

This book contains 11 specially commissioned essays by experts in their respective areas of specialization. Read in sequence they offer a syllabus for a survey course in contemporary metaphysics. The editors hope to have emphasized important topics of interest, for the realm of metaphysics is too broad for truly comprehensive coverage in just one book. The first essay concerns methodological and global themes that cut across the more specialized kinds of problems within metaphysics. The following nine essays focus on how many of the perennial metaphysical questions are currently being addressed by working metaphysicians. The final essay looks ahead to emerging questions and themes in metaphysics.

Research problems and methods

The domain of metaphysics is introduced by Amie Thomasson through a discussion of its history, central problems, and methods. She organizes her discussion around three kinds of question: existence questions, relational questions, and modal questions.

Existence questions define the subdiscipline of ontology, which attempts to give an account of what really exists (as opposed to what might exist only in name—e.g., "the economy" or "the English Premiere League"). Alternative accounts of ontology are discussed here against the background of alternative methodological approaches. Thomasson traces the development of contemporary views on ontology through the general framework of the debate between Quine and Carnap over how to determine our ontological commitments.

Relational questions address the issue of how things are constituted, founded, or grounded. Which objects are basic? How can the world in part or whole serve as a truthmaker for a statement? Thomasson focuses on these relational questions as an extension of the ontological issues introduced by existence questions—that is, how are complex entities related to simpler or more basic entities?

Modal questions concern how what exists must be, might be, or could not be, as well as the conditions under which we would say that entities are distinct or identical. Thomasson concludes her chapter with a useful discussion of extant and emerging methodological approaches as well as the importance of methodological debates conducted under the heading of meta-metaphysics.

Modality

The whole enterprise of metaphysics is regimented by what is actual, possible, impossible, and necessary. However, there is broad disagreement about how to understand the metaphysical significance of these categories. Must there be possible entities? Are the facts that ground the truth of modal claims different from those that ground ordinary claims about what is or is not the case? How one answers such questions colors how one approaches almost every other issue in metaphysics. In his chapter Tony Roy asks us to consider how claims about what is possible but not actual could be true. We say it is possible that my hair could be longer and that it is necessary that squares have four sides. Does this require that we accept the existence of a multitude of possible worlds, none containing squares with anything other than four sides? Must we believe there is a possible world where my long-haired counterpart is writing this sentence? To answer such questions we must first answer the question of what modal discourse is really about. Do its terms only refer to features of the actual world, or must we posit a wider domain of possible worlds or possible individuals to fully explain possibility and necessity? Do modal claims only apply to sentences (*de dicto*), or are some modal claims true of the things they speak of themselves (*de re*)?

Roy offers an extended examination of various approaches to possible worlds. According to the usual account, a proposition is necessarily true just in case it is true in all possible worlds, possibly true just in case it is true in at least one possible world. What this story leaves out is a fully developed theory about what possible worlds might be. Some hold that possible worlds are real, but distinct from and spatiotemporally and causally isolated from the actual world. Others hold that worlds are linguistic constructions, collections of sentences that would be true in a given world. In a domain of linguistic "ersatz" worlds a proposition is necessarily true just in case it is true in all world-sets of sentences, possibly true just in case it is true in at least one world-set of sentences.

Roy considers the viability and limitations of such linguistic approaches, especially whether or not they presuppose modality rather than explain it. He expands his discussion further to more contemporary accounts of modality as being determined, not by real or ersatz worlds, but rather by the relations that hold between abstract platonic properties.

Universals and abstract objects

If you meet three women, each named Sue, you do not ordinarily suppose that there is another thing SUE-ness in virtue of which each of the women is Sue. But, if you open your closet and find three red shirts, you might more readily believe in some entity RED-ness that explains their similarity with respect to being red.

Roy Cook's chapter begins by distinguishing universals (special entities posited to explain similarities) from abstract objects (particular entities that are outside of space, time, and the causal order, and that are mind independent, necessary, and unchanging). This distinction has historically been poorly drawn. For Plato, the Forms were abstract objects that were universals. Cook suggests that this historical coextension has led to a confusion of the two classes; a precise account of each requires that we recognize their distinctive characters.

Cook proceeds by considering the theoretical virtues of the main alternatives on offer in the literature: realism (or platonism), immanent realism, conceptualism (or psychologism), and nominalism. Platonic realism about universals is the view that universals exist as abstract objects and are mind independent. Immanent realism is the view that universals exist mind-independently, but are immanent in the world somehow, that is, they are not abstract entities. Conceptualism holds that universals exist, but are somehow dependent upon minds or thought. And nominalism asserts that universals do not really exist in any way. His comparison of these approaches is performed, in part, by addressing these issues through the special lens of mathematical objects, for it is in that domain that the arguments for abstracta and abstract universals can be most compelling. By extending these analyses into non-mathematical domains, the debates over abstracta and universals can be better understood on their own terms. Cook concludes, like Thomasson, by considering the prospects for adapting the neo-Fregean approach to non-mathematical cases.

Naturalism and physicalism

Depending upon how one defines the terms "naturalism" and "physicalism," one (or both) represents a dominant metaphysical framework in much of contemporary metaphysics. Indeed, it is often a form of praise to say of a view that it is "naturalistic" or "acceptable to the physicalist." The first several essays contain ample evidence of this. There we find approaches to modal notions, abstracta, and universals that have been developed specifically in order to harmonize these notions with a natural or physical ontology. Similarly, as we proceed, we will find that present-day discussions of the mind, of mereology, and of identity are all colored by these concepts. Thus, it seems appropriate that we try to get clear about what they really mean.

Gene Witmer starts off by addressing the terminological issue and by teasing apart the metaphysical sense of "naturalism" from the epistemic and methodological uses of the term. Witmer surveys formulations of naturalism found in the contemporary literature, but ultimately advances the thesis that naturalism is best understood as a claim about the essential sameness of those parts of the world of deep concern to human beings and all other parts of the world. This approach, Witmer suggests, helps to unify the metaphysical and epistemic senses of naturalism in contemporary philosophy.

Formulating physicalism, according to Witmer, requires that we settle on the relevant nature of "physical" and determine what the scope of physicalism is intended to be. Notoriously, the project of defining what counts as physical relative to some conception of the physical sciences is made more difficult by the evolving nature of science. Witmer surveys various replies to this problem and goes on to explore how best to formulate the extent of the physicalist position. A number of relational and reductive formulations are examined. Despite the fact that both the character of the physical and the extent of physicalism remain unsettled, Witmer concludes by considering the various arguments that are employed to justify the centrality of both naturalism and physicalism to contemporary metaphysics.

Mind

The ongoing debate over physicalism is nowhere more relevant in contemporary metaphysics than in discussion of how to address metaphysically the mind and consciousness. In this essay we begin to examine some of the narrower questions in metaphysics—specifically, how phenomena such as consciousness and mentality fit into a natural world. Historically, the main philosophical issue here has been how to reconcile the experienced inner, personal perspective of the mind with the perceived outer, impersonal perspective of the body. In this essay, Thomas Polger evaluates the various leading philosophical approaches toward the mind by examining how well they fare with respect to four theoretical desiderata: realism, physicalism, the causal efficacy of the mental, and the explanatory autonomy of psychology. Thus Polger hopes to find a view that takes the mental seriously and provides a basis for psychological science, but which can locate the mind in the physical world without having to make special allowances for mental causation (i.e., cases where mental states cause bodily behavior).

Before beginning his analysis in earnest, Polger offers an exegetical and historical overview of key positions on the mind–body problem before narrowing the field of contenders to three: identity theory, functionalism, and property dualism. Identity theory is usually thought to fall prey to the multiple realization objection. Property dualism is not strictly physicalist and so does not really account for mental causation. Functionalism, too, has trouble accounting for mental causation. However, as identity theory has a worry-free account of mental causation, Polger's claim that the force of multiple realization objections may be exaggerated does suggest that identity theory deserves another look.

Material constitution

Witmer and Polger both highlight the importance to contemporary physicalism of being able to give an account of objects and properties, where these things either are basically physical or are somehow built from or reducible to what is basically physical. The next three essays jointly address issues about identity— how to think about objects and how to distinguish them—primarily under the assumption of something like materialism or physicalism. The issue of how material objects might be related to their material structure, their material constitution, is the focus of Stephan Blatti's essay. He critically examines four leading accounts of material constitution. Material constitution is problematic to the extent that, for many, intuitions about relevantly similar cases yield different judgments about the degree to which changes in what constitutes an object necessitate a change in what an object is. What is at stake in this issue is the nature of a material object's identity in both space and time.

The familiar and traditional conception of identity as indiscernibility (i.e., the sharing of all properties) is central to three of the leading approaches. For example, if we consider a lump of clay and the bowl that is formed from the clay, shall we say that there is one object constituted by the clay or that there are two objects? We might say that there are two coincident objects (the clay and the bowl) or just the bowl. In the former case, we must accept that more than one nonidentical object can exist in the exact same spatiotemporal region, and that one can be destroyed without harming the other even though they are composed of the same matter and share all the same properties while coincident. In the latter case we can either hold that the bowl supersedes the lump of clay, or that the creation of the bowl temporarily annihilates the lump.

None of the approaches is without its problems. In the first case the two objects share all their properties for the duration of the bowl, but are not identical. In the second case, we must suppose that objects are identified with their intrinsic kinds, and that some kinds are able to dominate others ontologically. In the third case, the lump of clay, though real, pops in and out of existence depending on whether a bowl, a statue or something else is formed from the clay. The first case gives us an odd account of identity, the second and third cases give us odd accounts of objects. The fourth approach to the problem of material constitution is to reject the problem. If the problem results from conceiving of identity as having all the same properties, then perhaps a revision of the logic of identity is required. This resolves the problem of explaining how the same material object can both be and not be the lump of clay, but it requires that we globally revise our conception of identity. Blatti examines the virtues and possible failings to each of these approaches, and identifies where further research and methodological consideration are needed.

Endurantism and perdurantism

While the nature of an object's identity is central to the problem of material constitution, the question of how objects can be thought of as persisting in time is the focus of Nikk Effingham's essay. He explains that the problem of persistence has at least three versions, related to different ways of thinking about what persistence means. If persistence means that an object O exists at 2 o'clock and the same object also exists at each point in time for the next six hours, then we might say that O endures, that it is wholly present at each moment in time and that it might be divisible in space—it is a three-dimensional object, but is not divisible in time. Alternatively, some might say that O at 2 o'clock is merely a temporal part of an object O* that extends both in time and space—O* is a four-dimensional object. It is not wholly present at any single time, but is identical with the entity that occupies its footprint in both space and time, over the same six hours. O* in some sense persists by perduring.

Effingham analyses the distinction between endurantism and perdurantism in three ways: as a disagreement over what objects there are; as a disagreement over how many dimensions objects occupy; and as a disagreement over how objects are related to the regions of spacetime they occupy. Effingham also has occasion to address hybrid approaches such as stage theory. Effingham concludes, somewhat ironically, by noting that whether one accepts endurantism or perdurantism—three-dimensional or four-dimensional objects—it remains unclear if any of these theories truly captures the nature of persistence itself.

Personal identity

Both Blatti's discussion of material constitution and Effingham's treatment of persistence deal with the traditional problems of identity and mereology (the philosophical study of how parts are related to wholes). The problem of material constitution focuses on the issue of spatial parts, while the perdurantist and endurantist seem to disagree over the reality of temporal parts. These issues seem abstract when we are primarily concerned with, for example, lumps of clay, pottery bowls, statues, or icebergs. But issues of constitution, identity, and persistence become more personal when the object we must identify is the human person we ourselves are. This is the topic of David B. Hershenov's essay on personal identity.

Personal identity is the area of metaphysical inquiry most concerned with what kind of beings human persons are and what it takes for a person to persist from one time to another. Hershenov approaches the question of personal identity by separating the question of what a person is from the question of how persons might persist in time. The first question addresses what we are tracking, the criteria for personhood. Is it self-conscious beings, clusters of essential properties, the compound of a mind and body, a soul, a mind or a living organism? The second question addresses the criteria for sameness over time.

The problem of personal identity is often motivated by thought experiments similar to those that excite the problem of material constitution, but which focus on what our intuitions tell us about cases where a person might or might not survive a certain kind of change, for example, teleportation, loss of half a brain, body switching, and so on. Hershenov proceeds by surveying and assessing the viability of leading approaches on both questions. Various formulations of psychological criteria address the issue of personhood, but make sameness more problematic. Animalist approaches identify the persistence of a person with the survival of a specific organism, but run afoul of our intuitions about the importance of our self-consciousness and may require that we have more than one thing that is us. Four-dimensionalists maintain that persons are really objects extended in time and space, so that our familiar conception of ourselves merely reflects one or more temporal parts of the real person. Others hold that the animal and the person might be coincident objects, where the animal constitutes the person. Thus the issues discussed by Blatti and Effingham reemerge for the special case of the person.

Like Blatti, Hershenov concludes with suggestions for needed research. He places special emphasis on questions about whether the various moments of a person's existence are related by a form of identity or by some less-demanding relation of similarity. Likewise, questions about the identity of persons and their constitution may be eased by softening the concept of object in use. Our intuitions about personhood may be better served by thinking of persons as vague entities without sharp boundaries between self and world, or between moments.

Free will

The status of persons as agents is the focus of Kevin Timpe's essay. For many, the issue of human freedom is important because it is often understood to be the primary point of contact between metaphysics and the domain of morality.

Historical discussions of free will often focus on how free will might work. Following Augustine, most of these thinkers have assumed that free will exists and needs to have its place in reality explained. In his treatment of the issue Timpe gets behind the historical tradition and looks to the so-called *Existence Question*. Do humans have free will? Does human free will really exist?

Properly addressing the Existence Question requires that Timpe first clear the ground by surveying the alternative conceptions of free will on offer. He begins by distinguishing a thin conception of free will that echoes Peter van Inwagen's minimal "ability to do otherwise" criterion from a thicker conception of free will as the ability to control one's actions that is relevant to assessments of moral responsibility. Timpe adopts the morally thick account of free will, in large part due to the role of moral responsibility in treatments of the existence question.

Timpe develops a taxonomy of positions regarding free will by distinguishing first among the various positions on the axis running from free will skepticism (the denial of free will) to libertarianism (the view that we have free will and are not determined), including varieties of compatibilism (the view that humans can have free will even if determinism is true). He then further distinguishes between positions based on whether they reflect the notion of free will as the decision between or possession of alternative possibilities on the one hand, or as our being the source or origin of our own choices on the other.

The definitional and taxonomic preliminaries are here in the service of the Existence Question. Timpe surveys various strategies for arguing both for and against the existence of human free will. He distinguishes between attempts to argue for the existence of free will indirectly and those that attempt a direct proof of the existence of free will. The indirect strategy is to argue that free will is a necessary condition for some other factor or phenomenon X (e.g., moral responsibility or desert), argue that X obtains, and infer the existence of free will. The direct strategy is to argue directly from a conception of free will as such and such, plus the putative identification of cases of such and such, to the existence of free will.

Timpe's treatment of the Existence Question wraps up by examining options available to those who would argue against the existence of free will. Interestingly, the indirect strategy is not available to the denier of free will. To make an indirect argument against free will, one would need to falsify a conditional of the form "If X, then free will exists," that is, affirm that X obtains but that there is no free will. Such an approach would be a direct denial. Instead Timpe marks a distinction between contingent direct denials of free will—that is, that free will is possible in the metaphysically relevant sense but is not ever actual—and categorical denials of free will—that is, that the conception of free will in play is self-contradictory or entails a contradiction. Timpe makes no real attempt to answer the existence question; instead his chapter shows that there are as many existence questions to resolve as there are distinct conceptions of free will.

God

The final set of metaphysical questions examined in this volume concerns the place of God in metaphysical theorizing, especially against the background of naturalism and physicalism that dominates much of contemporary metaphysics. This is the focus of Graham Oppy's essay.

Metaphysical discussions about God often seem overwhelmingly complex due to the frequency with which tangential issues and independent theological commitments are brought in by many philosophers. In such cases, progress and development often take the form of redescribing or reconceiving the issues and questions involved. Oppy attempts to distill metaphysical debates about God down to two essential questions. First, can we meaningfully and consistently talk about God? Second, are there any clear cases where theistic explanations of phenomena are superior to naturalistic (nontheistic) explanations?

The first question is answered by considering two topics: the proper, coherent, and consistent way to conceive of God, and whether on such a conception meaningful discourse about God is possible. Oppy proceeds by surveying a wide range of ways to think about divine attributes—including what they might be and whether they are literally or analogically applied to God—and concludes that at a very schematic level it is almost certain that some acceptable conception of God is possible. It follows that metaphysical questions about God, and most centrally about God's existence, can be asked in a meaningful and noncontradictory way. A case in point is the role of God, if any, in creation. Here Oppy discusses how appeals to theistic explanation in specific cases like the grounding of logic, mathematics, morality, or even modality can be more problematic than many assume.

With respect to Oppy's second question, the general issue of theistic explanation is addressed under two very general headings. First, is appealing to God the best explanation of the world and its causal order? Second, is divine action the best explanation of the apparent fine-tuning of the universe for life? Oppy proceeds in a schematic, a prioristic and methodical manner to exhaustively consider various cases and alternatives under each heading. Here Oppy takes great pains to balance the argumentative ground and ensure only comparable cases are weighed, one against the other. In the end, he maintains that there is no case among those examined where a theistic account is preferable, in terms of theoretical and explanatory virtue, to its corresponding nontheistic naturalistic alternative.

Oppy concludes by considering whether divine explanations might be preferable to naturalistic accounts in special cases such as explaining how rationality or consciousness might come to be. Here the issue is left unsettled pending a final settlement of the sorts of issues that are raised in discussions of whether or not rationality or consciousness can be explained in naturalistic terms (a topic discussed in Polger's "Mind" essay). For Oppy's part, until the phenomenon of consciousness is itself better understood, it makes no sense to compare theistic and naturalistic explanations of what theists consider a mystery and many naturalists consider a settled question. Oppy's distillation therefore yields what he takes to be a theoretically neutral account of why, despite the fact that metaphysical questions about God can meaningfully be asked, none of the answers on offer from the theist are to be preferred to the theoretically simpler accounts on offer from the naturalist.

New directions in metaphysics

We close the circle and return to broader themes in the final essay. Tony Roy and Matthew Davidson offer an extended metaphysician's apology in favor of metaphysical tradition against the alternative approaches suggested by advocates of broadly deflationary or experimental approaches to metaphysical problems. Their essay advances three central claims. First, when the standard Quinean approach to ontology fails to eliminate all ontological commitments to abstract or queer objects, properties, relations, worlds, times, or ways of being, this is not necessarily a failure. Second, attempts to defuse disagreements over metaphysical questions by deflating them into disputes about language ultimately fail because the deflationary strategy implicitly assumes a neutral ground and neutral language into which the disputes can be translated. Roy and Davidson deny that such a neutral ground exists. Third, the attempt to illuminate metaphysical questions by appealing to empirical accounts of people's intuitions is misguided.

The canonical Quinean approach, argue Roy and Davidson, tightly binds together questions of ontological commitment and the presumption that every true statement can be given an enlightening extensional analysis. This approach handles many ordinary existence questions well, but runs into familiar problems when we attempt to describe the intensional or modal dimensions of metaphysical disputes. Further, there are, they claim, fairly ordinary cases that essentially seem to involve commitments to entities that are not aptly or easily given extensional analyses. The front lines of many of the metaphysical debates highlighted in this volume can be drawn directly over a map of disputes about how to address or explain these failures of the standard Quinean approach.

The deflationary strategy proposes that the best way to resolve these disputes is to assume a standpoint where the debates are best understood as complex verbal disputes or as turning upon how best to characterize the language within which the competing positions are expressed. Roy and Davidson suggest that either approach merely puts off the metaphysical dispute by recasting it. Neither approach, in their view, really deflates the deeper metaphysical issues.

The attempt to clarify metaphysical debates by investigating the ordinary intuitions that ground them is the matter of "experimental metaphysics." Here Roy and Davidson offer their take on the relevance of the emerging "experimental philosophy" movement to metaphysics in particular. They offer a quick survey of some recent experimental results demonstrating how various moral, emotional, and psychological factors appear to influence the judgments that nonphilosophers offer in response to questions about the connection between free will and moral responsibility or between personality types and judgments about personal identity. The authors maintain that these results are less informative than they might seem. Their concerns center on two main points. The first is that the very process of developing these experiments embeds complex metaphysical concepts, such that the responses of ordinary folk are unable genuinely to contribute anything to technical debates between philosophical experts. (This approach is a variety of what those sympathetic to experimental philosophy sometimes call the "expertise defense.") The second is that the only real upshot of empirical experimentation will be to highlight the existence of disagreements over metaphysical questions. But no one denies that there is disagreement, and so the authors worry that focusing on disagreement will lead to irrational and ungrounded skepticism.

In the end Roy and Davidson argue that the ultimate direction for metaphysics is to stay the course and build on the progress of the last century, where advances in the application of logical analysis to metaphysical confusions have provided us with a better and more detailed map of the logical and theoretical spaces where the work of metaphysics is done.[1]

Note

1   This introduction has benefited from the influence, encouragement, and criticism of Joe Ulatowski, Robert English, Terry Horgan, John Tienson, Stephan Blatti, Tom Polger, Jonathan Weinberg, Marie Barnard, and Neil A. Manson.

1

Research Problems and Methods

Amie L. Thomasson

The problems of metaphysics seem, at least on the surface, to be among the deepest and most important questions of philosophy. Thus, for example, Richard Taylor writes: "metaphysics is a foundation of philosophy. . . . One's philosophical thinking, if long pursued, tends to resolve itself into basic problems of metaphysics" (1992, p. 2), while Jaegwon Kim and Ernest Sosa call metaphysics "the most central and general subdivision of philosophy" (1995, p. xiii). Though the problems metaphysicians work on are superficially diverse, most may without too much distortion be divided into three major categories: existence questions, relational questions, and modal questions.

Questions regarding what exists belong to the subdiscipline of metaphysics known as ontology. Some existence questions, for example, "Does God exist?" and "Does matter exist?" have long been at the heart of metaphysics. More recently, especially over the past 60 years or so (under the dominance of a neo-Quinean picture of metaphysics I will say more about later), existence questions have proliferated and taken a more central place in metaphysics, as metaphysicians aim to articulate and defend competing "ontologies" — considered as views about what does (and does not) exist (or, alternatively, about what there is).[1] Thus among contemporary research problems pursued in metaphysics we now find not only traditional existence questions like "Does God exist?," but also questions about the existence of entities seldom questioned by nonphilosophers—for example, "Do tables and chairs exist?" "Do persons exist?" "Do events exist?" and "Does consciousness exist?" — and even existence questions raised about philosophical entities unfamiliar to nonphilosophers— for example, "Do temporal parts exist?" "Do mereological sums exist?" "Do universals exist?" and so on. Those doing ontology generally take themselves to be interested not merely in answering individual existence questions, taken separately, but also to be attempting to formulate an overall ontology that meets certain theoretic goals better than its competitors—goals such as empirical adequacy, explanatory power, unity, and (prominently) parsimony.

Metaphysicians are also typically concerned with relational questions; in Sellars' phrase, metaphysicians aim "to understand how things in the broadest possible sense of the term hang together in the broadest possible sense of the term" (1963, p. 1). How is, say, a statue related to the clay it is made of? Are they identical, connected by some kind of "constitution" relation, or what? More generally, how do such things as conscious beings, and social and cultural entities such as artifacts, works of art and nations, relate to the objects described by the physical sciences? Are there different "levels of reality," with the entities described by physics (perhaps) on the lowest level, and artifacts, social and cultural objects, or minds on higher levels? If so, what are the relations between entities of different levels? Do the "higher level" entities really exist? May they be "reduced to" lower level entities, or considered to provide no "real addition of being" with respect to them? In the earlier days of analytic philosophy, the goal was typically to reduce "higher-level" entities to the lower; as reductions proved problematic, talk turned more, especially in the 1980s and 1990s, to supervenience; more recently, there has been a turn to looking for lower level entities to serve as "truthmakers" for statements of higher level facts, or looking for the "ontological grounds" for higher level entities (about this more later). The list of options has been ever expanding, and of course has introduced new questions about what precisely the target relation (whether of reduction, supervenience, truthmaking, or grounding) consists in. Relational questions have not been confined to asking about relations between social and cultural entities and those of the natural sciences, however. A perennial set of ontological questions also involves questions about the relations among entities of the most basic ontological categories, for example, objects, facts, events, universal properties, and property instances (tropes). So, for example, questions such as "Are objects just bundles of tropes?" "Are properties just sets of possible objects?" and "Which is more basic: objects or facts?" may also be counted as relational questions.

Metaphysics is not only traditionally concerned with what exists, and with how things are related, but also with questions about the *natures* of things of various sorts. Thus other important problems in metaphysics are questions about the natures, for example, of persons, artifacts, or works of art. What are their essential properties? What does it take for something to be a person, an artifact, or a work of art? Are humans, artifacts, or works of art essentially tied to their origins? Related questions concern the identity and persistence conditions for things of various sorts. Metaphysicians writing about personal identity, for example, often aim to determine under what conditions persons A and B would be identical. Meanwhile, from the time of the ancients, metaphysicians have been concerned with puzzles about the conditions under which ships or other artifacts persist over time. All of these questions about natures, identity, and persistence conditions are *modal* questions: questions about the properties an object *must* have to be of a certain type, about what it *would take* for there to be something of a given type, about the conditions under which individuals *would be* identical, or under which a given thing *would or would not* persist.[2] Under this heading also come questions not about *whether* something of a given sort exists, but about *what it would take* for something of a given sort (or for an individual) to exist, about the existence *conditions* for things of various kinds. Questions about whether or not colors, numbers, or moral facts are "mind-dependent," for example, are modal questions about whether the existence of minds is necessary for the existence of things of these other sorts.[3]

This may not capture everything metaphysicians deal with, and the tripartite classification is certainly not the only way of dividing up the problems of metaphysics. Nonetheless, it provides, I think, a fair survey of the sorts of problems that have come to occupy center stage in metaphysical debates over the past 60 years or so, during the post-positivist revival of metaphysics. Furthermore, the division into three will provide a useful organization for considering the methodological issues below, as similar methodological issues arise, for example, for all existence questions and for all modal questions, despite superficial dissimilarities between, for example, questions about identity conditions and questions about essences (both of which are classified as modal questions).

Now, if those are among the central questions of metaphysics, the next question is how we are to go about answering them. While the methodology to be employed in the natural sciences has been clear and consistent for some time, the question of what methods are proper to answering metaphysical questions has become only more contested and more obscured over the past century.

A standard response—if you interrupt metaphysicians in the heat of a first-order debate to enquire about their methodology—is to brush off the question, saying that to answer metaphysical questions we simply "think really hard" and "see who has the best arguments." But this alone is no kind of answer to a very real and pressing question, for it only leads us back further to the underlying questions. What *sorts* of arguments are and are not appropriate, or suitable for providing support for metaphysical theses, say, about what exists, about identity and persistence conditions, or about the relation between higher and lower level entities? Do purely a priori arguments based on thought experiments and/or conceptual analysis provide the proper support? Or should we be suspicious of the idea that "intuitions" about imagined cases can be truth-tracking at all, or that conceptual analysis can tell us anything about what the world is like? Is empirical enquiry relevant, and can it alone be sufficient to tell us what ontology to adopt or what the natures of things of various kinds are? What role, if any, do the theoretic virtues play in justifying the adoption of a metaphysical theory? Do metaphysical theories aim to do the same sort of job as scientific theories, so that they may be evaluated on similar grounds, according to their theoretic virtues? Moreover, if we do take metaphysical questions to be answerable empirically, further questions arise about the sorts of empirical evidence that are relevant. If we want to know about the essence of a given kind of thing, say, persons or artifacts, do we study the things themselves, or should we, with experimental philosophers, undertake empirical study of those who use the corresponding terms or concepts?

None of these methodological questions are easy to answer, all are highly contested, yet how we answer them makes an enormous difference to how we go about entering into metaphysical debates and evaluating the merits of various proposals. Perhaps it's no wonder, then, that the controversies in metaphysics show so little hope of being resolved, and that the answers to metaphysical questions seem to keep proliferating and diversifying rather than converging on (what we hope is) the truth. The methodological problems are crucial, since without clarity about what we are doing in metaphysics, what sorts of consideration are and are not legitimate to resolving metaphysical debates, we can make little progress in adjudicating metaphysical disputes (at least where the disputants do, as is often the case, explicitly or tacitly employ different methodologies). These obscurities at the methodological level, and the proliferation in opinions that has resulted, have led some to doubt that these questions of metaphysics are as deep and important as they seem. Indeed, methodological doubts have led some to treat many core metaphysical questions as pseudo questions, as poorly formed and unanswerable questions, or as trivially answerable and so not suitable subjects for deep metaphysical debates.

While many practicing metaphysicians still prefer to brush off methodological problems, over the past ten years or so (as the post-positivist euphoria among those who wanted to just practice metaphysics unencumbered has died down, and as skeptics and deflationists have raised new worries), there has come to be an increasing sense of the importance of returning to examine these methodological issues. Tim Williamson, for example, speaks of a "current tendency towards increasing methodological self-consciousness in philosophy" (2007, p. 8), a tendency that can be witnessed in the prominent books and collections on the topic which have recently come forth or are in preparation (e.g., Chalmers et al. 2009; McGinn, 2011; Sider, 2011; Williamson, 2007). The clearest way to see how and why the confusion over the methods for addressing metaphysical debates has developed is to take a brief look back at the history of metaphysics—so I will pause now to provide a bit of that history, and then return to assess the current state of the debate.

Methodology in metaphysics: A very brief history

In the days of rationalism, philosophers doing metaphysics thought of themselves as aiming to discover fundamental truths about the world and its structure using a priori reasoning. Thus, for example, Descartes argued for the existence of God, and for the existence of two fundamentally different kinds of substance, from his armchair alone.

Empiricists grew suspicious of these lofty claims and sought to clarify the methods for resolving metaphysical disputes. Some traditional questions of metaphysics were held to be resolvable empirically if at all, whether through external observation or internal observation of our own psychological processes. So, for example, the question of the existence of God was thought to be resolvable (if at all) by empirical arguments about whether or not God is the best causal explanation of the (coming into) existence of the world, or of its apparent "design." Other questions of metaphysics were taken to be resolvable by way of grasping "relations among ideas" rather than "matters of fact." For example, through examining relations among our ideas, we can see that moral responsibility presupposes liberty in (and only in) the sense of doing what one wills, without external hindrance (Hume, 1748/1977). Purported metaphysical questions that cannot be resolved through either of these means were considered dubious. Thus, in what may have been the most famous early attack on rationalist metaphysics, Hume wrote:

> If we take in our hand any volume of divinity, or school metaphysics, for instance; let us ask, *Does it contain any abstract reasoning concerning quantity or*

number? No. *Does it contain any experimental reasoning concerning matter of fact and existence?* No. Commit it then to the flames. For it can contain nothing but sophistry and illusion. (1748/1977, p. 114)

Kant also raised suspicions against traditional metaphysics as illegitimately attempting to acquire knowledge about things in themselves, an attempt which reaches beyond our cognitive powers. His transcendental approach gave a new way of understanding metaphysical questions about, for example, the structure of space and time or the nature of freedom: neither by using experience to examine the world, nor by examining our concepts, but rather by ferreting out the transcendental presuppositions required for our experience of the phenomenal world to be possible or for our moral concepts to have application.

As the empirical sciences continued to develop, to become methodologically self-conscious and to break off from philosophy (ending with the separation between philosophy and psychology around the end of the nineteenth century), philosophers became increasingly concerned with methodological questions. The question of what philosophy is, how philosophy differs from science, how we should do it and what sort of knowledge we might hope to gain from it, as Gilbert Ryle puts it, didn't "begin seriously to worry the general run of philosophers until right around the beginning of the twentieth century" (1971, p. 366). But by the middle of the twentieth century, methodological concerns had become far more prominent—even a core obsession for many philosophers. Thus Ryle says of philosophers of his generation: "We philosophers were in for a near-lifetime of enquiry into our own title to be enquirers" (1970, p. 10).

The methodological crisis for metaphysics

In the early twentieth century, the dominant answers to the question "what are the proper roles and methods of philosophy?" deflated the goals and ambitions of metaphysics. The logical positivists of the Vienna Circle, as heirs to the Empiricist tradition, drew a clear distinction between metaphysics and science. Forms of traditional metaphysics that involved claims to knowledge of a reality transcending the world of science and common sense were roundly rejected as nonsensical. A. J. Ayer, who visited the Vienna Circle and aimed to promote its views to an English-speaking audience, put the point as follows: "no statement which refers to a 'reality' transcending the limits of all possible sense-experience can possibly have any literal significance, from which it must follow that the labors of those who have striven to describe such a reality have all been devoted to the production of nonsense" (1946/1952, p. 34). That is, on this view many of the statements (and debates) of traditional metaphysics are not *false,* but *nonsensical.*

On the positivist view, philosophy and science were seen as having distinct roles and distinct methods. Philosophy was seen as being concerned with a kind of linguistic or meaning analysis, which reveals analytic/necessary truths that are independent of any empirical assumptions; science, by contrast, was seen as engaged in empirical enquiry aiming to discover matters of fact (Ayer, 1946/1952, p. 57). Metaphysics was considered acceptable only to the extent that it could be seen not as attempting to state truths about the world, but only as concerned with *analytic* questions.[4] (And indeed, Ayer takes some pains to argue that a great deal of historical work in metaphysics—especially that of Empiricists such as Locke, Berkeley, and Hume—can be understood as engaged in analysis in this sense (1946/1952, pp. 51–5).) Analytic statements, as Ayer understood them, are tautologies that make no factual claims about the world. They are knowable a priori, express necessary truths, and are true just given the meanings of the terms involved. Empirical statements, by contrast, are true or false in virtue of both the meanings of the terms involved and the way the world is; they are attempts to describe the world. Thus Ayer would declare: "the function of philosophy is wholly critical" (1946/1952, p. 48)—the philosopher must "confine himself to works of clarification and analysis" (1946/1952, p. 51), where "the philosopher, as an analyst, is not directly concerned with the physical properties of things. He is concerned only with the way in which we speak about them" (1946/1952, p. 57).

With this view came an answer to the problem of how we can acquire knowledge of modal truths. Necessary truths positivists held to be analytic truths that "illustrate" or "convey" the conventions or the rules of use for our terms or concepts—a view that came to be known (perhaps rather unfortunately) as "modal conventionalism." Analytic propositions "simply record our determination to use words in a certain fashion. We cannot deny them without infringing the conventions which are presupposed by our very denial, and so falling into self-contradiction. And this is the sole ground of their necessity" (1946/1952, p. 84). Thus the modal portions of metaphysics (on this understanding) may be done by way of a form of conceptual or linguistic analysis that can help reveal or make explicit those analytic truths—which may, despite their analyticity, be complex and difficult for limited beings like ourselves to recognize.

What then about existence questions? Rudolf Carnap, one of the most important members of the Vienna Circle and proponents of logical positivism, famously argued that the existence questions of ontology could be understood in one of two ways. They may be *internal* questions—questions such as "Is there a prime number between 16 and 20?" or "Are there (still) any ivory-billed woodpeckers?" Internal questions, Carnap held, are asked within (or using) a linguistic framework, and the answers may be "found either by purely logical methods or by empirical methods, depending upon whether the framework is a logical or a factual one" (1956/1999, p. 14). That is, answers to questions like "Is there a prime number between 16 and 20?" may be found by mathematical reasoning; answers to "Are there (still) ivory-billed woodpeckers" may be found by empirical methods (e.g., placing motion-detector activated cameras around the woods of Arkansas). But existence questions may also be understood as *external* questions: questions about the existence or reality of *the system of entities as a whole*, for example, "Do numbers exist?" or "Do material objects exist?" These external questions are more like the existence questions that exercise metaphysicians. They are, on Carnap's view, questions asked outside of a linguistic framework: "They purport to assert the existence of entities of the kind in question not merely within a given language, but, so to speak, before a language has been constructed" (1963, p. 871).

As mentioned earlier, internal existence questions may be answered straight-forwardly, either through empirical or analytic means (or a combination of these). External questions, Carnap held, taken literally, are ill-formed pseudo questions. We can make sense of them only to the extent that we can understand them as disguised practical questions, involving practical decisions about "whether or not to accept and use the forms of expression in the framework in question" (1956/1999, p. 14). We should,

> replace the ontological theses about the reality or irreality of certain entities [expressed in answer to external questions], theses which we regard as pseudo theses, by proposals or decisions concerning the use of certain languages. Thus realism is replaced by the practical decision to use the reistic [thing-] language, phenomenalism by the decision to use only the phenomenal language. (1963, p. 869)

In sum, then, to the extent that the philosopher has anything to contribute to internal debates about existence, it is not by providing some kind of deep insight into what "really" exists, but merely by clarifying the question by using analysis to determine what it might take for entities of the relevant sort to exist. To the extent that the philosopher has anything legitimate to contribute to resolving external questions, the contribution will take the form of pragmatic arguments about what language to adopt (for a given purpose), not of arguments that can purport to show that numbers, material objects, or other disputed entities "really" do or do not exist.

Later analytic philosophers, especially in the ordinary language tradition, would grow skeptical about the idea that we could uncover true analyses of many of our most central philosophical expressions; but nonetheless the idea remained that (to the extent that it was legitimate, dealing in sense rather than nonsense) philosophy had a role completely separate from that of the natural sciences. Its role was largely seen as distinguishing sense from nonsense and avoiding mistakes that arise from being misled by language. Thus by the time he wrote *The Concept of Mind*, Ryle came to see philosophy as primarily concerned with avoiding mistakes (which lead to absurdities) that arise from mistaking the "logical geography of our concepts"—avoiding category mistakes by avoiding misconceptions about how certain terms work. The Wittgenstein of the *Philosophical Investigations* similarly held that philosophy is not concerned with discoveries of fact at all, but with avoiding nonsense: "The results of philosophy are the uncovering of one or another piece of plain nonsense and of bumps that the understanding has got by running its head up against the limits of language" (1953/1958, p. 119). On Wittgenstein's view, philosophy was to provide a kind of "therapy," a "cure for diseases of the understanding." "Philosophy is a battle against the bewitchment of our intelligence by means of language" (1953/1958, p. 109).

Despite the differences among positivists, ordinary language philosophers, and other early twentieth century philosophers,[5] philosophers in the first half of the twentieth century presented a rather unified front in terms of their basic understanding of the role of philosophy, its methodology and its relation to the sciences. On the dominant view, the roles of philosophy and the sciences were seen as separate: philosophy is an a priori study engaged in conceptual or meaning analysis, not in the discovery of matters of fact, while science is an *empirical* study concerned with matters of fact. Points of controversy tended to concern not that general picture, but rather details about how we should understand the meanings involved (whether we should take them as Platonic entities, as rules of use, or what; indeed, whether we should hypostatize meanings as "objects" at all) and over what meaning analysis involved (whether we could hope for positive analyses of key terms in the form of necessary and sufficient conditions, or could only hope for a critical role in avoiding problems and confusions engendered by misleading forms of language). In any case, for the first half of the twentieth century, to the extent that metaphysics was seen as legitimate at all, it was only seen as engaged in some sort of linguistic or conceptual analysis—whether in a fine-grained way (with focus on particular concepts such as knowledge or freedom) or in the broader spirit of what P. F. Strawson called "descriptive metaphysics," which aims "to lay bare the most general features of our conceptual structure" (1963, p. xiii). What was uniformly rejected was what we may call "serious metaphysics," understood as a metaphysical discipline that aims to provide knowledge of deep features of reality, without its methods being simply those of conceptual or linguistic analysis (nor even these combined with the empirical results from the natural sciences).

In this context, we can see quite clearly how Tim Williamson can say, of many of the recent giants of metaphysics such as Kripke, Lewis, van Inwagen, Armstrong, and Fine—none of whom would think of themselves as engaged only or even primarily in conceptual analysis—"On the traditional grand narrative schemes in the history of philosophy, this activity must be a throwback to pre-Kantian metaphysics: it ought not to be happening—but it is" (2007, p. 19).[6]

Why is it?

Metaphysical revival

The crucial change, enabling serious metaphysics to rise from the ashes of positivism, is usually traced to the debate between Quine and Carnap in the mid-twentieth century. In "On Carnap's views on ontology" (1951/1966), Quine denies that Carnap's division between internal and external existence questions has any significance.

Quine argues that Carnap's distinction between internal and external questions relies on a deeper distinction in the relationship between what we are inquiring into the existence of and what we are quantifying over when asking the existence question. The existential quantifier, usually represented as "$\exists$," is read "there is," and is said to "bind" variables (typically "x," "y" . . .) in its scope, which range over some domain of objects (they are those objects we are "quantifying over"). So existence questions may be posed using first-order logic as questions about whether or not "$\exists x(\ldots x \ldots)$," that is, as questions about whether or not there is something that meets the following conditions $(\ldots x \ldots)$. An existentially quantified claim of that form is true provided there is something in the domain of objects over which we are quantifying that, if substituted for the variable "x," would make the claim true.

When we ask an existence question of the form "Are there so-and-sos?," in some cases, the so-and-sos we are asking about (say, prime numbers between 16 and 20, or animals that are ivory-billed woodpeckers) would be just some among many of the things that we might be quantifying over (say, all the numbers or all the animals). So in asking existence questions like these, we are effectively asking: "Of all the xs (where 'x' ranges over numbers), are any primes between 16 and 20?," or "Of all the ψs (where 'ψ' ranges over animals), are there any that are ivory-billed woodpeckers?" These Quine calls "subclass" questions, since they are asking if there is anything of a particular *subclass* of the entities over which we are quantifying. Carnap's "internal" questions, Quine argues, are just subclass questions.[7]

In other cases, in asking "Are there so-and-sos?," we are asking about whether there is anything at all in the whole *category* of object our quantifier ranges over: whether there are any numbers (at all), or any animals (at all) (not just whether there are any numbers/animals *that have certain features* of interest). In these cases, as Quine puts it, the so-and-sos "purport to exhaust the range of a particular style of bound variables" (1951/1966, p. 207). That is, if our "xs" were supposed to range over all and only numbers, then the numbers (if any) would exhaust the range of this style of variable (and we might use a different style of variable, say, the "ψs," to range over material objects). Quine calls these "category" questions, and equates them with Carnap's *external* questions when asked "before the adoption of a given language" (1951/1966, p. 207).

But having recast the distinction in this way, Quine goes on to argue that we can always choose to adopt a single style of variable for all sorts of thing, for example, let "the xs" range over numbers *and* material objects. If we do that, then any existence question can be rephrased as a subclass question. So, for example, we could understand "Are there numbers?" as a subclass question: "Of all the *objects*, are there any of them that are *numbers*?" As a result, Quine argues, the distinction between category questions and subclass questions can't have any particular significance, since it varies given "logically irrelevant changes of typography" (1951/1966, p. 210).

Nonetheless, as Quine acknowledges, Carnap's approach to ontology can be preserved without relying on the internal–external distinction. For as long as he has the analytic-synthetic distinction, Carnap can hold that statements like "there are physical objects," "there are propositions," or "there are numbers" are analytic given rules for introducing the terms into the language (1951/1966, pp. 209–10).[8] Given the analytic–synthetic distinction, Carnap can also retain the idea that many statements thought of as ontological are disguised linguistic proposals, distinct from empirical existence claims like "there are black swans" (1951/1966, p. 210).

So the real basis of the dispute between Carnap and Quine comes down to the analytic–synthetic distinction: "if there is no proper distinction between analytic and synthetic, then no basis at all remains for the contrast which Carnap urges between ontological statements and empirical statements of existence. Ontological questions then end up on a par with questions of natural science" (1951/1966, p. 211).

This of course is exactly the point that Quine aims to argue for. He famously argues in "Two Dogmas of Empiricism" (1953/2001) that the analytic–synthetic distinction is ill-grounded. If we give up the analytic–synthetic distinction, we can no longer distinguish internal questions (as those to be answered by empirical or analytic means) from external questions (those best understood as pragmatic questions about what language to adopt). On Quine's view, no existence claim is purely empirical, nor is any language choice purely pragmatic. Choosing a language is empirically loaded, so it is wrong to think of alternate linguistic frameworks as equally acceptable systems of rules, with the choice between them merely pragmatic. Instead, there are better and worse theories/languages—the best one is that which best enables us to predict and explain events (Hylton, 2004, p. 134). Once we have chosen a best language-cum-theory, we can determine what exists according to (and so internally to) that theory/language, and have reason to accept those entities and to reject the posits of the lesser theories.

Quine was widely held to have won this debate and to have inaugurated a new golden age for metaphysics. Indeed Quine was not only seen as rescuing metaphysics, but also as granting it new respectability on grounds that its questions could be considered as not obscure matters for scholastic dispute, but rather as "on a par with questions of natural science." Scott Soames sums up the change in methodology inaugurated by Quine as follows: "For Quine, philosophy is continuous with science. It has no special subject matter of its own, and it is not concerned with the meanings of words in any special sense" (Soames, 2003, p. 224). It would be no exaggeration to say that most of those who currently practice serious metaphysics either explicitly embrace Quine's methodology or implicitly follow it. The new metaphysics, saved from the rubble of positivism, from a methodological standpoint, is by and large a neo-Quinean metaphysics.

The new metaphysics

Since the 1950s, serious metaphysics has been alive and well again—indeed, it has been quite a growth area in philosophy, especially in the last three decades. In this section I will try to discuss the revival of metaphysics and the major approaches that have been taken to the three core questions, and will return to discuss challenges for the new metaphysics in the section that follows.

Ontological issues

Quine explicitly laid out a methodology for the ontological part of metaphysics in "On what there is" (in 1953/2001). The question "What is there?" or "What exists?" may be divided into two parts. First, how do we know what the ontological commitments of a theory are—what a theory is committed to *saying* there is? Second, what theory should we accept? If we can answer both of these questions, we can figure out both what theory to accept and what it commits us to, and thereby know to what ontology we should commit ourselves.

To answer the first question—the question of what a theory is ontologically committed to—Quine gives this short, famous answer: "a theory is committed to those and only those entities to which the bound variables of the theory must be capable of referring in order that the affirmations made in the theory be true" (1953/2001, pp. 13–14). Let me explain.

Suppose you have a theory expressed in certain statements and you want to know what you will be committed to saying exists, if you accept the theory. According to Quine, you can't just look at what the statements of the theory, as expressed in ordinary English, say, or what names the theory uses in its statements, to determine what its commitments are. For suppose one statement of the theory is "Vulcan [the planet once hypothesized to orbit between Mercury and the sun] doesn't exist." It might on the surface seem that, in accepting the theory, you are committed to there being a planet between Mercury and the sun (to which we are referring with the name "Vulcan"), and asserting that it has the property of not existing. [It seemed so to Meinong, at any rate.] But, Quine argues, even if we accept the theory we are not really committed to the existence of Vulcan.

Instead of just looking at the surface claims of a theory, Quine argues, to find out what you are committed to in accepting the theory you must properly express the theory's claims in the more perspicuous notation of first-order quantified logic. Then we can see that the claim "Vulcan doesn't exist" would be properly expressed in the quantificational form: "~∃x(Vx)" (it is not the case that there is something that is-Vulcan—i.e., that is a planet orbiting between Mercury and the sun).[9] According to Quine's criterion of ontological commitment, the theory is committed only to whatever entities these bound variables have to range over for the theory's claims to be true. Once the theory's claim is expressed in that clearer way, we can see that accepting the truth of this statement as part of our theory does not commit us ontologically to the existence of Vulcan (1953/2001, pp. 7–8). For the statement to be true, the xs in the range of the quantifier need not include anything that is a planet orbiting between Mercury and the sun; it is enough merely that none of the xs over which the quantifier *does* range (me, my coffee cup, this parrot . . .) is something that is a planet orbiting between Mercury and the sun. So one can accept, as part of one's astronomical theory, that Vulcan doesn't exist, without being ontologically committed to Vulcan.

On the other hand, if a theory states "there are black holes," we restate this in quantified form as: "∃x(BHx)" (i.e., there is something that is a black hole). Once the theory has been expressed in quantificational form, we can determine what entities the bound variables of the theory must range over for the theory to be true. In this case, for the theory to be true, there does have to be something in the domain of the quantifier that is a black hole. So anyone who accepts this as part of a theory *is* ontologically committed to black holes.

But another facet of Quine's approach to ontological commitment needs to be brought out here: when we translate the statements of the theory into first-order quantified logic we are not constrained to using the most obvious or straightforward translation. Instead, we may aim to *paraphrase* the statements of the theory in a way that will minimize our ontological commitments. So, for example, suppose our theory says, "Venus has the property of being a planet." One obvious way of expressing this in first-order quantified logic is: ∃x∃P((Vx) & (x has P)), where "V" stands for "is-Venus" and "P" stands for "the property of being a planet." If we did express the theory this way, then we would be ontologically committed both to the existence of an individual (Venus) and to that of a property (the property of being a planet), since our quantifiers must range both over individuals (one of which must be Venus for the statement to be true) and over properties (one of which must be the property of being a planet). But on Quine's view we need not be so committed in virtue of accepting that statement as part of our theory. For the statement may be paraphrased as "Venus is a planet," which may be expressed in first-order logic as "∃x(Vx & Px)" ("there is something that is-Venus and is a planet"). In this rendering, we are quantifying only over individuals; for the statement to be true, something must lie in the range of the quantifier that is Venus and is a planet, but we are not quantifying over properties. Thus on Quine's view, someone who accepts the original theory may avail herself of a paraphrase like this and so need not be committed to the existence of properties (but only individuals). On the other hand, if our theory says "some zoological species are cross-fertile" we are committed to the existence of species "at least until we devise some way of so paraphrasing the statement as to show that the seeming reference to species on the part of our bound variable was an avoidable manner of speaking" (1953/2001, p. 13).

As a result, arguments about ontology since Quine have often centered on arguments about whether a given form of talk, apparently about numbers, fictional characters, properties, or other disputed entities, may be paraphrased into a form that does not require quantification over those suspect objects, thus enabling us to avoid ontological commitment to them. (I return to this issue in the discussion of relational questions below.)

On its own, Quine's criterion of ontological commitment does not tell us *what* there is, only how to find out what a given theory *says* there is—or, more properly, is *committed* to the existence of (1953/2001, p. 15). To provide anything like a method for doing ontology, we must answer the second question: how should we decide which theories to accept? Here, Quine's scientism does the work:

> Our acceptance of an ontology is . . . similar in principle to our acceptance of a scientific theory, say a system of physics: we adopt, at least insofar as we are reasonable, the simplest conceptual scheme into which the disordered fragments of raw experience can be fitted and arranged. Our ontology is determined once we have fixed upon the over-all conceptual scheme which is to accommodate science in the broadest sense. (1953/2001, pp. 16–17)

We may choose among theories by employing such familiar criteria as explanatory power, explanatory simplicity, ontological parsimony, and so on. Assuming that our scientific theories turn out to be the best theories, that will mean that we accept all and only those entities that our best scientific theories tell us there are (i.e., what they require there to be to render their affirmations true).

This methodology for doing ontology has been extremely influential; it plays a key role, for example, in Putnam's and Quine's own arguments for—and Hartry Field's subsequent argument against—the existence of numbers, and in Peter van Inwagen's argument for the existence of fictional characters (1983, pp. 67–8), to name some prominent examples. Important questions arise, however, about how broadly one should interpret "theories" here. Quine and Field are both directly concerned with whether our best *physical* theories can be formulated without quantifying over numbers. Van Inwagen, however, employs the notion of "theory" far more broadly, applying the Quinean strategy by arguing that our best *literary-critical* theories about fiction include commitment to fictional characters.

While all neo-Quineans pay homage to Quine's criterion of ontological commitment, an important distinction among neo-Quineans lies in whether they take Quine's methodology to require ontologists to *defer to* scientists or to *act like* scientists. That is, if we take Quine to be requiring that we accept the best total theory—on the scientist's own terms—and then use our philosophical/ logical skills merely to render it into the standard form of quantified logic and determine its commitments, then we have a view of ontology as merely a "formal finishing school" for science, in which ontologists merely await and interpret the results of the sciences—leading generally to rather sparse naturalist and physicalist ontologies.[10] Others, however, have interpreted the Quinean methodology as leaving a far bigger role for the metaphysician, insisting that there is no difference in kind between philosophy and science, as both (perhaps together) are in search of the best "total theory." Along those lines, a standard approach in metaphysical arguments has been to argue that accepting one's favored entities provides the best "total theory"—evaluated according to the scientific theoretic virtues, even if that "total" theory involves terms and posits no physicist ever dreamt of. One prominent example of this is David Lewis' argument for an ontology of a multitude of possible worlds, on grounds of its contributions to theoretical economy, unity, and fruitfulness (1986, p. 4).

Putting these differences aside, the resurgence of metaphysics—more particularly, of the ontological branch of metaphysics—over the past 60 years may largely be credited to the influence of Quine, and the methodology that has dominated has been a Quinean quasi-scientific methodology.[11] As Ted Sider puts it, the methodology of most metaphysicians today

> is rather quasi-scientific. They treat competing positions as tentative hypotheses about the world, and assess them with a loose battery of criteria for theory choice. . . . Theoretical insight, considerations of simplicity, integration with other domains (for instance science, logic, and philosophy of language), and so on, play important roles. (Sider, 2009, p. 385)

Indeed this quasi-scientific approach to metaphysics has become so dominant among its most prominent practitioners that David Manley calls it simply "mainstream metaphysics" (2009, p. 3).[12]

A prominent alternative to Quine's approach to ontology—that we should accept ontological commitment to whatever entities must serve as the values of the bound variables in our best theories—involves using the "Eleatic" criterion, promoted by David Armstrong: "Everything that exists makes a difference to the causal powers of something" (1997, p. 41). On this view, as it is usually interpreted, we should accept into our ontology all and only those entities that *make a causal difference*, or that have "distinct causal powers" "over and above" those of other entities we accept.[13] It is by wielding this principle (or rather, a version of it constrained to macrophysical objects), for example, that Trenton Merricks (2001, ch. 3) argues against the existence of ordinary objects such as tables and chairs, by arguing that they lack distinctive causal powers "over and above" those of the atoms that make them up.[14] It has also (sometimes under the name "Alexander's Dictum" that to be real is to have causal powers) played a prominent role in discussions about whether we should grant real existence to phenomenal consciousness (Kim, 1993, pp. 348–9).[15] Another alternative to Quine's approach is the truthmaker approach to ontological commitment (Armstrong, 2004; Cameron, 2010; Heil, 2003)—I will return to discuss this under "relational issues" below.

Relational issues

Relational questions have also played a central role in the revival of metaphysics. As Kit Fine puts it, "The history of analytic philosophy is littered with attempts to explain the special way in which one might attempt to 'reduce' the reality of one thing to another" (forthcoming, p. 6). The interest in relational questions has often been in service of the project of ontology. Initially, the goal was typically reduction of "higher level" entities to "lower level," where this was typically conceived of as requiring a translatability of talk of higher level entities into talk of the more basic entities. If we could paraphrase all talk of "higher level" entities into talk about lower level entities, so that we could say all that needs to be said without quantifying over the higher level entities, the Quinean criterion of ontological commitment would entail that we need not be committed to the higher level entities at all, leaving us with a more parsimonious ontology and thus (other things remaining equal) a better theory.

As such analytic reductions proved elusive, the standards shifted. The new goal was to account for higher level entities as "supervening" on lower entities, where again the hope (though much more controversial) was that the supervening entities would be a kind of "ontological free lunch," to use a phrase of David Armstrong's (1997, pp. 12–13). While there are many competing definitions of "supervenience," the core idea is that A-type properties supervene on B-type properties if no two possible worlds differ in their A-type properties without differing in their B-type properties; for example, moral properties are said to supervene on nonmoral properties if no possible worlds could differ in their moral properties (differ in who did something morally praiseworthy or reprehensible, say) unless they also differed in their nonmoral properties (i.e., differ in who performed which actions, with which results, etc.). But problems with the notion of supervenience emerged. For starters, this kind of covariation doesn't even ensure asymmetry or the dependence of A-type facts on B-type facts. More generally, to say that A properties supervene on B properties seems to report a superficial observation of correlations. The deeper metaphysical question is thought to be: *in virtue of what* does this supervenience relation hold? (Horgan, 1993; Heil, 2003, p. 37).

Thus (following a suggestion by C. B. Martin) the dominant terms of discussion for the relational question shifted again: to the project of finding the lower level *truthmakers* for higher level facts. As Armstrong puts it, a truthmaker is a part of reality in virtue of which a particular proposition is true (2004, p. 5). Thus, for example, one need not hold that statues are reducible to bits of clay (in the sense that all talk of the former may be translated into talk of the latter) to hold that *there being clay arranged in this way, by an artist, in these circumstances* is that in virtue of which "there is a statue" is true (cf. Heil, 2003, p. 48). According to those who defend a truthmaker definition of ontological commitment (Armstrong, 2004; Cameron, 2010; Heil, 2003), showing that sentences involving terms for higher level entities have as their truthmakers only lower level entities can ensure that we are *really* only committed to the existence of the more fundamental entities. As Ross Cameron puts it, "the ontological commitments of a sentence are not what the sentence quantifies over but rather what entities must be included in our ontology to ground the truth of the sentence—what entities must exist to make the sentence true" (2010, p. 252).[16]

Modal issues

One might say that what Quine did for existence questions, Kripke did for modal questions. Those in the logical positivist tradition had identified necessary truths with analytic statements knowable a priori by those who mastered the use of the relevant terms or concepts. As a result, they considered modal questions—about the essences of things of various types, the identity or persistence conditions of entities of various types, and so on—to be answerable in principle by a form of conceptual or linguistic analysis.[17]

But in *Naming and Necessity*, Kripke rejected the equation between necessary and a priori knowable truths, arguing that there are necessary a posteriori truths, and "probably contingent a priori truths" (1972/1980, p. 38). So, for example, consider the truth of an identity statement, for example, that Hesperus is Phosphorus. An identity statement, Kripke argued, must be *necessarily* true if it is true at all. But we can only learn that Hesperus is Phosphorus by doing empirical work in astronomy—it is not analytic, nor is it something we can learn just by linguistic competence with use of the names. Thus it provides an example of a necessary truth that is only knowable a posteriori. The same principle, Kripke argued, applies to theoretic identifications—such as that water is H_2O. This, if true at all, is necessarily true, yet it is only discoverable a posteriori by scientific means, not by any form of conceptual analysis. One may be as competent a user of the term "water" as one likes and yet still not know the necessary truth that water is H_2O. Kripke also argued that there are other necessary a posteriori truths, including statements of origin (e.g., that Margaret Truman is the daughter of Bess Truman) and of original composition (e.g., that this podium was made out of wood).

Kripke's work reinvigorated the idea that there are genuine modal features of the world, ripe for discovery, that could not simply be known a priori by those competent in wielding the relevant concepts. As Crawford Elder puts it, "we must learn from nature where there are real necessities. . . . These matters are not ours to fashion; they are fixed independently of us" (2004, p. xi). This inspired many serious metaphysicians to take up modal questions, the answers to which they took to be discoverable by serious metaphysical enquiry.[18]

And since modal facts were taken to be discoverable features of reality (not things we could somehow read off of our concepts or linguistic rules), conflict with what we would normally say about when two people are identical, or when a work of art persists, and so on, was typically rejected as counterevidence to a philosophical theory. Thus one result of the new robustly realist conception of modality has been a proliferation of revisionary positions in metaphysics over the past three decades or so. For example, Greg Currie defends the view that paintings are not individual material objects but rather are abstract action types that can survive the destruction of any canvas (1989, p. 7), and brushes off complaints that his view conflicts with what we would normally say about the identity and persistence conditions of paintings, saying "it is possible that we are mistaken about this" (1989, p. 87). Elder himself argues (2004, p. 149) that the real necessities we can discover in the world support the idea that there are members of some kinds of artifacts (there are members of what he calls "copied kinds"—kinds that have clusters of essential properties traceable to a common history of function), but should lead us to deny that there are general artifactual kinds such as tables and chairs, scarves and earrings.

New challenges for serious metaphysics

So where do we stand now, and where can we expect debates to head next in each of these areas? This can be assessed most precisely if we consider separately the three dominant sorts of questions in metaphysics: ontological questions, relational questions, and modal questions.

Ontological questions

Where ontology is concerned, new grounds have recently been raised for questioning the long-dominant Quinean approach. Quine's arguments against the analytic–synthetic distinction—which play such a crucial role in his rejection of Carnap's approach and his defense of the idea that philosophy and science are parts of a single continuous enterprise—no longer seem as compelling as they once did and have been subjected to much recent criticism.[19] Moreover, the idea that metaphysics and other areas of philosophy can and should proceed by a form of conceptual analysis has been recently revived, for example, by the Miami Analysts (McGinn, 2011; Thomasson, 2007).

If we can retain the analytic–synthetic distinction, or at least the idea that the truth of some sentences may analytically entail that of others (in the sense that—given logical principles and the meanings of terms involved—the truth of the first sentence guarantees the truth of the others), then certain existence questions may turn out to be trivially answerable (either *tout court* or given some empirical truths). Thus, for example, I have argued in *Ordinary Objects* (2007b) that the empirical fact that there are, say, particles arranged chairwise analytically entails that there is a chair. If that is the case, then the question of the existence of chairs and other ordinary objects is not a quasi-scientific question to be resolved by seeking the best "total theory," but rather a question that is trivially answerable by those who accept basic empirical truths such as that there are particles arranged chairwise here—empirical truths that even eliminativists about ordinary objects accept. Stephen Schiffer (2003), and neo-Fregeans such as Crispin Wright (1983) and Bob Hale (2001) have argued that trivial something-from-nothing transformations entail the existence other disputed entities, such as propositions, properties and numbers—transformations we can perform just by being competently introduced to the practices of using the relevant terms, without even the need to rely on any empirical truths. So, for example, those competently introduced to our use of property terms know that they are entitled to move from "Fido is a dog," to "Fido has the property of doghood," to "There is a property (doghood)"—and thus to infer the existence of properties.[20] Similarly, from "The cups and saucers are equinumerous" we are entitled to infer "The number of cups equals the number of saucers," from which we can infer "There is a number," giving us an "easy" argument for the existence of numbers (Wright, 1983).

These "lightweight" or "easy" approaches to ontology have received increasing discussion in recent years. Whether such "easy" arguments are acceptable in ontology hinges at least in part on the question of whether we can defend the idea that there are analytic or trivial entailments that can be used in leading to existential conclusions (for critical discussion see Hofweber, 2005, 2007; Yablo, 2002, 2005). If there are, then it seems we have reason to drop the "only if" side of Quine's criterion of ontological commitment: that "We are convicted of a particular ontological presupposition if, *and only if,* the alleged presuppositum has to be reckoned among the entities over which our variables range in order to render one of our affirmations true" (1953/2001, p. 13). For if there are trivial entailments committing us to the existence of entities not mentioned in the basic statements of the theory, then we may be entitled, indeed required, to accept the existence of far more entities than those explicitly quantified over in the basic statements of our best scientific theories (see also Jackson, 1998, pp. 4–5; Thomasson, 2007b, ch. 9).

Others have attempted to revive the idea that our terms have some sort of conceptual content which can license some form of conceptual analysis, without appealing directly to analyticity; see, for example, the two-dimensional semantics developed in (Chalmers, 2002a; Jackson, 1998). The viability of conceptual analysis as a method for doing metaphysics has thus recently come back into discussion, and often relies on views in the philosophy of language: about the defensibility of a notion of analyticity, about analytic or trivial entailments (and whether they may have existential consequences), or, more broadly, about whether our terms (or ways of referring to objects) have conceptual or intensional content.

Another worry about Quineanism and the heavy-duty metaphysics it inspired concerns whether the existence questions neo-Quineans dispute so seriously are genuine or merely verbal disputes. For the neo-Quinean, existence questions are to be formulated in quantificational terms, for example, of whether there is something that is (. . . a property, a mereological sum, a table . . . and so on for other disputed entities). But, following some ideas of Putnam's, Eli Hirsch (2002) has argued that the quantifier does not have a single, privileged meaning. If we allow that the meaning of the quantifier may vary, that raises the worry that existence disputes, for example, between those who accept and deny the existence of mereological sums, may be merely *verbal* disputes in which the disputants mean different things by their quantified expressions and so fail to express any real disagreement at all. As Hirsch puts it:

> If whenever you make an existential claim in metaphysics you are tacitly or unconsciously assuming that the claim has to be couched in terms of a quantificational apparatus that is in some sense the uniquely right one—the one that God would use—then this assumption is likely to lead you to futile and interminable pseudo-theoretical arguments. (Hirsch, 2002, p. 61)

Hirsch does not think that the use of the quantifier actually varies in ordinary English. But if we stick with the English use of the quantifier, he argues, the resolution to various ontological disputes (e.g., whether there is an object that is the mereological sum of my nose and the Eiffel tower) becomes laughably trivial. Since in *plain English*, the use of the quantifier precludes applying it to disjoint mereological sums, the answer is "no" (2002, p. 60). However, if those who think there is a more serious dispute here rely on using different senses of the quantifier (from the ordinary English sense, and from each other), then their dispute threatens to be a mere verbal dispute.

Against the threat of quantifier variance, Ted Sider (2009) argues that disputes in ontology can't readily be understood as classic verbal disputes, since there is no "neutral" formulation of the debate that both parties to the dispute would accept (which would show it to be only a verbal disagreement). In defense of serious ontology, Sider argues that there is a single best meaning for the quantifier. On Sider's view, the world not only has a structure into natural kinds (which can serve as reference magnets for our natural kind terms), but "the world's distinguished structure includes quantificational structure" (2009, p. 407). Given that the world has quantificational structure, we can plausibly hold that there is just one most natural meaning in the vicinity of EXISTENCE.

Whether or not our common English word "exists" employs the term in this sense depends on the relative weights that fit with usage and naturalness play in fixing its content. But regardless of whether this captures the sense of our ordinary English term, Sider argues, serious ontologists may make use of this sense of EXISTENCE to ensure that their debates are genuine (2009, p. 412). Thus despite the differences in where those who affirm and deny mereological sums would apply the word "exists," they may both be held to use "exists" in the same sense: a sense in "Ontologese," in which both agree to use the term in its most "natural" sense.

Thus a current focus of debate concerns whether the quantifier does or could vary, or if it has a single "best" or "most natural" meaning. Those who do think the quantifier has a "best" meaning face the further question: can this be understood as the ordinary meaning of the English phrase "there are," or does making sense of ontological disputes require shifting to a technical language such as Ontologese? (For further discussion in favor of introducing a technical language of Ontologese, see O'Leary-Hawthorne and Cortens [1995], Dorr [2005], and Cameron [forthcoming]; for critical discussion see Korman [forthcoming]. Thomas Hofweber (2009, pp. 266–75) rejects this and other technical terminology that plays a role in "esoteric" metaphysics.) If, to do ontology, we must use a technical sense of the quantifier different from the standard English sense of "there is," then a further question arises: if they are using a technical sense of the quantifier, can ontological theories really speak to the question, raised in ordinary English, of whether or not *there are* tables and chairs and other disputed objects?

In response to this, Sider (2011) argues that metaphysical debates are genuine, substantive debates to the extent that their crucial terms carve nature at the joints. Since the world has "logical joints," in conducting ontological debates, the disputants may stipulate that their quantifiers are to carve the world at its joints, and thereby ensure that their debates about EXISTENCE have depth—even if debates about existence, conducted in ordinary English, would not. While the answers we get by asking existence questions in Ontologese may be different answers (indeed answers to different questions) than those we would get if we stuck to ordinary English, the questions asked in Ontologese are said to be "better" questions, as they are asked in a "better" (joint-carving) language, giving us reason to care about those answers rather than the answers to trivial existence questions that can be posed in ordinary English (Sider, 2011, section 8.8).

A different sort of threat to the Quinean approach to "mainstream metaphysics" comes not from the thought that the quantifier might vary in meaning, but rather from the idea that the core questions used to motivate many ontological disputes—questions like "How many objects are there?," "Can two objects be in the same place at the same time?," or "Under what conditions do some things compose a larger thing?"—rely on an overly generic sense of "object." As has often been pointed out (e.g., Lowe, 1989, pp. 11–12 and 24–5; Hirsch, 1982, p. 38), in its core use in ordinary English, "object" is not a sortal term that comes associated with its own conditions of application and criteria of identity. Instead it functions as a "dummy sortal"—a placeholder for any other sortal—playing a "covering" role under which, from any claim of the form "there is an S" (where "S" is any genuine sortal term) one is licensed to infer that there is an object. But, according to some (Thomasson, 2007b), existence and counting questions are only answerable when they are expressed using a sortal term.[21] Thus on this view generic existence questions about how many "objects" there are, or what "objects" are here—if they are using "object" in a sortal-neutral sense—are simply ill formed and unanswerable questions.[22] If, on the other hand, we replace them with existence questions involving genuine sortal terms, asking, for example, "How many cups are there?" or "Under what conditions do pieces of wood compose a table?" then they are straightforwardly, indeed often trivially answerable—leaving no room for the kind of "deep" ontological debates characteristic of the new serious metaphysics (Thomasson, 2007b, pp. 110–25).

Relational questions

In recent work both the terms of the relational question and the goals of work on it have changed. As mentioned earlier, for a time the most prominent form of the relational question was to ask what the truthmakers were for our claims about entities of a certain sort. But the metaphysician's desire to focus on *objects* in the *world* rather than the *truth* of sentences or propositions has led to a further shift, from focusing on the *truthmakers* for *sentences or propositions about* higher level entities to the search to find the *grounds* for these facts and entities themselves. As Kit Fine puts it, "From the perspective of the theory of ground, truth-maker theory has an unduly restricted conception of what is grounded" (forthcoming, p. 8). For while truths may be grounded in their truthmakers (it is those *in virtue of which* the truths are true), it is not merely truths that are grounded, but also (more relevantly to the metaphysician) facts, objects, and so on; thus grounding is said to be the more general issue than truthmaking. Moreover, some have argued, we need a *metaphysical* conception of grounding to explain the connection between truths and truthmakers—to explain why it is that truthmakers are able to make certain propositions true. As Paul Audi puts it, "it is very natural to express the truthmaker principle as the idea that the truth of true propositions is *grounded* in what there is, or in what facts obtain" (manuscript, p. 10).[23] Thus the formulation of the core "relational" question seems to be shifting again, to focus on the notion of "grounding," and attempting to determine what entities are basic and how they ground the nonbasic entities.

The shift to an interest in grounding has often come with a shift in the very goals of addressing the relational question. As mentioned earlier, initially, interest in relational questions arose largely because they were thought relevant to the ontological question. It was thought that if we could reduce all talk of higher level entities to talk of lower level (and so avoid quantifying over the former), or could show that higher level entities supervened on lower, or could show that higher level claims were made true by lower level entities, then we wouldn't be ontologically committed to the higher level entities. But those ontological ambitions have been rejected by some recent defenders of grounding. Jonathan Schaffer, for example, argues against the Quinean conception of ontological commitment, and argues that finding the grounds for one sort of entity in another does not undermine the claim that the first "really exists." Audi (forthcoming, pp. 1–2) similarly argues that grounded entities are no less real than those entities that ground them.

Rather than using the relational question as a means of (more sparsely) answering the ontological one, Schaffer argues that we should give up the ontological question. For, he argues, most of the existence questions that have concerned metaphysicians are trivially answerable in the positive, given the validity of "easy" arguments for such things as numbers and properties (as discussed in "Ontological Questions")—for example, claims like "there are numbers" and "there are properties" may be trivially inferred from obvious truths like "there are prime numbers" and "there are properties that you and I share" (2009, p. 357). Instead of pursuing such ontological questions, he argues, we should focus on the old Aristotelian question of what grounds what (2009, p. 347). As Schaffer puts it, "metaphysics as I understand it is about what grounds what. It is about the structure of the world. It is about what is fundamental, and what derives from it" (2009, p. 379). In short, in its latest form, the relational question has been presented as a question to be pursued in its own right, not in the service of answering the ontological question of what (really) exists.

If a separate core problem for metaphysics is discerning what grounds what, we might well ask what the methods are supposed to be for addressing grounding questions. How can we discover what grounds what? About this, less has been said. Audi, for one, leaves this open, holding that we may discover grounding facts sometimes a priori (e.g., as we may discover that the fact that this is red is grounded in the fact that it's scarlet), sometimes empirically (e.g., as we discover that this being copper grounds this being electrically conductive) (Audi, forthcoming). Fine holds that grounding facts are themselves to be explained in terms of the natures of the things grounded (forthcoming, p. 50), and so one might expect that grounding facts may be discovered via the same route as facts about natures or essences. This leads us back to the questions of modal epistemology discussed earlier. As Fine writes:

> investigation into ground is part of the investigation into nature; and if the essentialist locus of ground-theoretic connections lies in the fact to be grounded and not in the grounds, then it is by investigating the nature of the items involved in the facts to be grounded rather than in the grounds that we will discover what grounds what. (forthcoming, p. 51)

At any rate, questions regarding not only what grounds what, but also what the grounding consists in and how one may discover or discern grounding facts, seem to be part of an emerging set of relational research problems in metaphysics.

Modal questions

As mentioned above, modal questions came once again to occupy a central role in metaphysics after Kripke's arguments were taken onboard in the 1970s. But while modal questions have been vigorously pursued, the deeper question that concerned the Empiricists and early analytic philosophers has once again come to the forefront. By what methods can we acquire knowledge of these modal facts? While there has been consensus since Kripke that there are modal facts that are not merely analytic facts, and cannot be discovered through mere conceptual analysis, there has been no consensus about how exactly the relevant modal facts about essences, identity, or persistence conditions *are* to be discovered.

Many mainstream metaphysicians carry on attempting to answer modal questions without engaging in the epistemological question of how we can know modal facts. But the problem is a virulent one: taking the metaphysically serious attitude of thinking that there are distinctively modal features of the world that metaphysics is (in part) in the business of discovering makes it particularly perplexing how we could hope to acquire that knowledge. For the modal facts of the world (assuming there are some) don't seem to be features to which we are in any way *causally* connected, making purported modal knowledge importantly disanalogous to perceptual knowledge. Moreover, many of the dominant views of what modal facts consist in (whether one takes them to involve facts about other concrete possible worlds or about possible worlds considered as abstract entities such as sets of propositions or the like) make it doubly clear that we can expect to have no causal interaction with the modal facts we aim to describe.

In fact, the problem of the epistemology of modality may deserve the notoriety of being one of the problems we have made the *least* progress in resolving in the last half-century. Peter van Inwagen puts it succinctly: "Modal epistemology is a subject about which little is known" (2001, p. 251).

In the face of the epistemic problem, some have advocated a form of skepticism about many modal claims in metaphysics. For example, van Inwagen allows that we do have knowledge of mundane possibilities (e.g., about where we could put that vase), but denies that this ability to acquire everyday modal knowledge carries over to enable us to know the truth of the sorts of modal proposition disputed in many metaphysical debates (e.g., whether it is possible for there to be a perfect being, whether it is possible that I exist and nothing material exists) (2001, pp. 243–5). Moreover, though he accepts that we have mundane modal knowledge, van Inwagen does not offer any account of how we may acquire such knowledge, saying simply "I regard much of this knowledge as mysterious" (2001, p. 250).

Others have likewise declined to even try to answer this epistemic question. For example, while David Lewis suggests that we often *do* arrive at modal opinions by reasoning from a principle of recombination, he offers no justification for *why* that should give us any knowledge about what is true in other possible worlds. The deeper problem of how we could acquire something that qualifies as *knowledge* of modal facts he simply punts on, saying "That is a fair request, and I regret that I cannot deliver the goods. But I don't see that this is especially my problem. It is a problem for everyone (certain skeptics and conventionalists excepted) . . ." (1986, p. 113). (Notice here what Lewis points out: that this is a problem that has particularly originated since the positivist's conventionalist treatment of modal questions was rejected—it is a problem for the new serious metaphysics that didn't arise [or at any rate was far less virulent, with a clear idea of the direction of reply] for the older, more modest sort of metaphysics that was regarded as acceptable even by the positivists.)

These epistemic worries, of course, haven't prevented many metaphysicians from claiming to know modal truths and using these centrally in their arguments. Many still appeal to claims about what is imaginable or, more broadly, conceivable, in arguments about when something, for example, would or would not survive. As Stephen Yablo puts it, "In the actual conduct of modal inquiry, our theoretical scruples about conceivability evidence are routinely ignored" (1993, p. 3). But if (as those practicing "serious" or deep metaphysics presuppose) modality is supposed to be a deep feature of the world, it's unclear why our imagination or conceptual abilities should provide knowledge of what is or is not possible (cf. Evnine, 2008, p. 666). Given the role of imaginative experiments and conceivability claims in arguments about what is possible, necessary, or impossible, a large part of the discussion of the epistemology of modality has centered on whether or not what we can imagine or conceive provides any guide to what is or is not possible. Some have defended the idea that conceivability provides some, even if fallible, guide to possibility. Stephen Yablo, for example, defends the idea that if something is conceivable we have a prima facie (though defeasible) reason for regarding it as metaphysically possible, where something is conceivable only if one can imagine a world that one takes to verify it (1993, p. 34). George Bealer (2004) argues that although modal intuitions are fallible, they nonetheless retain evidential force, and we can in principle root out these errors by a priori investigations.

Others have defended the idea that there is not just an *evidential* but a *constitutive* connection between conceivability and possibility. David Chalmers, for example, argues that, provided we understand the notion of conceivability properly, conceivability doesn't just provide evidence of possibility, it entails possibility (2002b). More precisely, he holds that the ability to positively conceive of P (on ideal rational reflection) entails that P is possible (that there is some possible world in which P is the case) and that being unable (on ideal rational reflection) to rule out P entails that P is possible (2002b, pp. 171–2).

A more minority approach has been to look for knowledge of modal facts not from our ability to imagine or conceive of situations, but rather from empirical, factual knowledge. That means holding that (contrary to Hume) modal facts about essences or natures can be purely empirically discovered—just as other facts are. So, for example, Crawford Elder argues that essential properties of objects may be purely empirically discovered by the ways in which properties cluster together—using what he calls the "test of flanking uniformities" (2004, p. 23).[24]

There has also been some renewed interest in deflationary approaches to modality as alternatives that might hope to crack the epistemic problem. For example, Alan Sidelle (1989) defends a neo-conventionalist approach to modality, and argues that a virtue of this view is that it enables us to explain why our modal intuitions may be thought to give us knowledge of modal facts (1989, pp. 110–11). On his view, all *general* principles of individuation are analytic and so knowable in virtue of our mastery of the relevant linguistic conventions. Our knowledge of Kripkean a posteriori necessary truths comes from combining our knowledge of general principles of individuation (e.g., that—if there is water—whatever chemical microstructure water actually has, it has necessarily) with empirical knowledge (e.g., that water actually has the chemical micro-structure H_2O). The modal force of the claim comes from the general principle of individuation, knowable a priori given our linguistic competence, but the full knowledge of the derivative modal claim (that water is necessarily composed of H_2O) comes only with the addition of empirical knowledge, accounting for its a posteriori status (1989, pp. 35–7 and 43–4).

Others (e.g., Blackburn, 1993; Brandom, 2008; Thomasson, 2007c) have argued for a different deflationary approach to modality, in the form of a nondescriptivist understanding of modal discourse. On Brandom's view, for example, talk about what is necessary has the function not of describing modal facts, but rather of making explicit certain norms governing the use of non-modal, empirical terms and concepts (2008, p. 99). This line of thought enables one to demystify modal knowledge by showing how our ability to utilize ordinary (non-modal—or at least not explicitly modal) vocabulary, combined with our ability to make explicit the rules governing those terms (in object-language modal indicatives), enables us to make true basic modal claims, and to acquire what modal knowledge there is to acquire (cf. Thomasson, 2007c, pp. 149–50).

Conclusion

While I have found it clearest to proceed by examining each type of research problem separately, some commonalities clearly reach across all three of these areas. In each area, the turn to concern with methodological questions is becoming more prominent. After the heady post-Quinean revival of simply doing first-order metaphysics, questions are once more being raised about how we can acquire knowledge in metaphysics, whether about issues of ontology, of grounding, or of modality. Methodological questions and meta-metaphysical questions are once again coming to the forefront, in ways that they had not for the past 60 years or more, but that are reminiscent of debates that held center stage in the earlier twentieth century, as "analytic philosophy" self-consciously emerged.

Where ontology is concerned, there *was* a methodological consensus that secured the revival and proliferation of ontology as a subdiscipline of metaphysics; the consensus was to adopt the Quinean approach to existence questions (putting aside difficulties about how exactly to interpret this). But this consensus is beginning to crack, as more philosophers are beginning to question the legitimacy of the scientistic approach, to question the arguments against the analytic–synthetic distinction that lie behind Quine's approach and to question its foundations in an absolutist interpretation of the quantifier. Interest is once again turning back to Carnap's side of the seminal Carnap–Quine debate, and a great many skeptical positions in contemporary meta-metaphysics may be identified as, in some sense, neo-Carnapian (see, e.g., Chalmers et al. 2009; Thomasson, 2007).

Where relational questions are concerned, there has been far less stability, as the very terms in which they are formulated have been constantly changing. In its current formulation, as considering questions of ground, little has been said about the proper methods for going about answering these questions, so here, too, much work remains to be done.

Finally, where modal questions are concerned, there previously *had been* a methodological consensus—that necessary truths were broadly speaking analytic truths and discoverable a priori by a form of conceptual analysis. That was rejected in light of Quine's arguments against analyticity and Kripke's discovery of necessary a posteriori truths. Yet there have been few plausible and informative suggestions of alternative methodologies for discovering modal truths, and that remains one of the most vexed problems in metaphysics. Without progress on that front, it is quite difficult to see how to evaluate the ongoing first-order debates about modal facts and properties in metaphysics.

In sum, research problems in metaphysics are increasingly methodological in focus. As the methodological worries have come to the forefront, there has also come to be a growing minority interested in deflationary alternatives to the robust neo-Quinean metaphysics that has held center stage for the past 60 years.

So, for example, we see increasing interest in minimalist or "easy" approaches to ontology (Schiffer, 2003; Thomasson, 2007b; Wright, 1983), as well as a small but growing interest in deflationary conventionalist or nondescriptivist approaches to modality (Blackburn, 1993; Brandom, 2008; Sidelle, 1989; Thomasson, 2007c). This has led in turn to increasing methodological sophistication and retrenching by those on the side of "mainstream" metaphysics (e.g., Sider, 2009, 2011; van Inwagen, 2009). The often surprising, revisionary views of mainstream metaphysicians also have led to increasing debate about the role of intuition and folk belief in resolving metaphysical disputes. Does conflict with philosophers' intuitions or with widespread beliefs among the folk count against a metaphysical "theory"? What strategies can, or need, a revisionist take in the face of apparent conflict with folk belief? (See Korman, 2009) The debates on these issues are very much in full swing, and will no doubt continue for some time to come. How the methodological questions get answered in turn will make all the difference to which research problems are pursued and which dismissed as unanswerable or pseudo problems, and to how they are pursued and how their competing answers are evaluated.[25]

Notes

1 I will speak of these as "existence questions," but of course allied questions are raised about what entities there *are*. Formulating the questions in those terms enables us to at least make superficial sense of the metaphysical question of whether there are nonexistent objects. Nonetheless, as most contemporary metaphysicians treat "there exist" and "there are" as equivalent, and as "existence questions" is a better phrase then "what there is questions," I will continue to speak of "existence questions" above—meaning to include also questions about what there *is,* where this is taken to be a broader question than one formulated in terms of what "exists."

2 Along with these first-order modal questions come also metaphysical questions about modality itself. Are there essences? Are there modal properties? Are there other possible worlds? These I would classify as existence questions *about* (alleged) modal entities rather than as first-order modal questions.

3 These issues of dependence also tend to play a core role in relational questions about what grounds what. I don't mean to suggest that these types of question are mutually exclusive.

4 Despite these acceptable forms, Ayer and other positivists tended to use the term "metaphysics" as a term of abuse.

5   As I have argued elsewhere (2002), phenomenologists such as Husserl and Heidegger employed a very similar methodology to that of "analytic" conceptual analysts, indeed one that seems to have been influential on the development of ordinary language philosophy.

6   This is not to suggest that Williamson himself thinks that, in a philosophical sense, it shouldn't be happening. He continues: "Many of those who practice it happily acknowledge its continuity with traditional metaphysics; appeals to the authority of Kant, or Wittgenstein, or history, ring hollow, for they are unbacked by any argument that has withstood the test of recent time" (2007, p. 19).

7   Subclass questions also include category questions "when these are construed as treated within an adopted language as questions having trivially analytic or contradictory answers" (Quine, 1951/1966, p. 207).

8   Carnap's approach in this regard is closely related to the later "easy" or "lightweight" arguments for the existence of numbers, propositions, etc. defended by Hale, Wright, Schiffer, and others. See "Ontological questions" below for discussion.

9   For simplicity, I will here treat "Vulcan" as shorthand for the description "the planet orbiting between Mercury and the sun." This is of course a contested issue itself, but is not at stake here, and the assumption will greatly simplify the exposition.

10 The phrase is from Huw Price (2006), who argues that even this may prove too ambitious a conception of metaphysics to properly attribute to Quine himself. For it is clear that on Quine's view philosophy is *continuous* with science, and there is no standpoint outside of science for the philosopher to take to separately ask, given those theories, how things really stand.

11 This is not to say that Quine himself would have endorsed the contemporary conception of metaphysics, or the work done under its name—indeed there have been powerful arguments suggesting that the neo-Quinean metaphysicians have often misinterpreted what Quine was really saying, or what the debate between Carnap and Quine was really about. See Price (2009) and Soames (2009).

12 For a further articulation and defense of this neo-Quinean metaontology, see van Inwagen (1998).

13 Graham Oddy (1982) discusses the difficulties in interpreting Armstrong's criterion.

14 For critical discussion of this argument see my (2007b), chapter 1.

15 Notice that Quine's criterion and the Eleatic criterion may lead to different results: for example, if numbers are indispensable to our best physical theories, then by the Quinean criterion we should accept their existence even if they do not, themselves, make a causal difference, but by the Eleatic criterion we should not.

16 For critical discussion of this approach, see Schaffer (2008).

17   Of course, Quine's criticisms of the notion of analyticity already cast doubt on this understanding of necessary truths—though Quine himself aimed to reject modal notions along with analyticity, not to revive a deeper metaphysical conception of modality.

18   I say many serious metaphysicians "took them to be" discoverable by metaphysical enquiry. Whether they were right to draw this lesson from Kripke's work is another matter—it is arguable that the proper lesson to draw instead is that some essences require empirical work to be discovered. But, as Sidelle has argued (1989), this is perfectly compatible with a general Empiricist approach that sees the work of metaphysics as lying only in conceptual analysis, and the work of science as undertaking empirical inquiry (see below), with no role remaining for "serious" metaphysics.

19   The earliest of which is Strawson and Grice (1956); but there has been a recent resurgence. See, for example, McGinn (forthcoming), Thomasson (2007b, ch. 2), Creath (2000), and Russell (2008, pp. 129–37). For a contemporary defense of the analytic–synthetic distinction, see Russell (2008).

20   Notice that this doesn't in fact rely on an empirical truth at all, since the same conclusion can be reached even if the original claim is false. From "Fido *isn't* a dog" we can similarly infer "Fido lacks the property of doghood" and then infer: "There is a property (lacked by Fido) (doghood)."

21   More precisely, answerable existence questions must be posed using a term with associated application conditions (which fix basic existence conditions for the entities, if any, falling under the term); answerable counting questions require that the term also be associated with co-application conditions (which fix basic identity conditions for the objects, if any, falling under it).

22   Unless they are using "object" in a covering sense in which it is clear which sortal terms are covered; in that case the question is straightforwardly answerable by answering the sub-questions for each covered sortal term.

23   For further discussion of the relation between grounding and truthmaking, see Fine (forthcoming), and Audi (manuscript).

24   For a discussion of problems with this approach, see my (2007a).

25   Many thanks to Simon Evnine, Dan Korman, Uriah Kriegel, and Ted Sider for very helpful comments on an earlier version of this chapter.

References

Armstrong, D. M. (1997), *A World of States of Affairs*. Cambridge: Cambridge University Press.

—(2004), *Truth and Truthmakers*. Cambridge: Cambridge University Press.

Audi, P. (forthcoming), "A clarification and defense of the notion of grounding," in
    F. Correia and B. Schnieder, eds, *Grounding and Explanation*. Cambridge: Cambridge
    University Press.
—(manuscript), "Modality and grounding."
Ayer, A. J. (1946/1952), *Language, Truth and Logic*. New York: Dover.
Bealer, G. (2004), "The origins of modal error." *Dialectica*, 58(1), 11–42.
Blackburn, S. (1993), "Morals and modals," in *Essays in Quasi-Realism*. New York:
    Oxford University Press.
Brandom, R. (2008), *Between Saying and Doing: Towards an Analytic Pragmatism*.
    Oxford: Oxford University Press.
Cameron, R. P. (2010), "How to have a radically minimal ontology." *Philosophical
    Studies*, 151, 249–64.
Carnap, R. (1956/1999), "Empiricism, semantics and ontology," reprinted in J. Kim and
    E. Sosa, eds, *Metaphysics: An Anthology*. Oxford: Blackwell.
—(1963), *The Philosophy of Rudolf Carnap*, ed. P. A. Schlipp. La Salle, IL: Open Court.
Chalmers, D. J. (2002), "On sense and intension," in J. Tomberlin, ed., *Philosophical
    Perspectives 16: Language and Mind*. London: Blackwell, pp. 135–82.
Chalmers, D. J., Manley, D., and Wasserman, R., eds (2002), "Does conceivability entail
    possibility?," in T. Gendler and J. Hawthorne, eds, *Conceivability and Possibility*.
    Oxford: Oxford University Press.
—(2009), *Metametaphysics: New Essays on the Foundations of Ontology*. Oxford: Oxford
    University Press.
Creath, R. (2000), "The initial reception of Carnap's doctrine of analyticity," in
    D. Follesdal, ed., *Philosophy of Quine: General, Reviews, and Analytic/ Synthetic*.
    New York: Garland.
Currie, G. (1989), *An Ontology of Art*. New York: St. Martin's Press.
Dorr, C. (2005), "What we disagree about when we disagree about ontology," in
    M. E. Kalderon, ed., *Fictionalism in Metaphysics*. Oxford: Oxford University Press,
    pp. 234–86.
Elder, C. L. (2004), *Real Natures and Familiar Objects*. Cambridge, MA: MIT Press.
Evnine, S. (2008), "Modal epistemology: our knowledge of necessity and possibility."
    Philosophy Compass, 3(4), 664–84.
Fine, K. (forthcoming), "Guide to ground," in F. Correia and B. Schnieder, eds,
    Grounding and Explanation. Cambridge: Cambridge University Press.
Gendler, T. and Hawthorne, J., eds (2002), *Conceivability and Possibility*. Oxford: Oxford
    University Press.
Heil, J. (2003), *From an Ontological Point of View*. Oxford: Oxford University Press.
Hirsch, E. (1982), *The Concept of Identity*. Oxford: Oxford University Press.
—(2002), "Quantifier variance and realism," in E. Sosa and E. Villanueva, eds, *Realism
    and Relativism: Philosophical Issues Vol. 12*. Oxford: Blackwell, pp. 51–73.
Hofweber, T. (2005), "A puzzle about ontology." *Nous*, 39(2), 256–83.

—(2007), "Innocent statements and their metaphysically loaded counterparts."
Philosophers' Imprint, 7(1), 1–33.

—(2009), "Ambitious, yet modest metaphysics," in D. J. Chalmers, D. Manley and
R. Wasserman, eds, *Metametaphysics: New Essays on the Foundations of Ontology.*
Oxford: Oxford University Press.

Horgan, T. (1993), "From supervenience to superdupervenience: meeting the demands
of a material world." *Mind,* 102, 555–86.

Hume, D. (1748/1977), *An Enquiry Concerning Human Understanding.* Indianapolis:
Hackett.

Hylton, P. (2004), "Quine on reference and ontology," in R. F. Gibson, Jr, ed., *The
Cambridge Companion to Quine.* Cambridge: Cambridge University Press.

Jackson, F. (1998), *From Metaphysics to Ethics: A Defence of Conceptual Analysis.*
Oxford: Oxford University Press.

Kim, J. (1993), *Supervenience and Mind.* Cambridge: Cambridge University Press.

Kim, J. and Sosa, E., eds (1995), *A Companion to Metaphysics.* Oxford: Blackwell.

Korman, D. (2009), "Eliminativism and the challenge from folk belief." *Nous,* 43,
242–64.

—(manuscript), "The language of the ontology room."

Kripke, S. (1972/1980), *Naming and Necessity.* Cambridge, MA: Harvard University
Press.

Lewis, D. (1986), *On the Plurality of Worlds.* Oxford: Blackwell.

Lowe, E. J. (1989), *Kinds of Being.* Oxford: Blackwell.

Manley, D. (2009), "Introduction: a guided tour of metametaphysics," in D. J. Chalmers,
D. Manley and R. Wasserman, eds, *Metametaphysics: New Essays on the Foundations
of Ontology.* Oxford: Oxford University Press.

McGinn, C. (2011), *Truth by Analysis: Games, Names and Philosophy.* Oxford: Oxford
University Press.

Merricks, T. (2001), *Objects and Persons.* Oxford: Oxford University Press.

Oddy, G. (1982), "Armstrong on the eleatic principle and abstract entities." *Philosophical
Studies,* 41, 285–95.

O'Leary-Hawthorne, J. and Cortens, A. (1995), "Towards ontological nihilism."
Philosophical Studies, 79, 143–65.

Price, H. (2006), "Quining naturalism." *Journal of Philosophy,* 104, 375–405.

—(2009), "Metaphysics after Carnap: the ghost who walks?" in D. J. Chalmers,
D. Manley and R. Wasserman, eds, *Metametaphysics: New Essays on the Foundations
of Ontology.* Oxford: Oxford University Press.

Quine, W. V. O. (1951/1966), "On Carnap's views on ontology," reprinted in *The Ways of
Paradox and Other Essays.* Cambridge, MA: Harvard University Press.

—(1953/2001), *From a Logical Point of View* (second edition). Cambridge, MA:
Harvard University Press.

Russell, G. (2008), *Truth in Virtue of Meaning.* Oxford: Oxford University Press.

Ryle, G. (1970), "Autobiographical," in O. P. Wood and G. Pitcher, eds, *Ryle*. New York: Doubleday.

—(1971), *Collected Papers. Volume 2*. Bristol: Thoemmes.

Schaffer, J. (2008), "Truthmaker commitments." *Philosophical Studies*, 141, 7–19.

—(2009), "On what grounds what," in D. J. Chalmers D., Manley and R. Wasserman, eds, *Metametaphysics: New Essays on the Foundations of Ontology*. Oxford: Oxford University Press.

Schiffer, S. (2003), *The Things We Mean*. Oxford: Oxford University Press.

Sellars, W. (1963), "Philosophy and the scientific image of man," reprinted in *Science, Perception and Reality*. Atascadero, CA: Ridgeview, pp. 1–40.

Sidelle, A. (1989), *Necessity, Essence and Individuation: A Defense of Conventionalism*. Ithaca, NY: Cornell University Press.

Sider, T. (2009), "Ontological realism," in D. J. Chalmers, D. Manley and R. Wasserman, eds, *Metametaphysics: New Essays on the Foundations of Ontology*. Oxford: Oxford University Press.

—(2011), *Writing the Book of the World*. Oxford: Oxford University Press.

Soames, S. (2003), *Philosophical Analysis in the Twentieth Century Volume 2: The Age of Meaning*. Princeton, NJ: Princeton University Press.

—(2009), "Ontology, analyticity, and meaning: the Quine-Carnap dispute," in D. J. Chalmers, D. Manley and R. Wasserman, eds, *Metametaphysics: New Essays on the Foundations of Ontology*. Oxford: Oxford University Press.

Strawson, P. F. (1963), *Individuals: An Essay in Descriptive Metaphysics*. New York: Doubleday.

Strawson, P. F. and Grice, H. P. (1956), "In defense of a dogma." *Philosophical Review*, 65(2), 141–58.

Taylor, R. (1992), *Metaphysics* (fourth edition). Englewood Cliffs, NJ: Simon and Schuster.

Thomasson, A. L. (2002), "Phenomenology and the development of analytic philosophy." *Southern Journal of Philosophy*, XL, 115–42.

—(2007a), "Review of Crawford Elder, *Real Natures and Familiar Objects*." *Philosophy and Phenomenological Research*, 74(2), 518–23.

—(2007b), *Ordinary Objects*. New York: Oxford University Press.

—(2007c), "Modal normativism and the methods of metaphysics." *Philosophical Topics*, 35(1 & 2), 135–60.

van Inwagen, P. (1983), "Fiction and metaphysics." *Philosophy and Literature*, 7, 67–77.

—(1998), "Meta-ontology." *Erkenntnis*, 48, 233–50.

—(2001), "Modal epistemology," in *Ontology, Identity and Modality*. Cambridge: Cambridge University Press.

Williamson, T. (2007), *The Philosophy of Philosophy*. Oxford: Blackwell.

Wittgenstein, L. (1953/1958), *Philosophical Investigations* (third edition), ed. G. E. M. Anscombe. New York: Macmillan.

Wright, C. (1983), *Frege's Conception of Numbers as Objects.* Aberdeen: Aberdeen University Press.

Yablo, S. (1993), "Is conceivability a guide to possibility?" *Philosophy and Phenomenological Research,* 53(1), 1–42.

—(2002), "Go figure: a path through fictionalism." *Midwest Studies in Philosophy,* 25, 72–102.

—(2005), "The myth of the seven," in M. E. Kalderon, ed., *Fictionalism in Metaphysics.* Oxford: Oxford University Press.

Modality

Tony Roy

There is a Humean problem about possibility and necessity: "Obama is president" is true insofar as it describes the way things actually are. But if it is true, "Obama could make it in the NBA" is true only because it describes a non-actual possibility. On its face, however, an appeal to that which is not actual seems absurd. Whence, then, the latter claim? I introduce this difficulty, and consider replies. In so brief an article, it will not be possible to survey views from the history of philosophy, or the full range of contemporary responses. Rather, a cross section of issues will be introduced in the context of a "possible worlds" reply, and especially *linguistic ersatzism* as a representative of this strategy. In the midst of objections, I try to keep things interesting, and see what there is to say on behalf of the ersatz approach.

The problem of modality

A proposition may be true (or false) *simpliciter*. But possibility and necessity are among modes of truth. Thus a proposition may be *possibly* or *necessarily* true. Among the modalities are propositions probably true, permissibly true, henceforth true, and more—where each of these raise philosophical questions about actuality and truth. Under the heading "modality" though, philosophers have been specially interested in the particular question raised by possibility and necessity. Some observations: (i) Possibility and necessity are inter-definable. Possibly Obama plays in the NBA, if and only if it is not necessary that he does not. And necessarily Obama is human if and only if it is not possible that he is not. Given this, an adequate account for either possibility or necessity is an account for both, and a problem for one is a problem for both. (ii) Possibility and necessity come in different varieties. Thus, in one sense, a bishop must move along a diagonal—for to do otherwise breaks the rules. But in another sense, the bishop can move from any square to one of a different color—for nothing is simpler than to pick it up and set it down wherever you please. And similarly different notions of possibility and necessity appear in a wide variety of contexts. (I sometimes ask students if it is possible to drive the 60 miles from our campus in San Bernardino to Los Angeles in 30 minutes. From natural assumptions about Los Angeles traffic, law enforcement, and the like, most say it is not. But some, under different assumptions, allow that it can be done!) Philosophers have been particularly interested in a broad, *metaphysical* sort of modality—described by Alvin Plantinga (1974, pp. 1–2) as "broadly logical." In this sense, it is not possible for something to be round and not round, or for a thing to be round and square; but it is possible for Obama to play in the NBA and for aliens to invade the earth. More controversially, water is necessarily H_2O; and it is possible for natural laws to be other than they are, and so, say, for a thing to travel faster than the speed of light. I shall concentrate on this modality, though the structure of the problem is parallel from one case to the next. Finally, (iii) in one variety or another, modal notions are ubiquitous. Fundamental components of logic depend on possibility and necessity. Even if philosophical results are not necessary, aspects of philosophical reasoning remain subject to necessary constraint. One encounters modal notions in science, for natural law, and in moral or decision theory, where it matters what one can and cannot do. And so forth. It is natural, then, to seek an adequate account of these notions. But it is not obvious that any such account is to be had.

Problems about possibility and necessity as such are parallel to traditional problems about knowledge of possibility and necessity. In each case, on a plausible account, supposed results outrun their actual grounds. So it may help to begin with a sketch about worries for knowledge. It is natural to think that knowledge of the world is derived from observation of the world. Suppose we observe that all crows are black. Is it possible that there be a non-black crow? The answer is not determined by our observation that all crows are black, for not every possible situation is actual. If it is possible for there to be a non-black crow, then some non-actual possibility is such that *if* it were actual there would be a non-black crow. But we observe only the actual world; there is no observation of what is non-actual. And if there is not any observation of what is not actual, then there is not any observation of correlations between the actual and the non-actual—it is not obvious how observations of the actual are relevant to what is merely possible. Thus, following a suggestion from Colin McGinn (1981, p. 181), consider a theory T with consequences for non-modal properties of the actual world and for non-actual possibilities, and some other theories whose actual-world consequences are the same as T, but whose non-actual consequences are different. Insofar as observation is of actuality, there is seemingly no observation to distinguish among the theories. So the empiricist, who grounds knowledge of the world in observation, has reason to hold that observation does not ground knowledge of truth or falsity for the various modal claims, and may find in these considerations the basis for a general skepticism about modal knowledge.

This skepticism rests on a metaphysical difficulty according to which the requirements for possibility and necessity exceed the resources of actuality. The basic elements of the problem lie not very far under the surface of the possible worlds picture of modality. Thus consider, for example, David Lewis's *modal realism* (1986). On his view, for every way a world can be, some world is. A thing is necessary if it is true in all worlds, possible if true in some. On this view, worlds are things very much like the universe in which we live, though different worlds are spatiotemporally and causally isolated; for Lewis, "actual" is analyzed indexically—the reason this world is actual for us is that it is the one we are in. Say a property is *categorical* if and only if it does not depend on properties at other worlds: so a thing's *being round* or *being 10 kilograms* is categorical, where its *being necessarily round* or *being possibly other than 10 kilograms* are not; for the former, but not the latter, do not depend on how things are in other worlds. On Lewis's view there is a plurality of worlds, where each has a distribution of its own categorical properties. In any world, every property, modal or otherwise, has a ground in the overall distribution of categorical properties. Modal properties in a world are not grounded merely in the categorical properties of their own world, but in the categorical properties of the plurality as a whole. Thus crows are possibly non-black in a world just in case there is some member of the plurality in which there is a non-black crow; crows are necessarily black just in case they are black in every world.

So on this worlds picture, modal properties are not wholly grounded in actuality. But this stands in tension with the natural thought that the very idea of a(n actual) property or truth not wholly grounded in actuality is bizarre or occult. Take a salt tablet. It is natural to say that it is soluble, and that it is soluble because of the categorical way it actually is. Diamonds, plastics, and the like are insoluble because they are categorically different. And similarly for a wide variety of properties. Suppose, for example, I claim to have "ultimate greatness" and insist that my dopplegänger in a world categorically the same as ours does not have it (or has it only on alternate Thursdays); when pressed for those features in virtue of which I have it and he does not, I respond, "It is a brute fact—there is no difference beyond our differing with respect to ultimate greatness." This is bizarre. Similarly for serious moral properties. And similarly for the modal properties with which we began.

But, if these reflections are right, we have a full-blown problem about modal truth. For we seem to accept,

> *MP*: Things actually have objective modal properties.
> *AC*: Any property has an actual categorical ground.
> *NG*: Actual categorical properties are not an adequate ground for modal
>   properties.

MP is from the ubiquity of modality. AC is the natural claim about actual grounds. And NG is illustrated by the worlds picture. But these are inconsistent. From MP and AC, some modal properties have an actual categorical ground. And by NG, no modal property has such a ground. Standard responses take the form of denying MP, that things actually have objective modal properties, as in some versions of empiricism; denying AC, that modal properties have an actual or a categorical ground, as in appeals to possible worlds or primitive modality; or denying NG and arguing for the sufficiency of some actual categorical ground. The history of philosophy suggests that it is no easy task to make sense of the world without modal properties. Thus we concentrate on attempts to account for modality: Assuming MP, that there are modal properties, we encounter each of the other options as we proceed.

Worlds as a solution

The standard semantics of modal logic incorporates a set of "worlds" which may or may not have restricted "access" from one to another. Assignments to basic sentences are made at these worlds. A sentence is possible at world w if and only if it is true at some world accessible from w, and necessary if and only if it is true at every world accessible from w. An argument is valid if and only if no such structure includes a world where the premises are true and the conclusion is not.[1] The worlds approach to modality structurally parallels the standard semantics for modal logic—only with some account of worlds that makes them more than mere indices for the arbitrary assignments of logic (let each world have access to all the others). As we have seen, Lewis (1986) develops an account on which worlds are things like the universe in which we live, with different ones spatiotemporally and causally isolated.

Against Lewis, however, it is natural to object that the required plurality of worlds does not exist and attempt to attain the benefits of his "paradise" on the cheap. Thus Lewis considers abstract entities that would, from his point of view, count as substitute (ersatz) worlds. One particularly straightforward proposal is *linguistic* ersatzism. On this account, worlds are some collections of sentences; an ordinary sentence is true in a world just in case it is a member of the world; then a thing is possible if and only if it is true in some world, and necessary if and only if it is true in all. Supposing that there are sets of sentences, the question becomes whether these entities are sufficient for an account of modality. I consider two broad objections, first with respect to the nature and second the relevance of such "worlds."

The metaphysics of worlds

An ersatz world substitutes for a universe, with all its myriads of detail. This puts burdens on the expressive power of the language for the sets of sentences—for the language should be sufficient to describe anything about a world. And, similarly, philosophers have been led to say ersatz worlds are *maximal*—that for any sentence *a*, either *a* or not-*a* is an element. I raise concerns related to each point.

Expressive power

An initial thought from Lewis (1973) is that there simply are not enough sets of sentences in a natural language to represent all the ways the world could be. Suppose there could be a Euclidean space with any combination of points filled by matter; then the number of ways the world can be is at least as great as the number of subsets of the set of all the points in the space. But sentences in a natural language are finite strings over a finite alphabet; and the number of worlds is no greater than the sets of such strings. So by straightforward cardinality considerations, it is not the case that there are as many sets of sentences as there are ways the world can be.[2] So the ersatz strategy misrepresents the possibilities.

Say this is right. In 1986, Lewis grants that linguistic entities for ersatz worlds need not be sentences of a natural language, and goes so far as to allow that worlds may be composed of a "Lagadonian" language on which each object functions as its own name, and each universal as its own predicate; sentences are set-theoretic constructions out of this "vocabulary" along with logical connectives and quantifiers (pp. 145–6; compare Swift, III.V). On this Lagadonian account, there are words and sentences corresponding to nothing ever spoken or contemplated by a human speaker (e.g., a sentence about some object in a distant galaxy). Thus Lewis gives the ersatzer a language of exceptional power. However, he goes on to object that, even so, the ersatzer's language does not have sufficient power to represent properly the facts of modality.

To see the worry, consider *indiscernible* individuals—as Napoleons in worlds of two-way eternal recurrence, or individuals that could, but do not exist. Then, though the language has the resources to describe the features of actual things down to the last detail, and to name whatever there actually is, it may seem to lack the resources to tell one Napoleon from another, or to say that a non-actual individual might have done this or might have done that. Thus, in a much-discussed example, Alan McMichael (1983) objects that the ersatzer cannot represent the possibility that JFK have had a second son who becomes senator, but who could have become an astronaut. It is simple enough to tell one story according to which JFK has a second son who becomes a senator, and another where he has a second son who becomes an astronaut. But just as someone other than John Jr. might have been the first son of JFK (say, one born years earlier and with a different mother), so different individuals might have been JFK's second son. And even a Lagadonian language does not name a second son of JFK. So given the one story according to which JFK has a second son who becomes a senator, the other is not one according to which *he*—the same individual—becomes an astronaut. So we do not represent the possibility that the individual who becomes a senator could have become an astronaut.

There are different responses available. Problems go away if in some sense there exist merely possible individuals, or essences for individuals that could but do not exist; for then the language might name a second son of JFK in some straightforward way (Plantinga, 1976; Zalta, 1983). But there exist also responses that do not require "extra" ontology (Roy, 1995; Sider, 2002). So, extend the Lagadonian language L to a language L^* with the addition of some extra constants. (Perhaps the pair $\langle N, x \rangle$ names object x and $\langle n, x \rangle$ is an extra constant; then there are as many extra constants as things and so, with sets as things, as many as sets.) Tell stories in the extended language. Then it might be that (α is a second son of JFK who becomes a senator) is true in some w_1 and (α becomes an astronaut) is true in w_2. Given the world where α becomes an astronaut (α is a second son of JFK who becomes a senator, and could have become an astronaut), is true in w_1. On this scheme, extra constants work as "placeholders" for individuals; stories in L^* use the constants to indicate the places. But the extra constants do not name anything; they rather indicate places something could occupy. So it is generalizations in the original L, indicating just the places, which represent real possibility. Thus, generalizing on α, (something is a second son of JFK who becomes a senator and could have become an astronaut) is true in w_1; and since there is such a world, we have that possibly something is a second son of JFK who becomes a senator and could have become an astronaut in actuality. Similarly, one might tell stories according to which there are qualitatively identical but distinct Napoleons. And similarly for related objections about properties that are indiscernible or could but do not exist.

Maximality

Suppose that for any proposition *a*, some sentence expresses *a* and some sentence expresses not-*a*. (Perhaps, depending on the metaphysics of propositions and the Lagadonian language, sentences just *are* propositions.) Then the supposition that worlds are maximal and so include one of *a* or not-*a* for every sentence is incoherent:[3] Consider a world *w*, and the set $P(w)$ which has as members all the subsets of *w*. By Cantor's Theorem, there are more sets of sentences in $P(w)$ than sentences in *w*. Trouble. But first, the Theorem.

Set A is a *subset* of set B if and only if every member of A is a member of B (this is understood to imply that the empty set φ, with no members, is a subset of every set). Set A has at least as many members as set B if and only if there is a one-to-one map from (some of) the members of A onto all the members of B. Suppose $P(w)$, the set of all the subsets of sentences from world *w*, does not have more members than there are sentences in *w*; then *w* has at least as many members as $P(w)$, and there is a one-to-one map *h* from members of *w* onto all the members of $P(w)$. Since *h* is a function from sentences to sets of sentences, we may ask if a given sentence *a* is itself a member of $h(a)$. Thus, with integers, if some function *f* has $f(2) = \{2,4,6\}$ and $f(3) = \{19,127\}$, then 2 is a member of $f(2)$ but 3 is not a member of $f(3)$. Consider $C = \{a \in w \mid a \notin h(a)\}$, the set of all elements *a* in *w* such that *a* is not a member of $h(a)$; C is formed by collecting every sentence *a* in world *w* which is not a member of the subset to which it is mapped by *h*. Any sentence in C is collected from *w*; so C is a subset of *w* and thus a member of $P(w)$. But C is designed so it differs from every $h(a)$ in membership of *a*: Consider an arbitrary $h(a) = A$; if *a* is a member of A, then by construction, *a* is not included in C, so $A \neq C$; if *a* is not a member of A, then by construction, a is included in C, and again A ≠ C; either way, $h(a)$ ≠ C. So there is no a such that $h(a)$ = C; so h does not map onto all the members of $P(w)$. This contradicts the specification of h; reject the initial assumption: there are more elements of $P(w)$ than of w.

And this generates a problem about the maximality of w. Suppose w is maximal; then given our assumption that there are sentences to express any proposition and its negation, for any A in $P(w)$, w includes one or the other of,

a_1 Some member of A is true; and
a_2 No member of A is true.

So w includes at least one sentence for each member of $P(w)$; so there are not more members in $P(w)$ than w. This is impossible; reject the assumption: w is not maximal.

So given a language with adequate expressive power, the very attempt to say everything about a world is self-defeating. But there is a reason for maximality in the account of necessity. Suppose non-maximal (partial) "worlds," and for some necessary a consider a world w that does not include a. Then, on the account we have offered, a is not true in w. So a is not true in every world and, on the usual account, a is not necessarily true, contrary to assumption. (Exercise for the reader: Adapt the above reasoning to show that there is no set of all necessary truths, so that any set of sentences is missing some necessary a. Hint: if members of A are necessary, then a_1 is necessary; and if A is empty, a_2 is necessary.)

A natural response is to obtain the function of worlds but without maximality (Humberstone, 1981; Roy, 1995). Thus, for example, require that a (partial) story be a *fully extended* set of sentences.

i. t *extends* s ($t \geq s$) if and only if t includes every member of s ($t \supseteq s$).
ii. s is *fully extended* if and only if for any a, some extension of s includes a or not-a.

Then say an ordinary a is *true* in s if and only if every $t \geq s$ has a $t' \geq t$ such that a is an element of t'. So a sentence is true in a story so long as, no matter how the story is extended, the sentence always shows up eventually. Consider stories that are possible in the sense that they could be true, and consider a story s and extension t of s. Where story t is possible, for any necessary a, $\{a\} \cup t$—the story that adds a to t—is possible as well. So among possible stories, every extension t has an extension with a as a member, and a is therefore true in s. Given this, proceed in the usual way: A thing is necessary if and only if it is true in all stories, possible if it is true in some.[4] Insofar as stories are not maximal, there is no problem about maximality—though there is the related requirement that stories be fully extended.

This strategy seems to accommodate related objections. Consider a case derived from Kit Fine (2003, pp. 169–71). Grant the possibility of "telepathic Cartesian egos." Suppose,

a. There could be at least one Cartesian ego.
b. If it is possible that there are some egos, it is possible that for any (sub)set of them, an ego is in telepathic communication with just the egos in that set.
c. If some egos can exist, it is possible that they all exist together.

From (c) there is a story (Descartes's story) according to which all possible egos exist, and from (a) according to Descartes's story there are some egos. From (b), one might conclude,

d. If it is possible that there are some egos, then possibly there are more egos than that.

So some story has more egos than Descartes's story. But (d) follows from (b) only with the assumption that the egos that exist according to any given story comprise a set. The immediate consequence of the Cantorian argument is that any set has more subsets than members; if there can be some set of egos, by (b) there can be an ego corresponding to every subset of it; so there can be more egos than are in the set. On our assumptions, however, there need not be a set of all the egos. Suppose there is a set A of egos according to story s; then there may be an extension t of s according to which there are all the egos in A and for any subset of A, some ego is in communication with just the egos in that set. Say the egos in t comprise a set B; then there may be an extension of story t according to which there are all the egos in B and for any subset of B some ego is in communication with just the egos in that set. And so forth. So it is possible that for any set of egos, there are more egos than are in it. And this seems just right, given the assumptions with which we began. All the possible egos appear eventually in extensions of Descartes's story, so according to Descartes's story they all exist; but no extension of Descartes's story has a set of all the possible egos. So attempts to show that ersatz entities (stories in this case) are "too small" to include everything are correct, but the force of them is undercut by allowing the ersatz entities to extend, just as a universe of sets (or egos) itself extends under Cantorian pressures.

The relevance of worlds

So far, we have addressed technical problems with technical solutions. If ersatz entities do not properly represent the facts of modality, then ersatzism cannot hope to provide an adequate analysis of modality. Suppose such problems are resolved, and some ersatz entities do adequately represent the facts of modality. Even so, there are reasons to question the adequacy of a worlds approach. Perhaps worlds exist as advertized, but still do not solve the problem. I turn now to concerns of this sort.

Lewis

Lewis does not appeal to modality in his specification of worlds. On his theory, there are some worlds; possibility and necessity are defined on them. And given the nature of his worlds, there is no question that their features are possible. But he objects that the ersatzer can give no such account (1986). Rather, he says, the ersatzer must appeal to modality in specification of her stories. It is not enough that stories are some fully extended sets of sentences (or whatever), for the stories must be possibly true. But an account which appeals to modality does not explain it. So if the ersatzer simply says, "stories are *possible* and fully extended sets of sentences," she does not account for modality; ersatz worlds may have some utility, but not for an account of modality as such.[5]

Lewis anticipates a reply according to which stories may be merely *consistent* relative to syntactic criteria—relative to some axioms and derivation rules. So if axioms include "No dog is a cat" and a story says Fido is both a dog and a cat, contradiction follows in the usual way, and the story is not consistent. So far, so good. But, says Lewis, any plausible specification of the axioms will itself rely on primitive modality.

> Primitive modality will not go away. The axioms to do the job may exist, but the ersatzer will not be in a position to specify them. He can only declare: the axioms shall include whichever sentences of such-and-such form are necessarily true. Once he says that, all his analyses from there on are modal. (Lewis, 1986, p. 154)

So, again, modality is required for a specification, and the ersatz stories do not suffice for an account of modality.

For the moment, grant that we are in no position to specify stories except by appeal to modality. Still, the ersatzer might attempt a "brazen" reply: Suppose some sets are all the possible stories, or sentences are a specification of all the axioms. Seemingly God, at least, could survey the sets or the sentences, "point out" the relevant ones, and say, "Thus I identify the possibilities." So God could give an analysis of modality in terms of linguistic entities making no appeal to modality. But for an adequate analysis of some feature of the world, it should not matter who does the analysis. Lewis says worlds are determinative of modality; the ersatzer, God in this case, says that particular sets and sentences do the job. Each points and says *"voilà."* And relative to God, the human ersatzer's problems may seem to be (merely) epistemic and practical. Lewis grants that the ersatzer may legitimately depend on knowledge of modal facts for axiom specification. But it is unlikely that some modal facts will ever be known. So the human ersatzer is in the position of being unable to determine whether certain sentences are axiomatic or not. And perhaps there are "too many" axioms for any finite being to specify them all. But, again, these are not problems for ersatzism as such. So far as primitive modality goes, then, Lewis and the ersatzer are in very much the same boat. When they "point," it is required that they point to all and only the possibilities. In either case, once this is done, the analysis is complete without appeal to modality.

Perhaps there is something deeply unsatisfying about "brazen linguistic ersatzism." Parity between Lewis and the ersatzer may motivate rejecting the views together, rather than accepting one or the other. One can point to any old entities, a stack of books or whatever, and say a thing is possible if true according to some, and necessary if true according to all. Even if a proposed analysis is extensionally correct, it may not immediately be clear how or why the entities constitute the modality. It is surely implausible that the modal facts are constituted by any stack of books! One wants to know what it is that connects modality to Lewis's worlds, or some abstract stories, or the books, or whatever. This concern underlies a critique developed by Michael Jubien, especially in his (2009); compare (Jubien, 1988, pp. 303–5) along with (Lycan, 1979, pp. 308–12) and (van Inwagen, 1986, p. 199).

Jubien

To set the stage, Jubien emphasizes that the "worlds" of semantics for modal logic are (mere) indices in a mathematical structure. By means of the structure, there are results for validity and invalidity of arguments. But the mathematics is not metaphysics. A theorist who accepts the "central tenet" of worlds theory according to which a thing is possible if and only if true in some possible world, adopts a position structurally parallel to the standard semantics for logic. But this is not a mathematical justification for the central tenet. Rather, a thesis about the metaphysics of modality requires metaphysical justification. In particular, the central tenet "cannot rise to the status of an analysis of the notion of possibility until we have been told *what the possible worlds are like and why what goes on in other possible worlds has anything to do with what is true in a given possible world*" (Jubien, 2009, pp. 69–70). Both Lewis and the ersatzer make headway toward accounts of what the worlds are like. This leaves the question about what other worlds have to do with what is true in ours. And, though worlds might reflect modal reality, Jubien maintains that they do not ground it.

Against Lewis, Jubien invites us to consider the "pure, untitled ontological picture of detached *realms*" (Jubien, 2009, p. 62). Suppose there are two such realms, or 27. Say the latter, but all of them include stars. On the face of it, the detached realms are not so much as relevant to the question whether stars are necessary beings. Similarly for a stack of 27 books, each asserting that there are stars. So far, the view lacks "modal oomph" to connect the realms to what can and must be. Lewis argues from theoretical fruit to the result that for every way a world could be some detached realm is that way. This fruit requires treating the realms as possibilities. But even the fruitful hypothesis that detached realms are the possibilities does not itself remove the question how or why this is so.

Lewis's counterpart theory may seem to provide the relevant oomph. On this theory, different worlds represent our world as being other than it is. So for example (parts of) worlds represent Hubert Humphrey, the former Vice President and 1968 United States presidential candidate.

> Humphrey may be represented *in absentia* at other worlds, just as he may be in museums in this world. The museum can have a waxwork figure to represent Humphrey, or better yet an animated simulacrum. Another world can do better still: it can have as part a Humphrey of its own, a flesh-and-blood counterpart of our Humphrey, a man very like Humphrey in his origins, in his intrinsic character, or in his historical role. By having such a part, a world represents *de re*, concerning Humphrey—that is, the Humphrey of our world, whom we as his worldmates may call simply Humphrey—that he exists and does thus and so. By waving its arm, the simulacrum in the museum represents Humphrey as waving his arm; by waving his arm, or by winning the presidential election, the other-worldly Humphrey represents the this-worldly Humphrey as waving or as winning. That is how it is that Humphrey—our Humphrey—waves or wins according to the other world. This is counterpart theory, the answer I myself favour to the question how a world represents *de re*. (Lewis, 1986, p. 194)

So other realms are relevant to our world to this extent: they represent it as different than it is. Given counterpart theory, then, Lewis and the ersatzer each offer representations of actuality.

Jubien argues that "no one could bring it about that an entity represents Humphrey without being causally connected to both Humphrey and the entity" (Jubien, 2009, p. 65). If this is right, Lewis's entities do not represent actuality, and to this extent, his view is at a disadvantage relative to ersatzism. But allow that similarities are sufficient to set up representation even without causal interaction. Then the worlds as representers land in very much the same boat as ersatz stories. A set of sentences can represent what is not possible. This is the reason for axioms, or the like, to constrain stories. But so a concrete entity may represent what cannot be. Thus Saul Kripke argues that, if Queen Elizabeth II is not in fact the natural daughter of the Trumans, it is metaphysically impossible for her to have been the natural daughter of the Trumans (Kripke, 1980, pp. 110–13). Say this is right. Still, "this would not prevent someone from staging a play in which she was represented as being the Truman's daughter" (Jubien, 2009, p. 66). One might require "similarity with respect to necessary features" for representation; but then worlds are not doing the modal work. One might postulate that other realms just have *making it possible that Humphrey won.* But, again, this is an appeal to modality best avoided.

So any worlds theory must appropriately connect its worlds to what is actually possible and necessary. But, says Jubien, there is a "deep and fundamental weirdness" in the supposition that any such connection exists.

> The weirdness is this. Suppose it's necessary that all **As** are **Bs**. The central-tenet *analysis* is that in every possible world, all **As** are **Bs**. So the necessity arises from what goes on in all the worlds taken together. There's nothing intrinsic to any **A**-containing world, even in all of its maximal glory, that *forces* all of its **As** to be **Bs**. It's as if it just *happens* in each such world that all of its **As** are **Bs**, that from the strictly internal point of view of any world, it's *contingent,* a mere coincidence.... The theory provides no basis for understanding why these contingencies repeat unremittingly across the board (while others do not). As a result, it provides no genuine analysis of necessity. . . . *Of course* if something is necessary, *and* there really are all these "possible worlds," then the something that is necessary will be true in each of them. But that doesn't tell us *why* it is true in each of them, in other words, what its necessity consists in. (Jubien, 2009, pp. 74–5)

So worlds do not explain necessity. And an account of whatever intrinsic features constrain worlds to be the way they are would seem to render the worlds superfluous for an analysis of modality, as the real work is done by the account of the intrinsic features.

Jubien himself holds that necessities are constrained by relations among Platonic properties—it is from these relations that we obtain the required modal oomph. According to Platonism, for something to be a horse is for it to instantiate the property *being a horse,* and for something to be an animal is to instantiate the property *being an animal.* This requires that the properties themselves have distinct intrinsic natures. Given the natures, the reason that necessarily horses are animals is that *"the two properties' intrinsic natures together guarantee it"* (Jubien, 2009, p. 93). Thus one property may *entail* another. Similarly, horses are possibly wild if the properties *being a horse* and *being wild* are *compatible* in the sense that neither entails the negation of the other. Jubien has "no opinion" about the details of property entailment (Jubien, 2009, p. 94). In particular, it is not a thesis about property constitution. Thus, when something instantiates *being a horse* it instantiates *not being a xylophone*—though the one is not a constituent of the other. For Jubien's analysis, it is sufficient to think of the entailment relations as primitive, if not simple. In the end, then, for "necessarily all horses are animals" and "possibly some horses are blue," Jubien gives, "necessarily anything that instantiates *being a horse* instantiates *being an animal,*" and "possibly something instantiates *being a horse* and *being blue.*" The first is necessary insofar as *being a horse* entails *being an animal.* The second is so if *being a horse* is compatible with *being blue.*

Worlds Again

So the charge is that worlds, ersatz or otherwise, are superfluous for an analysis of modality. But there may yet be a role for worlds. Begin with some simple analyses (compare Mondadori and Morton, 1976): A notion of entailment (or provability) is familiar from logic. But on the standard account,

D Sentence *a* is *provable* if and only if there is a derivation of it

where a *derivation* is a sequence of sentences such that each member is either an axiom or follows from previous members by a rule. Similarly, in a game of chess,

G White *can* win from position *p* if and only if some game overlapping *p* results in checkmate of black where a *game* is a sequence of moves respecting the rules of chess. Without an account of the derivations or games, it would be bizarre simply to point at some sequences of sentences and say, "*a* is provable if and only if one of these has *a* as its last element"; or to some sequences of moves and say "white can win if and only if a sequence overlapping *p* results in checkmate of black." As such, pointing leaves it open whether the relevant sequences respect the rules, and whether they are all the sequences under the rules. It is mysterious how entities not subject to the constraints could be relevant to the analyzed notions. But quantifications over proofs and games are relevant precisely because of the constraints to which they are responsible. Proofs and games become relevant insofar as they represent all the combinations subject to the constraints. The "modal oomph" results from their relation to basic rules functioning as a constraint on the range of combinations.

Similarly, one might think ersatz stories could be relevant to metaphysical modality. Suppose partial stories and truth in them as above. Then one might offer,

Q Sentence *a* is *possibly* true if and only if there is a consistent story according to which *a*

where we require of consistent stories that they respect some basic constraints. Let the constraints be precisely the ones to which Jubien appeals. Thus all consistent stories make it true that anything that instantiates *being a horse* instantiates *being an animal,* and the like. So the suggestion is that possibility is a quantification over stories; and stories become relevant insofar as they represent combinations subject to constraints grounded in the actual intrinsic natures of properties.

Jubien might allow the biconditional Q. He would not, however, allow it as an analysis of modality. Though worlds may represent possibilities by respecting intrinsic constraints, they are superfluous if the constraints do all the work: Necessities are given by property entailment; at best, stories merely exhibit what they are. But note that derivations and games are not superfluous to D or G. Their rules do not simply list all the entailments. Rather, rules function as basic constraints; the full range of entailments is fixed by rules only in combination with quantification over the derivations or games. In this way, the derivations and games are essential to accounts D and G.

Jubien accounts for all necessity by property entailments. With this done, there is no work left for stories to do. But even supposing his Platonism, not all property entailments are so straightforward as in the case of *being a horse* and *being an animal,* or *being a horse* and *being wild.* Consider whether pigs can fly. This does not seem to be a simple matter intrinsic to *being a pig* and *being a flying thing.* Rather, the possibility depends on some complex interaction between the density of pigs, the nature of gravity, the atmosphere, laws of flight and the like. One might respond that *being a flying thing* builds in features of gravity, the atmosphere and laws of flight, so the relations remain intrinsic. Even so, surely entailments of *being a flying thing* are not independent of entailments from *being gravity, being an atmosphere* and *being laws of flight.* It is natural to think entailments of a complex *being a flying thing* result from entailments of constituent properties. But if this is right, there remains room for a class of "basic" entailments from which others result. Pigs cannot fly when every combination of basic properties rules it out. But with entailments of complex properties given by combinations subject to basic constraints, one might offer quantification over all stories that respect the basic constraints (or maybe better, over complex properties) precisely in order to complete the account of entailment and compatibility. In this case, even under an entailment picture, stories have a non-weird role for an account of modality.

Of course, if stories are constrained by entailments, and the entailments are themselves modal, we appeal to modality for the account of the stories. Again, however, there is apparently no such appeal in D or G. Any derivation makes it true that each sentence is an axiom or results from previous sentences by a rule, and each of the games makes it true that a bishop moves along a diagonal. Then on the proposed accounts, modal notions are quantifications over all the entities with these features. So long as, with Jubien, we hold no opinion about the details of property entailment, the stories of Q are no doubt modal at bottom—for we appeal to basic and modal property entailments as constraints. But one might hope to lever the picture of property constituents into something like an account of the basic entailments. Thus one might accept,

cnj A thing has *being p and q* if and only if it has *being p* and *being q*
dsj A thing has *being p or q* if and only if it has *being p* or *being q*
neg A thing has *being not p* if and only if it does not have *being p*

Though any such suggestion must be controversial, perhaps a thing has *being not p* when it instantiates a property in a complement of *being p* relative to some background property class—as a thing is not a pine when it is a cedar, an oak or the like (Figure 1).

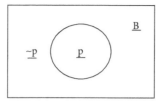

Figure 1

So if *being an animal* is a conjunctive part of *being a horse,* horses are animals. And if *being a horse* is a disjunctive constituent of *not being a xylophone,* then a thing that is a horse is not a xylophone. (So though *being a horse* is no part of *being a xylophone* it might, notwithstanding the above suggestion, be a part of *not being a xylophone*; in this case constituency does account for the entailment from *being a horse* to *not being a xylophone*.) I do not mean to offer an account of basic constraints! Perhaps there is no theory of properties sufficient for a complete account of entailments.[6] Still, the Platonist accepts that properties have some intrinsic natures. Supposing basic constraints are a function of intrinsic categorical features (as above or otherwise) then, even if a complete *specification* of them requires modality, the constraints themselves rest on an actual categorical ground. If this much is right then, on the model of D and G, Q contributes to a theory on which there is a categorical ground for modal reality.

Observe that the present approach does not somehow eliminate modality. At best, modal notions are "reduced" to ones that are non-modal in the sense that stories and quantification, themselves not modal, combine to constitute possibility and necessity. So stories play a non-weird role in a complete account of possibility and necessity. Or one might try for something less: perhaps stories exhibit combinations under basic, but modal constraints. Again, then, there is a non-weird role for worlds, though in something less than a complete account of modality.

Philosophers have not generally attempted so much. While there are different accounts of what worlds are like, in typical cases, either there is modality in the account, or it is left unclear how or why they matter.[7] So there is no single way an appeal to worlds addresses the problem with which we began. Lewis denies AC by denying that every property has an actual ground. This view, together with brazen ersatzism, faces relevance objections. With primitive modality, one denies AC by denying that every property has a categorical ground. Depending on how much is primitive, in this case, worlds may (or may not) play a role in something less than a complete account of modality. The present story account, in its strongest version, denies NG, by holding that actual categorical elements are an adequate ground for modal properties. So modality is explained on the basis of categorical elements alone.

De re modality

Traditionally, philosophers have distinguished between modality *de dicto* and modality *de re*—where "possibly there is a blue horse" is *de dicto* and "Possibly Obama plays in the NBA" is *de re*. On a worlds picture, *de re* modality "tracks" particular objects across worlds, where *de dicto* modality does not. So, for example, "Possibly Obama plays in the NBA" depends on how Obama is in different worlds; it is true just in case there is a world where he plays in the NBA. In contrast, "possibly there is a blue horse" depends on horses in the different worlds, but without respect to how a thing is from one world to the next; it is true if and only if there is a world where something is a blue horse. So *de re* modal claims, in contrast to *de dicto*, have to do with the modal properties of particular things.[8]

Though he is not enthusiastic about necessity and possibility on any account, it is well known that W. V. O. Quine, and many others, have thought that *de re* modality is particularly problematic (Quine, 1976, 1980). Suppose property entailments, or the like, underwrite *de dicto* results of the sort, "necessarily horses are animals" and "necessarily no horses are xylophones." Still, these entailments do not obviously suffice for the *de re* case. Given *de dicto* principles sufficient for the result that there is no story where something is both a horse and a xylophone, we do not yet have the result that something that is a horse in one world is not a xylophone in another. So we do not yet have that Seabiscuit, say, is not possibly a xylophone. Insofar as the entailments are necessary *de dicto*, they have no consequences for modal properties of particular individuals. So a solution to the problem of *de dicto* modality leaves the problem of *de re* modality intact.

But the difficulty is not merely that a solution to one leaves the other intact. Rather, Quine argues that there are special difficulties for the *de re* case. By the indiscernibility of identicals, if *x* is identical to *y*, then *x* has the same properties as *y*. Quine thinks this principle fails for supposed modal properties, and therefore that the very idea of a modal property is incoherent. Quine's own examples tend to depend on descriptions, and there are well-known replies. Here is a case, like Quine's, that illustrates the difficulty: "Necessarily the inventor of bifocals invents bifocals" seems true, and "Necessarily the first Postmaster General invents bifocals" false. But the inventor of bifocals is the first Postmaster General. At one level, then, Quine would like to see us as first granting and then withholding *being necessarily the inventor of bifocals* to Benjamin Franklin, and so as violating the principle. Arguably, however, these claims are not *de re* at all. It is enough that no world has something that is and is not the inventor of bifocals, but some world has a thing that is Postmaster General and not the inventor of bifocals. So there is no question about Franklin in different worlds. Against Quine, then, Ruth Barcan Marcus, Saul Kripke, and others have responded that it is important to separate proper names which may be *rigid* in the sense that they track with particular things across worlds, from descriptions which need not work this way; they suggest that if one does keep them and their roles distinct, problems evaporate (Kripke, 1980, pp. 6–15; Marcus, 1961; Plantinga, 1976, pp. 14–26; Smullyan, 1948).

Here is a case that seems to avoid such replies (Gibbard, 1975). Suppose God creates *ex nihilo* a clay statue, and later annihilates it into nothing. Then it is uncontroversial that the statue and the lump or mass of clay of which it is composed coincide over their entire career. On some occasion, a person points to the statue and says, "Let this statue be called '*s*'." Prima facie, "*s*" is as good a proper name as any. Similarly, on some occasion, a person points to the clay and says, "Let the clay of which this statue is composed be called '*c*'." The name enters the language and is transmitted in the usual way. Prima facie "*c*" is as good a proper name as "*s*." The statue and the clay have their actual categorical features: shape, weight, spatiotemporal location, and so forth, all in common. Thus one might think that $s = c$. But then there is a problem if we admit both of the (apparently) *de re* claims,

S Necessarily *s* is not as flat as a pancake
C Possibly *c* is as flat as a pancake

for then we seem to allow that *c* has *being possibly as flat as a pancake* but *s* does not. With $s = c$, then, there is conflict with the indiscernibility of identicals. But even if the statue is distinct from the clay, insofar as the statue and the clay are categorically the same but modally different, there is a difficulty about AG, the principle that any property has an actual categorical ground. Where both designators are plausibly rigid, it is not obvious how the standard anti-Quinean strategies apply. So it is important for this case that "*s*" and "*c*" are rigid, one no less than the other (see Della Rocca, 1996).

Responses to this problem are tangled with accounts of designation and of what it is to be a thing. If the statue and the clay are distinct things, then we may accept both S and C, but at the apparent cost of denying AG. Then there is no problem about the indiscernibility of identicals, insofar as $s \neq c$. If the statue and clay are a single thing, at least one of S or C is false—or, if we are to preserve the data, one of S or C is something other than a straightforward *de re* claim about the thing. So, for example, one might say that reference for relevant terms switches so that one of S or C is a true claim about some fictional object, process or the like (see Zimmerman, 1995). Or, finally, we might accept that neither S nor C is a straightforward *de re* claim about a thing, and accept some alternate analysis of both.

Without venturing so far as an analysis of S and C, it might be possible to say something about the modal reality underlying such claims. Again following Jubien for basic constraints, say a property is *singulary* if it cannot be instantiated by more than one thing at a given time. A *k-essence* is a property, like *being that specific dog* or *being this specific human* that, for kind *k,* must always be instantiated by the same *k. Being president of the United States* is singulary, but not a human essence—for it might be instantiated by different humans. On Jubien's account, for any kind *k* and entity *x* of kind *k* there is a *k*-essence (Jubien, 2009, p. 90). So there is *being this statue* and *being this clay.* Then, from property entailments in the usual way, necessarily nothing instantiates *being this statue* and *being as flat as a pancake*; and possibly something instantiates *being this clay* and *being as flat as a pancake.* More generally, we might accept principles according to which, if something instantiates a statue essence and has some shape, then necessarily a thing with that essence retains (roughly) that shape; and if something instantiates a lump-of-clay essence and has some shape, then possibly a thing with that essence has a different shape; and so forth. It seems possible to adopt this much independently of whether the statue and clay are distinct, and how "*s*" and "*c*" designate.

And nothing stops incorporating principles like these as basic constraints into stories. Thus we might accept principles according to which, if something instantiates a statue essence and has some shape, then in any story in which a thing has the essence, the thing has (roughly) that shape. Such principles may seem to result from the nature of properties as before. Suppose we have as a constraint that if something instantiates a horse essence, then in any story a thing with that essence is a horse. Then, supposing also that necessarily no horse is a xylophone, there is no case where a particular horse in one story turns out to be a xylophone in another. Given that stories are so constrained, we have already much of what is likely to be required of stories for a full analysis of things, and of S and C. And if the constraining principles rest on the categorical nature of properties, we have all the elements of the solution from before. Possibility and necessity are quantifications over consistent stories, where consistent stories respect basic constraints from the (categorical) nature of properties. So both modality *de dicto* and (what we have been able to say about) modality *de re* are explained on the basis of categorical elements.[9]

Notes

1   A semantics for modal logic is developed in Kripke (1963a, 1963b) and Hintikka (1963). Graham Priest (2008) is an accessible introduction.

2   For N the set of all natural numbers, the cardinality of the points in a Euclidean space, like that of the real numbers, is $P(N)$ the set of all the subsets of natural numbers; so there are $PP(N)$ sets of points in the space and, on our assumption, as many ways to distribute matter. But there are just N finite sequences of a finite vocabulary; and no more ersatz worlds than there are sets of sentences; so the number of worlds is at most $P(N)$. So by Cantor's Theorem, there are more ways the world can be than ersatz worlds. These basic cardinality claims arise in, say, the first couple chapters of Boolos et al. (2002). For Cantor's Theorem, see the discussion of "Maximality" just below.

3   This point is from Jubien (1988, p. 307), Grim (1991, pp. 91–124), and others. Jubien (2009, pp. 78–82) develops a nice version that does not depend on the specifically set-theoretic nature of worlds. He argues that no "world proposition" (or related entity) is both consistent and maximal in the sense that it *entails* every proposition or its negation.

4   On this account, a sentence may remain neither true nor false when some extensions of a story have *a* and some not-*a*. But this is a mere feature of story incompleteness, rather than of the world as such. Constraints on modal access, as in modal logic, are possible but introduce complications (see Humberstone, 1981).

5   So, for example, Robert Adams (1974, p. 225), "A [world story] is a set which has as its members one member of every pair of mutually contradictory propositions, and which is such that it is possible that all of its members be true together." And Plantinga (1974, p. 44) says a possible world is a possible and maximal state of affairs. Of course, these thinkers have other applications for worlds.

6 If there are entailments between basic properties, as between *having mass* and *having extension* where one is no part of the other, constituency does not take us the whole way. In this case, either there is more to say, or we are saddled with primitive modality. Perhaps there are no such entailments, or no basic properties. Or perhaps *having mass* and *having extension* are basic but "unsaturated" so that one is instantiated only in conjunction with the other (see Denkel, 1996).

7 A potential exception are the *combinatorial* theories of modality which take worlds to include all combinations of some basic entities. For a combinatorial theory, see David Armstrong (1989).

8 There is a corresponding formal distinction. Formally, a sentence is *de re* if and only if it has a subformula that, taken alone, has an individual constant or free variable inside the scope of a modal operator; a sentence is *de dicto* if and only if it is not *de re*. Thus, "possibly Obama plays in the NBA" and "there is a man such that possibly he plays in the NBA" with their natural symbolizations, "◊Po" and "∃x(Mx ∧ ◊Px)" are *de re*; "possibly there is a blue horse" with its symbolization, "◊∃x(Hx ∧ Bx)" is *de dicto*.

9 Thanks to the editors, along with Christina Roy, Rose Roy, and my colleague Matthew Davidson for helpful comments on this chapter.

References

Adams, R. (1974), "Theories of actuality." *Noûs*, 8, 211–31.
Armstrong, D. (1989), *A Combinatorial Theory of Possibility*. Cambridge: Cambridge University Press.
Boolos, G., Burgess, J., and Jeffrey, R. (2002), *Computability and Logic* (fourth edition). Cambridge: Cambridge University Press.
Della Rocca, M. (1996), "Essentialists and essentialism." *Journal of Philosophy*, 93, 186–202.
Denkel, A. (1996), *Object and Property*. Cambridge: Cambridge University Press.
Fine, K. (2003), "The Problem of possibilia," in M. Loux and D. Zimmerman, eds, *The Oxford Handbook of Metaphysics*. Oxford: Oxford University Press, pp. 161–79.
Gibbard, A. (1975), "Contingent identity." *Journal of Philosophical Logic*, 4, 187–221.
Grim, P. (1991), *The Incomplete Universe: Totality, Knowledge and Truth*. Cambridge, MA: MIT Press.
Hintikka, J. (1963), "The modes of modality." *Acta Philosophica Fennica*, 16, 65–79.
Humberstone, L. (1981), "From worlds to possibilities." *Journal of Philosophical Logic*, 10, 313–39.
Jubien, M. (1988), "Problems with possible worlds," in D. Austin, ed., *Philosophical Analysis*. Boston: Kluwer Academic Publishers, pp. 299–322.
—(2009), *Possibility*. New York: Oxford University Press.

Kripke, S. (1963a), "Semantical analysis of modal logic I: normal propositional calculi." *Zeitschrift für Mathematische Logik und Grundlagen der Mathematik,* 8, 67–96.

—(1963b), "Semantical considerations on modal logic." *Acta Philosophica Fennica,* 16, 83–94.

—(1980), *Naming and Necessity.* Cambridge, MA: Harvard University Press.

Lewis, D. (1973), *Counterfactuals.* Oxford: Basil Blackwell.

—(1986), *On the Plurality of Worlds.* New York: Basil Blackwell.

Lycan, W. (1979), "The trouble with possible worlds," in M. Loux, ed., *The Possible and the Actual.* Ithaca, NY: Cornell University Press, pp. 274–316.

Marcus, R. (1961), "Modalities and intensional languages." *Synthese,* 13, 303–22.

McGinn, C. (1981), "Modal reality," in R. Healey, ed., *Reduction, Time and Reality.* Cambridge: Cambridge University Press, pp. 143–87.

McMichael, A. (1983), "A problem for actualism about possible worlds." *Philosophical Review,* 92, 49–66.

Mondadori, F. and Morton, A. (1976), "Modal realism: the poisoned pawn." *Philosophical Review,* 85, 3–20.

Plantinga, A. (1974), *The Nature of Necessity.* New York: Oxford University Press.

—(1976), "Actualism and possible worlds." *Theoria,* 42, 139–60.

Priest, G. (2008), *An Introduction to Non-Classical Logic: From If to Is* (second edition). Cambridge: Cambridge University Press.

Quine, W. V. O. (1976), "Three grades of modal involvement," in Quine, *The Ways of Paradox and Other Essays.* Cambridge, MA: Harvard University Press, pp. 158–76.

—(1980), "Reference and modality," in Quine, *From a Logical Point of View.* Cambridge, MA: Harvard University Press, pp. 139–59.

Roy, T. (1995), "In defense of linguistic ersatzism." *Philosophical Studies,* 80, 217–42.

Sider, T. (2002), "The ersatz pluriverse." *Journal of Philosophy,* 99, 279–315.

Smullyan, A. (1948), "Modality and description." *The Journal of Symbolic Logic,* 13, 31–7.

Swift, J. (1996), *Gulliver's Travels.* Mineola, NY: Dover Publications.

van Inwagen, P. (1986), "Two concepts of possible worlds," in P. French, T. Uehling, and H. Wettstein eds, *Midwest Studies in Philosophy XI.* Minneapolis: University of Minnesota Press, pp. 185–213.

Zalta, E. (1983), *Abstract Objects.* Boston: D. Reidel Publishing Company.

Zimmerman, D. (1995), "Theories of masses and problems of constitution." *Philosophical Review,* 104, 53–110.

Universals and Abstract Objects

Roy T. Cook

Metaphysics is a discipline with many distinct facets. One of the most important of these is ontology—the study of the sorts of entities that exist and their nature. Two types of entity that have, jointly, received a great amount of attention within ontology are abstract objects and universals.

In this chapter we shall survey various stances one might take regarding the existence and nature of these two ontological categories. In "What is a Universal?" and "What is an Abstract Object?" we shall first outline what universals and abstract objects, respectively, are (if they, in fact, exist). In "Some Clarifications Concerning Terminology" we shall be concerned with sorting out some confusions in the language used to speak about these topics—in particular, we shall sort out some ambiguities in the use of the terms "platonism" and "nominalism" with regard to how these terms are applied both to particular views regarding universals and to particular views regarding abstract objects. We shall then, in "Universals, Mathematical Objects and Language," examine the most common form of argument for the existence of abstract objects and of universals, and briefly discuss why this type of argument, which focuses on particular ways we use language, seems more compelling in the case of abstract objects than as an argument for the existence of universals. In "Platonism vs Nominalism" we shall then survey four major types of position one can take towards the existence and nature of abstract objects and of universals: platonism, immanent realism, conceptualism, and nominalism. In "Connecting Platonisms: Logicism" the chapter concludes with a short discussion of neologicism, focusing on the prospects for using this framework, originally devised as a foundation for mathematics, as a means for examining the connections between universals and abstract objects more generally.

The approach taken here is primarily a positions-based approach. We shall concentrate on outlining particular (contemporary) positions and stances, evaluating arguments both pro and con regarding these positions, and defining and disambiguating specialized technical terminology used in these debates. No attempt shall be made to trace the historical origins of these ideas in any sophisticated sense. Nevertheless, with regard to both abstract objects and universals, contemporary debates can (as is almost always the case in philosophy) be traced back to issues which first arose in the work of Plato. Thus, we shall begin each of the following two sections with a brief note on where, exactly, the notions at issue arose in Plato's thought and what he had to say about them.

What is a universal?

In *Parmenides,* Socrates describes an argument presented by Zeno as follows: "What does this statement mean, Zeno? 'If things are many', you say, 'they must be both like and unlike. But that is impossible; unlike things cannot be like, not like things unlike'" (Plato, 2005, p. 922). The problem raised by this passage, appropriately called the *One Over Many Problem,* requires us to explain how two distinct objects (the "many") can nevertheless, in some sense, be the same (be "one"). Thus, given a red apple and a red salt shaker, the two objects are, by hypothesis, distinct, yet we must somehow account for the fact that they are nevertheless in some philosophically substantial sense the same, since the first is red and the second is red.

Formulated in more technical jargon, the One Over Many Problem consists in noting that individual objects (particulars) are sometimes qualitatively similar, sometimes qualitatively dissimilar—or, more carefully, that objects can be qualitatively similar in one respect and qualitatively dissimilar in another (such as our ball and salt shaker, which are color-wise similar and shape-wise dissimilar)—and asking of our metaphysics that it account for such differences.

Zeno's point, as summarized by Socrates in the *Parmenides,* is that we cannot solve the One Over Many Problem in terms of a primitive notion of "likeness," since our red apple and red salt shaker would need to be both like (in terms of their shared redness) and unlike (in terms of their distinct shapes). A pair of objects being both instances of the primitive likeness relation and instances of its contradictory—unlikeness—results in a prima facie contradiction. So how should we deal with the One Over Many Problem?

The answer, in one sense or another, is universals (or, more colloquially, properties, concepts, etc.). Loosely put, universals are entities which ground these similarities and dissimilarities by being (in one sense or another) jointly present in the particulars (or individuals) that share the relevant similarity and being absent in one or both of the objects that share the relevant dissimilarity. Thus, if REDNESS and ROUNDNESS are universals, then the similarity color-wise between our ball and our salt shaker is explained by the fact that REDNESS is somehow present in both of these objects, and the dissimilarity shape-wise between the two is explained (in part) by the fact that ROUNDNESS is present in the former but not the latter object.

Of course, postulating the existence of such seemingly bizarre entities without providing some account of their nature is useless. No matter how one works out the details, the defining characteristic of universals, which distinguishes them from particulars, is their repeatability. Our red ball cannot be (wholly) located in two distinct locations at the same time, but REDNESS is simultaneously located (wholly) in the red ball and (wholly) in the red salt shaker (or, at least, so our intuitions tell us—see the discussion of conceptualism and immanent realism below).

There are two important things to note at this point. First is that (with the parenthetical caveat from the end of the previous paragraph in mind) this repeatability is not merely a case of the universal being multiply located in the sense in which we might think that some particulars are multiply located. For example, if one thinks that Nicolas Bourbaki is a genuine particular (one need not, but please bear with the example), then this particular is located, in a certain sense, in many different particular locations—one for each of the mathematicians who collaborated under this pseudonym. Importantly, however, the particular denoted by "Nicolas Bourbaki" is not wholly located in any of these locations—rather, a part of Bourbaki is located in each location corresponding to each of the mathematicians who wrote under this name. Universals, on the other hand, are wholly located wherever they are located at all; thus REDNESS—and not merely some part of REDNESS—is wholly located in the red ball, and is also wholly located in the red salt shaker.

Second, it should be emphasized that properties (i.e., universals corresponding to unary predicates such as "is red") need not be the only universals. In addition, relations (corresponding to two-place predicates such as "is redder than . . .," three-place predicates like "is between . . . and . . .," etc.) might be universals. Nevertheless, it is often convenient to restrict one's attention to the simpler case of unary universals, a practice that shall be followed here, with the tacit assumption that whatever account we provide for this special case can be generalized to universals of all types with minimal modifications.

As a result, there would seem to be good reasons for thinking that universals are not material objects—or, at the very least, they are not the sort of simple material objects we are familiar with from everyday physical interactions. After all, material objects do not seem to be able to wholly locate themselves in two places at the same time. Further, even if we thought that (at least some) universals might "correspond" to complex material objects—thus, REDNESS might so correspond to the mereological sum of all red surfaces (see Quine, 1964)—it is not obvious that there are any material objects (mereologically complex or not) that correspond in this way to relations.

Before moving on to abstract objects, we should note that an explanation of qualitative similarities and dissimilarities between objects is not the only theoretical role that universals might be play in our theorizing. A successful account of the nature of universals promises to provide important ingredients to the solution of a number of philosophical conundrums, which might include, but need not be limited to, providing us with philosophically substantial accounts of the nature of: (a) possible worlds; (b) propositions; (c) second- and higher order quantification; (d) semantic values of predicates[1]; and (e) scientific laws. Of course, some of these are more or less closely related to others, and one need not accept any of these particular applications in order to grant that questions regarding the nature and existence of universals are interesting and important. Before moving on to a direct investigation of such questions, however, we shall examine another odd type of entity—abstract objects.

What is an abstract object?

Like the case of universals in the previous section, any discussion of abstracta (i.e., abstract objects—the singular is "abstractum") must begin with Plato. In *Phaedo* he gives an elegant summation of his reasons for accepting the existence of abstract objects.

> Do we recognize such a thing as absolute uprightness? . . . And absolute beauty and goodness too? . . . Have you ever seen any of these things with your eyes? . . . Well, have you ever apprehended any of them with any other bodily sense?

By "them" I mean not only absolute tallness or health or strength, but the real
nature of any given thing—what it actually is. Is it through the body that we get
the truest perception of them? . . . Don't you think that the person who is most
likely to succeed in this attempt is the one who approaches each object, as far as
possible, with the unaided intellect . . .? (Plato, 2005, p. 48)

Here we have Plato introducing his infamous theory of Forms. The Forms (e.g.,
absolute uprightness, beauty, and goodness) are characterized here in two ways.
First, the Forms are genuine objects. Second, the forms are (both ontologically
and epistemologically) independent of any of our bodily senses. As we shall see,
such causal inefficacy is one (but not the only) important characteristic typically
attributed to abstract objects. (It is worth noting that Plato seemed to believe that
universals [i.e., his Forms] were not the only type of abstract object.[2]) A fuller
discussion of Plato's views is beyond the scope of this chapter, but suffice it to
say that Plato's metaphysics, although likely the first account of the nature of
abstract objects, is but one of a multitude of different ways to work out such a
metaphysics.

Many (but certainly not most!) modern-day philosophers, even if they
do not accept every aspect of Plato's particular account of abstract objects
(and, in particular, even if they do not accept the central epistemological role
attributed to them by Plato), nevertheless accept that there is a type of object
distinct from everyday material objects—that is, distinct from concrete objects.
Abstract objects are usually identified, and distinguished from concrete objects,
in terms of being some or all of the following: (a) causally inert; (b) mind
independent; (c) necessary; (d) nonspatial; (e) nontemporal; (f) nonphysical;
and (g) unchanging. Abstract objects are thus particulars with some or all of
these properties. As we shall see, there is room on the conceptual map for entities
which are abstract but which are not particulars, hence we shall reserve the term
"abstract object" (or "abstracta") specifically for objects.

The careful reader will have noticed an uncomfortable fact regarding the
list—all of the characteristics of abstracta (or other abstract entities) given
above are merely negations of characteristics which we usually take most or all
everyday, material objects to have. David Lewis (1986) calls such an account
of abstract objects the "Way of Negation"—we say nothing positive regarding
the nature of abstracta, but instead characterize them in terms of their lacking
features shared by more pedestrian material objects. In other words, we have
said nothing regarding what abstracta *are*, and have instead only said what they
are not! This leaves us in an uncomfortable position where we might suspect

that we have not, as of yet, said anything interesting or substantial regarding the actual nature of these entities.

If abstracta are anything, however, then they are, first and foremost, objects. This suggests a second means for distinguishing between abstract objects and concrete objects—by ostension. According to this strategy, we would explain the nature of abstract objects by identifying a number of typical or paradigmatic cases. Unfortunately, there is little agreement regarding which, if any, objects are abstract. Typical candidates include: (a) fictions; (b) logical objects; (c) numbers (or the subject matter of other mathematical theories); (d) possible worlds; (e) propositions; (f) types (as opposed to their tokens); and (g) universals. None of these can be thought of as genuinely typical or paradigmatic examples of abstract objects, however, since none of these are cases where there is genuine agreement that the objects in question are, in fact, abstract (nor is there, in most of these cases, even general agreement regarding the existence of the relevant objects at all). Thus, this second method of drawing the abstract–concrete distinction seems no more successful that the first.

Setting aside these difficulties in formulating the abstract–concrete distinction precisely,[3] there does seem to be some general implicit agreement regarding what these objects are and to what uses, philosophically, they might be put. In fact, the list of purported "examples" of abstract objects given above also provides a useful guide to the topics within which abstract objects might play a significant explanatory role.

Before moving on, it should be noted that, contrary to the typical manner of presenting the notions of abstract and concrete, these two concepts in question might be neither exhaustive nor exclusive. For example, certain sorts of dualists regarding the mental might think that there are objects that are neither concrete physical objects nor abstract objects (since the latter must presumably be, among other things, unchanging, atemporal, and mind-independent), and thus that the two categories discussed above are not exhaustive. The possibility that the categories of abstract and concrete are not exclusive arises when we consider the so-called "impure" abstract objects such as {Mr. Decatur} (i.e., the set containing exactly Mr. Decatur as its only member). While we might believe that pure sets such as the empty set are nonspatial, nontemporal, etc., it would seem that such "mixed" objects as {Mr. Decatur} are neither wholly concrete nor wholly abstract. Regardless of the existence of cute terminology such as "impure abstracta," which has been cleverly formulated for the sole purpose of obscuring this complication, the existence of such objects makes it clear that the abstract–concrete distinction is neither as precise nor as clear as we might like. Nevertheless, the comments above are enough to move on to our examination of the different positions one might take regarding the existence and theoretical role of such entities. Before doing so, however, a number of clarifications regarding the terminology used in these debates is in order.

Some clarifications regarding terminology

Often platonism regarding universals is equated with the view that universals are a particular species of abstracta. This might be true of some ways of working out platonism, but as a general description of the philosophical terrain it is misleading in a number of interconnected respects. First, universals are typically taken to be the semantic values of predicates (and are a potential candidate for the range of higher order quantification), while abstracta are taken to be the semantic values of terms (and are the range of first-order quantification (for more on these issues, see "Universals, Mathematical Objects and Language" later). Second, if universals are to be of use in explaining qualitative similaries and dissimilarities among particulars, then they will need to play this role for abstract particulars as well as for concrete particulars. Thus, it will serve us well, in what follows, to not *assume* that universals, even if they exist, are abstract— they might turn out to be concrete, or alternatively, they might turn out to be abstract, but nevertheless metaphysically distinct, in the relevant sense, from the kind of abstract *particulars* that are, for example, the subject matter of mathematics on platonist accounts. Thus, the point is not that universals are not abstract objects, but rather that their abstractness and their particularity are two distinct issues.

This brings us to another terminological difficulty—ambiguities in the use of the terms "platonism" and "nominalism." As we have already seen, platonism comes in (at least) two distinct varieties: the acceptance of universals and the acceptance of abstracta. Along similar lines, nominalism is either a denial of the existence of universals or a denial of the existence of abstract objects. This use of the term "nominalism" comes (unfortunately) with two distinct, additional and systematic ambiguities—one of which occurs in both applications to universals and to abstracta, and another that is specific to the case of abstract objects.

First, as already noted, nominalism is either the denial that universals are abstract entities, or that the subject matter of mathematics consists of abstracta. The first ambiguity occurs, however, as a result of the fact that such rejections come in two different "strengths." We can identify two formulations that nominalism might (and often does) take in each case—nominalism regarding universals could amount to either of the following.

Strong Universal Nominalism: There are no universals.
Weak Universal Nominalism: Universals exist but are not abstract.

There are analogous formulations with respect to the subject matter of mathematics.

Strong Mathematical Nominalism: There are no mathematical objects.
Weak Mathematical Nominalism: Mathematical objects exist but are not abstract.

These demonstrate that the usage of "nominalism" in the philosophy of mathematics is similarly ambiguous. In what follows we shall reserve the term "nominalism" for the strong formulations in each case, using other established terms for positions which amount to acceptance of merely the weak thesis.

Second, "nominalism" has, even when restricted to the debate over the existence of abstract objects, been used to refer either to the denial of the existence of abstract objects or to the denial of the existence of special objects that are the subject matter of mathematics (i.e., the denial of the existence of abstract objects that are the subject matter of mathematics). The two usages are equivalent, of course, only if the only (potential) abstract objects are those objects (whatever they are) that (potentially) serve as the subject matter of mathematics, and vice versa, but we need not make this assumption.

This latter ambiguity highlights the fact that debates regarding the existence of abstract objects are not, and need not be, restricted to the special case of mathematical entities. On the contrary, a positive answer to "Are there abstract objects?" still leaves open both whether the subject matter (if any) of mathematics is composed of abstract objects and whether there are abstract objects that are not mathematical. Nevertheless, much of the discussion of abstract objects centers on the mathematical case, and we will follow tradition here. It should be clear as we go along, however, that the arguments and positions outlined below with regard to the subject matter of mathematics can be generalized to other types of abstract object, such as those catalogued in the previous section.

Universals, mathematical objects, and language

As should already be evident from the previous sections, there are intimate connections between the issues under discussion here—the existence and nature of universals and of mathematical objects—and the ways that we use language. Among other things, it is natural to think that universals—if such exist—are the semantic values of, or somehow correspond to, our predicates (or, at least some of our predicates)—hence REDNESS, if such a universal exists, is of interest to us because of the usefulness of the predicate expression "is red." Along similar lines, one of the reasons we might be tempted to believe in abstract objects is the fact that mathematical language is filled with singular terms that seem to refer to abstract objects, if they refer at all. This latter intuition, in fact, can be strengthened to provide an argument, originally due to Gottlob Frege (1884), for the claim that the subject matter of mathematics is abstract.

The Singular Term Argument for Abstracta

1. If a simple subject–predicate statement of the form "t is P" is true, then t must refer.[4]
2. Arithmetic contains an infinite sequence of distinct such true statements (e.g., "0 is a number," "1 is a number," "2 is a number," etc.).
∴3. The terms of arithmetic refer (and refer to infinitely many distinct objects).
4. Only abstract objects could be the referents of these terms.
∴5. Abstract objects exist.[5]

The Singular Term Argument for Abstracta, in both its original Fregean form and in more sophisticated contemporary variants (see, e.g., Wright, 1983), underlies most contemporary accounts of mathematics as being about abstract objects. Furthermore, we can modify the argument so that the new version concludes that universals exist and are abstract. The modified argument proceeds as follows.

The Predicate Argument for Universals

1. If a simple subject–predicate statement of the form "t is P" is true, then P must have a semantic value.[6]
2. Everyday (and scientific) discourse contains a multitude of true statements of this form (e.g., "The ball is red," "The salt shaker is red," "The stoplight is red," etc.).

∴3.   These predicates must have semantic values.

4.   Only (abstract) universals could be the semantic values of these terms.

∴5.   Universals exist (and are abstract).

Interestingly, the Predicate Argument for Universals is typically taken to be much less compelling than the superficially quite similar Singular Term Argument for Abstracta. As we shall see in the next section, W. V. O. Quine—one of the most vocal defenders of one form of the Singular Term Argument for Abstracta—is also one of the most vocal critics of the Predicate Argument for Universals. Before moving on to that discussion, however, it is worth noting one additional issue regarding universals that is highlighted by attending to the Predicate Argument for Universals: the abundance or sparseness of these entities.

An account of universals is abundant if there is a universal corresponding to every arbitrary collection of objects, and is sparse if there are stricter criteria for universal existence. For example, a sparse account of universals might claim that only those universals that "carve reality at the joints" exist, or only those universals that correspond to a simple predicate exist, etc.[7] Even if one accepts the validity of the Predicate Argument for Universals, it is worth noting that, depending on how one works out the details, the argument need not entail the existence of a universal for each arbitrary collection of particulars—or even one for each complex predicate—in the same manner that the Singular Term Argument for Abstracta implies the existence of an object for *each and every* genuine singular term.[8] The issue, of course, hinges on what predicates can occur in statements of the form "t is P" such that the statement in question is simple in the sense relevant to the Predicate Argument for Universals. To see the issue, consider the following two statements:

Mr. Decatur is tall.
Mr. Decatur is tall and handsome.

If we analyze these statements as having the following logical forms:

T(d)
T(d) ∧ H(d)

then the Predicate Argument for Universals entails the existence of the abstract universal TALLNESS (and would, of course, entail the existence of a second universal, HANDSOMENESS), but does not entail the existence of a "conjunctive" universal TALL-AND-HANDSOMENESS. If, on the other hand, we analyze the logical form of the second statement as:

$$\lambda x[T(x) \wedge H(x)](d)$$

where $\lambda x[T(x) \wedge H(x)]$ denotes a single complex predicate that holds of exactly those objects that are both tall and handsome, then the Predicate Argument for Universals would apply to the predicate:

$$\lambda x[T(x) \wedge H(x)]$$

and we would obtain, in addition to REDNESS and TALLNESS, a universal TALL-AND-REDNESS. In short, whether the Predicate Argument for Universals entails the existence of a complex univeral TALL-AND-REDNESS depends on whether we analyze the sentence as one with two distinct predicates T and H, in which case the expression is not simple in the relevant sense, or as one involving a single predicate expressing tall-and-redness, in which case the sentence is simple.

While typical extant arguments over the sparseness vs abundance issue tend to hinge on nonlinguistic issues (e.g., Lewis, 1986), the above emphasizes that the connections between universals and predicates are crucial to our understanding not only of what universals are, but of the number and nature of the universals that do exist (if any).

Platonism vs nominalism[9]

As already noted in "Some Clarifications Concerning Terminology" earlier, the terms "platonism" and "nominalism" have been systematically overused. (Here I adopt the convention by which we use the lower case "platonism" when talking about realist accounts of universals, abstracta, and so on, reserving "Platonism" for the views actually held by Plato.) The former refers to a number of different stances involving the claim that either abstract universals or abstract objects genuinely exist. The latter refers to a number of different stances that involve the rejection of the existence of whichever of these types of entity is under discussion. Hence we will take care to distinguish between the platonism vs nominalism issue regarding universals and the platonism vs nominalism issue regarding abstracta. Nevertheless, the uniformity of nomenclature in these two distinct debates suggests that there will be profound connections between the two debates—connections that we shall explore further in the following section, but which already motivate our treating the various options at one go in the present section.

The disjunctive form of the subtitle to this section is, of course, somewhat misleading—there are, in fact, a continuum of approaches one can take toward the existence of both universals and abstracta, with platonism (in its strongest, face-value reading) and nominalism (in its strong form; see "Some Clarifications Concerning Terminology" earlier) occupying the extreme endpoints. This spectrum conveniently divides into four main sub-approaches, however. It should be noted in what follows that I have made no attempt to compile complete bibliographic surveys of every option within these four main approaches, and have instead merely highlighted one or two particularly important or illuminating examples of each approach.

The first of these is, as we have already indicated, *platonism.* Platonists about universals take universals talk at face value—as entailing the genuine existence of abstract universals. Platonists about mathematics (and other discourses) whose face-value reading suggests the existence of abstracta likewise take such discourse at face value—and as entailing the genuine existence of abstracta.[10] Thus, according to someone who is a platonist with regard to universals, in addition to the existence of everyday red objects, there is an abstract universal REDNESS, and red objects are red in virtue of their exemplification of (or participation in, or instantiation of) this universal. Along similar lines, a platonist with regard to mathematics will regard arithmetic as referring to abstracta—numbers, in this case—and "1 + 1 = 2" is true on this account in virtue of appropriate relations holding between the abstracta referred to by "1" and "2."

The most forceful objection to platonism of either variety is what has come to be called *the Epistemological Argument* (see Benacerraf, 1973; Field, 1989). Abstracta and abstract universals are nonspatiotemporal and causally inert. Reference to, and knowledge about, an entity seems to require some sort of causal connection between the referrer/knower and the entity being referred to or known.[11] Such a causal connection is impossible with abstract universals or abstract objects. Hence, abstract universals and abstract objects, even if they exist, can neither be referred to nor known. This is a powerful and influential argument, and we shall return to it later. For now, however, let us use the epistemological argument as motivation for moving on to alternative accounts of universals and of the subject matter of mathematics.

The second general approach toward universals and mathematical objects is *immanent realism* (or *Aristotelianism*). Immanent realism regarding either universals or mathematics accepts the platonist thesis that universals, or mathematical objects, exist, and further agrees that such entities are mind-independent. Where immanent realists disagree with platonists is in rejecting the abstractness of universals or mathematical objects. Instead, immanent realism with regard to universals involves universals being parts of the material world (and immanent realists with regard to mathematical objects regard mathematical objects as parts of the material world).

For example, according to David Armstrong (1989), universals are physical—albeit of a very different nature than more commonplace physical objects—and thus universals like REDNESS are constituents of red objects. Note the use of the term "constituent" here—Armstrong's view is not that REDNESS is a part of the ball in the same, spatial sense that its lower hemisphere is a part of it (which would violate the principle that universals are wholly present in each of their instances). Rather, each universal is a complex material object that is wholly, and nonspatially, contained in every particular that instantiates it (note that this sort of account, unlike platonism, entails that no un-instantiated universals can exist).

Another immanent realist approach to universals involves the notion of tropes (or "particularized" universals). Trope theorists such as D. C. Williams (1953a, 1953b) and George F. Stout (1914) reject the idea, common to both platonism and Armstrong's version of immanent realism, that universals are mereologically simple objects that are wholly located in their instances. Instead, each object that is an instance of REDNESS contains, as either a part or a non-mereological constituent, a trope: its own particular "redness." The universal REDNESS is then the "sum" of all the individual trope instances.[12]

Along similar lines, an immanent realist with regard to mathematics will regard arithmetic as being about the material world. Immanent realist accounts of purportedly abstract objects, however, tend not to identify the referents of mathematical terms such as "3" with single, physical objects. Instead, apparent singular terms that appear to denote abstract objects, such as "3," instead are shorthand for more complex expressions involving collections of, or, more commonly, operations on physical objects.[13] For example, John Mayberry (2001) argues that (at least some) ancient Greek thinkers (including, notably, Aristotle) accepted a form of immanent realism, arguing that there is no such thing as the number three, but instead that we are just faced with numerous "three"s (triples of material objects). Differing in the details, but still squarely within the immanent realist approach, is the account proposed by Philip Kitcher (1985), who, following John Stuart Mill (1874), argues that arithmetic is a theory regarding possible physical operations on material objects.[14]

One of the main problems with mathematical versions of immanent realism (one that can also be applied to the conceptualist approaches discussed later) is that there does not seem to be enough "stuff" in the material universe to underwrite contemporary classical mathematics. Classical mathematics requires an immensely large ontology (a proper class, in technical jargon). As a result, it is simply implausible that the material world is either numerous enough or complex enough to allow for a reconstruction of mathematical ontology along immanent realist lines. It is important to note that this objection does not depend on the assumption that the material universe is finite—although the mere possibility of a finite material universe is enough, on the immanent realist approach, to strip mathematics of its necessity! If the immanent realist is to be able to account for modern set theory, then the material universe must not only be infinite, but it must contain an extremely "large" infinite collection of entities.

A similar problem plagues many versions of immanent realist accounts of universals, since immanent realism involves the idea that the existence of particular universals is dependent on the existence of "underlying" concrete particulars—hence the comment above regarding the impossibility of uninstantiated universals on immanent realist accounts.

The third approach to the metaphysical status of universals and mathematical objects is *conceptualism* (or *psychologism*). Conceptualism holds that these entities exist, but they are neither abstract nor material (and thus they are not mind-independent). Instead, universals and mathematical objects are mental entities of some sort—ideas, thoughts, mental constructions, and so on.

Perhaps the most well-known and relatively recent version of conceptualism is the conceptualism regarding mathematical objects found in the writings of L. E. J. Brouwer (1913 and 1949)—and, in a somewhat less explicit form, in later intuitionists such as Arend Heyting (1966) and Michael Dummett (1975). Intuitionists hold that the subject matter of mathematics consists of mental constructions, and thus "2" does not refer to an abstract object, but rather to a construction present in the mind of the mathematician. The revisions to classical mathematics that intuitionists propose based on this account are well known (and are lucidly surveyed in Dummett [2000]). Nevertheless, revisionary or not, conceptualism retains the intuition that mathematics has a genuine—albeit mind-dependent—subject matter.

There are a number of interconnected problems with conceptualism, most of which apply to both conceptualism about mathematical objects and to conceptualism about universals, and many of which are forcefully developed in Frege's celebrated dismantling of psychologism regarding these issues in *Die Grundlagen der Arithmetik* (1884/1980). (Frege's work is likely the primary reason for the comparative scarcity of conceptualist positions within metaphysics and the philosophy of mathematics during the twentieth and twenty-first centuries). Among these, the following two considerations seem most worrisome. First, there is a cardinality worry similar to the one seen above for immanent realism. There are, and have been, only finitely many thoughts, ideas, concepts, and so on—human beings are finite, and, to put it bluntly and loosely, we have collectively had only finitely many thoughts. Arithmetic requires that there be infinitely many distinct numbers, however, and (depending on how abundant one's conception of universals is) there seems to be no guarantee that there are enough mental entities to supply a theoretically useful domain of universals (see Burgess [1983] for more details). Second, ideas, thoughts, etc. cease to exist when the thinker does. As a result, on conceptualist accounts mathematics was false (because it lacked a subject matter) before humans existed and will be false again once we become extinct. Along similar lines, if color universals such as REDNESS are mental entities of some sort, then objects were not colored (in fact, had no properties whatsoever) before the existence of humans and will cease to be colored once we all die.[15]

As a result of these well-known problems, conceptualism has not been a particularly popular node on the map of approaches to either universals or mathematical objects. Nevertheless, conceptualists at least agree with platonism and immanent realism that, in one sense or another, universals exists (and similarly, platonism, immanent realism, and conceptualism about mathematics involve an admission that mathematical objects of some sort exist). The differences between these three views hinge on what sort of entities universals (or mathematical objects) are. The fourth, and final, approach is quite different from the first three. Nominalists deny outright the existence of universals (or, in the case of mathematical discourse, nominalists deny the existence of any objects—abstract or not—that mathematical theories are "about").

Of course, the nominalist cannot just deny the existence of the relevant entities and be done with it. The much harder task is to explain why we don't need the entities in question in the first place—in other words, the nominalist owes us some sort of explanation of how we can explain qualitative similarities and dissimilarities without universals, or how we can account for the (apparent) truth, and undeniable utility, of mathematics without mathematical entities to serve as its subject matter.

As a practical matter, this task is typically carried out in very different ways by nominalists regarding universals and nominalists regarding mathematical entities. Nominalists about universals usually mobilize some variant of Quine's famous argument from "On What There Is" (1948), emphasizing the metaphysical "weirdness" of universals, and then arguing that such bizarre entities are not needed in order to account for qualitative similarity and dissimilarity anyway.

> One may admit that there are red houses, roses, and sunsets, but deny, except as a popular and misleading manner of speaking, that they have anything in common. The words "houses," "roses," and "sunsets" denote each of sundry individual entities which are houses and roses and sunsets, and the word "red" or "red object" denotes each of sundry individual entities which are red houses, red roses, red sunsets; but there is not, in addition, any entity whatever, individual or otherwise, which is named by the word "redness," nor, for that matter, by the word "househood," "rosehood," "sunsethood." That the houses and roses and sunsets are all of them red may be taken as ultimate and irreducible, and it may be held that McX[16] is no better off, in point of real explanatory power, for all the occult entities which he posits under such names as "redness." (Quine, 1948, pp. 29–30)

The point is simply this: faced with explaining the redness of our ball and our salt shaker, invoking strange multiply-located entities—that is, universals—seems no better to Quine and like-minded nominalists, all things considered, than treating their redness as brute facts about the ball and the salt shaker themselves.

Nominalists about mathematical objects, however, tend to pursue a different approach. As already noted, they need to provide some sort of account of why mathematical talk—which on their account is false if taken at face value—is nevertheless so useful in our dealings with the world. Typically, the nominalist will provide an argument that mathematics is in some sense or another a useful fiction. The most influential such account along these lines is Hartry Field's (1980), where he argues that mathematics, while false, is nevertheless *conservative* over everyday and scientific discourse. Put simply, on Field's account, mathematics does not allow us to learn anything new about the physical world that we could not have discovered without mathematics, but mathematics does often simplify considerably the arguments involved in obtaining that knowledge.

The four positions we have just outlined can be summarized in the following table (for reasons of space I have restricted the table to universals—a similar chart obviously applies to, e.g., the subject matter of mathematics):

	Universals are abstract	Universals are mind-independent	Universals exist
Platonism	Yes	Yes	Yes
Immanent realism	No	Yes	Yes
Conceptualism	No	No	Yes
Nominalism	No	No	No

Note that if we assume that abstractness entails mind independence and mind independence (and hence abstractness) in turn entails existence, then the four approaches we surveyed above exhaust the available options.

We should note, of course, that one can, prima facie, inhabit different positions on the platonism/immanent realism/conceptualism/nominalism spectrum with regard to universals and abstracta. For example, we might (as Quine did at various points) accept platonism with regard to the subject matter of mathematics while remaining a nominalist regarding universals. Nevertheless, there is a view in the philosophy of mathematics which shows some promise for connecting platonism with regard to one of these domains to platonism with regard to the other. The view is known variously as neologicism, neo-fregeanism, and abstractionism (we shall use the former term).

Connecting platonisms: Logicism

Now that we have a general framework for thinking about universals and abstract objects in place, in this final section we shall look at the connections between these two, seemingly distinct, realms of entities. Of course, there are numerous ways one might attempt to draw connections between the existence and nature of universals and the existence and nature of abstract objects. Here we shall focus on one of those, albeit one with an important and influential philosophical pedigree: neologicist accounts of abstract objects as abstractions from equivalence classes of other entities.

The neologicist approach to the existence of abstract objects begins, of course, as its name suggests, with the original logicist: Frege. Frege, in his *Die Grundlagen der Arithmetik* (1884/1980) and *Grundgesetze der Arithmetik*

(1893/1903), developed a foundation for mathematics based on higher order logic plus his *Basic Law V*:

$BLV: (\forall X)(\forall Y)(\S(X) = \S(Y) \leftrightarrow (\forall z)(Xz \leftrightarrow Yz))$

where "§" is a term-forming operator (i.e., a function symbol denoting a function from concepts—or, for our purposes, universals—to objects). Given BLV, Frege was able to define cardinal numbers as the extension of the (second level) concept holding of equinumerous (first level) concepts, directions as extensions of concepts holding of parallel lines, etc., and he was able to derive the basic laws of arithmetic (and other mathematical theories) using these definitions of mathematical entities.

Of course, Frege's project was doomed, as Bertrand Russell's famous paradox (1902) demonstrated, but recently the neologicists, led by Crispin Wright (1983), have developed a modified (and arguably consistent) version of the view. On the neologicist account, we introduce distinct abstraction principles for each distinct mathematical concept—these abstraction principles serve as (something like) implicit definitions of the concept in question. Thus, *Hume's Principle*:

$HP: (\forall X)(\forall Y)(\#(X) = \#(Y) \leftrightarrow X \approx Y)$

(where "#" is a term-forming operator mapping concepts to objects—their cardinal numbers—and "$\approx$" abbreviates the purely second-order logical formula expressing that there is a one–one onto function from the Xs to the Ys[17]) serves as something like an implicit definition of the concept "cardinal number."

The main interest of the neologicist approach, within philosophy of mathematics, is that it promises to provide an answer to the epistemological argument against platonism (at least, with respect to platonism regarding the subject matter of mathematics). Abstraction principles such as HP, if they can be viewed as something akin to implicit definitions, promise to provide us with a tractable epistemology of these abstract objects, since their biconditional form equates knowledge of (identities between) mathematical objects (such as identity claims regarding cardinal numbers in the case of HP) and knowledge of purely logical claims (such as the existence of one–one onto functions between the extensions of concepts in the case of HP).[18] Since logical knowledge—whatever its ultimate nature—presumably does not require interaction with mysterious noncausal entities, this would provide an indirect but epistemologically respectable route to knowledge of mathematics.[19]

While the prospects for defusing the epistemological objection to platonism already make neologicism of interest in the present context, it turns out that the general approach, if successful, promises to shed even more light on the connection between universals and abstract objects. The general form of an abstraction principle is:

$$AP_E: (\forall\alpha)(\forall\beta)(@(\alpha) = @(\beta) \leftrightarrow E(\alpha, \beta))$$

where @ is an term-forming operator mapping entities of the type ranged over by variables α and β (typically objects, concepts—which, as already noted, can be treated as identical to, or at least corresponding to, universals in the present context—or relations) to objects, and E is an equivalence relation on the type of entities ranged over by α and β. While restricting E to logical formulas (or perhaps logical formulas supplemented with previously defined abstraction operators) might be required when using abstraction principles to provide a foundation for mathematics (since in that case there is prima facie reason to reduce mathematical identities to logical or previously defined mathematical facts), there seems to be no reason to so restrict abstraction principles in general. As a result, it would seem that abstraction principles could be used to introduce not just mathematical abstract objects, but abstract objects of any sort whatsoever.

An example: Anthony Wrigley (2006) proposes that propositions are obtained via abstraction by invoking an abstraction principle, which he calls $P^=$, of the form:

$$P^= : (\forall p)(\forall q)(P(p) = P(q) \leftrightarrow \Phi(p, q))$$

where p and q range over sentences, P is a term-forming operator mapping sentences to propositions, and Φ is the synonymy relation. The details need not detain us here (and, needless to say, Wrigley spends many pages working out the details regarding what, exactly, is meant by both "sentence" and "synonymy"). The point is that the abstractionist approach is, in the end, not just an account of the abstract objects that are to be the subject matter of mathematics, but also of abstract objects more generally, including propositions, possible worlds, types, and so on.

Returning more explicitly to the topic of this chapter, the interest of abstraction principles—and especially abstraction principles of the sort Wrigley considers, where the equivalence relation E on the right-hand side might invoke nonlogical machinery—in the present context is that they draw tight connections between universals and abstract objects. An abstraction principle AP_E can be understood as providing a single abstract object for each equivalence class of entities of the relevant sort (relative to E). These equivalence classes in turn can be understood in terms of the universal that holds of exactly the entities falling in that equivalence class (assuming that universals are abundant enough that there exists one for each such equivalence class).

For example, let us call the second-level universal that holds of all first level universals with exactly three instances THREE-ITY. Then, according to the abstractionist picture sketched earlier, Hume's principle assigns the abstract object THREE to the universal THREE-ITY (since THREE-ITY corresponds to one of the equivalence classes of universals "carved out" by the equivalence relation in HP).

As a result, abstraction principles can be viewed as providing a corresponding abstract object for each universal that has, as its instances, the class of entities that constitute that equivalence class. In other words, the neologicist approach associates each universal with an object-level analogue (the abstract object corresponding to it) knowledge of which is provided by the appropriate abstraction principles.

As a result, the general neologicist framework (divorced from its rather narrower origins as merely a means for providing a foundation for mathematics), if successful, might provide a means for drawing tight connections between abstract objects and universals. This particular aspect of the approach has not been examined in the sort of detail that it warrants. One notable exception, however, is Matti Eklund's (2006) exploration of the idea that neologicist abstraction can be used to defend a metaphysical view called "maximalism."

Roughly put, maximalism is the view that, for any (sortal[20]) universal Φ, if it is consistent that Φs exist, then Φs exists. Eklund's idea for obtaining maximalism via neologicism, simply put, is this. If the existence of instances of some universal Φ is consistent, then their existence can be guaranteed by invoking an appropriate abstraction principle whose equivalence relation provides identity conditions for those instances. If Eklund is right, and the neologicist approach does entail, or at least allows one to develop a version of, maximalism, then this would—in addition to the rather substantial metaphysical consequences that would follow from such a view—constitute a deep insight into the relationship between universals and abstract objects.

Nevertheless, there are serious worries regarding the neologicist approach—worries which must be overcome if the approach is to play any central role either in the foundations of mathematics or in a more general metaphysical account of universals, abstract objects, and the connections between the two. First and foremost among these are *the Bad Company Objection* and *the Caesar Problem.*

The Bad Company Objection amounts to the observation that we have no general criteria for separating the "good" abstraction principles (such as, presumably, HP and some form of Wrigley's P=) from the "bad" principles (such as the inconsistent BLV). Although presumably necessary, neither consistency nor conservativeness are sufficient for "goodness," since there are pairwise-incompatible abstraction principles that have these properties (see Weir [2004] for details). This observation also shows that Eklund's formulation of maximalism sketched in the previous paragraph is too broad, since presumably the problems with consistency as a sufficient criterion for "goodness" of Φs will fail there as well.

The Caesar Problem stems from the fact that abstraction principles, while requiring the existence of abstract objects to serve as the range of the abstraction operator, fail to entail that these abstract objects are not identical to concrete, physical objects. Presumably, however, any adequate account of abstract objects (and of the connection between them and universals) will need to entail that abstract objects are a metaphysical category distinct from physical objects (and from universals, for that matter). After all, their nonmateriality is a fundamental tenet of the "Way of Negation" characterization of abstract objects discussed earlier, and that view was criticized for being too weak, not too strong. Thus, additional resources are required if such an account is to provide an adequate account of the nature of abstract objects, at least if adequacy involves, at a minimum, entailment of the negative characteristics catalogued in our earlier discussion of the "Way of Negation."

If these two well-known worries regarding neologicism can be assuaged, however, then the approach does seem to hold promise as a response to the epistemological worry regarding platonism, and it would also provide a means for investigating and understanding more completely the intimate connections between universals and abstract objects. The impact of either of these should not be underestimated. In the former case the consequences would be profound, since the epistemological argument against abstract objects is not only an objection to platonism, but also seems to be the main positive motivation for contending views such as immanent realism, conceptualism, and nominalism. Without this argument, much of the motivation for adopting non-platonist views disappears. In the latter case, the advantages are evident. Success would bring with it a deeper understanding of both types of entity, but it might also bring with it a solution to one of the other problems plaguing accounts of abstract objects: our failure (discussed in "What is an Abstract Object?" earlier) to provide a positive account of their nature. On the neologicist account, abstract objects are presumably exactly the objects that fall in the range of abstraction operators. The hope here is that, as we study the philosophical and mathematical characteristics of abstraction principles, consequences for the philosophical and mathematical nature of the objects that they provide will be forthcoming.

As noted, however, neologicism is not the only way to connect the existence of abstract objects to the nature of universals. Although there are many other ways one might attempt to connect these two distinct subject matters, of particular interest are other modern-day revamped versions of logicism such as those found in Edward Zalta (2000) or Neil Tennant (2004). Exploration of these matters is left to the interested reader.

Notes

1 The semantic value of an expression is the entity "picked out," or denoted, by that expression. Simple terms (i.e., names) uncontroversially refer to objects, but other expressions might pick out other types of object or entity. In particular, it is tempting, although not uncontroversial, to think that predicates pick out universals or properties, and that sentences pick out truth values.

2 As Plato's allegory of the Line makes clear (see *The Republic*, Book VI), there is, in addition to the Forms, a realm of "intermediate" or "hypothetical" or "mathematical" objects which, in modern terminology, are abstract (like Forms) but which (unlike Forms) can be indistinguishable from one another.

3 See Burgess and Rosen (1997) for more discussion.

4 Of course, this premise requires that the expression "t is P" is genuinely simple, and not a paraphrase of some more complex, possibly quantificational expression, as with Bertrand Russell's (1905) infamous King of France example.

5 Another argument for the existence, and abstractness, of mathematical objects is the Quine–Putnam indispensability argument (Putnam, 1971; Quine, 1948, 1956), which, simply put, argues that the indispensability of mathematics within science entails that mathematics is true and should be taken at face value (and, hence, is about abstracta). This argument can, with little mutilation, be seen as a sub-argument supporting premise (2) in the singular term argument.

6 Of course, as before (see note 4), this premise requires that the expression "t is P" is genuinely simple, and not a paraphrase of some more complex, possibly quantificational expression not involving the predicate P.

7   This distinction seems to have been introduced in Lewis (1983).

8   The correctness of this last bit requires that we treat apparent singular terms such as Russell's "the present King of France" as not being singular terms at all. In other words, we need to treat "The present King of France is bald" as a statement not involving a singular term at all, rather than as a statement containing a singular term, but only appearing to be simple.

9   The organization and content of this section owes much to the excellent piece by Mark Balageur (2009).

10 Hale (1988) provides a forceful Fregean defense of abstract objects of various sorts, and we shall examine another front-running account of Platonism regarding mathematics—one closely connected to Hale's work—in the following section.

11 Note that acceptance of this premise falls short of a full acceptance of what has come to be known as the causal theory of knowledge (e.g., Goldman, 1967).

12 I am, for simplicity's sake, glossing over some important distinctions between various ways of working out the details of trope accounts; the reader is encouraged to consult Williams (1953a, 1953b), Stout (1914) or the excellent discussion found in Michael Loux (2002) for more details.

13 Of course, reinterpreting number talk as talk about operations is, on a literal reading, not an instance of immanent realism at all, but is instead a form of nominalism, since proponents of such an approach will deny the literal existence of mathematical objects. Nevertheless, the similarity in spirit of these approaches justifies our including them here.

14 Although it does not fall neatly into any of the four approaches discussed here, Geoffrey Hellman's (1989) modal structuralism, which treats mathematical theories as "about" possible collections of physical objects, clearly has much in common with immanent realist accounts.

15 Of course, a denial of conceptualism, either about universals or about mathematical objects or both, does not entail a denial of the existence of ideas or other mental entities. On the contrary, these mental entities obviously exist (although their exact nature is a matter of some lively debate). The point is that mental entities are not plausible candidates for playing the theoretical roles required of either universals or mathematical objects.

16 McX is W. V. O. Quine's fictional Meinongian opponent.

17 If f is a function from A to B, then f is *one–one* if and only if, for every x and y in A, if $x \neq y$ then $f(x) \neq f(y)$, and f is *onto* if and only if, for every z in B, there is a w in A such that $f(w) = z$. Thus, loosely speaking, f is a one–one onto function from A to B if and only if f associates each member of A with a unique member of B and vice versa.

18 The following fact is worth noting: neologicism is obviously committed to the idea that the subject matter of mathematics is the objects in the range of abstraction

operators occurring in acceptable abstraction principles. As far as the author knows, however, no neologicist has committed, in print, to the stronger thesis that all abstract objects whatsoever are in the range of appropriate abstraction operators. Nevertheless, the neologicist authoring this chapter will now admit to holding this stronger view.

19 For arguments both pro and con regarding the prospects for this approach as a foundation for mathematics, the reader is encouraged to consult the articles collected in Cook (2007).

20 The exact definition of a sortal concept, or sortal universal, is a matter of some controversy, but for our purposes a universal is sortal if and only if its instances can be counted. For further discussion, see (Wiggins, 2001).

References

Armstrong, D. (1989), *Universals: An Opinionated Introduction*. Boulder, CO: Westview Press.

Balageur, M. (2009), "Platonism in metaphysics." *Stanford Encyclopedia of Philosophy*. Available online at: http://plato.stanford.edu/entries/platonism.

Benacerraf, P. (1973), "Mathematical truth." *Journal of Philosophy*, 70, 661–9. Reprinted in Benacerraf and Putnam (1983), pp. 403–20.

Benacerraf, P. and Putnam, H., eds (1983), *Philosophy of Mathematics: Selected Readings*. Cambridge: Cambridge University Press.

Brouwer, L. (1913), "Intuitionism and formalism." *Bulletin of the American Mathematical Society*, 20, 81–96. Reprinted in Benacerraf and Putnam (1983), pp. 77–89.

—(1949), "Consciousness, philosophy, and mathematics," in E. Beth, H. Pos and J. Hollak, eds, *Proceedings of the 10th International Congress of Philosophy: Amsterdam 1948 III*. Amsterdam: North Holland. Reprinted in Benacerraf and Putnam (1983), pp. 90–6.

Burgess, J. (1983), "Why I am not a nominalist." *Notre Dame Journal of Formal Logic*, 24, 93–105.

Burgess, J. and Rosen, G. (1997), *A Subject with No Object*. Oxford: Oxford University Press.

Cook, R. ed. (2007), *The Arché Papers on the Mathematics of Abstraction*, Dordrecht: Springer Verlag.

Dummett, M. (1975), "On the philosophical significance of intuitionistic logic," *Studies in Logic and the Foundations of Mathematics*, 80, 5–40. Reprinted in Benacerraf and Putnam (1983), pp. 97–129.

—(2000), *Elements of Intuitionism* (second edition). Oxford: Oxford University Press.

Eklund, M. (2006), "Neo-fregean ontology." *Philosophical Perspectives*, 20, 95–121.

Field, H. (1980), *Science without Numbers*. Princeton, NJ: Princeton University Press.

—(1989), *Realism, Mathematics, and Modality*. New York: Basil Blackwell.

Frege, G. (1884/1980), *Die Grundlagen der Arithmetik* (trans. J. Austin). Evanston, IL: Northwestern University Press.

—(1893/1903), *Grundgezetze der Arithmetik, vols. I and II*. Jena: Verlag Hermann Pohle.

Goldman, A. (1967), "A causal theory of knowing." *Journal of Philosophy*, 64, 355–72.

Hale, R. (1988), *Abstract Objects*. Oxford: Blackwell.

Hellman, G. (1989), *Mathematics without Numbers: Towards a Modal-Structural Interpretation*. Oxford: Oxford University Press.

Heyting, A. (1966), *Intuitionism: An Introduction* (second edition). Amsterdam: North Holland.

Kitcher, P. (1985), *The Nature of Mathematical Knowledge*. Oxford: Oxford University Press.

Lewis, D. (1983), "New work for a theory of universals." *Australasian Journal of Philosophy*, 61, 343–77.

—(1986), *On the Plurality of Worlds*. Oxford: Blackwell.

Loux, M. (2002), *Metaphysics: A Contemporary Introduction* (third edition). New York: Routledge.

—(2008), *Metaphysics: Contemporary Readings* (second edition). New York: Routledge.

Mayberry, J. (2001), *The Foundations of Mathematics in the Theory of Sets*. Cambridge: Cambridge University Press.

Mill, J. S. (1874), *A System of Logic*. New York: Harper and Brothers.

Plato (2005), *The Collected Dialogues of Plato: Including the Letters*. ed. E. Huntington and H. Cairns. Princeton, NJ: Princeton University Press.

Putnam, H. (1956), "Mathematics and the existence of abstract entities." *Philosophical Studies*, 7, 81–8.

—(1971), *Philosophy of Logic*. New York: Harper and Row.

Quine, W. V. O. (1948), "On what there is." *Review of Metaphysics*, 2, 21–38.

—(1964), *Word and Object*. Cambridge, MA: MIT Press.

Russell, B. (1902), "Letter to Frege." Reprinted in Van Heijenoort (2002), pp. 124–5.

—(1905), "On denoting." *Mind*, 14, 479–93.

Stout, G. (1914), "On the nature of universals and propositions," British Academy Lecture. Reprinted in Stout (1930), pp. 384–402.

—(1930), *Studies in Philosophy and Psychology*. London: MacMillan.

Tennant, N. (2004), "A general theory of abstraction operators." *Philosophical Quarterly*, 54, 105–33.

Van Heijenoort, V. (2002), *From Frege to Godel: A Sourcebook in Mathematical Logic 1897–1931*. Cambridge, MA: Harvard University Press.

Weir, A. (2004), "Neo-Fregeanism: an embarrassment of riches." *Notre Dame Journal of Formal Logic*, 44, 13–48. Reprinted in Cook (2007), pp. 383–420.

Wiggins, D. (2001), *Sameness and Substance Renewed*. Cambridge: Cambridge University Press.

Williams, D. (1953a), "The elements of being I." *Review of Metaphysics,* 7, 3–18.

—(1953b), "The elements of being II." *Review of Metaphysics,* 7, 171–92.

Wright, C. (1983), *Frege's Conception of Numbers as Objects.* Aberdeen: Aberdeen University Press.

Wrigley, A. (2006), "Abstracting propositions." *Synthese,* 151, 157–76.

Zalta, E. (2000), "Neo-logicism? An ontological reduction of mathematics to metaphysics." *Erkenntnis,* 53, 219–26.

Naturalism and Physicalism

D. Gene Witmer

Two influential "Ism"s

Over the last several decades a great deal of work in metaphysics has been motivated by an allegiance to views most commonly known by the labels "naturalism" and "physicalism" (sometimes "materialism"). The influence of these commitments is most easily seen in work in the philosophy of mind, but both doctrines aim to have more general import, constraining one's overall view of the world.

Exactly what these labels are meant to denote is not always clear, and this problem is exacerbated by an occasional tendency to use them more as a badge of respectability than as a useful indication of philosophical commitments. The two terms are certainly not used interchangeably. One obvious difference is that "naturalism" is often deliberately used to name something other than a metaphysical thesis, signifying instead a commitment to a method of inquiry, perhaps accompanied by a theoretical account of that method's status. Call this "epistemic naturalism." By contrast, "physicalism" is normally used only to signify a metaphysical thesis. The two terms differ, further, in that physicalism seems to be a thesis logically stronger than (metaphysical) naturalism. The label "naturalist dualist" is not only intelligible but actually claimed by some philosophers (e.g., Chalmers, 1996, pp. 124–9; see also the "panpsychist naturalism" of Sellars, 1927). By contrast, it is harder to see how one could make sense of a declared anti-naturalist physicalist, though the combination sounds intelligible if the naturalism rejected is a purely epistemic thesis independent of the metaphysical physicalist claim.[1]

The present entry is divided into three main sections. In the first, after setting aside epistemic construals of naturalism, I survey some of the ways in which metaphysical naturalism might be understood. I also suggest a general interpretation of "naturalist" talk, the "nothing special" interpretation, according to which adherents of metaphysical naturalism are motivated by the core idea that humanity and our interests are not special in the overall order of things. This formulation does not yield a determinate metaphysical thesis but does provide a schema into which such theses may be fit—including physicalism as a version of naturalism.

The second section is devoted to physicalism and its formulation. The simple thesis that everything is physical will not be adequate, as there are recognizably physicalist positions that allow for entities which are strictly speaking not physical but which bear some appropriate relationship to the physical. More precisely, such positions allow for entities such that their existence and character are determined by the physical in a way that makes it appropriate to say that those entities are "nothing over and above" the physical entities involved in that determination. A thorough understanding of physicalism will require attention to this relation, but there are two other parameters that need clarification as well. Exactly what does it mean to describe an entity as "physical" in the first place? And just how extensive is the reach of the physicalist claim? That is, just what does the "everything" range over in the claim that everything is appropriately related to the physical? Does it include, for instance, abstract objects?

The third and final section addresses the ways in which one might justify either of the two doctrines. Challenges to them are well known; with regard to physicalism, the most prominent prima facie problem is to accommodate mentality. In this chapter I only address the question of how the claims may be supported in the first place. Given the widespread allegiance to these doctrines and the often casual way in which they are invoked to motivate various moves in contemporary philosophy, it is easy to suspect that there is more dogma than argument behind their endorsement. Nonetheless, we can identify a number of important lines of support, all of which turn in some way on the success of the natural sciences, especially physics.

Interpreting "Naturalism"

In the introduction to his book *Philosophical Naturalism*, David Papineau writes:

> What is philosophical "naturalism"? The term is a familiar one nowadays, but there is little consensus on its meaning. For some philosophers, the defining

characteristic of naturalism is the affirmation of a continuity between philosophy and empirical science. For others the rejection of dualism is the crucial requirement. Yet others view an externalist approach to epistemology as the essence of naturalism.

I shall not engage directly with this issue. It is essentially a terminological matter. The important question is which philosophical positions are right, not what to call them. I suspect that the main reason for the terminological unclarity is that nearly everybody nowadays wants to be a "naturalist," but the aspirants to the term nevertheless disagree widely on substantial questions of philosophical doctrine. The moral is that we should address the substantial philosophical issues first, and worry about the terminology afterwards. (Papineau, 1993, p. 1)

While Papineau is right to stress the substantive question over the terminological one, it may nonetheless be a good idea to have a plausible account of what *inclines* us to think of one position as "naturalist" and another not, since that may help us uncover just what makes the positions categorized as naturalist seem attractive to so many. With such an account on hand, we may be able to see good reasons for or against substantial positions that were not previously open to view.

As noted earlier, "naturalism" is sometimes used to denote either an epistemic thesis or a commitment to a method of inquiry; this is illustrated in the quick gloss offered by Papineau. After a very brief discussion of such I turn to our main focus: metaphysical naturalism.

Epistemic naturalism

Epistemic naturalism is associated with two familiar slogans:

(1) There is no first philosophy.
(2) Philosophy is continuous with the sciences.

The first slogan may be taken as the claim that philosophers should not try to arrive a priori at conclusions that are then used to evaluate, limit or otherwise regulate nonphilosophical inquiries. While the first slogan denies, the second affirms: there *is* a legitimate role for philosophy in our investigation of the world, but there is nothing distinctive or special about its methods.

Exactly what would it take for philosophy to be *dis*continuous with the sciences? Just what does (1) prohibit? It might be taken as a ban on all a priori theorizing, and this is certainly how many self-proclaimed naturalists see their commitments, though this is not true of all of them (Goldman, 1999). Such naturalists often name W. V. O. Quine as an important influence, and Quine of course famously denies the existence of a priori knowledge. Perhaps the most commonly cited work is Quine's "Epistemology Naturalized" (Quine, 1969), the main focus of which is not a denial of a priori knowledge but his recommendation that we make free use of empirical science in theorizing about the relations between theory and evidence, and this recommendation is in turn driven by his rejection of a certain project, namely, that of using philosophical argument to *legitimate* the pursuit of scientific inquiry and its results. One way philosophy might be distinctive, then, is if it were capable of properly pursuing that project. The epistemic naturalist rejects this idea: philosophy has no special resources that would enable it to take this lofty perspective on other areas of inquiry. As Penelope Maddy puts it, the "fundamental naturalistic impulse" is "a resolute skepticism in the face of any 'higher level' of inquiry that purports to stand above the level of ordinary science" (Maddy, 2001, p. 39). She cites Quine approvingly as ruling out any "supra-scientific tribunal" that would be in a position to "justify or criticize science on extra-scientific grounds" (Maddy, 2001, p. 43).

Why should "naturalism" be used as a term covering both this epistemic commitment and a metaphysical thesis that rules out such things as ghosts and gods—things that are "supernatural"? If one is convinced that the only way philosophy could play the special legitimating role would be if philosophers had access—putting it bluntly—to *magic,* then it is easy enough to see the connection. (Critics of a priori knowledge often speak of alleged "occult faculties" that would underwrite such knowledge.) Of course, one might think that philosophy can play such a role without pretending to be magical (whatever, exactly, being magical is supposed to come to), and in that case one would find the common nomenclature inappropriate.

Metaphysical naturalism

Just how should the metaphysical thesis be understood? "Naturalism" (here-after to designate the metaphysical claim) is plainly meant to rule out the existence of certain unwelcome entities—those characterized as the "supernatural" or the "non-natural."[2] We might take (3) as a suitable starting point:

(3) Every entity is a natural entity.

This does not help much until we have some grip on what it is for an entity to be "natural," of course.[3]

Many remarks about metaphysical naturalism lean on examples of the unwelcome entities in order to fix the thesis at issue. For instance, John Dupré offers us the following:

> By antisupernaturalism I mean something like the denial that there are entities that lie outside of the normal course of nature. It is easier to point to some of the things that are agreed to lie outside the normal course of nature than it is to characterize the normal course of nature. Central cases of such outliers are immaterial minds or souls, vital fluids, and deities. (Dupré, 2004, p. 36)

Mario De Caro lists several examples of things contrary to naturalism: "spiritual entities, Intelligent Designers, immaterial and immortal minds, entelechies and prime movers unmoved" (De Caro, 2010, p. 367). As De Caro points out, however, these examples don't help much once we move "beyond the simple cases toward more problematical ones, such as values, abstract entities, modal concepts, or conscious phenomena" (De Caro, 2010, p. 367). Are those supernatural or nonnatural? How are we to tell? Certainly it won't help to ask if they involve "magic."

A remark by Barry Stroud aims at something more general: "By 'super-naturalism' I mean the invocation of an agent or force that somehow stands outside the familiar natural world and whose doings cannot be understood as part of it" (Stroud, 2004, p. 23). Dupré invokes the "normal course of nature"; Stroud here speaks of something being apart from the "familiar natural world." But appeals to familiarity or regularity don't seem quite appropriate. There seems nothing odd about the idea that nature may contain very unfamiliar elements; indeed, avowed naturalists are often insistent on the potential strangeness of the natural world.[4] Nor does it seem out of keeping with our intuitive grasp of the natural to say that some natural events may be very infrequent (think of the Big Bang) or irregular (think of quantum indeterminacy).

One well known use of "naturalism" as a metaphysical thesis is due to David Armstrong, who offers an account that doesn't lean on examples of this sort. He defines naturalism as the claim that "[t]he world is nothing but a single spatiotemporal system" (Armstrong, 1978, p. 126). Let us then consider (4):

(4) Every entity is located in a single spatiotemporal system.

In the same work, Armstrong explicitly distinguishes "materialism" from naturalism, describing materialism as the thesis that "the world is completely described in terms of (completed) physics" (p. 126). If we presume that a completed physics will only posit things that are located in a single spacetime but that some possible spatiotemporal entities would not be included in such a physics, we have the result that materialism is logically stronger than naturalism, given Armstrong's definitions.

But (4) is not just weaker than materialism; it is surely weaker than what advocates of naturalism have in mind. Being located in space and time does not, on its own, do very much to constrain the kinds of items that might be thus located (see also Kim, 2003). It is far from clear, for instance, that (4) rules out the existence of ghosts as traditionally conceived. Such things have very odd and surprising properties, to be sure, but the man on the street would have no trouble thinking of ghosts as existing at particular places and at particular times. Nonetheless, it is safe to say that avowed naturalists would reject such entities as belonging to the category of the "supernatural."[5]

One can find throughout the writings on naturalism an emphasis on spatio-temporal location—and, often, an emphasis on a "space–time–causal system."[6] For a contemporary example, consider how George Gasser introduces a recent anthology of papers on naturalism. He first describes the epistemic naturalist thesis as the claim that "all knowledge we can acquire is obtainable only or fore-most through the application of the scientific method" (Gasser, 2007, p. 4) but follows this with:

> This epistemological thesis often comes hand in hand with an *ontological thesis* claiming that all that exists is what (in principle) can be studied by science. Science studies the spatio-temporal world. Most naturalists would insist that the whole world is spatio-temporal and all the entities to be found in this world are studied by science. (Gasser, 2007, p. 4)

This suggests that the emphasis on spatiotemporal location is the result of a more fundamental understanding of the natural as that which can be investigated by scientific means. If so, we might be better off with a formulation like (5):

(5) Every entity is of a kind such that things of that kind can, in principle, be successfully investigated by science.

The "successfully" is meant to avoid trivialization, since one could presumably *attempt* to investigate anything in a scientific fashion. Even given this, however, it's not obvious that (5) can rule out the unwelcome entities. If by "science" we mean just any appropriately disciplined and rational enquiry, how much can (5) rule out? Certainly on that reading of "science" it is not strong enough to rule out ghosts, entelechies, God, and other unwelcome entities; there is no reason to suppose such things could not be successfully investigated in a rational, disciplined fashion. Even if we restrict "science" to empirical investigations, such entities are not obviously ruled out.

In light of this point, one might be tempted to the view that it is just a mistake to try to treat "supernatural" or "non-natural" as picking out a kind of entity. A striking thought experiment due to Ludwig Wittgenstein points in that direction:

> [W]e all know what in ordinary life would be called a miracle. It obviously is simply an event the like of which we have never yet seen. Now suppose such an event happened. Take the case that one of you suddenly grew a lion's head and began to roar. Certainly that would be as extraordinary a thing as I can imagine. Now whenever we should have recovered from our surprise, what I would suggest would be to fetch a doctor and have the case scientifically investigated and if it were not for hurting him I would have him vivisected. And where would the miracle have got to? For it is clear that when we look at it in this way everything miraculous has disappeared. (Wittgenstein, 1965, p. 10)

Perhaps we should say that there is no difference between things that we see as "miraculous" and those that are natural, that the felt difference lies entirely on the side of our attitudes. Being a naturalist might then amount simply to a readiness to investigate in a rational, disciplined fashion whatever phenomena one might encounter.[7] There would be no such thing as metaphysical naturalism.

If we give "science" more content, however, (5) might still yield a distinction between the natural and the unwelcome. A tempting thought here is that we should define metaphysical naturalism by reference specifically to the *natural sciences*—physics, chemistry, biology, geology, and so on. There are at least two different ways to pursue this thought. On one option, which parallels (5) closely, metaphysical naturalism becomes the claim that the *techniques* specific to the natural sciences are adequate for investigating the relevant kinds of things:

(6) Every entity is of a kind such that things of that kind can, in principle, be successfully investigated using the techniques specific to the natural sciences.

On a rather different option, the focus is not on the techniques specific to the natural sciences but on the substantive content of the theories developed in the natural sciences:

(7) Every entity can be fully described using the theories developed in the natural sciences.

One advantage of (7) is that it suggests a simple parallel with physicalism or materialism, where the latter doctrine might be understood simply as (7) with "physics" replacing "the natural sciences."

Neither thesis is satisfactory as it stands. It is not obvious that there are techniques specific to the natural sciences; nor is it clear how the "in principle" in (6) should be understood. With (7) the question arises as to just which theories developed in the natural sciences are at issue, and of course the "fully described" clause leaves much to be desired as well. Questions of this sort are taken up in the literature on formulating physicalism, and parallel questions could be pursued for naturalism.

Depending on one's motivations for being a naturalist, (6) and (7) may seem objectionably arbitrary; those who count themselves as epistemic naturalists may insist there is no reason to focus on natural science in particular, so long as *philosophy* is deprived of any special authority. Such naturalists may accept the deliverances or techniques of the social sciences as providing warrant for philosophical claims even while denying (6) and (7).

The "nothing special" interpretation

Is there a way to make sense of the variety of different suggestions for how to understand naturalism? One promising avenue is what I call the "nothing special" interpretation.[8]

The discussion of what might count as a "natural entity" led us to a focus on the natural sciences; those sciences are "natural" presumably because they study the world *apart from humans.* The domains proper to physics, chemistry, biology, geology, meteorology, astronomy, and so on are understood without reference to human activity or special human interests. These sciences deal with "nature" in the specific sense of the world apart from humanity, while the others deal with humanity itself—those which, to use the older jargon, comprise the *moral sciences.* Metaphysical naturalism, I suggest, is best seen as the view that this division does not reflect any deep difference: humanity is *nothing special,* but just another part of nature.

The "nothing special" interpretation can explain why naturalists are united in rejecting certain entities—for example, ghosts, gods, and immaterial minds. One aspect of these examples is that such entities, if they exist, operate in a way quite foreign to the rest of the "natural" world, at least as we understand that world to operate. But that is not on its own enough to account for their being intuitively supernatural; the discovery of a unique and unanticipated kind of energy would not thereby tempt us to declare naturalism falsified. However, another aspect of at least many of these examples is that the entities in question are akin to human beings in some relevant respect. In particular, they are often understood as agents endowed with free will. Crudely put: what makes ghosts objectionably supernatural is not just their being inexplicable in terms of the existing theories of natural science but, further, their being *people,* or at least *agents.* If we were to learn that ghosts exist, then we would conclude that there *is* a deep division between humanity, or at least human-like things, and the rest of nature.[9]

Not every example of an unwelcome entity is one of a human-like entity; recall Dupré's example of vital fluids and De Caro's example of "prime movers unmoved." Nonetheless, where the example is of an entity that is akin to a human being, we may say that it runs counter to naturalism because it requires a serious divide between *things like us* and the rest of the world. And even with these other examples, the entities plausibly are ones that are of special significance to humans. Consider entelechies—entities unlike anything one finds in the inorganic realm that play a crucial role in making life possible. We take special interest in living things, whether or not we find them especially similar to us. Such things as entelechies plausibly strike us as contrary to naturalism because of their combination of (i) being essentially involved in something of special interest to us (namely, life), and (ii) not being explicable in terms of the sciences that deal with those things that are *not* of special interest to us.

As a way of testing the "nothing special" interpretation, we might manipulate some examples to see just when the threat to naturalism intuitively appears. Consider the earlier example of a newly discovered, unprecedented kind of energy; on its own, this seems compatible with naturalism. Now let us add that this energy is alleged to be directly controlled by the thought processes of appropriately situated humans. With that addition, we are much more likely to find the posit suspiciously "supernatural."

Can the "nothing special" interpretation give us a clear metaphysical thesis? It suggests at least a schema. First, we delineate a number of phenomena that are of special interest to humans; call these the "Human Interest Phenomena," or the HIP for short. (The acronym is deliberate; that which is "hip" is the cool, the trendy, the thing that people celebrate and are interested in.) Second, there is the rest of the universe, that in which we have no special interest apart from our general intellectual curiosity; this is the non-HIP, which is akin to "nature" as the HIP is akin to "man," as potentially set apart from nature. Metaphysical naturalism might then be expressed thus:

(8) The HIP are not fundamentally different from the non-HIP.

At bottom, the idea is that there's nothing special about *us,* or about those things that are of special concern to us. This "nothing special" idea is of course quite vague, and this vagueness is reflected in (8). "Fundamentally different" admits of more than one reading, and the class of HIP does not have sharp boundaries. Nonetheless, this seems to capture well the core metaphysical conviction of the naturalist, and insofar as we want a *diagnosis* of what people have in mind, such indeterminacy is only to be expected.

This core idea can be found in declarations of naturalism reaching back to the early twentieth century. In 1927, in clarifying his understanding of "naturalism," John Dewey credits his naturalism for finding incredible any view that posits a "gulf . . . between nature and man," adding that, on his view, "human affairs . . . are projections, continuations, complications, of the nature which exists in the physical and prehuman world" (Dewey, 1927, p. 58). In the present day we can find clear echoes of this basic idea. In a review of a recent anthology of papers on naturalism, Joseph Rouse suggests that one strand of naturalist thought is driven by an opposition to "humanism":

> Here lies the motivation for some naturalists' hostility to folk psychology, freedom, transcendental reason, the irreducibility of consciousness or first-person standpoints, and above all, any conception of normativity as *sui generis.* Human beings live in a world indifferent or even hostile to our interests, desires, values, or perspectival priorities, and the sciences provide our primary access to this anthropo-peripheral world to which we must accommodate ourselves. This anti-humanist strain of naturalism aspires to a hard-headed, resolute commitment to a thoroughly scientific self-understanding that can free us from the residual strands of self-aggrandizing illusion or wishful thinking that still confer disproportionate significance upon our all-too-human preoccupations. (Rouse, 2008)

It is, I think, fair to say that contemporary declarations of naturalism are often accompanied by a vivid awareness of just how tempting it is for us to endorse views of the world that are self-congratulatory in the way Rouse describes.

The "nothing special" interpretation makes it plain just why, despite the variation in how exactly "naturalism" is understood, we have near-unanimity in seeing naturalism as opposed to *theism*. After all, if theism is correct, the HIP are decidedly different from the non-HIP, since the lives of human beings are located at the very purpose of the universe and the non-HIP merely provide a stage for the human drama. The present suggestion also makes it easy to see why the mind–body problem should loom so large in the concerns of naturalists without their conviction being *limited* to the status of the mind. There is no question that mentality is included in the HIP; whether we can see it as not fundamentally different from the rest of the world is thus a key question for the naturalist.

Another advantage of (8) is that it makes sense of the fact that some surprising metaphysical views might be seen as metaphysically naturalistic despite nonstandard elements. Consider a version of theism according to which all of nature is equally sacred in the divine plan, where humans occupy no special place in the universe. Or consider a panpsychist view according to which the human mind is indeed of a piece with the non-HIP, as everything in the universe is endowed with mentality. In such cases, the HIP and non-HIP are fundamentally similar, but the similarity is achieved at the cost of a rather radical revision of how we understand the non-HIP, for example, giving up the ordinary view that microphysical particles lack mental properties.

The deliberate vagueness of "fundamental similarity" in (8) also enables us to see how a property dualist could (without radical revision of our understanding of the physical) take himself to be a naturalist. When, for example, David Chalmers describes the dualism defended in *The Conscious Mind* (1996) as naturalistic, he stresses the similarities between phenomenal properties and physical properties on the dualist view, which similarities are primarily a matter of being governed by laws of nature and being subject to similar causal explanations.[10]

The "nothing special" interpretation is offered as a diagnosis more than as a recommendation, and it does not handle all cases of naturalist talk equally well. For instance, it is not as easy to see how it can make sense of the emphasis on spatiotemporal location we saw above with (4).[11] Two additional aspects of it are worth pointing out, however. First, it helps connect epistemic naturalism with metaphysical naturalism, since the key epistemic naturalist view might be described as the conviction that there is nothing special about what *philosophers* can do, and hence no position of special authority we can wield in adjudicating the development of science. Second, and most important for present purposes, it makes sense of the idea that physicalism is a *version* of metaphysical naturalism, as we'll see later.

Formulating physicalism

Let us take the core idea of metaphysical naturalism to be (8). Presumably the physical realm is a decidedly non-HIP realm; there is nothing about physical entities as such that is of special interest to humanity. If we then formulate physicalism as the claim that everything is either physical or at least nothing over and above the physical, and that "everything" ranges over all the HIP, then physicalism counts as a version of metaphysical naturalism. The significance of the physical, on this view, lies precisely in its being a realm that is both indifferent to human interests and plausibly believed to be what ultimately makes up those things that are of special interest to us.

A formulation of physicalism needs to address at least three aspects of the claim: its extent, what is meant by "physical" and the relation that everything in the extent is supposed to bear to the physical.

The extent of physicalism

The question of the extent or scope of physicalism has received less attention than the other two questions of formulation. This may be due to the fact that controversies about the doctrine tend to revolve around cases that are obviously within its scope, such as actually existing mental phenomena. The preceding discussion of naturalism suggests that the physicalist claim ought to extend at least far enough to include everything that we might consider HIP—including biological phenomena, moral phenomena, and perhaps more.

What the physicalist claims about these phenomena will not be limited to the claim that the particular objects involved are physical objects. This is made clear by the fact that "property dualism" as a position on the mind–body problem is considered incompatible with physicalism. The thesis should imply that all of the relevant properties and relations are either physical or—at least, when actually instantiated—appropriately nothing over and above the physical.

If properties are understood as abstract objects, this claim can strike one as very puzzling; after all, how can an abstract entity be a physical entity? Depending on how we want to understand "physical," however, this may make perfectly good sense. For instance, classifying a property P as physical may mean only that it is a property in the domain of the relevant physical theory, where P itself can be construed along traditional Platonic lines as a necessarily existing entity not located in space or time. Most contemporary physicalists aim to be neutral on questions about the reality of abstract entities, and this stance is vindicated by the availability of such readings of "physical."

The focus on properties raises several other questions about the extent of physicalism. If we allow that there are uninstantiated properties, must they be included as well? Perhaps we can exclude those that are necessarily uninstantiated, but not those that are merely by luck uninstantiated. And there are nice questions about those that are necessarily instantiated—for example, being such that $2 + 2 = 4$. One promising suggestion here is that the claim should extend just to those properties that are capable of being contingently instantiated.[12] Obviously, the significance of one's answers to these questions depends as well on just how many properties or relations one is willing to recognize in the first place, though the more permissive one is the more important it is to get clear on this parameter.

Further, we should ask whether an attention to properties is sufficient. The physicalist is perhaps obliged to make a further claim about objects, events, laws, facts, or other entities. Consider objects: since they are plausibly not just bundles of properties, a claim only about the properties of objects might not say enough to satisfy physicalist scruples. For another example, consider laws: depending on one's view of laws of nature, even if all the actual instances of properties are caught in the physicalist net, this may not be enough to rule out laws of nature that the physicalist should reject.[13]

Nonetheless, for the remainder of this chapter I will focus solely on actually instantiated properties (understood hereafter as including relations), as it is at least obvious that the physicalist will claim that those are physical or (at least on each actual occasion of instantiation) appropriately nothing over and above the physical.

Specifying the "physical"

Let us start by considering a distinction drawn in the middle of the last century in thinking about the mind–body problem. In a classic discussion of emergentism, Paul Meehl and Wilfrid Sellars (1956) defined "physical$_1$" and "physical$_2$" as follows:

> *Physical$_1$*: an event or entity is *physical$_1$* if it belongs to the space–time network.
> *Physical$_2$*: an event or entity is *physical$_2$* if is definable in terms of theoretical primitives adequate to describe completely the actual states though not necessarily the potentialities of the universe before the appearance of life. (Meehl and Sellars, 1956, p. 252)

The physical$_2$ might be more loosely described as the *inorganic*; Meehl and Sellars' qualification regarding the "potentialities" of such things is meant to make room for the possibility that after the appearance of life new, unpredictable features may emerge. Those features would not need to be named in an account adequate to describing the pre-organic world, however, and hence would not count as physical$_2$.

"Physical$_1$" is reminiscent of an approach to the mind–body problem associated more with the term "materialism" than "physicalism," namely, defining the fundamental category as *matter,* where matter is understood in the Cartesian fashion as that which is extended in space. It should also remind us of the formulation of naturalism as the thesis that everything is located in one space–time network. As argued earlier, that attempt to make sense of naturalism is problematic. The notion indicated with "physical$_2$" comes closer to being an adequate account of the natural, as the inorganic seems clearly to belong to the realm of things that fail to be of special human interest.

If the physicalist makes use of "physical$_2$," her doctrine threatens to be equivalent to metaphysical naturalism, whereas it seemed at first to be a logically stronger thesis. To restore that strength one could keep the approach exemplified in the definition of "physical$_2$" and narrow the domain of relevant explananda. In fact, if we think of physics as a discipline charged with explaining some range of phenomena less expansive than "the inorganic," we might define the physical by reference to physics, or, rather, to some idealized version of physics—a version that succeeds in explaining those target phenomena.

This is the route taken by what is likely the most popular contemporary approach for specifying the physical. Plausibly, the popularity of this strategy turns on the fact that physicalism is itself motivated in some way by the impressive success of physics. Insofar as what motivates the physicalist is the success of some broader science—say, the physical sciences, as opposed just to physics itself—then a definition in terms of this broader set of theories may be in order, including perhaps chemistry, astronomy, and more. At one extreme what may impress the physicalist might be nothing more than the "natural sciences"—in which case we are driven back to metaphysical naturalism.

There are two reasons one might want to focus on physics in particular—or, more precisely, that part of physics that is fundamental by physicists' own lights, quantum mechanics and microphysical theory. First, the entities at issue in the other "physical sciences" seem likely to be appropriately "nothing over and above" the entities delineated by physics, so including them in the domain of the physical is unnecessary. One could use "physical" to encompass both that which counts as physical by the criteria we are now searching for and that which is appropriately nothing over and above the physical according to that first criterion, but that is likely to court confusion. In this chapter I will use "physical" to mean that which qualifies as physical according to the initial criterion, and will occasionally use "properly physical" to stress this point when necessary.

The second reason one might want to limit the (properly) physical to that part of physics concerns the justification of physicalism. One of the most popular and promising ways of supporting the doctrine appeals specifically to the thesis that physics is causally complete—more precisely, the thesis that all physical events can be given entirely adequate causal explanations solely by appeal to other physical events and laws. The easiest way to justify that claim, in turn, is by understanding the properly physical in terms of the domain of quantum mechanics and microphysical theory (Sturgeon, 1998).

If it is agreed that the physical should be limited in this way, then one must bear in mind the fact that much discussion of physicalism has been conducted as if the "physical" includes a broader range of properties. For instance, J. J. C. Smart's celebrated defense of the identity theory (Smart, 1959) focused on the identity of mental properties with *neurophysiological* properties—which would not count as properly physical on the present suggestion. If such properties really are appropriately nothing over and above the physical as delimited by theory, then this is a harmless practice, but it may help avoid confusion to distinguish an ordinary notion of the physical on which we enjoy an intuitive grip from the official notion tied to theory.[14]

The proposal that we specify what "physical" is to mean by referring to physical theory has prompted a considerable skeptical literature (Crane and Mellor, 1990; Crook and Gillett, 2001; Montero, 1999; van Fraassen, 1996; Stoljar, 2010, ch. 5). The core worry can be traced to Carl Hempel (Hempel, 1969) and is now often referred to as "Hempel's Dilemma." It may be put as follows. The theory by reference to which the "physical" is to be defined is either some actually existing theory or some theory that exists only in some ideal, possible future. In light of the history of science, it is likely that present theories are false, even if they are in some sense closer to the truth than past theories. As a result, the physicalist who takes the former option will be defining physicalism by reference to a false theory, which seems an unhappy result.[15] On the other hand, if the physicalist chooses the latter option, the resulting notion faces two important worries.[16]

The *obscurity* objection is that an appeal to an ideal physical theory leaves the physicalist thesis too obscure to be properly evaluated. If we don't know what the ideal physical theory looks like, we don't know what sorts of properties will count as physical properties; how, then, can anyone support, attack, or otherwise assess the physicalist thesis? The *inappropriate extension* objection (to use the apt term from Wilson, 2006) is that the appeal to an ideal theory allows for the possibility that intuitively nonphysical entities could count as properly physical by being included in the ideal physical theory. Suppose that there are metaphysically fundamental mental events that make a causal difference to the behavior of physical particles, and an ideal physical theory will, because it must succeed in explaining the behavior of such particles, end up positing those mental entities. The result in that case is that such entities count trivially as physical, which seems an inappropriate extension of the category.

One important response to Hempel's Dilemma is that offered by Andrew Melnyk (Melnyk, 2003, pp. 223–37; also see Melnyk, 1997). Melnyk defends the first option (appealing to current physical theory) by arguing that physicalism is itself a scientific hypothesis, and hence, the attitude the physicalist takes toward it should be the same attitude that scientific realists take toward what they consider to be the best of current scientific theories. As scientific realists usually recognize that current theories are likely to be false, the attitude in question need not be one that is rendered irrational by that recognition. On Melnyk's account of the appropriate attitude, one assigns the theory in question a higher probability than any of its *relevant rivals,* where not every incompatible theory counts as a relevant rival. As a result, the physicalist can take this attitude toward current physical theory without thinking it true or even likely true. Even if we accept Melnyk's account of the relevant attitude, it's not clear that it resolves our dilemma. One reaction is to say that *both* the scientific realist and the would-be physicalist face a problem: shouldn't they be able to tell us what they *do* think is likely true?

Other responses to the dilemma can be classified as either blunting the second horn or avoiding both by understanding "physical" without reference to theory at all. Among the former (Papineau, 1993; Wilson, 2006) is the strategy of dealing with the problem of inappropriate extension simply by stipulating that the "physical" is *not* to include anything mental unless it is nothing over and above something else that qualifies as physical.[17] This move helps somewhat with the obscurity objection, since one can then know something about what is *not* included in the physical. An importantly different response to the dilemma is to define the physical in an entirely negative way. This may be called the Via Negativa response: what is meant by a physical property simply is a non-mental property—or, more precisely, one that can be understood in a way that doesn't characterize it in mental terms.[18] Another variant is to drop talk of the "physical" altogether and simply identify a metaphysical thesis as, say nonmentalism: everything is either nonmental or nothing over and above the non-mental (Papineau and Spurrett, 1999). Both versions should be distinguished from the approach that combines an appeal to ideal physical theory and a negative stipulation, as that offers an indirect link to current physical theory, the impressiveness of which is again part of the motivation for many physicalists (for discussion, see Gillett and Witmer, 2001; Montero and Papineau, 2005).

The "Nothing Over and Above" claim

Suppose an account is available that tells us when a property counts as (properly) physical in the first place. As mentioned, many physicalists want to allow properties that are not themselves properly physical but are nonetheless related in the right way to the physical. Before focusing on how that "right way" might be understood, it will prove instructive to get clear on why a simple identity approach is unpopular. Why not opt for (9)?

(9) Every property is identical with a properly physical property.

Common lore has it that (9)—known also as the *type identity* thesis—was overthrown by the recognition that there are properties that can be *multiply realized,* that is, instantiated at different times by virtue of quite different physical features (Boyd, 1980; Fodor, 1974; Putnam, 1967). It is important to distinguish two aspects of multiple realizability. When it is said that a given property F is multiply realizable, one part of the claim is a denial that there is any physical property P such that F and P are necessarily coextensive. This claim is one that an *opponent* of physicalism might urge in attacking the doctrine; it can hardly motivate dropping (9) as a requirement for physicalism.

The other aspect of multiple realizability, however, is that in the cases under consideration, the relation between the physical and F is plainly one in which it is misguided to see the instantiation of F as something requiring more than what is already given in the relevant physical conditions. This is easiest to see (and historically was made most evident) when the property F is already understood as a functional property, that is, the property of having some property that plays such and such a role. Where the property that plays the role is physical, and its playing that role is due entirely to physical events and laws, then the instantiation of F comes along "for free"; it is not genuinely additional to the physical conditions there satisfied. It is what Armstrong has called an "ontological free lunch" (Armstrong, 1997, pp. 12–13).

The relation exemplified in these examples has come to be known as "realization": the property F is *realized* by some physical property or properties in a way that satisfies physicalist requirements. Exactly how the term "realize" is best used has been a matter of some contention (Gillett, 2002; Polger, 2007; Shoemaker, 2007); the present point, however, is just that the relevant examples illustrate how a property could fit into a physicalist world without being strictly identical with any physical property. Indeed, even if the examples are entirely fictional, so that no properties are ever actually multiply realized, if their possibility is allowed, that would be enough to show that (9) is not necessary for the truth of physicalism. This is an important point to keep in mind in light of the renewed controversy over whether there really are multiply realized properties (Heil, 1999; Kim, 1992; Polger, 2002; Shapiro, 2000).[19]

The foregoing discussion sheds some light on the relation between physicalism and "reductionism"—at least in some sense of that vexed and politically loaded term. While "reductionism" is often associated simply with the type identity thesis, the rationale for not requiring such identity is that we can, without that requirement, secure something that still has a "reductive" sound to it, namely, the claim that nonphysical properties are nothing over and above the physical. It is far from obvious, however, just how this reductive commitment may or may not be related to claims about intertheoretic reduction as discussed in the philosophy of science (e.g., in such seminal texts as Churchland, 1979; Hooker, 1981; Kemeny and Oppenheim, 1956; Nagel, 1961; Nickles, 1973; Schaffner, 1967).[20]

Thus far, we might formulate physicalism as (10):

(10) Every property is either physical or, on every actual occasion of instantia-
     tion, nothing over and above the physical conditions that actually obtain.

One may wonder, of course, just how this "nothing over and above" talk is to be understood. Such talk is certainly not without intuitive appeal, and it is associated with talk that has wide currency in philosophy generally, especially talk of *grounding* one property in another, or talk of something's having one property *in virtue of* having another. It is also associated with talk of *truthmaking,* and the physicalist is plausibly committed to the claim that when a nonphysical property F is actually instantiated, the physical facts make true the proposition that F is thus instantiated (Melnyk, 2003, p. 59).

In moving beyond (10), we might aim to eliminate the "nothing over and above" talk entirely in favor of more familiar notions, finding it objectionably obscure. Even if we don't think such elimination necessary to have a respectably articulated thesis on the table, we will likely want to clarify (10) by getting clear on just what it is meant to entail.

The notion of *supervenience* has been widely thought to help in this regard. Briefly, one family of properties supervenes on another family just in case there can be no difference in the former without some difference in the latter. In other words, the total state of something with regards to one family of properties (the "subvenient" if you will) suffices for its total state with regards to the supervenient family. An easy example to use to keep the idea clear is that of aesthetic and nonaesthetic properties. Plausibly, if two items differ in their aesthetic properties, they must also differ in some nonaesthetic properties; there cannot be a *bare* aesthetic difference. This is in turn a function of the derivative status of aesthetic properties; if something is ugly, something *makes* it ugly.

If the nonphysical properties are an ontological free lunch, fixing the physical properties should fix the nonphysical properties; and this is just what an appropriate supervenience thesis delivers. The qualifier "appropriate" is crucial, however, since there are many different ways in which the basic idea of supervenience can be fleshed out. In particular, the relevant comparisons can be understood in a variety of ways. What sorts of objects are to be compared for sameness and difference in the relevant properties, and how exactly are the relevant pairs to be selected? We might compare objects, regions, or entire worlds, and we might even compare the state of one thing with respect to its supervenient properties with the state of a distinct thing to which it is mapped with respect to its subvenient properties. Permutations of these parameters can result in a wide variety of distinct supervenience claims (see Kim, 1993; Savellos and Yalçin, 1995; Stalnaker, 1996).

Perhaps the most popular supervenience thesis in contemporary work is that which makes use of the notion of a "minimal physical duplicate," a term introduced by Frank Jackson (Jackson, 1998, pp. 11–13) to enable us to formulate a kind of global supervenience thesis, one that compares entire possible worlds. A minimal physical duplicate of a world *w* is, intuitively, what one would get if one were to take the physical description of *w* as a recipe, building a new world out of nothing but the ingredients spelled out in that recipe. No additional objects, events, or properties are added; nothing is in that world except what comes along necessarily given the recipe. The supervenience thesis now available is (11):

(11) Any minimal physical duplicate of the actual world is a duplicate simpliciter of the actual world.

The need for minimality arises from an important complication. Consider the property of being the happiest person in the world. Even if mental properties are in fact as the physicalist envisages, it is clear that fixing all the physical properties will not on its own suffice for someone's having this property. To see this, consider a possible world *w* just like this one in every physical respect, yet in addition, *w* contains an extra mind that is entirely independent of the physical. Even if the mental state of each actual individual is as the physicalist imagines, if the extra individual in *w* enjoys a level of happiness greater than that of each actual individual, this addition will make a difference as to who has the property of being the *happiest,* and as a result *w* differs from the actual world with respect to some nonphysical property without differing in any physical respect.[21]

In light of this complication, it may be incorrect to describe the physicalist's commitment as requiring that the way things are generally is nothing over and above the way things are physically; after all, to get something that suffices for distribution of nonphysical properties one needs not *just* the way things are physically but that in combination with a kind of totality fact—the fact that nothing is added to the situation beyond that which comes for free with the physical properties. This totality fact is presumably not best classified as just a fact about the properly physical.

Suppose (as many hold) that (11) is necessary for physicalism; is it also sufficient? It will clearly not be sufficient if the range of possible worlds at issue in (11) is implicitly restricted in some way—say, to only those worlds with the same laws of nature as the actual world. In that case, the truth of (11) could be explained in a way incompatible with physicalism. There is no prima facie difficulty in supposing there could be laws of nature that link distinct entities in such a way as to guarantee that fixing the physical fixes everything else, even though the "everything else" includes things that are indeed something over and above the physical. For (11) to come close to a sufficient condition, the relevant minimal physical duplicates must be drawn from among all the possible worlds, without restriction.[22]

Even with this clarification, there are reasons to suspect that (11) is not sufficient. For one, we might worry that there could be "brute" metaphysical necessities, that is, necessities not explainable in terms of anything deeper, so that physical entities are simply related to nonphysical entities in a way that makes (11) true without having any consequences for the nature of those nonphysical entities (Melnyk, 2003, pp. 58–9). For another, the contrast between metaphysical and nomic necessity presupposed in the previous paragraph might be a false one, in which case even the "full strength" reading of (11) might be explained by laws of nature, which apparently undermines its significance (see Wilson, 2005). Finally, there is a general lesson from the philosophy of science that seems applicable. The physicalist will want to say that the nonphysical properties are instantiated in virtue of the physical properties, which is an explanatory claim. But the familiar lesson from philosophy of science is that sufficiency is not itself sufficient for explanation; we may suspect, then, that a merely modal thesis such as (11) cannot ensure the relevant explanatory import of physicalism. In general, with each of these worries, the point is that there may be ways of explaining the truth of (11) that run counter to the physicalist thesis. What is needed is not just supervenience but, to use Terence Horgan's terminology, superdupervenience: supervenience that is explainable in a physicalistically acceptable fashion (Horgan, 1993; Kim, 1990; McLaughlin, 1995).

In light of this, we might try formulating physicalism in terms of some set of possible relations that actually instantiated properties might bear to the physical, each of which would make available the kind of explanation of the sufficiency of physical facts that is wanted, an explanation that would vindicate the "nothing over and above" talk. Consider (12):

> (12) Every actually instantiated property is either (i) identical with some properly physical property or (ii) a functional property, where on each actual occasion of instantiation, it is realized by physical properties.

The idea that physicalism is best formulated as (12) has gained in popularity in recent years, largely because it seems better placed to provide a sufficient condition on the doctrine (Kim, 1998, pp. 23–7; Melnyk, 2003).

Advocates of (12) will naturally focus on the notion of realization, given its central role and the fact that, unlike the clear and simple relation of identity, clarification is surely in order. On some accounts of realization, only properties that are functional in a suitably broad sense can be realized, where a property is functional in the sense used earlier, namely, being a property expressible as the property of having some property that plays role R (for a careful overview of some options here, see Shoemaker, 1981). A property R realizes such a functional property just in case it in fact meets condition C. This is a very simple and tidy account, but it exacts a considerable cost: any actually instantiated property that is not plausibly identified with a properly physical one needs to be functional in the relevant way, and it is far from obvious so many properties could be plausibly construed as functional in this way.

Not all accounts of realization tie the notion to functional properties understood in this fashion, however. Some alternative accounts lean on a certain increasingly popular background view, namely, that properties in general are individuated by the causal powers they contribute to their bearers. Suppose that a property F is associated with a set C(F) of causal powers in this way and that R is likewise associated with a set C(R) of causal powers. On the "subset view" of realization, R realizes F just in case C(F) is a proper subset of C(R) (Clapp, 2001; Shoemaker, 2001, 2007). Since C(R) includes members not in C(F), R is a distinct property from F, but since every member of C(F) is a member of C(R), once R is instantiated, F is thereby automatically instantiated as well.

An aspect of the subset view of realization that makes it especially appealing for the physicalist is that it seems to promise an account of how a property could be distinct from its physical realizer yet connected to it in a way that appears to avoid duplicating causal powers. When F is realized by R, it is not as if there are two sets of causal powers at work; there is just one set that is operative in the situation, while the two distinct properties are related in different ways to that one set of causal powers. This might alleviate several worries about the causal role of properties that are not themselves properly physical, although the matter is quite controversial.[23]

Support for naturalism and/or physicalism

The doctrines of naturalism and physicalism enjoy extremely widespread support in contemporary philosophy, so much so that they seem often taken for granted. Nonetheless, there are at least two important ways in which physicalism has been supported, and there is a rough (and rarely articulated) argument for the more general and nebulous doctrine of metaphysical naturalism. I start with the latter.

Naturalism and a general trend of dethronement

How can the thesis of metaphysical naturalism be supported? If the "nothing special" interpretation is adopted, it is not hard to see how someone could find metaphysical naturalism compelling. Again, let "HIP" stand for the Human Interest Phenomena—minds, life, morality, and perhaps other things—and consider (8) as an expression of metaphysical naturalism:

(8) The HIP are not fundamentally different from the non-HIP.

It has often been said that there were a number of powerful historical moments in leading humanity to disabuse itself of the idea that it was at the center of the universe: there was the Copernican revolution, so that our planet is literally not at the center of the solar system; there was the Darwinian revolution, which assimilated mankind to the rest of the kingdom of life; and there was the impact of Freud, forcing us to take seriously the effects of our nonrational nature. These three famous moments seem to exemplify a more general trend of *dethronement* of humanity in the development of the sciences. It is not clear that one could specify this trend with any precision; it is nonetheless quite plausible to say that such a trend has shaped the thinking of contemporary philosophers—not to mention contemporary thought in general. The idea is simple and familiar: science has repeatedly debunked those views on which humanity and our interests occupy a special place in the world.

Whether this idea can be worked up into a powerful argument for metaphysical naturalism as per (8) is a good question. We could stipulate a more precise meaning for "not fundamentally different," taking as our cue the formulation of the "nothing over and above" aspect of physicalism. The more difficult task lies in thinking about how one could appropriately *project* from examples of the HIP that have been shown to be nothing over and above the non-HIP to the general conclusion that the same is true of all the HIP. Suppose that the class of the HIP is akin to the class of *grue* things (Goodman, 1983), so that generalizing from the naturalistic status of some of them to all of them is unwarranted. Similarly, the category of the non-HIP may be heterogeneous as well, undermining such a generalization.

A distinct strategy here would be to develop an argument aimed not at supporting (8) directly but instead at the conclusion that we should not give any epistemic weight to any inclination we may have to treating the HIP as special—or, perhaps, more weakly, that we should treat them as prima facie unjustified, given their poor historical track record. On its own, this does not motivate endorsing (8); general considerations of simplicity may, however, tilt the scales here. If our inclinations to deny (8) are not to be trusted, and in general we should aim for simpler theories, then this may give us good reason to treat the truth of (8) as at least a default view.

Of course, if we have independent evidence for physicalism, and physicalism implies (8), then we have much more reason to endorse metaphysical naturalism.

Physicalism: Inductive arguments

The first of the two influential routes to justifying physicalism is roughly inductive in character: argue that since a wide variety of phenomena have already been shown to be nothing over and above the physical, the physicalist is justified in making the inductive leap to conclude that all actual phenomena are likewise grounded wholly in the physical.

One way to develop this argument is by appealing to an alleged history of successful intertheoretic reductions. That is certainly the justification imagined by those philosophers writing in the middle of the twentieth century who were concerned to defend a physicalist theory of the mind (see especially Oppenheim and Putnam, 1958). As they saw it, the work had already been done in showing that the sciences—at least, most of those other than psychology and those dependent on psychology—reduce, in order, to biology, to chemistry, and ultimately to physics. In effect, on this view, physicalism as a view about everything other than the mental had already been demonstrated by a string of successful reductions, so that all that remained was to justify the extension of physicalism to the realm of the mental.

There are two important problems facing this approach. First, it is not entirely clear how intertheoretic reduction, understood as a phenomenon studied in the philosophy of science, is to be related to the key metaphysical claims of the physicalist. The literature on the former is bound up with epistemic concerns about the preservation of epistemic virtues across theory change, which is not directly relevant to the physicalist's claim. In particular, the best-known account of intertheoretic reduction—the derivational account offered by Ernest Nagel (1961)—is subject to important worries regarding its significance for metaphysical debate (Kim, 1998).

Second, and most pressing, the view that intertheoretic reductions are widespread in actual science is now widely rejected by philosophers of science.

The claim that biology has been shown to be reducible to chemistry, for example, is far from being uncontroversial. No one doubts that all sorts of interesting intertheoretic links have been found and developed, but the controversy is over the proper interpretation of those achievements (see Garfinkel, 1981, ch. 2; Kitcher, 1984; Smith, 1992; Sklar, 1999; and for a book-length treatment of the significance of "post-reductionist philosophy of science," see Horst, 2007).[24]

Even if the physicalist cannot find a history of successful intertheoretic reductions, she may still find a history in which physicalist commitments are repeatedly vindicated. One very detailed development of this strategy can be found in the last chapter of Melnyk's *A Physicalist Manifesto* (2003), in which he reviews a variety of examples from natural science (ranging from such things as chemical bonding to cardiac musculature), to argue that the scientific results give us the resources for defending many identity hypotheses of the sort that vindicate physicalism. On his view, physicalism requires every particular entity to be either physical or physically realized, where realization is tied to the notion of a functional type. The scientific results will not speak directly to this, of course, since they won't speak of "realization" directly or focus on these questions; but it may be that, as Melnyk argues, the results do enough to show that if we make the needed identifications, we are able to explain all that needs explaining about the relevant phenomena.

The general strategy may be illustrated with what Melnyk says about solidity. As he stresses, "the *physicist's* account of solids just sketched is not yet a *physicalist* account of solids" (Melnyk, 2003, p. 241). The former implies that solidity includes certain properly physical features, which features can explain a wide variety of explananda—for example, the fact "that solid items retain their size and shape despite the effects of gravity, and despite the application to them of (a restricted range of) mechanical forces" (p. 242). Still, this is consistent with saying that solidity involves something in addition to what is needed to explain those things. The key move is then made by pointing out that, so far as those explananda are concerned, "there is no theoretical need to construe solidity as anything more than a physical or a functional-but-physically-realized property" (p. 242). Given the general principle that we should minimize our commitments, this gives us reason to think that the best explanation of those facts is one that vindicates the physicalist hypothesis regarding solidity. If this can be repeated for many and varied cases, this can serve as powerful evidence for physicalism in general.

The task is far from trivial. One potential difficulty turns on the fact that the relevant explananda might be described in the first instance in terms far removed from the properly physical, so that even if the physicalist hypothesis can adequately explain the physical aspects of target explananda, it may fail to explain all that needs explaining. Further, there are important questions about how inference to the best explanation is to work when supporting identity claims in general (Kim, 2005), and those may force some rethinking of this strategy.[25]

Physicalism: Causal arguments

A rather different kind of approach to supporting physicalism makes use of a general thesis regarding the physical, namely, the causal completeness of physics (also often called the "causal closure" of physics). The idea, informally put, is that one never needs to advert to anything other than physical events and the laws of physics to provide an adequate causal explanation of physical events. Physics thus provides a domain which is complete in that it is never lacking for the resources to provide causal explanations of events in its own domain.

The completeness thesis does *not* say that the only legitimate causal explanations of physical events are ones that appeal exclusively to physical factors; its claim is only that, for every physical event which can be causally explained at all, there exists a causal explanation of it that appeals only to physical conditions and laws and is entirely adequate on its own, so that *if* that were the only explanation to be had, there would be nothing unsatisfactory about that explanation. As such, it is the sort of thesis that can be supported by considerations internal to physical theory, by judging the success of physical theory in producing such explanations, without having to rely on any claims about the relation of physical theory to anything else. This is a considerable advantage, as any such claims are likely to be philosophically contentious.

If the causal completeness of physics is granted, the physicalist may press the following point. Consider some property M that is not, at least not obviously, a properly physical property. If, as seems likely, M is involved in the causation of some physical event, then, unless we say that M is either identical with some physical property or appropriately nothing over and above such properties, we face a puzzling situation. If e is the physical event at issue, we know from the causal completeness of physics that it can be given an adequate explanation adverting only to other physical conditions; since M is also involved in causing e, its role would seem as a result to be redundant—a consequence that seems at least odd, and intolerable if we were forced to accept it as a widespread occurrence. If the only way to avoid this unhappy consequence is to accept that M conforms to the physicalist thesis, then we have what seems a tidy and apparently powerful argument for physicalism (Papineau, 1993; Sturgeon, 1998).[26]

The argument is not as tidy as it may first appear, however. A major complication arises from the fact that causation appears to be a relation between events, yet the above argument attempts to draw conclusions about the nature of the property M, which I described as being "involved" in the causation of a physical event. If we stick simply with events, we can perhaps draw the conclusion that every event is either identical with a physical event or nothing over and above some physical event. As noted earlier, however, the physicalist commitment clearly extends to properties. So it is crucial that the causal argument be development with careful attention to the role of properties in causation. It is easy enough to say that a property may have "causal relevance" in a given cause–effect pair just in case the cause event was a cause in virtue of instantiating that property; but how should this complication be incorporated into the argument for physicalism?

Another considerable difficulty concerns the relationship between avoiding the conclusion that the putatively nonphysical property is causally redundant and establishing that it is either properly physical or nothing over and above the physical. The argument presumes that the only way to avoid an offensive kind of overdetermination is to embrace physicalism about the relevant property, at least as it is then and there instantiated. But it's not obvious just how to establish this. There is again a considerable literature related to this issue, though its relation is somewhat indirect. Much of the literature is devoted to what Kim has made well known as the "exclusion problem": this is the problem for the would be "nonreductive" physicalist who wants to maintain the causal relevance of those properties that he nonetheless counts as not reducing to the physical (Bennett, 2007; Heil and Mele, 1993; Horgan, 2001; Kim, 1998). It is not always clear just how "reductive" and "nonreductive" are being used in this discussion, though if we take "reductive" to mean a commitment to a simple type identity hypothesis, we can see the dispute as revolving around the following question: How can anything less than strict identity avoid the threat of problematic overdetermination? Answers to this question will be indirectly relevant to the more general question: Exactly what are the possible ways in which a problematic kind of overdetermination can be avoided? Addressing that question, in turn, is crucial for assessing the causal argument for physicalism.

Notes

1   If epistemic naturalism forbids a priori knowledge, then someone like Frank Jackson (1998), who embraces both physicalism and a priori knowledge, would count as a kind of anti-naturalist physicalist. I would count myself in this camp as well (Witmer, 2006).

2   There is a nice question as to how "supernatural" and "non-natural" are to be distinguished from each other. The latter seems designed to be less offensive than the former, with perhaps the "super" indicating precisely the same unwanted aspect as does the "supra" in Maddy's talk of a "supra-scientific tribunal"—that is, some kind of authority or power over the merely natural.

3   There is a use of "natural property" in contemporary metaphysics that must be distinguished from the use of "natural entity" in the current context. As used by David Lewis (1983) and many others influenced by him, the natural properties are those such that their instances genuinely have something in common, so that positing a universal is tempting, whereas the nonnatural properties are merely classes of possible individuals, where they may have nothing genuinely in common. Plausibly, if we say that some predicates correspond to something in reality other than the individuals that satisfy them while others don't, the former pick out the "natural" properties and the latter don't. To see that this notion of "natural property" is not what is currently at issue, consider the property of being a ghost. If there were ghosts, then that property would surely count as natural in the Lewisian sense, but presumably it would still be objectionably supernatural in the sense at issue in metaphysical naturalism.

4   For example, when James Ladyman and Don Ross explain why it is "anti-naturalist" to give weight to intuitions, they claim that doing so "requires ignoring the fact that science, especially physics, has shown us that the universe is very strange to our inherited conception of what it is like" (Ladyman and Ross, 2007, p. 10).

5   Only one page after his account of "naturalism" Armstrong says that to accept naturalism "is to reject such entities as Cartesian minds, private visual and tactual spaces, angelic beings and God" (Armstrong, 1978, p. 127). Armstrong presumably can appeal to his official doctrine (4) to rule out each of these. Cartesian minds, angels, and God are presumably not located in both space and time, while private visual and tactual spaces may be located in some way but not in the *same* spatiotemporal system as ordinary objects. Armstrong's emphasis on a single spatiotemporal system thus does play a role. Unhappily, however, this same emphasis renders the thesis too strong. Suppose the world were to consist of two distinct spatiotemporal systems, each containing nothing but what is describable by current physics. I doubt any naturalist would decry such a world as contrary to his doctrine simply because of the disconnect between two otherwise perfectly "natural" systems.

6 For example, consider Roy Wood Sellars' remarks in 1927: "[N]aturalism takes nature in a definite way as identical with reality, as self-sufficient and as the whole of reality. And by nature is meant the space–time–causal system which is studied by science and in which our lives are passed" (Sellars, 1927, p. 217).

7 Consider in this light the following remark from Gerhard Vollmer in a recent anthology of papers on naturalism: "We understand naturalism as a natural-philosophical anthropological position. It can be characterized briefly by the thesis: everywhere in the world everything can be explained rationally" (Vollmer, 2007, p. 35).

8 This interpretation is presented in (Witmer, unpublished).

9 An interesting case: suppose we discovered that ghosts exist, are psychologically much like us, but actual human beings are fully understandable in physical terms. Would naturalism be falsified? I expect many would say that it still is. This is one reason I suggest a formulation in terms of "human interest phenomena"—which would include things that are not themselves human but are still human-like.

10 As he puts it, the view in question "is naturalistic because it posits that every-thing is a consequence of a network of basic properties and laws" (Chalmers, 1996, p. 128).

11 There might nonetheless be an intelligible link between the privileging of the natural sciences and the focus on spatiotemporal location we find in (4). Consider the following striking fact about the entities posited by the most admired of natural sciences, namely, physics: physical entities pervade all of space and time, including those regions we ourselves occupy. Taking this for granted, one might implicitly suppose that anything *in contrast* to the entities described by the natural sciences would have to be separate from this single spatiotemporal system. Being spatiotemporally located would not, on its own, confer the status of being natural, but the pervasiveness of entities already deemed natural *conjoined* with this claim could motivate one to think that anything that is fundamentally different from those natural entities would need to be located elsewhere, thus giving rise to (4) as an expression of naturalism.

12 A notable discussion of the extent of physicalism can be found in Andrew Melnyk's book *A Physicalist Manifesto* (2003), in which he proposes that the claim extend to all causal or contingent tokens (pp. 10–11). The "causal" is not redundant; if a necessarily existing God existed but still has a causal impact, that token would also need to be caught in the physicalist net.

13 I have argued (Witmer, 2001) that the physicalist should include a claim about laws so as to ensure that physicalism is not a lucky accident, though I don't think we should make physicalism a necessary truth.

14 Papineau appeals to "paradigmatically physical" events (1993, p. 30); see also the discussion of the ordinary–physical as it relates to the theoretical–physical in (Witmer, 2000).

15   It is worth noting that the mere falsity of current physical theory wouldn't matter; the physicalist is only exploiting the theory for its inventory of entities. The problem arises only insofar as one thinks that current physical theory makes an error in including or leaving out entities that an ideal theory would not.

16   An additional worry is sometimes aired that is not, in my view, very serious. This is the *triviality* worry: if the ideal physical theory is ideal in the sense that it succeeds as a theory about all those phenomena which the physicalist believes to be ultimately physical, then those phenomena are trivially counted as physical simply by virtue of being the subject matter of the ideal physical theory. This worry can be set aside, however, as the physicalist can define the ideal theory as one that succeeds as a theory about all phenomena *of interest to the physicist*— which is less than all those believed by the physicalist to be ultimately physical. (This point is related to the one in the main text about exploiting Meehl and Sellars's definition of "physical$_2$.")

17   Similarly, if one wants to ensure that physicalism is a species of naturalism, one might expand this prohibition to include anything that is HIP—so that, for instance, there are no basic biological properties among the physical.

18   The Via Negativa needs to be spelled out in a way that doesn't commit the physicalist to the falsity of the classical identity theory; we cannot characterize the view, then, by saying that on it physical properties are defined simply as those properties not identical with any mental properties. Some more elaborate characterization as that given in the main text is needed.

19   It's worth pointing out, too, that even if functional properties are deemed impossible for some reason, there are other kinds of cases in which a property appears to "come for free" given other, more basic properties, for example, when a determinable is instantiated by a determinate.

20   For a useful discussion of one example of how different literatures on "reduction" can become confusingly entangled, see Robinson (2001).

21   This example presumes that physicalism can be contingently true, so that even if all actual mental properties are nothing over and above the physical, there are possible instances that conform to the dualist's view of things. Functionalists have generally allowed such a possibility, but there has been some dispute over the availability of this position (Levine and Trogdon, 2009).

22   It should be noted that the minimal physical duplicates plausibly need to duplicate the laws of physics in the actual world, since such laws would be included in the physical "recipe"; the point is that no other laws, if there are any other laws, should be held constant.

23   The worries in question revolve around the "exclusion problem"—roughly, the problem of finding a suitable causal role for nonphysical properties given the (presumed) fact that physical properties already provide adequate causal

explanations on their own. For representative discussions, see Bennett (2007), Heil and Mele (1993), Heckmann and Walter (2003), Horgan (2001), and Marcus (2001).

24 It is a nice question whether or not the shift in attitude between the middle of the last century and now is due more to changes in how carefully philosophers of science attend to the details of actual science or more to shifting standards of what is needed for something to count as a genuine "intertheoretic reduction." The answer to this question is relevant to the prospects for the argument strategy discussed in the following paragraph.

25 A somewhat different way one might use the history of science to argue for physicalism is via what one can call the argument from *proven methodological utility*. Instead of focusing on the content of scientific results, this argument would turn on the claim that scientific practice has often presupposed that physicalism is true, and this presupposition is at least partly responsible for its success. If the history of science shows that it pays to presume physicalism, we could argue that the best explanation of this is that physicalism *is* true. One important difficulty with this strategy arises simply from the general difficulty in adjudicating claims about presuppositions. Even if it is plausible to say that actual scientists have presumed physicalism, more work is needed to show that this presumption— and not, perhaps, some less weighty or significant presumption—played an important role in shaping the theories constructed, experiments designed, or the like (Gillett, 2001).

26 The causal argument should be sharply distinguished from the traditional attack on Cartesian dualism that questions the intelligibility of causation spanning the mental and physical divide. The argument does not concern the mental–physical divide in particular, nor does it turn on claims about intelligibility at all. It should also be distinguished from Davidson's famous argument (Davidson, 1970) for the thesis that every event is a physical event. While there are a few (indirect) relations between this argument and Davidson's, the latter turns fundamentally on the claim that there are no strict laws that can be given in nonphysical terms, whereas the present argument could happily allow such laws. For an excellent discussion of these different arguments and their independence from each other, see chapter 6 of (Foster, 1991).

References

Armstrong, D. M. (1978), *Universals and Scientific Realism 1: Nominalism and Realism.* Cambridge: Cambridge University Press.

—(1997), *A World of States of Affairs.* New York: Cambridge University Press.

Bennett, K. (2007), "Mental causation." *Philosophy Compass* 2(2), 316–37.

Boyd, R. (1980), "Materialism without reductionism: what physicalism does not entail," in N. Block, ed., *Readings in the Philosophy of Psychology*. Cambridge, MA: Harvard University Press, 67–106.

Chalmers, D. J. (1996), *The Conscious Mind: In Search of a Fundamental Theory*. Oxford: Oxford University Press.

Churchland, P. M. (1979), *Scientific Realism and the Plasticity of Mind*. Cambridge: Cambridge University Press.

Clapp, L. (2001), "Disjunctive properties: multiple realizations." *Journal of Philosophy*, 98(3), 111–36.

Crane, T. and Mellor, D. H. (1990), "There is no question of physicalism." *Mind*, 99(394), 185–206.

Crook, S. and Gillett, C. (2001), "Why physics alone cannot define the 'physical': materialism, metaphysics and the formulation of physicalism." *Canadian Journal of Philosophy*, 31(3), 333–60.

Davidson, D. (1970), "Mental events," in L. Foster and J. W. Swanson, eds, *Experience and Theory*. Amherst, MA: University of Massachusetts Press, pp. 79–101.

De Caro, M. (2010), "Varieties of naturalism," in R. C. Koons and G. Bealer, eds, *The Waning of Materialism*. New York: Oxford University Press, pp. 365–74.

Dewey, J. (1927), "Half-hearted naturalism." *Journal of Philosophy*, 24(3), 57–64.

Dupré, J. (2004), "The miracle of monism," in M. De Caro and D. Macarthur, eds, *Naturalism in Question*. Cambridge, MA: Harvard University Press, pp. 36–58.

Fodor, J. (1974), "Special sciences, or the disunity of science as a working hypothesis." *Synthese*, 28, 97–115.

Foster, J. (1991), *The Immaterial Self*. New York: Routledge.

Garfinkel, A. (1981), *Forms of Explanation*. New Haven, CT: Yale University Press.

Gasser, G., ed. (2007), *How Successful Is Naturalism?* Frankfurt: Ontos.

Gillett, C. (2001), "The methodological role of physicalism: a minimal skepticism," in Gillett and Loewer (2001), pp. 225–50.

—(2002), "The dimensions of realization: a critique of the standard view." *Analysis*, 64(4), 316–23.

Gillett, C. and Loewer, B., eds (2001), *Physicalism and Its Discontents*. Cambridge: Cambridge University Press.

Gillett, C. and Witmer, D. G. (2001), "A 'physical' need: physicalism and the via negativa." *Analysis*, 61(4), 302–9.

Goldman, A. I. (1999), "A priori warrant and naturalistic epistemology." *Philosophical Perspectives*, 13, 1–28.

Goodman, N. (1983), *Fact, Fiction and Forecast*. Cambridge, MA: Harvard University Press.

Heckmann, H. D. and Walter, S., eds (2003), *Physicalism and Mental Causation: the Metaphysics of Mind and Action*. Charlottesville, VA: Imprint Academic.

Heil, J. (1999), "Multiple realization." *American Philosophical Quarterly*, 36(3), 189–208.

Heil, J. and Mele, A., eds (1993), *Mental Causation*. New York: Clarendon Press.

Hempel, C. G. (1969), "Reduction: ontological and linguistic facets," in S. Morgenbesser, P. Suppes and M. White, eds, *Philosophy, Science and Method: Essays in Honour of Ernest Nagel*. New York: St Martin's Press, pp. 179–99.

Hooker, C. A. (1981), "Towards a general theory of reduction—parts 1-3." *Dialogue: Canadian Philosophical Reviews,* 20, 38–59, 201–36, 496–529.

Horgan, T. (1993), "From supervenience to superdupervenience: meeting the demands of a material world." *Mind,* 102(408), 555–86.

—(2001), "Causal compatibilism and the exclusion problem." *Theoria,* 16(40), 95–116.

Horst, S. (2007), *Beyond Reduction: Philosophy of Mind and Post-Reductionist Philosophy of Science*. New York: Oxford University Press.

Jackson, F. (1998), *From Metaphysics to Ethics: A Defence of Conceptual Analysis*. New York: Oxford University Press.

Kemeny, J. G. and Oppenheim, P. (1956), "On reduction." *Philosophical Studies,* 7, 6–17.

Kim, J. (1990), "Supervenience as a philosophical concept." *Metaphilosophy,* 21(1–2), 1–27.

—(1992), "Multiple realization and the metaphysics of reduction." *Philosophy and Phenomenological Research,* 52, 1–16.

—(1993), *Supervenience and Mind: Selected Philosophical Essays*. Cambridge: Cambridge University Press.

—(1998), *Mind in a Physical World: An Essay on the Mind–Body Problem and Mental Causation*. Cambridge, MA: MIT Press.

—(2003), "The American origins of philosophical naturalism," in R. Audi, ed., *Philosophy in America at the Turn of the Century*. Charlottesville, VA: Philosophy Documentation Center, pp. 83–98.

—(2005), *Physicalism, or Something Near Enough*. Princeton: Princeton University Press.

Kitcher, P. (1984), "1953 and all that: a tale of two sciences." *Philosophical Review,* 93, 335–74.

Ladyman, J. and Ross, D. (2007), *Every Thing Must Go: Metaphysics Naturalized*. New York: Oxford University Press.

Levine, J. and Trogdon, K. (2009), "The modal status of materialism." *Philosophical Studies,* 145(3), 351–62.

Lewis, D. (1983), "New work for a theory of universals." *Australasian Journal of Philosophy,* 61, 343–77.

Maddy, P. (2001), "Naturalism: friends and foes." *Philosophical Perspectives,* 15, 37–67.

Marcus, E. (2001), "Mental causation: unnaturalized but not unnatural." *Philosophy and Phenomenological Research,* 63(1), 57–83.

McLaughlin, B. (1995), "Varieties of supervenience," in Savellos and Yalçin (1995), pp. 16–59.

Meehl, P. E. and Sellars, W. (1956), "The concept of emergence," in H. Feigl and M. Scriven, eds, *The Foundations of Science and the Concepts of Psychology and Psychoanalysis*. Minneapolis: University of Minnesota Press, pp. 239–52.

Melnyk, A. (1997), "How to keep the "physical" in physicalism." *Journal of Philosophy,* 94(12), 622–37.

—(2003), *A Physicalist Manifesto: Thoroughly Modern Materialism.* Cambridge: Cambridge University Press.

Montero, B. (1999), "The body problem." *Nous,* 33(2), 183–200.

Montero, B. and Papineau, D. (2005), "A defence of the via negativa argument for physicalism." *Analysis,* 65(287), 233–7.

Nagel, E. (1961), *The Structure of Science.* New York: Harcourt Brace World.

Nickles, T. (1973), "Two concepts of intertheoretic reduction." *Journal of Philosophy,* 70, 181–201.

Oppenheim, P. and Putnam, H. (1958), "Unity of science as a working hypothesis," in H. Feigl, M. Scriven and G. Maxwell, eds, *Minnesota Studies in the Philosophy of Science Vol. 2.* Minneapolis: University of Minnesota Press, pp. 3–36.

Papineau, D. (1993), *Philosophical Naturalism.* Oxford: Blackwell.

Papineau, D. and Spurrett, D. (1999), "A note on the completeness of 'physics'." *Analysis,* 59(1), 25–9.

Polger, T. W. (2002), "Putnam's intuition." *Philosophical Studies,* 109(2), 143–70.

—(2007), "Realization and the metaphysics of mind." *Australasian Journal of Philosophy,* 85(2), 233–59.

Putnam, H. (1967), "Psychological predicates" (later retitled "The nature of mental states"), in W. H. Capitan and D. D. Merrill, eds, *Art, Mind and Religion.* Pittsburgh, PA: University of Pittsburgh Press, pp. 37–48.

Quine, W. V. O. (1969), "Epistemology naturalized," in *Ontological Relativity and Other Essays.* New York: Columbia University Press, pp. 69–90.

Robinson, H. (2001), "Davidson and nonreductive materialism: a tale of two cultures," in Gillett and Loewer (2001), pp. 129–51.

Rouse, J. (2008), "Review of G. Gasser (2007), *How Successful is Naturalism?,*" in Notre Dame Philosophical Reviews. http://ndpr.nd.edu/review.cfm?id=12284.

Savellos, E. E. and Yalçin, Ü. D., eds (1995), *Supervenience: New Essays.* New York: Cambridge University Press.

Schaffner, K. F. (1967), "Approaches to reduction." *Philosophy of Science,* 34, 137–47.

Sellars, R. W. (1927), "Why naturalism and not materialism?" *The Philosophical Review,* 36(3), 216–25.

Shapiro, L. A. (2000), "Multiple realizations." *Journal of Philosophy,* 97(12), 635–54.

Shoemaker, S. (1981), "Some varieties of functionalism." *Philosophical Topics,* 12(1), 83–118.

—(2001), "Realization and mental causation," in Gillett and Loewer (2001), pp. 74–98.

—(2007), *Physical Realization.* New York: Oxford University Press.

Sklar, L. (1999), "The reduction (?) of thermodynamics to statistical mechanics." *Philosophical Studies,* 95(1–2), 187–202.

Smart, J. J. C. (1959), "Sensations and brain processes." *Philosophical Review,* 68, 141–56.

Smith, P. (1992), "Modest reductions and the unity of science," in D. Charles and K. Lennon, eds, *Reduction, Explanation, and Realism*. New York: Oxford University Press, pp. 19–43.

Stalnaker, R. (1996), "Varieties of supervenience." *Philosophical Perspectives,* 10, 221–4.

Stoljar, D. (2010), *Physicalism*. New York: Routledge.

Stroud, B. (2004), "The charm of naturalism," in M. De Caro and D. Macarthur, eds, *Naturalism in Question*. Cambridge, MA: Harvard University Press, pp. 21–35.

Sturgeon, S. (1998), "Physicalism and overdetermination." *Mind,* 107, 411–32.

Van Fraassen, B. C. (1996), "Science, materialism, and false consciousness," in J. Kvanvig, ed., *Warrant in Contemporary Epistemology: Essays in Honor of Plantinga's Theory of Knowledge*. Lanham, MD: Rowman and Littlefield, pp. 149–81.

Vollmer, G. (2007), "Can everything be rationally explained everywhere in the world? Theses and declarations for naturalism," in Gasser (2007), pp. 25–48.

Wilson, J. (2005), "Supervenience-based formulations of physicalism." *Nous,* 39(3), 426–59.

—(2006), "On characterizing the physical." *Philosophical Studies,* 131(1), 61–99.

Witmer, D. G. (2000), "Locating the overdetermination problem." *British Journal for the Philosophy of Science,* 51(2), 273–86.

—(2001), "Sufficiency claims and physicalism: a formulation," in Gillett and Loewer (2001), pp. 57–73.

—(2006), "How to be a (sort of) a priori physicalist." *Philosophical Studies,* 131(1), 185–225.

—(Unpublished), "Making sense of 'naturalism.'"

Wittgenstein, L. (1965), "A lecture on ethics." *Philosophical Review,* 74, 3–12.

Mind

Thomas W. Polger

The enduring metaphysical question about minds and mental phenomena concerns their nature. At least since Descartes this question—the mind–body problem—has been understood in terms of the viability or necessity of mind–body dualism, the thesis that minds and bodies are essentially distinct kinds of substance. Assuming that the nonmental ("body") portions of the world are constituted of physical stuff, a question remains. Are minds or mental phenomena essentially distinct nonphysical substances, or phenomena that essentially involve such distinct kinds of substances?

By the middle of the twentieth century there was broad philosophical and scientific consensus that the answer to this classical question about minds is negative. Minds and mental phenomena are not essentially distinct substances, nor are they phenomena that essentially involve distinct kinds of substances. There are at least two broad trends and one specific argument that lead to this conclusion. One trend is the decreasing influence of specifically theological arguments and commitments in philosophical argumentation, so that religious belief in immortal souls was no longer given much weight in the ontology of mind. The second trend, perhaps related to the first, is the increased demand that metaphysical theories bear explanatory fruits, so that the postulation of an immaterial and essentially mental substance appears to be an abdication from explanatory duties rather than a useful proposal. The argument, known to Descartes from the very beginning, is that there has never been an adequate account of how two essentially distinct and incompatible substances could causally interact.[1] Descartes' solution was inadequate and brute, and his followers struggled with the problem—leading to Leibniz's parallelism and Malebranche's occasionalism, among other views. The problem of mental causation, then, is the central difficulty that undermines substance dualism.[2]

The negative answer on the question of substance dualism, however, only increases the pressure for some monistic account of the nature of minds. In particular, given the assumption that the one kind of substance is physical or material substance, there is a need for an account of minds consonant with physicalist or materialist monism.[3] As Jaegwon Kim puts it, "the mind–body problem—our mind–body problem—has been that of finding a place for the mind in a world that is fundamentally physical" (1998).

Today the most widely disputed metaphysical theories in philosophy of mind are proposals for how to locate the mind in a fundamentally physical world, or else proposals to weaken the commitments of physicalist monism in order to locate the mind in a nonetheless mostly physical world. Likewise, the challenges faced by the various proposals are mainly questions about their adequacy to the task of locating the mind in a fundamentally or mostly physical world.

Before moving on to the examination of these theories, it is worth noting the range of phenomena that are covered by metaphysical theories of mind. It is common to distinguish between theories of contentful mental states and theories of conscious mental states. Theories of contentful mental states cover beliefs, desires, wishes, hopes, and other intentional mental states (Dennett, 1971, 1987) or propositional attitudes (Fodor, 1978, 1985, 1987, 1991). Theories of conscious mental states cover phenomena such as sensations, feelings, and perhaps moods or emotions—though it is controversial where to locate moods and emotions in this crude dichotomy (Montague, 2009). Some theorists hold that either conscious states (e.g., Searle, 1992) or intentional states (e.g., Dennett, 1991; Dretske, 1995; Lycan, 1987) are more fundamental and that the complement can be explained in terms of the more fundamental kind. Other theorists (e.g., Block, 1996) appear to hold that the two general kinds of mental states are equally fundamental but given distinct explanations. And there is a growing group of philosophers who think that neither is more fundamental than the other and that both must be explained together (e.g., Horgan and Tienson, 2002; Horgan and Kriegel, 2008; Loar, 2003; Pautz, 2008; Pitt, 2004, 2009; Siewert, 1998). In what follows, except where explicitly noted I will mainly ignore the distinctions among these approaches and the range of phenomena that they intend to cover. Despite this, you can often tell from the examples given and the objections raised whether it is, say, beliefs or sensations that are at stake. There is no question that certain views are more plausibly applied to some phenomena. But in focusing on specifically metaphysical issues about the mind, I am taking the liberty of ignoring some of the other variations that are no less relevant to the total assessment of the theories.

Preliminary census

It will be useful to have a brief census of the main views on the table in contemporary philosophy of mind: behaviorism, identity theory, eliminativism, functionalism, anomalous monism, and emergentist and fundamentalist property dualisms. All of these views are varieties of substance monism in that they assert that there is only one kind of substance in the world, or at least that the ontology of minds does not require adding more kinds of substances to our ontology. And the most prominent versions are all versions of physicalist monism; they hold that the one kind of substance in the world is physical substance.[4] While there is an ongoing dispute about how exactly to characterize physicalism and the physical (see the paper "Naturalism and Physicalism" in this volume), it will be enough for present purposes to think of the physical substance as that of which at least the majority of the nonmental world is constituted and that which is canonically studied by physics, perhaps with the additional (or redundant) qualification that physical substance is not fundamentally mental.[5] Finally, with the exception of metaphysical behaviorism, the views are all minimally realist (or at least conditionally realist) about mental phenomena: they all presume that mental phenomena are mind- and language-independent internal states of thinking or feeling creatures, or would have to be in order to be counted in our ontology.[6] Beyond these basic commonalities, the views are quite diverse and have met with quite different fates.

Behaviorism, the king of the hill in early- to mid-twentieth century psychology and philosophy, has largely fallen out of favor. The explanatory and methodological rigor that scientific behaviorism brought to psychology remains highly influential, but adherence to any metaphysical view about the nature of minds is not essential to rigor. The metaphysical behaviorists, if ever there were any, hold that there are no internal mental states, events, or properties, but only a whole organism's syndromes of behavior and dispositions to behave.[7] Reasons for holding such a view were always sparse, and usually involved prior commitment to either scientific behaviorism or to so-called logical behaviorism (Putnam, 1963). Scientific behaviorism faltered due to its inability to explain complex flexible behaviors such as language use, and because of its inability to state individuation conditions for stimuli and responses that were independent of the phenomena being studied (e.g., Chomsky, 1959). Logical behaviorism is the special application of the verification criteria of meaning to psychological vocabulary, so that the meanings of mentalistic terms are held to be exhausted by the syndromes of behavior and behavioral disposition that they pick out. But these views are antiques. Metaphysical behaviorism has not had any serious defenders since the downfall of scientific behaviorism in psychology and the abandonment of verification criteria of meaning in philosophy.

Identity theories, by which I mean physical type identity theories, hold that mental state types can be identified with physical state types, canonically brain state types, broadly construed. These kinds of theories enjoyed brief popularity in the 1950s and 1960s, especially in the United States and Australia. The theory has experienced a small renaissance around the turn of the twenty-first century.[8] The chief virtues of the identity theory are its simplicity and that it arguably provides the only workable account of mental causation. But it also suffers from some difficulties. Early objections that it is logically incoherent were adequately rebuffed by U. T. Place (1956), Herbert Feigl (1958), J. J. C. Smart (1959), and David Lewis (1966, 1972). But there are lingering concerns about whether the theory is empirically adequate, and in particular whether it can be reconciled with the full diversity of actual and possible psychological creatures. This concern is most clearly articulated in Hilary Putnam's "multiple realization" objection to such theories (1967). And the identity theory is at least minimally reductionist in that it does not recognize mental states as independent existents in their own right. That has led many philosophers to worry that the identity theory might entail reductionism in some stronger or more problematic sense, if not downright eliminativism (Fodor, 1974, 1997).

Eliminativists hold that there are no internal mental or psychological objects, states, events, or properties. The motivation for holding an eliminativist theory has two parts. The first part is the belief that the reality of mental states would require their reduction to physical states in more or less the way imagined by identity theorists. The second part is acceptance of critiques of the identity theory, to the effect that no such reduction of mental states is possible. Consequently, the eliminativist concludes that there are no mental states. The most well-known eliminativist arguments were due to Richard Rorty (1965, 1970) and Paul Feyerabend (1963) in the 1960s, and to Patricia and Paul Churchland in the 1980s (1981, 1982, 1983). Eliminativism has almost always been a fall-back position, one arrived at only reluctantly. The obvious reason is that our lived experience gives us strong, if fallible, reason to think that we have beliefs, desires, pains, pleasures, emotions, and other mental states. So it seems that it will almost always be an option to reject some philosophical premise of any argument for eliminativism—for example, that real kinds must be reducible to physical kinds—rather than deny our prima facie rich experienced mental life. This is not to say that one could never be convinced by a philosophical or scientific argument to give up a belief that seems obvious, only that the bar is set quite high.

And indeed, for just those sorts of reasons recent philosophy of mind has been dominated by advocates of so-called nonreductive physicalist theories that reject the reductionist requirement. These theories aim to stay true to physicalist substance monism without falling into the excesses of either behaviorism or the identity theories, and without arriving at the eliminativist's deflationary conclusion. The two most familiar forms of nonreductive physicalism are functionalism and Donald Davidson's anomalous monism. Davidson's theory, though widely discussed, was never widely held. Components of the theory— that there are no physical-to-mental bridge laws, and that the brain–mind relation might be a supervenience relation—have been extremely influential. But the core package of claims is not often jointly held: that there are no strict psychological laws, that causation requires strict laws, that mental events are causes only because they fall under strict physical laws and that mental events are "token identical" to physical events. And it has become fairly clear that the central "token identity without type identity" thesis amounts to a kind of property dualism. So, as with behaviorism, the bits and pieces of anomalous monism have been absorbed into other theories, in particular into functionalism and self-avowed property dualism.

Functionalism is the theory of the nature of mind first articulated by Hilary Putnam in terms of computing devices (1960, 1967, 1972). It is the theory that mental states are abstract states of abstract systems that are "realized" by but not identical to brain states in human beings. Initially the abstract systems that Putnam had in mind were a variety of finite state automa. But over the 1970s and 1980s this literal conception of mind as computing device was elaborated so that the Turing-style computing program was replaced by an empirical or analytic psychological theory. In the elaboration, the causal laws of psychology replace the machine state instructions. These laws may be probabilistic and local, and otherwise fall short of strict laws. And in the most recent versions, laws and the entities they govern are thought of as selected by natural selection, so that a kind of biological teleology is brought into the nature of mental states (Dretske, 1981, 1988, 1995; Lycan, 1987; Van Gulick, 2011). This teleological functionalism is in some ways the cutting-edge version of functionalism, and when that teleology is understood in terms of a selected-effect account of teleological functions, the result is etiological variations on functionalism.

Functionalism promises to deliver all the benefits of identity theories but without the "chauvinistic" (Block, 1978) restriction that all psychological beings have brains similar to our own, and thus promises to allow for a more general theory of the metaphysics of minds. But functionalism stands in a tension that has long been recognized: the stronger the realization relation, the more secure the physicalist credentials and causal claims of the functionalist; but so too, the more the view turns out to be a version of reductionist identity theory. The looser the strength of the realization relation, the more distinct from the identity theory; but, in that case, functionalism faces increasing difficulties in accounting for mental causation, and threatens to turn into a version of emergentism or property dualism.

In the 1980s and 1990s functionalists (and nonreductive physicalists generally) attempted to resolve this tension by formulating the mind–body relation in terms of supervenience relations, hoping that Davidson's speculation would pan out and deliver a relation strong enough to ground a physicalist theory of minds without entailing a reductive or identity theory. By the 1990s it was widely accepted that supervenience is the wrong tool for the job—at least on its own (Horgan, 1993; Kim, 1993, 1998; Wilson, 2005). Consequently, in the early part of the twenty-first century there has been new attention to understanding the key realization relation for functionalism (e.g., Gillett, 2002, 2003, 2007; Keaton, 2010, 2011; Kim, 1998; Polger, 2004, 2007; Polger and Shapiro, 2008; Shoemaker, 2001, 2007; Wilson and Craver, 2007), and also reexamination of the merits and costs of identity theory (e.g., Polger, 2004) and property dualism (e.g., Chalmers, 1996). Just how bad would it be if functionalism turns out to be a version of one of those, after all?

Some philosophers have concluded that the costs of property dualism are worth paying, and have adopted either emergentist (Clayton and Davies, 2006; Humphreys, 1997) or fundamentalist (Chalmers, 1996) versions of the view that although there is only one kind of substance in the world (physical substance), nevertheless there are two *sui generis* kinds of properties: physical properties and mental properties. Self-avowed property dualists usually argue that distinctive mental properties are necessary to explain the subjective aspects of conscious mental life—"what it's like" to have experiences, in Thomas Nagel's well-known phrase (1974). Other theorists who do not adopt property dualism have been accused of falling into the position in virtue of espousing nonreductive theories of various sorts. Some philosophers even include property dualism (or distinctness) as a key tenet of nonreductive physicalism, for example, Jaegwon Kim (1998, 2005) and Karen Bennett (2003, 2008).

The live options

Our preliminary census allowed us to get a sense of which views are the main candidates on the contemporary field, and find some hints about the kinds of desiderata and critiques in play. We can safely set aside behaviorism, which proved to be both philosophically and scientifically suspect. Anomalous monism can also be neglected, as its main insights were absorbed into functionalism and property dualism. And eliminativism requires little further explanation; it can remain in the wings, an option of last resort. This leaves three main contenders: identity theory, functionalism, and property dualism in its fundamentalist and emergentist forms. Almost all theorists consider at least one of these three options to be obviously wrong, but explaining why will require us to know more about the theories. In the remainder of this section we will consider each in turn.

Identity theory, and four desiderata

Let us begin with the type identity theory, the theory that—as J. J. C. Smart (1959) famously puts it—"sensations are brain processes."[9] The distinctive claim of the identity theorist is that mental state kinds (psychological kinds) are strictly identical to brain state kinds. These identities are frequently represented by the toy example of the identification of pain sensations with the firings of neural c-fibers; but this example is a placeholder, known to be empirically inadequate. More important than the specific example is the general idea that the purported mind–brain identities should be understood on the model of such scientific identifications as that water is identical to H_2O, that gold is identical to the substance kind with atomic number 79 and that temperature (in a gas) is identical to mean molecular kinetic energy. The original identity theorists held that these identities are contingent because they are empirically discovered. But since the groundbreaking work of Saul Kripke (1971, 1972/1980), identity theorists recognize these scientific identities as examples of a posteriori necessities, and they hold that the mind–brain identities are also necessary a posteriori.

The identity theory was the first contemporary physicalist theory of the metaphysics of the mind that is also realist about internal mental states, *contra* behaviorism. But now most contemporary philosophers believe that the identity theory, whatever its philosophical merits, is empirically mistaken. Indeed, the development of our other contenders—functionalism and property dualism—is largely a process of responding to perceived defects in the identity theory. To understand the rise and fall of the identity theory, and its current modest renaissance, it will be useful to be explicit about some desiderata on a metaphysical theory of minds which were only alluded to in our initial census.

Identity theories are *realist* theories. As we saw above, in the brief discussion of eliminativism, realism is a widely shared desideratum on metaphysical theories of mind. Any theory that denies that mental states, properties, or events are real must provide overwhelming reason to abandon this requirement. The identity theory is a realist theory. It says that mental states can be identified with brain states, and *ipso facto* have the same realist status as brain states and biological states in general. That said, the requirement for realism is not cut and dried. Any theory might deny the reality of some of our familiar mental state kinds. To use an archaic example, we do not expect a theory of the nature of minds to be realist about the Victorian mental state *melancholy.* And we might well accept even significant revisions to our folk psychological categories as not violating the realist demand. For example, we would well expect the generic kind *memory* to be vindicated not as a singular kind but as a family of kinds, as per the current sciences of memory. Perhaps we will be realist about some or all of short-term memory, long-term memory, episodic memory, semantic memory, spatial memory, and so on. As with most philosophical issues, there is little reason to think that we could set in advance a specific standard for how much realism is to be expected and how much revision is to be tolerated. That does mean that there is room for disagreement about which theories are realist and on whom the burden of proof falls, but such is the nature of the beast. In general philosophers have been able to agree, for example, that behaviorism is not sufficiently realist, and that the identity theory and property dualism are indeed sufficiently realist. Disagreement arises over, for example, Daniel Dennett's quasi-realist "intentional stance" account of beliefs and desires; and Dennett's "multiple drafts" model of consciousness (1971, 1987, 1991) is sometimes accused of being flatly eliminativist.

That we cannot say ahead of time just how much realism is required of a theory of mind does not mean that we are entirely adrift. There are other desiderata that are closely related to one another and to the requirement for realism. Indeed, it may be that they are the reason that realism is required, or vice versa. Three of these desiderata are *physicalism,* the *causal efficacy* of the mental and the *explanatory autonomy* of psychology.

An important desideratum for most if not all theorists is *physicalism:* mental states, properties, and events are physical states or properties or events in the broad sense. That is, they are either fundamental physical states, or else they are fully dependent on and constituted by basically physical states, properties, and events.[10] Physicalism is, in the first case, the denial of dualism, be it traditional substance dualism or contemporary property dualism. The identity theorist is a physicalist who holds that mental state kinds are identical to brain state kinds, and who supposes that brain state kinds are physical in virtue of depending on and being constituted by fundamentally physical entities, states, processes, and so on. The functionalist, as we shall see, aims to satisfy the requirements of physicalism without identifying mental state kinds with brain state kinds.

To say that physicalism is a desideratum on metaphysical theories of mind is already to bias the scale against dualist theories, even those that are only dualist about properties. But just as most eliminativists adopt their position only reluctantly, so too most property dualists adopt that view only reluctantly. The requirement for a physicalist theory of the mind is not absolute, but it is not unfair to say that it is a desideratum. All of the well-known arguments for property dualist theories are arguments about the limits of physicalism, and its inability to account for some phenomenon—usually sensations and consciousness (Chalmers, 1996; Jackson, 1982; Kripke, 1972; Nagel, 1974).

The second desideratum is the causal efficacy of the mental. The identity theory holds that mental states are identical to brain states, and (as with realism, above) that they *ipso facto* have the same causal powers as brain states. Indeed, as we shall see, one of the biggest selling points for the identity theory is that it appears to have the strongest claim to satisfy the demand that mental states be causally efficacious. There are two motivations behind that demand, one that is quite general and the other that is specific to the metaphysics of minds. The general reason is connected to the requirement for realism via the thesis that Jaegwon Kim (1998, p. 10) calls *Alexander's Dictum*: "To be real is to have causal powers."[11] Such a principle makes causal power a condition on real existence, at least for contingent particular entities. (One might invoke some other criteria for *abstracta,* such as numbers or sets.) This reason usually operates as a negative constraint in philosophy of mind: if Alexander's Dictum is right, then epiphenomenalist theories—those that fail to establish the causal efficacy of the mental—accrue the double debt of turning into versions of eliminativism. We'll discuss this difficulty further when we examine functionalism and property dualism.

The mind-specific reasons for requiring causally potent mental states are more theoretically constructive. These reasons for the desideratum stem from the central role that mental states play in theories of knowledge, action, and responsibility. Consider, for example, the role that mental states play in the acquisition of knowledge and production of behavior. If an organism is to be responsive to events in its environment, then it must be that the environment can cause changes in the organism and that the organism can cause changes in the environment, such as changes in its location within in the environment. Of course this interaction could be entirely reflexive. But in human beings and likely some other animals these responses involve mental states of perception, belief, desire, emotion, and so on. And if an organism is going to count as having beliefs or knowledge about the environment—that is, mental states whose content is about the environment—then it seems that those mental states must be causally connected to the environment. And if those mental states are to guide the organism's behavior, then it seems that the connection must be a two-way connection: mental states must be both caused by and causes of events in the environment. This little sketch is not without its problems. But the basic idea is clear enough: it is highly plausible that accounts of knowledge and of action presuppose that there is mental causation. The stakes are only further raised when we consider questions of moral or political responsibility. Most theories of responsibility hold us morally responsible for those effects for which we are also causes; and many accounts of responsibility excuse us from responsibility for events for which we are not causes. These kinds of connections between mental causation and other philosophical issues lead Jerry Fodor to proclaim,

> if it isn't literally true that my wanting is causally responsible for my reaching, and my itching is causally responsible for my scratching, and my believing is causally responsible for my saying . . . if none of that is literally true, then practically everything I believe about anything is false and it's the end of the world. (Fodor, 1991, p. 156)

Like the requirement for realism about the mental, the requirement for causal efficacy is deeply ingrained. It can be rejected, but it is clear what sort of argumentative burden would be taken on by a denier of causal efficacy.

The final desideratum is the explanatory autonomy of psychology. This requirement consists of a pair of demands that are usually held together but can be separated. The first is that psychological explanations are legitimate, and the second is that psychological explanations are in some sense "autonomous" of other kinds of explanations. Jerry Fodor, quoted above with respect to the causal efficacy of the mental, has been a forceful advocate of the combination. The first part is the affirmation that psychological explanations are genuine explanations, that psychology is a genuine science. On the lingering post-positivist conception of explanation that is prevalent in metaphysics and philosophy of mind, explanations are genuine when they invoke laws of nature and those laws are causal laws. Thus the desideratum that psychological explanation be genuine turns out to be tied closely to the causal efficacy desideratum. Moreover, on the prevailing "ontic" conception of explanation, what exists is what our best explanations tell us exists. So the desideratum for psychological explanation is also bound up with the desideratum for realism about the mental.

The identity theory says that mental states are real, broadly physical, and causally efficacious because they are identified with brain states, which are presumed to be uncontroversially real, broadly physical, and causally efficacious. Psychology, on this view, is a science that explains the interactions of brain states even though it does not pick them out in terms of their explicitly neuroscientific properties or characteristics. So the identity theorist holds that psychology is an explanatory science. However critics worry that although the identity theory can validate psychological explanations, it cannot validate them *qua* psychological explanations but only *qua* neuroscientific explanations, for it seems that any putative psychological explanation could be "reduced to" (in the sense of "replaced by") a neuroscientific explanation. Indeed, the identity theory is the canonical reductionist view of the metaphysics of mind. Both the identity theory and functionalism explain mental phenomena in terms of nonmental phenomena. As Fodor says with respect to intentional mental states, "If aboutness is real, it must be really something else" (Fodor, 1987, p. 97).

The above line of criticism tacitly invokes a strong reading of the second part of the explanatory desideratum, that psychology turn out to be an autonomous science. In its strong form, this requirement becomes the demand that psychological explanation be not only permissible but also mandatory—that psychological explanations cannot be reduced to or replaced by any others. Louise Antony and Joseph Levine write, "a property is real (or autonomous) just in case it is *essentially* invoked in the characterization of a regularity" (Antony and Levine, 1997, p. 91). And Fodor (1997, p. 149) puts it thus:

> I will say that a law or theory that figures in bona fide empirical explanations, but that is not reducible to a law or theory of physics, is *ipso facto autonomous*; and that the states whose behavior such laws or theories specify are *functional* states.[12]

If one has these kinds of concerns, then one will argue that the identity theory fails to vindicate the explanatory import of psychology because it fails to deliver psychological kinds that are explanatorily autonomous on the strong reading of that requirement. A weaker reading of the autonomy requirement might be that the explanatory authority of psychology is independent of the explanatory resources of other sciences. Why, one might ask, should it be a defect of psychological explanations that there are also other explanations in the offing?

The question we're now considering, regarding autonomy and scientific explanation, has consequences for how we evaluate the candidate metaphysical theories of minds. But its answer will have to do with very general questions about explanation that are not themselves dependent on, and will not be decided solely by consideration of, the metaphysics of mind. We need not resolve them here. The present goal has been to introduce one theory and its purported merits, thereby introducing a general framework for evaluating candidate accounts of the metaphysics of minds. So far we've seen that identity theories measure up fairly well: they are realist and physicalist, they vindicate the causal powers of mental states and they can ground the legitimacy of psychological explanation so long as the autonomy requirement is not as strong as Antony, Levine, and Fodor require. But we began by noting that most contemporary philosophers regard the identity theory as false, indeed as a nonstarter. And now it is time to see why.

According to the identity theory, mental state kinds are identical to brain state kinds, just as water is identical to H_2O. Identity, we noted, is a necessary relation. And it is also a one-to-one relation: identity is the relation that everything has to itself and to nothing else. The trouble, say critics, is that it is not in fact true that mental states stand in a one-to-one relation to brain states. Rather, the same mental state kind, such as pain or hunger, can be had by creatures with a wide variety of kinds of brains, and thus a wide variety of kinds of brain states. As Hilary Putnam famously puts it, the identity theory requires "that the physical–chemical state in question must be a possible state of a mammalian brain, a reptilian brain, a mollusc's brain (octopuses are mollusca, and certainly feel pain), etc." (Putnam, 1967/1975, p. 436). But Putnam thinks that we know this is not true. So the identity theory, whatever its philosophical merits, is empirically falsified. This line of reasoning is the so-called *multiple realization* objection to the identity theory. And this objection has convinced the vast majority of philosophers that the identity theory is known to be false.

Putnam's inference from the diversity of pain- or hunger-experiencing creatures to the diversity of brain states mediating pain or hunger is rather dubious.[13] But in subsequent years the multiple realization argument was strengthened in two ways. First, it was argued that the phenomenon of neural plasticity shows that within species and even within individuals over short periods of time, the same kinds of mental states are associated with diverse brain state kinds, for example, in the work of Ned Block and Jerry Fodor (1972). Second, beginning with Block and Fodor and codified in Fodor's classic "Special Sciences" paper (1974), it was argued that even if it turned out that all known mental state kinds can be identified with brain state kinds, still it is possible that there are terrestrial or extraterrestrial creatures that are counterexamples to the hypothesis, and indeed we should expect that to be the case because psychological kinds are functional kinds. Putnam subsequently adopted this view as well (1972/1975). So there was a shift from the claim that mental states are in fact multiply realized to the argument that they are in principle multiply realizable. Because it was recognized that mind–brain identities would have to be necessary, the mere possibility of their failure is enough to undermine the identity hypothesis.

A consequence of the widespread belief that the identity theory is false has been the immediate need for alternatives. In particular, both Putnam and Fodor used the multiple realization and realizability objections to the identity theory to motivate Putnam's functionalist theory of the metaphysics of mental states. That theory quickly became the most widely held physicalist theory of the nature of minds. Before we examine it directly, we should say a few things about the current status of the identity theory.

First, there was always a small minority who doubted that the multiple realization and realizability arguments had the devastating consequences that were claimed for them. The main lines of resistance were to argue that the truth of multiple realization does not preclude that all mental states have some physical property or properties in common (Adams, 1979; Kim, 1972). Additionally, it was argued that to the extent that there is genuine diversity it can be accommodated by making appropriately fine-grained distinctions among mental states (e.g., pain-in-humans, pain-in-dogs, etc.) and relativizing the identity claims to those kinds (e.g., Kim, 1972; Lewis, 1969).[14]

Second, it has become plain that the empirical evidence for actual multiple realization is less clear than Putnam supposed. The controversial but widely cited critique of multiple realization from William Bechtel and Jennifer Mundale (1999) argues that the appearance of multiple realization can often be explained away as a failure to correctly match the "grain" of psychological and neurological kinds. It is no surprise that very many fine-grained brain states can be associated with a coarse-grained mental state like pain, just as it is unsurprising that very many kinds of things fall under the coarse grained category *vehicle.* Moreover, given the actual practices of neuroscience and psychology, particularly in their comparative (cross-species) forms, we should generally expect to find mind–brain identities. One of the goals of this research is precisely to identify anatomically and functionally isomorphic areas in the brains of different individuals and species. And the methodological practice of averaging across trials for and between individual subjects seems to presuppose that such registration is possible. In fact, Bechtel and McCauley (1999) argue that such identities are widely used heuristics of the brain and cognitive sciences. As such, it would be surprising if the resulting sciences produced taxonomies that cannot be brought into identification with one another, and thus surprising if there was a great deal of evidence for multiple realization. Still, the prospects for this line of argument are hotly disputed.

Finally, it is evident that the philosophical arguments for multiple realizability (in the absence of evidence of actual multiple realization) are not decisive. This is because the generally functionalist view that supports the multiple realizability arguments has some notable problems to go along with its significant attributes. To get a sense of those, we must first understand the functionalist approach.

Functionalism

The identity theory, recall, meets many of the desiderata for a good metaphysical theory of mind: it is realist, it is physicalist, it secures the causal efficacy of the mental and it vindicates psychological explanation so long as strong autonomy is not required. The troubles for the identity theory are that it might be empirically false if there is not a one-to-one correlation between mental state kinds and brain state kinds, and that strong autonomy might be required. The key to both of these problems is multiple realization. If there is multiple realization, then there is not a one-to-one relationship between sensations and brain processes, and the identity theory is falsified. However, if there is multiple realization, then that could justify the need for a distinct and autonomous science of the mental, one that ranges across kinds that cannot be reduced to or identified with the kinds of other sciences. Both Putnam and Fodor argued that mental states can be multiply realized and autonomous if they are functional kinds.

Functionalism is the view that mental states are functional states. Although functionalism does not entail physicalism, its most familiar versions are physicalist. The physicalist functionalist holds that mental states are functional states that are not identical to particular physical states (there is no one-to-one correlation) but can be realized by various physical states (i.e., multiply realized.) The core idea of functionalism is the distinction between functional roles and realizers.[15] Putnam (1967/1975) introduced this distinction and the theory of functionalism with the example of computing machines. A computer program describes the operation of a machine in terms of the system's inputs and outputs, and the relations among various states or variables that mediate between the inputs and outputs.

A simple example, discussed by Ned Block (1978), is an old-fashioned coin-operated vending machine. The input to the machine are coins of various denominations, the output is, for example, a can of soda, and the internal states of the machine include a register that tallies the value of the coins. The program describes the behavior of the machine in terms of the inputs, outputs, and internal states, and the instructions can all be stated by relations that are independent of the particular construction of the machine. For example, an instruction might say that when the tally of inputs is equal to a certain value, then an output should be produced. This instruction need not say anything about what the machine is made of: steel, plastic, or—or, as Putnam said—"copper, cheese, or soul" (1972/1975, p. 292). And the same machine instructions can as easily dispense juice as cola, or take inputs in Euros or Pounds. Consequently there is no single physical description that applies to all machines operating the same program— programs are multiply realized and multiply realizable. Think of the familiar example of a piece of software such as a web browser that runs on a Macintosh, on a PC and on a phone.[16] This is possible because the program is characterized in terms of "functional roles" or relations that characterize its inputs, outputs, internal computational ("functional") states, and the functional relations among them. The physical device that operates by these principles is said to *implement* the program, to *play* or to *occupy* the role, or to *realize* the computing device. Some metal parts inside the vending machine realize the vending program. Various silicon chips and bits of metal and plastic realize the word processing software on which I am typing this chapter.

The idea of functional roles and realizers generalizes beyond computing machines. For example, the functional role of a mousetrap can be realized by various physical devices that are characterized (roughly) by the program: input live mouse, output dead mouse. Indeed, most versions of functionalism today are characterized by causal relations rather than computational relations, and they regard these causal relations as the empirical laws of psychology. Some theorists, as was briefly mentioned earlier, hold that the psychological states also have biological functions that are the result of their history of natural selection. This so-called teleological functionalism combines elements of causal role functionalism with a theory of biological function, such as those theories developed by Ruth Millikan (1984, 1989) or Karen Neander (1991).

The most prominent current versions of functionalism are representational theories, according to which mental states have the causal and/or teleological function of representing objects or properties in the world. The representational view is the most widely accepted account of contentful mental states, due in no small part to its advocacy by Jerry Fodor (1978, 1985, 1987, 1991). But it has also been extended to sensory and other conscious mental states as well, for example, by Michael Tye (1995, 2000), William Lycan (1987), and Fred Dretske (1995). There is quite a bit of dispute about the suitability of the representation-alist version of functionalism, particularly when it is applied to explain not just the content of mental states but also the conscious character or feel of sensory states. That said, it is plainly a comprehensive and formidable theory.

At this point we can see the attraction of functionalism. It is a realist theory of mental states because it holds that mental states are functional states of a total system. While it does not entail physicalism, it has physicalist versions: if the realizers of the functional states are themselves physical states, then the resulting system will be a wholly physical system. But because there is not a one-to-one relation between functional states and physical states, the functional states can be the objects of an explanatory schema (i.e., psychology) that is autonomous from and not reducible to physical explanation. Finally, because the functions are at least partially characterized by their causal relations, it seems plausible that causal-functional states have causal powers; so mental states could be causally efficacious if they are causal-role functional states. So functionalism looks like it matches or beats the identity theory.

For most of the history of functionalism its main challenge has been to figure out exactly what the constitutive functional roles are for various mental states, and to figure out how to characterize them to correctly encompass all of the systems that are thought to have mental states (i.e., to accommodate multiple realizability) without also including things that should not count as having mental states (e.g., thermostats) or including everything at all (Putnam, 1988). This is what Block called the problem of inputs and outputs. If the problem can be solved, then functionalism looks very attractive. But if it cannot be solved, then multiple realization turns out to be just as much a challenge for functionalism as for identity theory.

Another classic problem for functionalism has been its inability to handle cases in which intrinsically different systems have the same functional profiles. Functionalism is most plausible as an account of propositional attitudes, and less so for sensory states. This problem is a hangover from functionalism's behaviorist ancestors (cf. Putnam, 1967). The trouble is that relational theories like functionalism and behaviorism hold that the nonrelational facts or properties are irrelevant, but in some cases that seems to yield the wrong answers. It seems to make a difference whether the functional roles of vision are realized in the normal way, or in a way in which red and green sensations are systematically inverted; or whether the role of memory is realized by neurons, or the entire population of China talking on radios, or tiny people in microscopic spacecraft (Block, 1978). Indeed, some philosophers hold that this problem with functionalism generalizes to all forms of physicalism, so that physicalist theories cannot rule out the possibility of a philosophical "zombie" who has no sensations at all but functions exactly like a normal human. They take this possibility to show that there are properties of sensations for which physicalism has no adequate explanation, and therefore that physicalism is false (Chalmers, 1996). We'll return to consider this kind of "functional duplicates" problem later when we discuss property dualism.

Recently, however, attention has been focused on a different problem for functionalism, namely its adequacy on the desideratum for mental causation. There are two problems, in fact: the problem of wide content and the problem of causal exclusion. Hilary Putnam (1975) and Tyler Burge (1979) convincingly argued that some words and beliefs have contents that depend constitutively on the subject's relation to the world. It is not merely that my beliefs about water are caused by stuff in the world. Rather, the fact that the beliefs that I have using the concept or word "water" are in fact about water depends on the fact that water is the stuff of my acquaintance. Someone else who is exactly like me behaviorally, functionally, or even microphysically could use the token "water" to think about a different substance that is not in fact water, if they lived in a place whether the familiar water-like substance was not in fact H_2O. The content of such beliefs or thoughts is said to be "wide" because it constitutively depends on what is in the world around the subject, in contrast to the traditional "narrow" conception of the content of beliefs being fully determined by local facts about what is literally or metaphorically in the speaker's head. The trouble is that causal powers are almost universally agreed to be narrow, in this case to be dependent on properties and events that are in the head or at least the body of the subject. So it seems that if some mental states are wide but all causal states are narrow, then some mental states will not be causally efficacious: the fact that my belief is about water rather than some other substance is causally irrelevant to my behavior, for the same behavior would have been caused by a non-water belief or even a physically similar state that has no content and therefore isn't a belief at all. The consequence is that at least some mental states turn out to be epiphenomenal.

The most common replies to the problem for mental causation raised by wide content is to attempt to establish that wide content states can be causally or explanatorily relevant even if they are not strictly speaking locally causally efficacious (Dretske, 1988; Jackson and Pettit, 1990; Yablo, 1992, 1997). But these responses have always seemed somewhat inadequate. After all, the requirement was for genuine causal efficacy of the mental, not a close substitute. Some authors have instead argued that enough mental states have causally efficacious narrow content to satisfy the causation desideratum (Fodor, 1987, 1991).

Importantly, this sort of problem does not yield any advantage back to the identity theorist, for most identity theorists apply their theory only to sensations, not to beliefs and other wide-content cognitive states. So the identity theorist does not as such have any better account of wide content states to offer, and may well be open to functionalist treatments of those states (e.g., Block, 1996). The second problem of mental causation that faces the functionalist does have a tendency to favor the identity theory, or so argues Jaegwon Kim (1989, 1992, 1993, 1998, 2005).

The causal exclusion problem arises for narrow or local mental states, and it exploits the central features of physicalist functionalism.[17] First, because the functional state is realized by a physical state, the causal powers of the functional state will simply be the causal powers of the physical state or a subset of them. Second, the functionalist holds that the functional state is not identical to the physical state. And third, as a physicalist the functionalist is committed to the causal closure of the physical—that anything that has a cause has a sufficient physical cause. But these commitments create a puzzle. If my mental state causes a behavior, it does so in virtue of the causal powers of its physical realizer. But if the causal powers of the physical realizer are sufficient for causing the behavior, then what work is left for the mental state left to do? Mental causation seems to be excluded by physical causation. Put another way, the mental state may be said to cause the behavior only *qua* physically realized, not *qua* mental state (Robb, 1997). The distinctive and autonomous realized functional properties appear to be epiphenomenal. And, if we follow Alexander's Dictum, that will also undermine the functionalist's claim to realism about mental states.

The most widespread response to the causal exclusion worries is to argue that they must be defective because the problem generalizes to undermine the causal power of any high-level properties, such as the solidity of tables and so on (e.g., Bontly, 2002). Kim tries to mitigate this complaint by distinguishing between realized properties and micro-based properties, and arguing that the exclusion problem does not apply to the latter; thus the extent of the generalization is limited (Kim, 1998). The extent to which the exclusion argument generalizes remains a matter of dispute, as does the question of how damaging generalization would be. Even if the generalization concerns were taken to show that something is wrong with the exclusion argument, it would not yet tell us exactly what is the problematic step.

One concrete response to the causal exclusion problem is to permit systematic causal over-determination: the mental and physical properties are both causally efficacious. Although this is not an initially attractive position, it has gained a certain amount of popularity (e.g., Sider, 2003). Another response is to argue that the two causes do not compete, perhaps because they stand in some logical relation to one another and are therefore not distinct causes at all (Yablo, 1992). This seems much more promising, though it has been shown that the specific accounts of that relationship on offer are not correct (Funkhouser, 2006; Haug, 2010). And it's hard to see how that kind of response can be leveled with the desiderata for strong autonomy. Kim's favored response is to give up strong autonomy and the claim that mental states are distinct from their physical realizers (1998, 2005). We can then solve the problem by opting for a reductive account like the identity theory.

The upshot of these lingering concerns about functionalism is that its success is not beyond question. While it remains the most popular general approach to the metaphysics of mind, many details remain to be worked out and there is reason to expect that compromises will have to be made. That means that functionalism has not yet earned the decisive victory over the identity theory that many have assumed it achieved before 1970. Particularly given new doubts about the empirical evidence against identity theories, it seems more fair to say that the identity theory's problems with the strong autonomy desiderata are no more damaging to it than functionalism's problems with mental causation are to it, and maybe less so. But the lingering dispute also tends to lend credibility, or at least sympathy, to those who think that no progress can be made if we limit ourselves to physicalist theories. Thus in the last 15 years a surprising contender has appeared on the scene, challenging any empirically driven physicalist theory of the metaphysics of mind.

Property dualism: Fundamentalism and emergentism

From the introduction of behaviorism and identity theory in the 1950s until the 1990s, physicalism was assumed by almost all philosophers of mind. A few iconoclasts worried that physicalist theories are not fully explanatory (Levine, 1983; Nagel, 1974) or are simply false (Jackson, 1982). But physicalist theories, especially versions of functionalism, carried the day. And in many circles nonphysicalist theories were simply not taken seriously.

More than anyone, David Chalmers (1996) gets the credit or blame for reviving an unapologetic form of dualism as a serious option in the mid-1990s. The stage was set for Chalmers' neo-dualism by the return, in the early 1990s, of philosophical and scientific interest in theories of consciousness. Consciousness had always been a recalcitrant if not downright mysterious phenomenon for theorists, and it was an especially thorny problem for functionalists. Chalmers's direct argument against physicalist theories of consciousness was of the functional duplicates sort, involving the possibility of zombies who are physically identical to human beings but who lack conscious experiences altogether. Left at that, physicalists would have no special concern. But Chalmers managed to ground his argument with a very clever development of Max Black's objection to J. J. C. Smart's identity theory. Black's was the famous Objection 5, to which Smart (1959) was least confident that he had successfully replied.[18] The concern is that even if the identity theorist can show that mental states are identical to brain states, it does not follow that mental properties are identical to brain properties. In fact, given that we have different "mentalistic" and "physicalistic" terms by which we refer to mental events and brain events, even if they are identical events there must be some distinct properties by which we recognize them as mental and physical, respectively. Otherwise we would know a priori that they are identical; but we do not. Smart's response was to argue that mentalistic terms do not refer to essentially mental items, but that they are "topic neutral" terms that are uncommitted as to the essential nature of the things to which they refer. According to Smart "I am experiencing a yellowish after-image" should be understood as saying, "there is something going on in me which is like what occurs when I view a yellow lemon," or something similar.

The full details of Chalmers' argument go beyond the scope of this brief survey.[19] The key premise is that if physicalism is true then from the fundamental facts of micro-physics, a conceptually competent ideal reasoner could derive a priori all of the other facts about the world, such as the locations of chairs and people, and the occurrence of conscious experiences. Chalmers and Frank Jackson say that the physical facts "entail" all the facts only if the other facts are a priori determinable in this special way, and they say that physicalism requires that the strictly physical facts entail all the facts (Chalmers and Jackson, 2001).[20] The possibility of philosophical zombies purportedly demonstrates that some facts are not a priori entailed, in particular facts about conscious experience.[21] And Smart's response is no help, because he concedes that the connection between the physical and the mental is not known a priori, but rather is empirically discovered.[22]

So it can seem that Chalmers has successfully amplified concerns about the explanatory power of physicalism into a metaphysical argument. We're in no position to fully assess Chalmers' argument. Suffice it to say that it invokes several highly contested epistemic, semantic, and metaphysical premises. Its wide influence may owe in part to the way the abbreviated presentation of the reasoning resembles the familiar and much more simplistic functional duplicates arguments, while also apparently deriving a much more radical conclusion. Additionally, growing dissatisfaction with the leading physicalist functionalism, and continued skepticism about the empirical viability of identity theories, contributed to a general hunger for new alternatives. If behaviorism and substance dualism are nonstarters, if identity theory is false, and if functionalism has unresolved issues . . . then maybe a not-too-spooky property dualism is worth considering? After all, the strong autonomy thesis endorsed by functionalists already asserts the non-identity of the mental and the physical, which is by some estimates tantamount to property dualism.[23]

Chalmers' version of property dualism is fundamentalist in that it posits novel mentalistic properties as part of the fundamental ontology of the universe. Some philosophers have thought that a better approach for property dualism is emergentist, according to which the new mental properties arise at higher levels of nature, for example, when certain kinds of complex systems are assembled.[24] The simple model for emergentism is the apparently novel properties of forests, which are not properties of any individual tree, or the apparently novel properties of fluids, which are not properties of individual molecules and are even surprising from the molecular perspective. Whether there are any prima facie examples of emergence is controversial.[25] And, if so, whether any of those are cases of "strong emergence," where the novelty is in some sense metaphysical and not just epistemically surprising or unpredictable, is very much up in the air. If there are any cases, they will be cases of emergentist property dualism. As such, they will have all of the defects of property dualism, plus an additional problem. The additional problem is that they violate the rule of thumb that brute or fundamental properties and entities normally occur at the most basic or fundamental scales of nature, and not at higher levels. We would have to have very good reasons to admit this kind of emergence; so in the short term it seems clear that the fundamentalist property dualist has a slight edge on this count.

Whether in its fundamentalist or emergentist versions, property dualism is certainly not a physicalist theory. It is realist and it delivers the strong autonomy of psychology. However, unless the property dualist is prepared to implausibly deny the causal closure of the physical, property dualism must be a self-consciously epiphenomenalist position. This is a serious defect in the theory, and one that has not been sufficiently appreciated. The basic lesson is that any controversial premise in the argument for property dualism will have to be more certain than the facts of mental causation. Otherwise we are free to regard the argument for property dualism as a reductio ad absurdum of the controversial premise.

At the present time, property dualism is nevertheless surprisingly popular. It is particularly fashionable among those who are primarily interested in metaphysics or basic ontology, who perhaps have fewer qualms about rejecting the traditional desiderata of philosophers of mind and psychology. Among philosophers interested in perception, action, psychological explanation, or philosophy of science, property dualism is not a serious candidate for the reasons surveyed above. This divergence of views perhaps reveals something of a strange and unfortunate disconnect between those theorists who work on basic ontology and those who work on what has been called the metaphysics of science.

Score keeping

At this point it is worth pausing for a bit of explicit score keeping. The four key desiderata on a metaphysical theory of mind are that it is (1) realist, (2) physicalist, (3) underwrites the causal efficacy of the mental, and (4) justifies the explanatory autonomy of psychology.

The identity theory is realist and physicalist, and it has an almost uncontroversial account of the causal efficacy of mental states. It can deliver on a modest kind of explanatory autonomy for psychology, though not the strong sort. However, if the multiple realization argument is correct, then the identity theory is false. But if the multiple realization argument is flawed (perhaps because multiple realization is much more rare than usually supposed) or can be met, the identity theory has a claim to be a serious contender. Modulo multiple realization, we have to give the identity theory at least 3 points, and maybe 3 1/2.

Functionalism is also realist and physicalist, so long as the realizers are physical. And it has the potential to deliver a strongly autonomous science of psychology. But functionalism has significant problems with securing mental causation, so it can only earn 3 points. And it still faces the traditional problems of inputs and outputs, and of functional duplicates, that seem to show that purely relational accounts of the mind are inadequate.

Property dualism purports to be an advance, but in fact its attractiveness is limited. It is prima facie realist and delivers an autonomous science of psychology. But it purchases the latter by giving up physicalism and thereby giving up on causal efficacy. So it can earn no more than 2 points. And if we follow Alexander's Dictum that to be is to be a cause, then property dualism's prima facie realism is only an illusion, and it is an eliminativist theory; that would earn it only 1 point for autonomy, and a dubious point at that.

Advocates of property dualism will argue that this measure under-values the theory: if identity theory and functionalism are false, then property dualism is the only contender left standing. In that case we would be justified in overriding our initial desiderata. This Sherlock Holmes argument for property dualism—"when you have excluded the impossible, whatever remains, however improbable, must be the truth"—is not very constructive. In philosophy, especially, one should be quite cautious of arguments that rely on the premise that all other views are false. In the present case, it is evident that the arguments for property dualism are not straightforward arguments concerning first-order questions about the metaphysical nature of minds. They also include a significant metametaphysical component that is hotly debated.[26] So the claim that all other theories fail is extremely contentious, as is the claim that property dualism is internally consistent and viable.

The state of play

In this chapter I have organized the discussion around the three most prominent metaphysical theories about minds, and around some desiderata on such accounts. One could just as well organize the discussion around the questions or "puzzles" that arise in philosophy of mind and then sort the views according to how they solve those puzzles. The questions would correspond to the desiderata: the problem of other minds and our own, the mind–body problem, the problem of mental causation, the puzzle of psychological explanation. We could then run through the pros and cons of proposals to answer each question, and try to assemble a theory that dodges all bullets. This story can be extracted from the present review, I think.

Where does that leave us? Despite the anomaly of the popularity of property dualism, the main live candidates for metaphysical theories of minds are still the identity theory and functionalism. The remaining candidates—behaviorism, eliminativism, anomalous monism, and property dualism itself—operate as foils, much as skepticism operates mainly as a foil in epistemology. There are few who directly endorse those views; more often they are raised only in order to press particular explanatory or ontological challenges. Functionalism remains the leading view, despite its widely recognized faults. And the identity theory is widely disregarded, despite growing concern that it is not contravened by the available evidence. It remains to be seen where we will be in the coming years.

Notes

1   That the problem of mental causation arises for physicalist theories as well is what Jaegwon Kim calls "Descartes' Revenge" (1998).

2   Relatedly, as David Papineau has emphasized, the scientific evidence for physicalism via the causal closure of the physical became increasingly well-confirmed (2001).

3   Recently some writers have thought to distinguish between physicalism and materialism, reserving the latter for a particular and perhaps archaic form of physicalism tied to an outdated notion of matter. See the chapter "Naturalism and Physicalism" in this volume.

4   There are still a few advocates of neutral monism, according to which mental properties and physical properties both inhere in a substance that is not itself essentially physical or mental (e.g., Stubenberg, 1998).

5   Here and throughout I use "constitution" generically to cover a variety of ontological dependence or "making up" relations, including identity, realization, and composition. For more on the so-called *via negativa* characterization of the physical, see Montero and Papineau (2005).

6 Thus construed, the eliminativist is a conditional realist who denies the existence of mental states precisely because they fall short of the realist standard.

7 The usual examples of metaphysical behaviorists, Wittgenstein and Ryle, each denied that they were behaviorists at all (Armstrong, 1968).

8 For example, Christopher Hill (1991) (who now has reservations), John Bickle (1998) (who no longer endorses the view), Jaegwon Kim (1993, 1998), Thomas Polger (2004), and Brian McLaughlin (2005).

9 In what follows I will usually characterize the theory in terms of mental states, by which I mean kinds of mental states; but it is just as often stated in terms of events, processes, entities, and properties. Following David Lewis (1966), I will use the notion of mental states generically to cover all of those options. Moreover, I follow the standard practice of speaking in terms of brain states, where that is a placeholder for neuroscientific states that almost certainly involve neurological facts not limited to the brain and may involve bodily facts that are not limited to neurons. Brain states, then, are whatever the various explanatory units of the neurosciences turn out to be.

10 I am unaware of any philosophers who hold that mental states are basic physical states in their own right; the dependence view is the standard version.

11 Others call this the *Eleatic Principle* (e.g., Colyvan, 1998).

12 Fodor continues, parenthetically: "In fact, I don't know whether autonomous states are *ipso facto* functional. For present purposes all that matters is whether functional states are *ipso facto* autonomous" (1997, p. 149).

13 There has been quite a bit of scrutiny of the multiple realization claim in recent years. In addition to the sources cited in the text, see Aizawa and Gillett (2009), Bickle (1998), Clapp (2001), Craver (2001), Endicott (2005), Heil (1999), Polger (2002, 2008b, 2009), Sober (1999), and Shapiro (2000, 2004, 2008).

14 This line of reasoning was a precursor to Kim's "disjunction argument" against multiple realization (1992, 1993, 1998).

15 For a more detailed discussion, see Polger (2004).

16 For many kinds of software, it is misleading to say that the same program is running on each machine; more likely, different programs that were compiled from a single source are running on the different machines, which is another kind of multiple realization. But in some cases—especially, for example, Java applets—it is more accurate to say that the same program runs on each machine.

17 For a more elaborate and detailed reconstruction, see Bennett (2003, 2008).

18 He had. See Polger (2011).

19 See "Naturalism and Physicalism" in this volume.

20 See Chalmers and Jackson (2001) for a few other qualifications on what has to be derivable from what.

21 And about causation, as well, but Chalmers downplays the significance of the fact that even by his own standards consciousness is not unique in its failure of entailment (e.g., Chalmers, 1996, p. 86).

22 A former dualist, Frank Jackson now believes that all the facts, including facts about consciousness, are indeed a priori entailed in just this way. David Lewis might have held this view, as well (1994); but "analytic" or "a priori" physicalism is not a widely held view about the mind or anything else.

23 As noted, some writers simply call that a form of dualism, for example, Kim (1998) and Bennett (2003, 2008).

24 The now classic introduction to emergence is McLaughlin (1992).

25 See Boogerd et al. (2005), for example.

26 About which see Block and Stalnaker (1999), Byrne (1999), Hill and McLaughlin (1999), Jackson (1998), Lycan (2003), McLaughlin (2005), Polger (2008a), Wright (2007), and Yablo (1999, 2000).

References

Adams, F. (1979), "Properties, functionalism, and the identity theory." *Eidos,* I, II, 153–79.

Aizawa, K. and Gillett, C. (2009), "The (multiple) realization of psychological and other properties in the sciences." *Mind & Language,* 24, 181–208.

Antony, L. and Levine, J. (1997), "Reduction with autonomy," in J. Tomberlin, ed., *Philosophical Perspectives 11: Mind, Causation, and World.* Boston: Blackwell Publishers, pp. 83–105.

Armstrong, D. (1968), *A Materialist Theory of Mind.* London: Routledge and Kegan Paul.

Bechtel, W. and McCauley, R. (1999), "Heuristic identity theory (or back to the future): the mind–body problem against the background of research strategies in cognitive neuroscience," in *Proceedings of the 21st Annual Meeting of the Cognitive Science Society.* Mahwah, NJ: Lawrence Erlbaum Associates, pp. 67–72.

Bechtel, W. and Mundale, J. (1999), "Multiple realization revisited: linking cognitive and neural states." *Philosophy of Science,* 66, 175–207.

Bennett, K. (2003), "Why the exclusion problem seems intractable and how, just maybe, to tract it." *Noûs,* 37(3), 471–97.

—(2008), "Exclusion again," in J. Hohwy and J. Kallestrup, eds, *Being Reduced.* Oxford: Oxford University Press, pp. 280–305.

Bickle, J. (1998), *Psychoneural Reduction: The New Wave.* Cambridge, MA: MIT Press.

Block, N. (1978), "Troubles with functionalism," in C. W. Savage, ed., *Minnesota Studies in the Philosophy of Science, Vol. IX.* Minneapolis: University of Minnesota Press, pp. 261–325. Reprinted in Block (1980), pp. 268–305.

—, ed. (1980), *Readings in Philosophy of Psychology, Volume One.* Cambridge, MA: Harvard University Press.

—(1996), "Mental paint and mental latex." *Philosophical Issues,* 7, 19–49.

Block, N. and Fodor, J. (1972), "What psychological states are not." *Philosophical Review,* 81, 159–81.

Block, N. and Stalnaker, R. (1999), "Conceptual analysis, dualism, and the explanatory gap." *Philosophical Review,* 108(1), 1–46.

Bontly, T. (2002), "The supervenience argument generalizes." *Philosophical Studies,* 109(1), 75–96.

Boogerd, F., Bruggeman, F., Richardson, R., Stephan, A. and Westerhoff, H. (2005), "Emergence and its place in nature: a case study of biochemical networks." *Synthese,* 145, 131–64.

Burge, T. (1979), "Individualism and the mental." *Midwest Studies in Philosophy,* 4, 73–121.

Byrne, A. (1999), "Cosmic hermeneutics." *Philosophical Perspectives,* 13, 347–83.

Chalmers, D. (1996), *The Conscious Mind: In Search of a Fundamental Theory.* New York: Oxford University Press.

Chalmers, D. and Jackson, F. (2001), "Conceptual analysis and reductive explanation." *Philosophical Review,* 110(3), 315–61.

Chomsky, N. (1959), "Review of *Verbal Behavior* by B. F. Skinner." *Language,* 35, 26–58.

Churchland, P. M. (1981), "Eliminative materialism and the propositional attitudes." *Journal of Philosophy,* 78, 67–90.

—(1982), "Is 'thinker' a natural kind?" *Dialogue,* 21(2), 223–38.

Churchland, P. S. (1983), "Consciousness: the transmutation of a concept." *Pacific Philosophical Quarterly,* 64, 80–93.

Clapp, L. (2001), "Disjunctive properties: multiple realizations." *Journal of Philosophy,* 98, 111–36.

Clayton, P. and Davies, P., eds, (2006), *The Re-Emergence of Emergence.* Oxford: Oxford University Press.

Colyvan, M. (1998), "Can the eleatic principle be justified?" *Canadian Journal of Philosophy,* 28(3), 313–36.

Craver, C. (2001), "Role functions, mechanisms and hierarchy." *Philosophy of Science,* 68, 31–55.

Dennett, D. (1971), "Intentional systems." *The Journal of Philosophy,* 68, 87–106.

—(1987), *The Intentional Stance.* Cambridge, MA: MIT Press.

—(1991), *Consciousness Explained.* Boston: Little, Brown, and Co.

Dretske, F. (1981), *Knowledge and the Flow of Information.* Cambridge, MA: MIT Press.

—(1988), *Explaining Behavior.* Cambridge, MA: MIT Press.

—(1995), *Naturalizing the Mind.* Cambridge, MA: MIT Press.

Endicott, R. (2005), "Multiple realizability," in *The Encyclopedia of Philosophy* (second edition). New York: MacMillan.

Feigl, H. (1958), "The 'mental' and the 'physical'," in H. Feigl, G. Maxwell and
    M. Scriven, eds, *Minnesota Studies in the Philosophy of Science 2*. Minneapolis:
    University of Minnesota Press, pp. 320–492.
Feyerabend, P. (1963), "Mental events and the brain." *Journal of Philosophy*, 40, 295–6.
Fodor, J. (1974), "Special sciences, or the disunity of science as a working hypothesis."
    Synthese, 28, 97–115. Reprinted in N. Block (1980), pp. 120–33.
—(1978), "Propositional attitudes." *Monist*, 61(4), 501–23. Reprinted in N. Block
    (1980), pp. 45–63.
—(1985), "Fodor's guide to mental representation: the intelligent auntie's vade-mecum."
    Mind, 94, 373, 76–100. Reprinted in Fodor (1992), pp. 3–30.
—(1987), *Psychosemantics*. Cambridge, MA: MIT Press.
—(1989), "Making mind matter more." *Philosophical Topics*, 17(11), 59–79.
—(1991), "A modal argument for narrow content." *Journal of Philosophy*, 88, 5–26.
—(1992), *A Theory of Content and Other Essays*. Cambridge, MA: MIT Press.
—(1997), "Special sciences: still autonomous after all these years," in Tomberlin (1997).
Funkhouser, E. (2006), "The determinable-determinate relation." *Noûs*, 40(3), 548–69.
Gillett, C. (2002), "The dimensions of realization: a critique of the standard view."
    Analysis, 64(4), 316–23.
—(2003), "The metaphysics of realization, multiple realizability, and the special
    sciences." *The Journal of Philosophy*, 100(11), 591–603.
—(2007), "Understanding the new reductionism: the metaphysics of science and
    compositional reduction." *The Journal of Philosophy*, 104(4), 193–216.
Guttenplan, S., ed. (1994), *A Companion to the Philosophy of Mind*. Oxford: Blackwell
    Publishers.
Haug, M. (2010), "Realization, determination, and mechanisms." *Philosophical Studies*,
    150, 313–30.
Heil, J. (1999), "Multiple realization." *American Philosophical Quarterly*, 36(3),
    189–208.
Hill, C. (1991), *Sensations: A Defense of Type Materialism*. Cambridge: Cambridge
    University Press.
Hill, C. and McLaughlin, B. (1999), "There are fewer things in reality than are dreamt of
    in Chalmers' philosophy." *Philosophy and Phenomenological Research*, 59, 445–54.
Horgan, T. (1993), "From supervenience to superdupervenience: meeting the demands
    of a material world." *Mind*, 102, 555–86.
Horgan, T. and Tienson, J. (2002), "The intentionality of phenomenology and the
    phenomenology of intentionality," in David J. Chalmers, ed., *Philosophy of Mind:
    Classical and Contemporary Readings*. Oxford: Oxford University Press, pp. 520–32.
Horgan, T. and Kriegel, U. (2008), "Phenomenal intentionality meets the extended
    mind." *The Monist*, 91, 347–73.
Humphreys, P. (1997), "Emergence, not supervenience." *Philosophy of Science*, 64,
    S337–45.
Jackson, F. (1982), "Epiphenomenal qualia." *The Philosophical Quarterly*, 32(127), 127–36.

—(1998), *From Metaphysics to Ethics: A Defense of Conceptual Analysis*. Oxford: Oxford University Press.

Jackson, F. and Pettit, P. (1990), "Program explanation: a general perspective." *Analysis,* 50, 107–17.

Keaton, D. (2010), "Two kinds of role property." *Philosophia,* 38, 773–88.

—(forthcoming), "Kim's supervenience argument and the nature of total realizers." *European Journal of Philosophy.*

Kim, J. (1972), "Phenomenal properties, psychophysical laws, and identity theory." *Monist,* 56(2), 177–92. Excerpted in Block (1980) under the title "Physicalism and the multiple realizability of mental states."

—(1989), "The myth of nonreductive materialism." *Proceedings and Addresses of the American Philosophical Association,* 63(3), 31–47. Reprinted in Kim (1993).

—(1992), "Multiple realization and the metaphysics of reduction." *Philosophy and Phenomenological Research,* 52, 1–16.

—(1993), *Supervenience and Mind.* New York: Cambridge University Press.

—(1998), *Mind in a Physical World: An Essay on the Mind–Body Problem and Mental Causation.* Cambridge, MA: MIT Press.

—(2005), *Physicalism, or Something Near Enough.* Princeton, NJ: Princeton University Press.

Kripke, S. (1971), "Identity and necessity," in M. Munitz, ed., *Identity and Individuation.* New York: New York University Press, pp. 135–64.

—(1972/1980), *Naming and Necessity.* Cambridge, MA: Harvard University Press.

Levine, J. (1983), "Materialism and qualia: the explanatory gap." *Pacific Philosophical Quarterly,* 64, 354–61.

Lewis, D. (1966), "An argument for the identity theory." *Journal of Philosophy,* 63, 17–25.

—(1969), "Review of art, mind, and religion." *Journal of Philosophy,* 66, 23–35. Excerpted in Block (1980) as "Review of Putnam."

—(1972), "Psychophysical and theoretical identifications." *Australasian Journal of Philosophy,* 50, 249–58. Reprinted in Lewis (1999), pp. 248–61.

—(1994), "Lewis, David: reduction of mind," in S. Guttenplan, ed., *A Companion to the Philosophy of Mind.* Oxford: Blackwell Publishers, pp. 412–31.

—(1999), *Papers in Metaphysics and Epistemology.* New York: Cambridge University Press.

Loar, B. (2003), "Phenomenal intentionality as the basis of mental content," in M. Hahn and B. Ramberg, eds, *Reflections and Replies: Essays on the Philosophy of Tyler Burge.* Cambridge, MA: MIT Press, pp. 229–58.

Lycan, W. (1987), *Consciousness.* Cambridge, MA: MIT Press.

—(2003), "Vs. a new a priorist argument for dualism." E. Sosa and E. Villanueva, eds, *Philosophical Issues,* 13, 130–47.

McLaughlin, B. (1992), "The rise and fall of british emergentism," in A. Beckermann, H. Flohr, and J. Kim, eds, *Emergence or Reduction?* Berlin: Walter de Gruyter, pp. 49–93.

—(2005), "A priori versus a posteriori physicalism," in C. Nimtz and A. Beckermann, eds, *Philosophy—Science—Scientific Philosophy. Main Lectures and Colloquia of GAP. 5, Fifth International Congress of the Society for Analytical Philosophy.* Paderborn, Germany: Mentis, pp. 267–85.

Millikan, R. (1984), *Language, Thought, and Other Biological Categories.* Cambridge, MA: MIT Press.

—(1989), "In defense of proper functions." *Philosophy of Science,* 56, 288–302. Reprinted in R. Millikan (1993), pp. 13–29.

—(1993), *White Queen Psychology and Other Essays for Alice.* Cambridge, MA: MIT Press.

Montague, M. (2009), "The logic, intentionality, and phenomenology of emotion." *Philosophical Studies,* 145(2), 171–92.

Montero, B. and Papineau, D. (2005), "A defence of the via negativa argument for physicalism." *Analysis,* 65(3), 233–7.

Nagel, T. (1974), "What is it like to be a bat?" *Philosophical Review,* 83(4), 435–50.

Neander, K. (1991), "Functions as selected effects: the conceptual analyst's defense." *Philosophy of Science,* 58, 168–84.

Papineau, D. (2001), "The rise of physicalism," in C. Gillett and B. Loewer, eds, *Physicalism and its Discontents.* Cambridge: Cambridge University Press, pp. 3–36.

Pautz, A. (2008), "The interdependence of phenomenology and intentionality." *The Monist,* 91(2), 250–72.

Pitt, D. (2004), "The phenomenology of cognition, or, what is it like to think that P?" *Philosophy and Phenomenological Research,* 69(1), 1–36.

—(2009), "Intentional psychologism." *Philosophical Studies,* 146, 1.

Place, U. T. (1956), "Is consciousness a brain process?" *British Journal of Psychology,* 47, 44–50.

Polger, T. (2002), "Putnam's intuition." *Philosophical Studies,* 109(2), 143–70.

—(2004), *Natural Minds.* Cambridge, MA: MIT Press.

—(2007), "Realization and the metaphysics of mind." *Australasian Journal of Philosophy,* 85(2), 233–59.

—(2008a), "H_2O, 'water', and transparent reduction." *Erkenntnis,* 69(1), 109–30.

—(2008b), "Two confusions concerning multiple realizability." *Philosophy of Science,* 75(5), 537–47.

—(2009), "Evaluating the evidence for multiple realization." *Synthese,* 167(3), 457–72.

Polger, T. (2011), "Are sensations still brain processes?" *Philosophical Psychology,* 24(1), 1–21.

Polger, T. and Shapiro, L. (2008), "Understanding the dimensions of realization." *Journal of Philosophy,* 105(4), 213–22.

Putnam, H. (1960) "Minds and machines," in H. Putnam (1975), *Mind, Language and Reality: Philosophical Papers, Volume 2.* New York: Cambridge University Press, pp. 362–85.

—(1963), "Brains and behavior," in Ronald J. Butler, ed., *Analytical Philosophy: Second Series*. London: Blackwell, pp. 1–19.

—(1967/1975), "The nature of mental states," in H. Putnam, *Mind, Language and Reality: Philosophical Papers, Volume 2*. New York: Cambridge University Press, pp. 429–40.

—(1972), "Philosophy and our mental life," in H. Putnam (1975), *Mind, Language and Reality: Philosophical Papers, Volume 2*. New York: Cambridge University Press, pp. 291–303.

—(1975), "The meaning of 'meaning'," in K. Gunderson, ed., *Language, Mind and Knowledge: Minnesota Studies in the Philosophy of Science, VII*. Minneapolis: University of Minnesota Press, pp. 215–71.

—(1988), *Representation and Reality*. Cambridge, MA: MIT Press.

Robb, D. (1997), "The properties of mental causation." *The Philosophical Quarterly*, 47(187), 178–94.

Rorty, R. (1965), "Mind–body identity, privacy, and categories." *Review of Metaphysics*, 19, 24–54.

—(1970), "In defense of eliminative materialism." *Review of Metaphysics*, 24, 112–21.

Searle, J. (1992), *Rediscovery of Mind*. Cambridge, MA: MIT Press.

Shapiro, L. (2000), "Multiple realizations." *The Journal of Philosophy*, 97, 635–54.

—(2004), *The Mind Incarnate*. Cambridge, MA: MIT Press.

—(2008), "How to test for multiple realization." *Philosophy of Science*, 75, 514–25.

Shoemaker, S. (2001), "Realization and mental causation," in C. Gillett and B. Loewer, eds, *Physicalism and Its Discontents*. Cambridge: Cambridge University Press, pp. 74–98.

—(2007), *Physical Realization*. Oxford: Oxford University Press.

Sider, T. (2003), "What's so bad about overdetermination?" *Philosophy and Phenomenological Research*, 67, 719–26.

Siewert, C. (1998), *The Significance of Consciousness*. Princeton, NJ: Princeton University Press.

Smart, J. J. C. (1959), "Sensations and brain processes." *Philosophical Review*, 68, 141–56.

Sober, E. (1999), "The multiple realization argument against reductionism." *Philosophy of Science*, 66, 542–64.

Stubenberg, L. (1998), *Consciousness and Qualia*. Amsterdam: John Benjamins.

Tomberlin, J., ed. (1997), *Philosophical Perspectives 11: Mind, Causation, and World*. Boston: Blackwell Publishers.

Tye, M. (1995), *Ten Problems of Consciousness: A Representational Theory of the Phenomenal Mind*. Cambridge, MA: MIT Press.

—(2000), *Consciousness, Color, and Content*. Cambridge, MA: MIT Press.

Van Gulick, R. (2011), "Non-reductive physicalism and the teleo-pragmatic theory of mind." *Philosophia Naturalis: Journal for the Philosophy of Nature* 47/48, 103–23.

Wilson, J. (2005), "Supervenience-based formulations of physicalism." *Nous,* 39(3), 426–59.

Wilson, R. and Craver, C. (2007), "Realization," in P. Thagard, ed., *Handbook of the Philosophy of Science, Volume 12: Philosophy of Psychology and Cognitive Science.* Dordrecht: Elsevier, pp. 81–104.

Wright, W. (2007), "Explanation and the hard problem." *Philosophical Studies,* 132, 301–30.

Yablo, S. (1992), "Mental causation." *Philosophical Review,* 101, 245–80.

—(1997), "Wide causation." *Philosophical Perspectives,* 11, 251–81.

—(1999), "Concepts and consciousness." *Philosophy and Phenomenological Research,* 59, 455–63.

—(2000), "Textbook Kripkeanism and the open texture of concepts." *Pacific Philosophical Quarterly,* 81, 98–122.

Material Constitution

Stephan Blatti

Everyday life and discourse is shot through with puzzles of material constitution. We often wonder what kind of material makes up certain physical objects. Of a traffic sign on the road, for instance, we might ask whether it is made of aluminum or steel. Seemingly implicit in such a question is a distinction between the sign, on the one hand, and the piece of metal that constitutes it, on the other hand. But what could be the basis for distinguishing the sign from that particular hunk of matter? Then again, consider the criminals who profit from melting down stolen copper pipes. If such pipes were nothing more than the portions of copper of which they were made, then we should say that the pipes persist in molten form. Yet, quite the contrary, we think that melting is a way of destroying these pipes.

Such examples confirm that even our pre-philosophical intuitions about material constitution strain in opposite directions. On the face of it, it seems bizarre to suggest that a physical object is something distinct from the particular piece of material of which it is made: surely what we see when we see a traffic sign is not multiple objects simultaneously occupying the same space. If this commonsense thought is correct, then the relationship between a physical object and the hunk of matter that makes it up is one of identity: the object *just is* its constitutive matter. But how are we to reconcile this thought with the equally intuitive thought about the copper pipes? If the portion of copper but not the pipe survives the melting process, then it cannot be that the pipe and the copper were one and the same thing, since prior to the melting, the portion of copper instantiated the ability to survive melting down while the pipe did not. A moment's reflection on this example, then, seems to suggest exactly the opposite of the lesson drawn from the traffic sign example: material constitution is *not* identity.

Sustained reflection on cases like these has played an integral role in contemporary discussions of material constitution. Here we will focus on two such puzzles—one concerning a clay statue, the other a tailless cat. Though different in important respects, both examples qualify as puzzles of material constitution because each presents a case in which two objects seem to share all of the same parts and yet relate to those parts in different ways.[1] Other notable puzzles include the Ship of Theseus, the "paradox of increase" (also known as the "growing argument"), and the case of Lumpl and Goliath.[2] Nearly all of these puzzles are centuries old, having been first introduced by ancient Greek philosophers (e.g., Epicharmus, Chrysippus) and later revived and, in some cases, modified by medieval (e.g., William of Sherwood, Peter Abelard), modern (e.g., Thomas Hobbes, Thomas Reid), and contemporary (e.g., Allan Gibbard) philosophers.[3]

Clay statue

Consider a sculptor who one morning begins to work with a particular lump of clay; call it "Lump." By the afternoon she has molded Lump into a figurative statue; call it "Statue." Dissatisfied with her creation, the sculptor crushes her work in the evening, destroying Statue but leaving Lump intact. Now ask yourself: is Statue one and the same thing as Lump? At first it seems that the answer is obviously yes. The sculptor appears to devote the day to working on just one thing: something that was amorphous in the morning, shaped in the afternoon, and amorphous again in the evening. Even when Statue is on the scene in the afternoon, it shares all of its physical properties with Lump: weight, shape, location, height, and so on. Yet further reflection seems to reveal that Lump and Statue differ in important respects. The most obvious difference is that Lump exists at times when Statue does not: both in the morning and in the evening. And since Statue and Lump cannot be one and the same thing if they differ in even one of their properties (e.g., the property *having existed in the morning*), we are left puzzled. If Statue and Lump are identical (as our ordinary ways of thinking and speaking suggest), then how are we to account for their apparent differences? But if common sense is systematically incorrect and Statue and Lump are not identical, then just what *is* the relationship between an object and its constitutive matter? And why would common sense lead us astray?

Tibbles the cat

Tibbles is a normal housecat. But whereas "Tibbles" refers to the whole cat, let "Tib" name a proper part of Tibbles—specifically, everything but his tail. Tib, in other words, is Tibbles's tail-complement, incorporating everything to which "Tibbles" refers *except* the tail. Notwithstanding the strangeness of naming a tail-complement, it is clear enough that the referents of these names are nonidentical: Tibbles weighs more than Tib, Tib has one fewer appendage than Tibbles, etc. Now consider what happens when a minor accident results in the loss of the tail. Since none of Tib's parts are affected, there seems no reason to deny that Tib survives the accident. But what about Tibbles? Either he survives or he does not. If he survives, then the accident results in two, wholly coincident, tailless cats. But not only would it be strange if the *destruction* of a whole's proper part were responsible for the *creation* of a second whole of the same kind, the prima facie impossibility of two objects of the same kind simultaneously occupying the same space strongly suggests that Tibbles does not survive the accident.[4] Yet if Tibbles does not survive, then we are left with the implication that things cannot survive the loss of even inessential proper parts. And that would be truly bizarre, for it would mean that you will not survive your next finger clipping, nor I my next haircut.[5]

Philosophers have engaged these puzzles from a variety of angles and have generated a large scholarly literature in the process. In the next four sections we will review four prominent strategies for addressing the problem of material constitution. Each of these strategies has been developed and defended by multiple philosophers. It is almost inevitable, therefore, that the scholarly literature should be marked by both discrepancies in presentation and intramural debates over matters of detail. But while we shall occasionally register these disagreements, for the most part emphasis will be placed on the broad outlines of, and some of the more prominent objections faced by, each general approach. The first such approach affirms the possibility of multiple objects sharing the same space at the same time (see "The Orthodox View: Coincident Objects"). On this view, "constitution" names a phenomenon in need of explaining rather than a problem in need of solving. According to the second strategy, the problem of material constitution dissolves in the light of a previously unrecognized possibility, viz. that a single object can be an instance of two kinds while nevertheless instantiating the essential properties of only one of those kinds (see "Dominant Kinds"). For advocates of the third approach, the problem of material constitution is best answered by denying the very existence of at least one of the objects involved in each of the cases described earlier (see "Nihilism"). The fourth and final strategy involves revising our commitment to Leibniz's Law and its standard conception of identity, without both of which the problem of material constitution seems not to arise in the first place (see "Revising the Logic of Identity").[6] I will conclude with some very brief reflections on the likely directions of future research.

The orthodox view: Coincident objects

Rather than reject the possibility of coincident objects like Statue and Lump (in the afternoon) and Tibbles and Tib (after the accident), advocates of what has become the standard response to the problem of material constitution *affirm* it. On their view, nonidentical objects *can* share all of the same parts at the same time; things can compose two objects at once. Thus, Tibbles survives the loss of his tail and is nonidentically colocated with Tib; Lump and Statue are non-identical and yet both present in the afternoon. While this strategy is pursued in different ways, all those who defend the orthodox account are committed to denying the "identity assumption":

(IA) $(\forall x)(\forall y)(\forall p)(\forall t)$ [(the ps compose x at t & the ps compose y at t) → $x = y$],

where "the ps" refers to an object's parts. In other words, wholly coincident, nonidentical objects are possible.[7]

By affirming this possibility, advocates of the orthodox account face the task of explaining the relationship between coincident objects. If it is not identity, what is it? Their answer: *constitution*.[8] The constitution relation may be distinguished from identity by the fact that, unlike identity, constitution is asymmetric. Whereas from the fact that a is identical with b it follows that b is identical with a, if a constitutes b, then it is not the case that b constitutes a.[9] Thus, for instance, it is held that Statue is constituted by Lump, but not vice versa.[10]

But why should we agree that Statue and Lump are nonidentical in the afternoon, when they share all of the same parts? The constitutionalist's answer is that they belong to different kinds: whereas Statue is a work of art, Lump is a piece of clay. It is this difference in kind-membership that explains the fact that Lump can (and does) survive squashing, while Statue cannot (and does not): unlike statues, lumps of clay just are the sort of thing that can survive even drastic reshaping. (Imagine melting down the copper that makes up the Statue of Liberty, reshaping it into the form of a mule and then trying to reassure the American public that the Statue of Liberty persists nevertheless.) The difference in kinds corresponds to a difference in sortal properties: Statue instantiates the property *being a work of art* but not the property *being a piece of clay*; conversely, Lump instantiates the property *being a piece of clay* but not the property *being a work of art*. This difference in kind-membership explains why Lump instantiates various modal and temporal properties that Statue lacks, including the properties *being able to survive reshaping* and *having existed in the morning*. Ultimately, then, despite sharing all of their parts, Statue and Lump are nonidentical because they differ in their sortal, modal, and temporal properties.

As the orthodox account, constitutionalism has been challenged from a variety of different angles. Here we will consider three of these objections.

The grounding problem

We can approach the first by noting the prima facie peculiarity of sortal properties like *being a work of art*. The instantiation of primitive, intrinsic properties (e.g., shape, size) can be explained in terms of the organization of an object's parts. But for coincident objects that share all of their parts, the instantiation of nonprimitive properties cannot be explained this way. Statue's instantiation of the sortal property *being a work or art*, for example, cannot be determined by the organization of its parts, since Lump's parts are organized in precisely the same way. Likewise for modal and temporal properties. Those who defend the orthodox view, then, must explain how it is that, despite their many similarities, coincident objects nevertheless instantiate different nonprimitive properties. This objection is known as "the grounding problem."[11]

Various answers to this problem have been offered. Karen Bennett (2004), for example, recommends a way of regarding sortal and modal properties as primitive. Ryan Wasserman (2002) contends that, contrary to appearances, coincident objects do differ in their parts and that this fact explains the difference in nonprimitive properties. Perhaps the most provocative reply to the grounding problem is due to Lynne Rudder Baker (2000), who argues that the difference in nonprimitive properties reflects a difference in relational properties. On Baker's view, Statue's status as a work of art consists in its being related to an artworld; it is the sort of thing whose existence is intended by an artist, given a title, exhibited in galleries, discussed by critics, and so on. In this way, *being a work of art* is a relational property. By contrast, *being a piece of clay* is a nonrelational property because it requires only that a particular atomic structure be intrinsic to a piece of matter.

The mereology problem

The second objection to the orthodox view directly attacks the very possibility of colocated objects by reminding us that we typically do not distinguish between a whole object, on the one hand, and the sum of its parts, on the other. Indeed, it would seem that the orthodox view conflicts straightforwardly with the "principle of mereological extensionality":

(ME) $(\forall x)(\forall y) [x = y \leftrightarrow (\forall z)(z$ is a part of x $\leftrightarrow z$ is a part of $y)]$.[12]

If ME is correct, then any complex object is equivalent with all of its parts. So, since they share all of the same parts, there simply is no basis for distinguishing between, say, Tibbles and Tib. To insist on the distinctiveness of coextensive objects is to engage in a kind of absurd double-counting. Call this "the mereology problem."

Various engagements with the mereology problem have featured in recent discussions of the constitution view.[13] Short of simply rejecting ME, arguably the most radical reply to this problem involves disambiguating different senses of the "is a part of" locution in ME.[14] From the fact that x and y share all of their material parts, advocates of this strategy insist, it does not follow that $x = y$ because x and y may differ in their *non*material parts. The challenge then becomes how to cash out a plausible conception of nonmaterial parts. Among the options here is Michael Rea's (1998) Aristotelian proposal that we construe material objects as hylomorphic composites of form and matter and that we count among its parts an object's nonmaterial form. On this view, despite sharing all of their material parts, Statue and Lump are nonidentical because Statue but not Lump has the form *artwork* as a nonmaterial part. Another option would be to follow Laurie Paul (2002) in claiming that material objects are mereologically composed of their properties. In any case, despite allowing their proponents to endorse both the orthodox view and ME (suitably modified), proposals like Rea's and Paul's face significant criticisms, not least from those who regard as bedrock their commitment to the wholly material nature of objects like cats and statues.

The arbitrariness problem

While the mereology and grounding problems have generated sizable scholarly literatures, the last objection we shall consider has received less attention. First raised by Ernest Sosa (1987, sec. H.1) and recently reinvigorated by Ted Sider

(2001, pp. 154–8), the "arbitrariness problem" charges that the constitution view lacks any principled grounds for restricting the number of objects present in cases of material constitution to the constituted (e.g., Statue) and constituting (e.g., Lump) objects only. If, for example, the aggregate of material simples that make up both of these objects is itself an entity of some sort, then matters quickly grow complicated, with not only the Statue–Lump relationship requiring explanation, but also the Simples–Statue and the Simples–Lump relationships. Nor does there seem to be any nonarbitrary reason to disqualify additional and even more bizarre objects. At the core of this objection is the thought that it is little more than anthropic hubris to presume that reality is carved up in such a way that all existing objects correspond precisely with human sortal concepts like *artwork, cat, lump of clay,* and so on. Sider directs this objection to David Wiggins in particular, but it may be that an answer can be developed, whether based on resources marshaled from Wiggins (2001, ch. 5) or otherwise.[15]

Dominant kinds

If the problems facing the constitutionalist account of material constitution seem insurmountable, we might reconsider how the puzzle cases were described and reject one or more of the assumptions built into these descriptions. In the clay statue case, for instance, it is assumed that Lump survives from the morning, through the afternoon, and into the evening. The constitutionalist is led to explain the relationship between Statue and Lump only once it is taken for granted that both exist. According to the dominant kinds view, however, we should deny that Lump survives the creative process. On this view, Lump ceases to exist when it is shaped into a work of art. Only one object exists in the afternoon, viz. Statue. Consequently, no explanation of relationship between nonidentical objects is required.[16]

On its face, the suggestion that Lump exits the ontological stage in the afternoon seems highly implausible. After all, lumps of clay are able to survive reshaping, and all that the sculptor does is to reshape Lump. To appreciate the dominant kinds view, then, it will help if we step back from the standard presentation of the clay statue case. To begin, let us provisionally set aside the labels "Lump" and "Statue." Let us further agree that at least one thing exists in the afternoon—possibly two (or more), but at least one. Call whatever thing(s) exist(s) in the afternoon "ϕ." Now, just as in everyday contexts we would accept "soup can" and "piece of aluminium" as equally true descriptions of the object in one's kitchen's pantry, so too "lump of clay" and "work of art" are equally true descriptions of ϕ. The problem emerges only when it is acknowledged that contradictory properties seem to be instantiated where ϕ is: considered as a lump of clay, ϕ instantiates the property *able to survive reshaping*, whereas considered as a work of art, ϕ instantiates the property *unable to survive reshaping*. And recall from above the constitutionalist's thought that modal properties like these are associated with sortal kinds: objects of the kind *work of art* being unable to survive reshaping, objects of the kind *lump of clay* being able to survive reshaping. But since one thing cannot be both a work of art and a lump of clay if this means being both able and unable to survive reshaping, the inference that at least two things must be located where ϕ is seems inescapable.

Dominant kind theorists, however, resist precisely this inference by rejecting the principle on which it is based. On this view, an object can be an instance of a sortal kind without instantiating the modal properties associated with members of that kind. In the case at hand, ϕ can be *both* a work of art and a lump of clay while being *either* able *or* unable to survive reshaping. Whether ϕ is or is not able to survive reshaping depends on which of the sortal kind concepts—*work of art* or *lump of clay*—is ϕ's primary, or "dominant," kind. According to Michael Burke's formulation of this view, when a single object satisfies more than one sortal kind concept, its dominant concept is "the one whose satisfaction entails possession of the widest range of properties" (1994b, p. 610). Because an object can satisfy *lump of clay* merely by instantiating particular physical properties, and because an object can satisfy *work of art* only by instantiating both physical properties and aesthetic properties, in a case like ϕ's where both concepts are satisfied, *work of art* dominates *lump of clay*. Consequently, ϕ is unable to survive reshaping. Returning now to the original case, this is why Lump goes out of existence in the afternoon: not because the lump of clay itself ceases to exist, but because the sortal concept satisfied by Statue comes to dominate.

Several objections to the dominant kinds view (sometimes called "sortal essentialism") have been raised.[17] Jonathan Lowe (1995), for instance, blanches at the peculiarity of the dominant kind theorist's claim that something as durable as Lump—able to survive infinitely many other rearrangements of its atoms—could be destroyed so easily, by one particular reshaping, viz. one that molds it into a statue.[18]

Another objection focuses on the notion of dominance itself—specifically, Burke's criterion for determining which kind concept is dominant. On Burke's view, every composite object (that is not a mere aggregate) satisfies at least two sortal kind concepts—possibly more—although only one of these is the dominant kind that determines that object's modal properties (and more generally its persistence conditions) (1994b, p. 608). Thus, while the container of chicken noodle soup satisfies both *soup can* and *piece of aluminium*, the former is its dominant sortal because *soup can* is the concept whose satisfaction entails possession of the widest range of properties. But what if the Campbell's Soup container in question were also a Warholesque work of pop art? Between *work of art* and *soup can* it is not at all obvious which concept has associated with it the wider range of properties. Nor is it clear how one would go about measuring such a thing. On the face of it, Burke's view seems to presume a stepwise hierarchy of sortal kind concepts, no two of that entail possession of equally wide ranges of properties by the single object which satisfies them. This is possible, of course, but it seems both artificial and unrealistic.

Although Burke acknowledges the vagueness of his criterion of dominance, after surveying what he takes to be a representative range of cases, he insists that it is serviceable. As he puts it, the criterion's "vagueness seldom prevents a clear-cut decision," and except in atypical cases "its rulings are the ones we want" (1994b, pp. 604 and 610). Rea also endorses the dominant kinds view, but he disagrees with Burke on this last point, charging both that "there seem to be many cases which are clearly not atypical and which are nevertheless such that Burke's criterion does not give us a clear decision" and that "there seem to be many obviously non-atypical cases in which Burke's criterion gives us the *wrong* decision" (2000, p. 184). The problem with Burke's account, Rea argues, is that it determines an object's dominant kind based solely on a comparison of the various kinds of which that object is a member. According to Rea, the object's essential properties must also contribute to this determination. In place of Burke's criterion of kind dominance, then, Rea proposes the following alternative (ibid., p. 187):

> (KD) For any x, K is x's dominant kind just in case (i) x is essentially a K, and (ii) for any kind K' such that x is essentially a K', x's being a K entails x's being a K'.

Rea then argues that this alternative formulation not only gives clear and correct answers to the key examples, but also respects the intuition that kind concepts can sometimes dominate and other times be dominated. While few have attacked it, the jury remains out on whether this modification will satisfy all critics of the dominant kinds view.

Nihilism

Whereas the dominant kind theorist dissolves the problem of material constitution by showing how a single object can exemplify multiple kinds, the nihilist *rejects* the problem by denying the very existence of one or more of the objects concerned. Various formulations of and rationales for this response have been offered. Here we shall consider two.

Extreme nihilism

The view we might call "extreme nihilism" insists that the only objects that exist are those without proper parts: mereological simples. Objects with proper parts—composite objects—do not exist, on this view. If extreme nihilism is correct, then there are no cats, tail-complements, statues or lumps of clay, in which case the demand for how to explain the relations between such things disappears. Under the headings of "nihilism" or "mereological nihilism," this view is often attributed to the early work of Peter Unger (1979a, 1979b). But in fact Unger's position was not quite this stark. His view would be more aptly labeled *"conditional* extreme nihilism," since he held only that *if* composite objects exist, then they fail to satisfy our ordinary sortal terms.[19] Unger's defense of this claim relies on what he calls the "sorites of decomposition" argument.

1. There is at least one stone.
2. For anything there may be, if it is a stone, then it consists of many atoms but a finite number.
3. For anything there may be, if it is a stone (which consists of many atoms but a finite number), then the net removal of one atom, or only a few, in a way which is most innocuous and favorable, will not mean the difference as to whether there is a stone in the situation.

(Unger 1979b, p. 120)

Unger claims that the preceding propositions are jointly inconsistent. If, following proposition (3), one or more atoms are removed until none remain, (3) tells us that a stone would nevertheless be present. Yet this prediction contradicts (2), since the stone that allegedly remains would consist of no atoms. From this Unger concludes that (1) ought to be rejected, and along with it our commitment to other ordinary objects, so long as these objects are thought to satisfy sortal terms (e.g., "stone," "statue," "cat"). The only composite objects immune to this argument are those with precise existence conditions, like "physical object," since removing atoms from a physical object always leaves either a composite physical object or a simple physical object, and in the latter case removal of the last atom results in no object. Thus, Unger's conditional conclusion: if composite objects exist, they will not be the objects to which we customarily refer.

Modest nihilism

Unger (1990) has since abandoned his extreme nihilist view. But its close cousin—what we might call "modest nihilism"—is defended by Peter van Inwagen (1981, 1990), among others.[20] Like the extreme nihilist, the modest nihilist accepts the existence of mereological simples and denies the existence of (most) composite objects. The modesty emerges from van Inwagen's answer to what he calls "the special composition question" (1990, ch. 2). The special composition question asks, "when is it the case that there exists an object y such that the xs compose y?" The answer, according to van Inwagen, is "if and only if the activity of the xs constitutes a life" (1990, p. 82). For the modest nihilist, in other words, the only composite objects that exist are living organisms.

Van Inwagen's argument for this position relies on his *rejection* of what he calls the "doctrine of arbitrary undetached parts":

(DAUP) For every material object M, if R is the region of space occupied by M at time t, and if sub-R is *any* occupiable sub-region of R *whatever*, there exists a material object that occupies the region sub-R at t. (van Inwagen, 1981, p. 123)

In essence, DAUP claims that for any given sub-region of an area occupied by a material object, a smaller object exists that occupies just that sub-region. But according to van Inwagen, if DAUP were true, then prior to the accident not only does Tibbles exist, so too does Tib. Assuming it is possible for a cat to survive the loss of his tail, the accident causes Tibbles to become one and the same thing as Tib. But since two things cannot become one thing, *either* a cat cannot survive the loss of its tail *or* Tib did not exist in the first place. Faced with this choice, van Inwagen contends, clearly it is the commitment to the existence of Tib that should be abandoned. And because this commitment followed only from our provisional acceptance of DAUP, it must be that DAUP is false.

In sum, then, the problem of material constitution simply does not arise for the modest nihilist. Inanimate composite objects do not exist, so that rules out Statue and Lump (and with them any need to explain their relationship). Living organisms like Tibbles do exist, but arbitrary undetached parts like Tib do not, so again no problem arises.[21]

Both forms of nihilism—extreme and modest—have generated vast literatures and spirited debates. They have also been subjected to a variety of criticisms, not least what David Lewis (in a different context) once termed "incredulous stares" (Lewis, 1973, p. 86). "Surely," this stare would say if it could speak, "it is just delusional—a philosopher's fantasy—to deny the existence of something as patently real as Statue." In its most forceful form, this incredulity may reflect a Moorean objection of the form, "any argument whose conclusion denies the existence of ordinary objects must rely on premises which are less plausible than the rejection of the conclusion itself."

Modest nihilists like Trenton Merricks and van Inwagen have tried to answer this objection by offering paraphrases of existential claims and commitments concerning everyday objects.[22] Roughly, the idea here is that, even though nihilists reject the existence of statues and tables per se, the truth-conditions for a proposition like "there is a statue over there" are the same as they are for "there are mereological simples arranged table-wise over there." While this paraphrastic strategy allows us to retain our ordinary ways of talking, such talk is loose and imprecise at best. At worst, some critics have charged, these paraphrases do not blunt the Moorean charge after all.[23]

Revising the logic of identity

In the clay statue case, we noted that Statue and Lump differ with respect to various types of properties: temporal properties, modal properties, kind properties, and so on. We then inferred from these differences that Statue could not be identical with Lump. Likewise in the case of Tibbles the cat, we granted that, prior to the accident, "Tibbles" and "Tib" referred to nonidentical objects on the grounds that Tibbles and Tib differ in their weight, number of appendages, and so forth.

The conception of identity at work here is of a relation that is absolute, permanent, and necessary. And the principle that licenses an inference from a difference in properties to numerical nonidentity is Leibniz's Law (sometimes referred to as "the indiscernibility of identicals"). Leibniz's Law describes a kind of constraint on the identity relation: *identical individuals cannot differ in any of their properties*. In other words, *it is a necessary condition for two things to be identical that they share all of their properties.* Expressed more carefully still, Leibniz's Law asserts the following:

(LL) For all x and y, if x is identical with y, then x and y share all of the same properties.[24]

If LL were false, then the inferences from property differences to nonidentity would not go through.

According to one broad line of thought, the problem of material constitution is not a problem about material objects per se—clay statues, tailless cats, and the like. Rather, the apparent problem arises from a misunderstanding of the logic of identity. On this view, instead of seeing the problem of material constitution as the unavoidable consequence of LL's application to these cases, it is the slavish adherence to LL and/or its attendant conception of identity that should be abandoned. As with many philosophical problems, the question here is what should be held fixed, and those who advocate revising the logic of identity submit that if the application of LL results in the conclusion that Statue and Lump are nonidentical, then so much the worse for LL and the conception of identity on which it relies. What should be inferred from the fact that Statue and Lump do not share all of their properties, in other words, is *not* that Statue and Lump are nonidentical. Rather, since Statue and Lump *are* identical (in some sense yet to be specified), it must be LL that is mistaken (for reasons yet to be explained). Seen in this way, the burden facing these revisionary logicians is the justification of their rejection of LL and the explanation of their alternative conception of the identity relation. According to the three most notable strategies for meeting this burden, identity (a) can be a contingent relation, (b) is never absolute but always relative to a kind, or (c) can be a temporary relation. We will consider each view in turn.

Contingent identity

In defending the contingency of identity, Gibbard (1975) advances the following claim:

(CI) $(x = y)$ & $\lozenge$ $[(x \text{ exists } \& y \text{ exists}) \& x \neq y]$.

In other words, even if x and y are identical, it is possible that they might not be. What the alleged nonnecessity of identity has to do with LL becomes apparent once we register that each and every thing is necessarily identical with itself: self-identity is a property that everything necessarily instantiates. Conjoined with LL, then, *x*'s instantiation of the property *being necessarily identical with x* generates the result that *x* is identical with *y* just in case *x* has the property of being necessarily identical with *y* and *y* has the property of being necessarily identical with *x*. Consequently, if LL is true, then it seems that CI must be false. Put the other way round, if Gibbard is correct that the identity relation is not necessary but contingent, then this would seem to justify the rejection of LL.

Gibbard's overarching aim is to demonstrate how Saul Kripke's (1971, 1980) attacks on the contingency of identity, while largely successful, nevertheless fail to dispense with all contingent identities. In making this case, there emerges in Gibbard's discussion an alternative to Kripke's theory of proper names as rigid designators (very roughly, the view that proper names refer to the same things even in contexts that express possibility and necessity). So if CI is true, then its implications extend well beyond the problem of material constitution. Nevertheless, Gibbard's case for CI turns crucially on an example involving material constitution, and this case has subsequently influenced debates concerning not only the problem of constitution in particular, but also the logic of identity and the semantics of proper names in general.

In Gibbard's example—a twist on the standard clay statue case—a sculptor's statue of the infant Goliath is prepared in two pieces: a top part (above the waist) and a bottom part (below the waist). Once the two halves have been completed independently, the sculptor sticks them together, simultaneously bringing into existence both a new piece of clay and a new statue. To the statue thus created the sculptor gives the name "Goliath," and to the new lump of clay she gives the name "Lumpl." Afterwards, the statue is smashed, simultaneously annihilating Goliath and Lumpl both. Unlike our original clay statue case, then, in the Lumpl and Goliath example, the statue and the piece of clay persist during exactly the same window of time. Describing this example, Gibbard insists,

> the statue and the piece of clay are identical. They began at the same time, and on any usual account, they had the same shape, location, color, and so forth at each instant in their history; everything that happened to one happened to the other; and the act that destroyed the one destroyed the other. If the statue is an entity over and above the piece of clay in that shape, then statues seem to take on a ghostly air. (Gibbard, 1975, p. 191)

But, Gibbard continues, if

> the statue and the piece of clay are the same thing, then their identity is contingent. . . . For suppose I had brought Lumpl into existence as Goliath, just as I actually did, but before the clay had a chance to dry, I squashed it into a ball.

At that point . . . the statue Goliath would have ceased to exist, but the piece of clay Lumpl would still exist in a new shape. Hence Lumpl would not be Goliath, even though both existed. (Gibbard, 1975, p. 191)

In this way, Gibbard concludes, the example of Lumpl and Goliath gives us a prima facie plausible instance of CI.

Of course, constitutionalists and others will object that, although they share all of their intrinsic, relational, and temporal properties, Lumpl and Goliath nevertheless differ in their modal properties (*being able to survive squashing* and *being unable to survive squashing*, respectively) and that these modal properties, in turn, ground Lumpl's and Goliath's different sortal properties (*being a lump of clay* and *being a statue*, respectively). Gibbard's reply is that, contrary to our ordinary ways of thinking and speaking, objects do not instantiate modal properties like those that allegedly distinguish Lumpl from Goliath. This is a convenient turn in Gibbard's argument, since the property of *being necessarily self-identical* is also a modal property. If objects lack even this property, then CI does not violate LL after all.

One's satisfaction with Gibbard's defense of contingent identity will depend on whether one accepts his alternative construal of our attributions of modal properties to material objects and ultimately his non-Kripkean theory of how proper names function in modal contexts. Very roughly, on Gibbard's view, a proper name cannot refer to an object *simpliciter*; a proper name refers only to an object considered under a sortal concept. In this way, "Goliath" and "Lumpl" each refer to the same thing but in different ways: "Goliath" to the object considered as a statue, "Lumpl" to the same object considered as a lump of clay. The attribution of modal properties to the referents of proper names, then, proceeds only via the sortal concepts under which those referents are considered. Thus, the claim "Lumpl but not Goliath is able to survive squashing" neither differentiates two objects (one of which can, the other of which cannot, survive squashing) nor attributes to one object a property impossible to instantiate (viz. *being both able and unable to survive squashing*). Indeed, on Gibbard's view, nothing per se instantiates or fails to instantiate the property *being able to survive squashing*; there are only sortal concepts under which a thing may be considered that make the attribution of this property true or false. Ultimately, then, it would seem that the prospects for CI depend on the appeal of Gibbard's account of how proper names function in modal contexts. And, though certainly not all, many metaphysicians have been reluctant to abandon their commitment to the view that modal properties are instantiated by material objects themselves.

Temporary identity

The second strategy relies on a distinction between different senses of "numerical identity." The first sense—what we can call "strict" numerical identity—is the equivalence relation depicted in LL and other standard characterizations of numerical identity. On this strict understanding, it is true that Statue and Lump are nonidentical. But there is another sense of numerical identity that we can call "temporary" identity, according to which x and y can be identical at one time and nonidentical at another time. Indeed, on this view, x and y cannot coincide at a time without being (temporarily) identical at that time. Thus we can say, for instance, that after its tail is removed, Tibbles and Tib are temporarily identical despite being strictly nonidentical. Likewise, though strictly non-identical, Statue and Lump are nevertheless temporarily identical while they occupy exactly the same space.

There is something appealing about the idea of temporary identity. When first confronted with the clay statue case, for instance, one might well be tempted to respond, "But why should we insist on the nonidentity of Statue and Lump *in the afternoon* simply because of what will happen to them *later in the evening?*" (Sider, 2001, p. 166). But while it nicely captures this intuitive response, the temporary identity view has attracted few adherents besides its two principal exponents, André Gallois (1998) and George Myro (1986). The objections voiced against Gallois's more recent presentation have been fairly technical in character—involving competing formulations of LL, the debate between three-dimensionalists and four-dimensionalists, and the debate between A-theorists and B-theorists about time.[25]

Relative identity

A third approach is associated principally with the work of Peter Geach.[26] Geach and fellow advocates of "relative identity" reject LL because they deny that there is any such thing as absolute identity. On this view, identity is not the bare relation reflected in "$x = y$"; such assertions are incomplete on this view. Rather, identity is always relative to a sortal kind concept (e.g., *artwork, cat*), as reflected in such claims as "x is the same F as y" ($x =_F y$) and "x is not the same G as y" ($\sim[x =_G y]$), where "F" and "G" serve as placeholders for predicates denoting sortal kind concepts. Indeed, the possible truth of the conjunction of these two claims represents the hallmark thesis of the relative identity view, viz.

(RI) ◊ (x and y are the same F but different Gs),

where "same *F*" and "same *G*" reflect relative identity relations and where "*x* and *y* are different *Gs*" is understood to mean that "*x* and *y* are *Gs* but *x* and *y* are not the same *G*."

If the relative identity thesis is correct, then the traditional puzzles of material constitution are inaccurately formulated. From a relativist perspective, it makes sense neither to affirm nor to deny flatly that, say, Statue is identical with Lump, for there is no such relation as identity *simpliciter* or nonidentity *simpliciter*. The nonidentity *simpliciter* of Statue and Lump cannot be inferred merely from the fact that they differ in various respects: though not the same piece of clay as Lump, Statue is nevertheless identical with Lump relative to the sortal concept *artwork*. Likewise for Tibbles and Tib, who, despite their different histories (one once had a tail, the other did not), are nevertheless one and the same cat: though different individuals, Tibbles and Tib are the same cat.

But despite the expansive literature it has generated, relativism about identity (like the temporary identity view) has gained little currency either as an account of identity in general or as a solution to the problem of material constitution in particular.[27] Most of the resistance to this view's application to the problem of material constitution, however, is grounded in alternative theories of the same problem. For instance, since the relativist solution ("different individuals but same cat") does not apply unless Tibbles and Tib exist, the modest nihilist's rejection of DAUP—and with it the existence of such things as tail-complements—amounts to an indirect rejection of relative identity. Likewise for the dominant kinds theorist, who, without denying Tib's existence, nevertheless denies that Tib survives the accident. In addition, Wiggins (1980, 2001)—Geach's most strident critic over the years—denies that Tibbles and Tib could be the same cat, since he denies that Tib is a cat at all (2001, pp. 173–5).

Future research

Future research regarding the problem of material constitution is needed in at least three areas. First, despite the fairly entrenched positions surveyed here, philosophers are still uncovering previously unexplored wrinkles of the problem of material constitution. For instance, in a recent article, Laurie Paul (2010) locates and develops three new puzzles at the intersection of the problems of material constitution and mereological composition. A second area where further research may be needed concerns how theories of material constitution are extended to particular cases. In weighing which theory best accounts for the clay statue case, for instance, discussions have generally assumed a top-down character—the assumption being that the conclusions drawn about Statue's relation to Lump will apply (*mutatis mutandis*) to similar examples of art objects. It may be, however, that examples (or types of examples) are *sui generis,* such that the analysis of the concept *work of art* as it applies in the case of a traditional, representative clay statue does not extend to applications of the same concept in, say, experimental, nonrepresentative works of installation art.[28] Finally, and not unrelated, the apparent intractability of many metaphysical problems— including the problem of material constitution—has philosophers in a reflective mood about the business and methods of metaphysics itself. Further work at the level of meta-metaphysics is needed to evaluate the status of the debate over material constitution (see "Research Problems and Methods" in this volume). Is it, for instance, merely a verbal dispute? Can it ever be resolved? If so, what sort of argument or piece of evidence do we lack? And if not, why not?[29]

Notes

1　This is Michael Rea's informal gloss (1997, p. xxi). In fact, as he has demonstrated (Rea, 1995, pp. 526–8), the problem of material constitution can be characterized more formally than this, as the product of a set of individually plausible and yet jointly incompatible assumptions. Thus construed, any solution to the problem will involve the rejection of at least one of these assumptions. While informal, the current discussion is intended to be consistent with this formal presentation.

2　While the Ship of Theseus example is widely known and the Lumpl and Goliath case will be discussed later (see "Revising the Logic of Identity"), the "paradox of increase" is perhaps less familiar. In this connection, see Chisholm (1976, pp. 157ff.) and Olson (2006).

3　See Rea (1997, pp. xv–xx) for a helpful overview of the provenance of these puzzles.

4　For a defense of the claim that it is impossible for two objects of the same kind to occupy the same place at the same time, see Wiggins (1968).

5　This example—sometimes called the "body-minus argument"—was introduced in the contemporary literature by Wiggins (1968), but the puzzle is an ancient one. Chrysippus raised the same questions with an analogous case involving a human being named "Dion" and his right-foot-complement named "Theon." A sample of recent discussions of the Dion and Theon puzzle includes Burke (1994a), McGrath (2005), and Olson (1995, 1996).

6 The most notable account not discussed here involves four-dimensionalism, according to which material objects are not wholly present at every moment at which they exist. Rather, by consisting of earlier and later temporal parts, objects are temporally as well as spatially extended. In the jargon of this literature, material objects do not endure through time; they *perdure*. Those who advocate four-dimensionalism include Lewis (1976), Quine (1963), and Sider (2001). Because four-dimensionalism represents an ontological framework whose impetus and challenges extend far beyond its application to the particular problem of material constitution, I have elected to set aside this view here and to operate (without defense and tacitly) within the standard three-dimensionalist framework, according to which objects are wholly present at every moment they exist. Readers interested in four-dimensionalism in general are encouraged to consult the chapter by Nick Effingham in this volume ("Endurantism and Perdurantism"). Readers interested in the application of the four-dimensionalist framework to the problem of material constitution in particular should see especially Sider (2001, ch. 5).

7 The name "the Identity Assumption" is due to Rea (1997, p. xxiii). Wiggins (1968) adds the further qualification that being of different kinds is a necessary condition of material colocation. He rejects the possibility that nonidentical things of the same kind can be colocated. Also, and while the meaning of "compose" is contentious, in this context, "the *p*s compose *x*" should be understood as the claim "the *p*s are all parts of *x*, no two of the *p*s overlap, and every part of *x* overlaps at least one of the *p*s" (likewise *mutatis mutandis* for "the *p*s compose *y*"); see van Inwagen (1990, pp. 28ff.).

8 As the standard response to the problem of material constitution, this view has many defenders. Among the most notable are Baker (1997, 2000, 2007), Doepke (1982), Fine (2003), Johnston (1992), Lowe (1989, 1995), Thomson (1983), and Wiggins (1967, 1968, 1980, 2001).

9 While this is an intuitive description of the constitution relation, some defenders of this view deny that constitution is asymmetric. On their view, it is the case both that Lump constitutes Statue and that Statue constitutes Lump. (For Paul, the question of how to explain this asymmetry presents a challenge analogous to that posed by the grounding problem [see below]; she calls it "the asymmetry puzzle" (2002, p. 583).) Among constitutionalists there is also some dispute over whether the relation is reflexive—whether, in other words, objects constitute themselves. I shall not engage these intramural disagreements here.

10 An incisive discussion of the constitution relation is given by Wasserman (2004).

11 The grounding problem is variously presented, but see especially Burke (1992), deRosset (2011), Olson (2001), and Zimmerman (1995).

12 ME corresponds to a fundamental set-theoretic axiom according to which two sets are identical just in case they share all of the same members. It differs from IA principally in that IA is temporally quantified.

13 In addition to those discussed here, see especially Doepke (1982), Johnston (1992), and McDaniel (2001).

14 The door to this strategy was opened by Johnston (1992, pp. 92ff.), who pointed out that it is unclear what kinds of parts ME is supposed to concern.

15 In this connection, see also Bennett (2004) and Olson (2007, pp. 65ff.).

16 A similar view (*mutatis mutandis*) about the case of Tibbles is advanced in Burke (1994a). In the interest of simplicity, I shall focus in this section on the application of the dominant kinds view to the clay statue case.

17 In addition to those mentioned here, other critical discussions can be found in Carter (1997), Noonan (1999), Olson (1997), Sider (2001, pp. 161–5), Stone (2002), and Burke (2004).

18 Rea (2000, p. 180) denies sharing the intuition that this is a peculiar way of destroying an object.

19 This wrinkle is often overlooked in presentations of Unger's early work. Sider (2001, p. 187) is one of the few to correct the record. Interesting discussions of Unger's sorites argument and its relation to subsequent debates about vagueness are given in Elder (2000) and Thomasson (2007, ch. 5).

20 Modest nihilism is also defended by (Merricks, 2001), whose view is roughly that if inanimate composites existed, they would be causally redundant; but since causal interactions among inanimate composites are not overdetermined by those objects' proper parts, inanimate composite objects do not exist. In the interest of simplicity, however, I will concentrate here on van Inwagen's line of argumentation.

21 In connection with the case of Tibbles and DAUP, see also Olson (1995) and Parsons (2004).

22 See, for example, Merricks (2001, ch. 7) and van Inwagen (1990, chs 10, 11, and 13).

23 Regarding this last charge, see McGrath (2005).

24 The converse of this principle, "the identity of indiscernibles," holds that it is a *sufficient* condition for the identity of x and y that they share all of the same properties. That is: for all x and y, if x and y share all of the same properties, then x is identical with y.

25 See, for instance, discussions in Hawley (2001, pp. 154–6), Hawthorne (2003, pp. 123–8), and Sider (2001, pp. 165–76).

26 See Geach (1967, 1972, 1980). Related views and relevant discussions can be found in Chandler (1971), Chisholm (1969, 1976), Griffin (1977), Noonan (1980), and Quine (1963). Deutsch (2007) and Noonan (1997) provide especially insightful overviews of the debate concerning relative identity.

27 Regarding relativism's wide-ranging implications for the philosophy of language, philosophical logic and mathematics, see, for instance, Dummett (1981, 1993), Gupta (1980), Hawthorne (2003), Perry (1970), and Wiggins (1980, 2001).

28 One arena where the particularities and nuances of the applied context have received greater respect is the debate over personal identity. See, for instance, Olson (2007, ch. 3), as well as the relevant sections from the chapter by David Hershenov in this volume ("Personal Identity").

29 Many thanks to Eric Olson for helpful comments on an earlier draft of this chapter.

References

Baker, L. R. (1997), "Why constitution is not identity." *Journal of Philosophy,* 94, 599–621.

—(2000), *Persons and Bodies: A Constitution View.* Cambridge: Cambridge University Press.

—(2007), *The Metaphysics of Everyday Life: An Essay in Practical Realism.* Cambridge: Cambridge University Press.

Bennett, K. (2004), "Spatio-temporal coincidence and the grounding problem." *Philosophical Studies,* 118, 339–71.

Burke, M. (1992), "Copper statues and pieces of copper: a challenge to the standard account." *Analysis,* 52, 12–17.

—(1994a), "Dion and Theon: an essentialist solution to an ancient problem." *Journal of Philosophy,* 91, 129–39.

—(1994b), "Preserving the principle of one object to a place: a novel account of the relations among objects, sorts, sortals, and persistence conditions." *Philosophy and Phenomenological Research,* 54, 591–624. Reprinted in Rea (1997), pp. 236–69.

—(2004), "Dion, Theon, and the many-thinkers problem." *Analysis,* 64, 242–50.

Carter, W. R. (1997), "Dion's left foot (and the price of Burkean economy)." *Philosophy and Phenomenological Research,* 57, 317–79.

Chandler, H. (1971), "Constitutivity and identity." *Noûs,* 5, 313–9; reprinted in Rea (1997), pp. 313–19.

Chisholm, R. (1969), "The loose and popular and strict and philosophical senses of identity," in N. Case and R. H. Grim, eds, *Perception and Personal Identity.* Cleveland, OH: Case Western Reserve University Press.

—(1976), *Person and Object: A Metaphysical Study.* La Salle, IL: Open Court.

DeRosset, L. (2011), "What is the grounding problem?" *Philosophical Studies,* 156(2), 173–97.

Deutsch, H. (2007), "Relative identity," in E. Zalta, ed., *Stanford Encyclopedia of Philosophy.* Available at: http://plato.stanford.edu/entries/identity-relative.

Doepke, F. (1982), "Spatially coinciding objects." *Ratio,* 24, 45–60. Reprinted in Rea (1997), 10–24.

Dummett, M. (1981), *The Interpretation of Frege's Philosophy*. Cambridge, MA: Harvard University Press.

—(1993), "Does quantification involve identity?" in *The Seas of Language*. Oxford: Oxford University Press, pp. 308–27.

Elder, C. (2000), "Familiar objects and the sorites of decomposition." *American Philosophical Quarterly*, 37, 79–89.

Fine, K. (2003), "The non-identity of a material thing and its matter." *Mind*, 112, 195–234.

Gallois, A. (1998), *Occasions of Identity*. Oxford: Oxford University Press.

Geach, P. T. (1967), "Identity." *Review of Metaphysics*, 21, 3–12.

—(1972), *Logic Matters*. Oxford: Blackwell.

—(1980), *Reference and Generality* (third edition). Ithaca, NY: Cornell University Press.

Gibbard, A. (1975), "Contingent identity." *Journal of Philosophical Logic*, 4, 187–221. Reprinted in Rea (1997), 93–125.

Griffin, N. (1977), *Relative Identity*. Oxford: Oxford University Press.

Gupta, A. (1980), *The Logic of Common Nouns*. New Haven, CT: Yale University Press.

Hawley, K. (2001), *How Things Persist*. Oxford: Oxford University Press.

Hawthorne, J. (2003), "Identity," in M. Loux and D. Zimmerman, eds, *The Oxford Handbook of Metaphysics*. Oxford: Oxford University Press, pp. 99–130.

Johnston, M. (1992), "Constitution is not identity." *Mind*, 101, 89–105. Reprinted in Rea (1997), pp. 44–62.

Kripke, S. (1971), "Identity and necessity," in M. Munitz, ed., *Identity and Individuation*. New York: New York University Press, pp. 135–64.

—(1980), *Naming and Necessity*. Cambridge, MA: Harvard University Press.

Lewis, D. K. (1973), *Counterfactuals*. Cambridge, MA: Harvard University Press.

—(1976), "Survival and identity," in A. Rorty, ed., *The Identities of Persons*. Berkeley, CA: University of California Press, pp. 17–40.

Lowe, E. J. (1989), *Kinds of Being*. Oxford: Blackwell.

—(1995), "Coinciding objects: in defense of the 'standard account'." *Analysis*, 55, 171–8.

McDaniel, K. (2001), "Tropes and ordinary physical objects." *Philosophical Studies*, 104, 269–90.

McGrath, M. (2005), "No objects, no problem?" *Australasian Journal of Philosophy*, 83, 457–86.

Merricks, T. (2001), *Objects and Persons*. Oxford: Clarendon Press.

Myro, G. (1986), "Time and essence." *Midwest Studies in Philosophy*, 11(1), 331–41.

—(1993), "Constitution is identity." *Mind*, 102, 133–46.

—(1997), "Relative identity," in B. Hale and C. Wright, eds, *A Companion to the Philosophy of Language*. Oxford: Blackwell, pp. 634–52.

Noonan, H. (1999), "Tibbles the cat: reply to burke." *Philosophical Studies*, 95, 215–8.

Olson, E. (1995), "Why I have no hands." *Theoria*, 61, 182–97.

—(1996), "Composition and coincidence." *Pacific Philosophical Quarterly*, 77, 374–403.

—(1996), "Dion's foot." *Journal of Philosophy*, 94, 260–5.

—(2001), "Material coincidence and the indiscernibility problem." *The Philosophical Quarterly*, 51, 337–55.

—(2006), "The paradox of increase." *The Monist*, 89, 390–417.

—(2007), *What Are We? A Study in Personal Ontology*. New York: Oxford University Press.

Parsons, J. (2004), "Dion, Theon, and DAUP." *Pacific Philosophical Quarterly*, 85, 85–91.

Paul, L. A. (2002), "Logical parts." *Noûs*, 36, 578–96.

—(2010), "The puzzles of material constitution." *Philosophy Compass*, 5(7), 579–90.
   Available at: http://philosophy-compass.com

Perry, J. (1970), "The same f." *Philosophical Review*, 79, 181–200.

Quine, W. V. O. (1963), *From a Logical Point of View* (revised second edition).
   Cambridge, MA: Harvard University Press.

Rea, M. (1995), "The problem of material constitution." *Philosophical Review*, 104, 525–52.

—ed. (1997), *Material Constitution: A Reader*. Lanham, MD: Rowman and Littlefield.

—(1998), "Sameness without identity: an Aristotelian solution to the problem of
   material constitution." *Ratio*, 11, 316–28.

—(2000), "Constitution and kind membership." *Philosophical Studies*, 97, 169–93.

Sider, T. (2001), *Four-Dimensionalism: An Ontology of Persistence and Time*. New York:
   Oxford University Press.

Stone, J. (2002), "Why sortal essentialism cannot solve Chrysippus's puzzle." *Analysis*,
   62, 216–23.

Thomasson, A. (2007), *Ordinary Objects*. New York: Oxford University Press.

Thomson, J. J. T. (1983), "Parthood and identity across time." *Journal of Philosophy*, 80,
   201–20. Reprinted in Rea (1997), pp. 25–43.

Unger, P. (1979a), "I do not exist," in G. F. Macdonald, ed., *Perception and Identity:
   Essays Presented to A. J. Ayer with His Replies to Them*. New York: MacMillan,
   pp. 235–51. Reprinted in Rea (1997), pp. 175–90.

—(1979b), "There are no ordinary things." *Synthese*, 41, 117–54.

—(1990), *Identity, Consciousness, and Value*. New York: Oxford University Press.

van Inwagen, P. (1981), "The doctrine of arbitrary undetached parts." *Pacific
   Philosophical Quarterly*, 62, 123–37. Reprinted in Rea (1997), pp. 191–208.

—(1990), *Material Beings*. Ithaca, NY: Cornell University Press.

Wasserman, R. (2002), "The standard objection to the standard account." *Philosophical
   Studies*, 111, 197–216.

—(2004), "The constitution question." *Noûs*, 38, 693–710.

—(2009), "Material constitution," in E. Zalta, ed., *Stanford Encyclopedia of Philosophy*.
   Available at: http://plato.stanford.edu/entries/material-constitution.

Wiggins, D. (1967), *Identity and Spatio-Temporal Continuity*. Oxford: Blackwell.

—(1968), "On being in the same place at the same time." *Philosophical Review*, 77, 90–5.
   Reprinted in Rea (1997), pp. 3–9.

—(1980), *Sameness and Substance*. Oxford: Blackwell.

—(2001), *Sameness and Substance Renewed*. Cambridge: Cambridge University Press.

Zimmerman, D. (1995), "Theories of masses and problems of constitution."
   Philosophical Review, 104, 53–110.

Endurantism and Perdurantism

Nikk Effingham

Introduction

Terms of art

If you do not know what "perdure" or "endure" mean then do not worry, you're in good company. Even among contemporary metaphysicians, there is a great deal of dissent when agreeing what these terms mean. This chapter does not seek to resolve which is the "correct" definition. Indeed, when it comes to terms of art it is wrong headed to think there is a correct usage (Hawthorne, 2006, p. 85). What it does do is lay out three different ways of understanding what "perdurance" and "endurance" have been taken to mean. The *populationist* says that the difference between the two is over what objects there are. The *dimensionalist* says that the difference is over how many dimensions objects are extended in. Finally, the *occupationalist* thinks the difference concerns how objects are related to regions of spacetime. We'll then turn to the arguments for the populationist versions of the theories before turning to arguments for the dimensionalist and occupationalist portrayals. While I survey fewer arguments in the case of the latter two, this is because many of the arguments for the populationist versions do double duty, for example, an argument for the populationist version of perdurantism can often double as an argument for the dimensionalist version. This isn't surprising, for that these arguments can be shared, and that the positions are very similar, is what has resulted in the confusion over what "perdure" and "endure" mean. Finally, having made clear the different ways to understand the terms, and surveyed the arguments for the various positions, I end with some concluding thoughts and a brief sketch of some more ways of defining the terms.

A rough (and misleading) sketch of persistence

Before we begin, a rough sketch for the beginner is in order. Objects are extended over regions of space and have spatial parts (a car has wheels; my body has a hand; a cup has a handle). Caricature perdurantists think objects are both stretched out in time (i.e., are four-dimensional) and have parts analogous to spatial parts—*temporal* parts. So I have a 1979 temporal part of me, which is all of me from my birth to the end of 1979; a 1980 temporal part of me; a 1981 temporal part of me, etc. Should I live to be a hundred, I would be composed of a hundred such year-long temporal parts. Nor need they be a year-long, for temporal parts can be more fine-grained. If I perdure I have day-long temporal parts, minute-long temporal parts, and even instantaneous temporal parts.

The caricature endurantist denies just that. We are three-dimensional objects that *move* through time rather than simply occupying it in a way analogous to how spatially extended objects occupy the regions that they do. Objects have no temporal parts, instead being *wholly present* at every instant at which they exist (i.e., whenever you find the object you find the entire object and *all* of its parts).

This traditional view of endurance/perdurance is crude at best, and at worst portions have been thought to be unintelligible gibberish. For instance, everyday mereological relations are temporally relativized (my car has a wheel *at a certain time*, I have my hand as a part *right now*, etc.). But the caricature perdurantist says that there is an *atemporal* parthood relation, which temporal parts stand in to their respective wholes (so I just have my temporal parts as parts *simpliciter*, with no temporal qualification). Not everyone understands this "atemporal parthood," nor does everyone understand what a temporal part is meant to be. So caricature perdurantists have a problem even making themselves understood (Chisholm, 1976, p. 143; Geach, 1972, p. 311; van Inwagen, 1981, p. 133).

Similar problems plague the endurantist. If perduring objects do not "move" through time whereas endurers do,[1] then we might wonder what this "moving" amounts to (Gilmore, 2006, pp. 205–6; Sider, 2001, p. 54). Or we might take issue with understanding "wholly present," fearing that we cannot define that term such that everyday objects meet it, while simultaneously ensuring that perduring objects do not (Carrara, 2005; Crisp and Smith, 2005; Hughes, 2005; Sider, 2001, pp. 63–8). That is why the rough sketch of persistence has been clarified over the years, albeit in different, competing ways.

Temporal parts

One such clarified term is "temporal part."[2] The most popular definition currently used is Ted Sider's.[3] Taking seriously the fear that "atemporal parthood" might be unintelligible, Sider gives his definition in terms of temporally relativized mereology (Sider, 2001, pp. 53–62):

> x is a temporal part of y during interval $T =_{df}$ (i) x is a part of y at every moment during T; (ii) x exists during, but only during, T; and (iii) for any sub-interval t of T, x overlaps every part of y at t.

So an instantaneous temporal part, the most commonly discussed type of temporal part, would be a temporal part of something that existed at but one instant. Given the definition uses the readily intelligible relations of temporally relativized mereology, everyone should admit that they can understand what it means. Further, as the section "Against Perdurantism$_p$" explains, everyone can say the existence of such things is contentious, therefore worthy of a rigorous philosophical examination. For the rest of this chapter I'll stick to using Sider's definition, concentrating instead on the variation between the definitions of the theories of persistence.[4]

Populationism

Populationist definitions

The most popular implicit understanding of perdurantism is as a commitment to things having temporal parts.[5] Endurantism, then, would be the denial that things have temporal parts.[6] Call this position populationism, and let the populationist definitions be:

> *Perdurantism$_p$*: All objects have an instantaneous temporal part at every instant that they exist at.
> *Endurantism$_p$*: Perdurantism$_p$ is false.[7]

Populationists think the persistence debate concerns what material objects exist, i.e. what the population of the world is. Both endurantist$_p$ and perdurantist$_p$ may agree that there are, say, cars, but they disagree over whether there are *in addition* lots of instantaneous temporal parts of cars. The vast bulk of the extant arguments for (or against) perdurantism concentrate on a populationist reading, offering arguments for (or against) the existence of such instantaneous temporal parts.

Against perdurantism$_p$

The arguments for perdurantism dwarf the arguments for endurantism. Most endurantists instead rest content with believing perdurantism to be counterintuitive, offering no benefits to outweigh such counterintuitions, and thus believing it is false and endurantism is true. Their first claim, that perdurantism is counterintuitive, proves tricky if we are dimensionalists or occupationalists. Both of those positions make perdurantism a thesis concerning the spacetime regions at which an object is exactly located. But, given that the notion of spacetime is a technical one, it would be tricky to say we have strong intuitions about the location of objects within it.

The counterintuitiveness of endurantism is, however, more straightforward given populationism. For perdurantists$_p$ there are scads of extra objects in the universe. God could never *just* create a tree in the quad; God must create a tree *plus* an infinite number of instantaneous temporal parts. Such objects, says the endurantist$_p$, don't exist according to our folk ontological beliefs; either they say that we don't perceive such temporal parts when we observe objects persisting (Gibson and Pooley, 2006, p. 158) or that it just seems weird that an infinite number of instantaneous objects keep appearing *ex nihilo* and then vanishing again (Sider, 2001, pp. 216–18; Thomson, 1983, p. 213). So there appears to be a prima facie case for them being strange entities.[8] Populationism, then, gives us a good reason for thinking that perdurantism$_p$ comes with costs (and endurantism$_p$ is the default option). Not that these are the only costs one might think perdurantism$_p$ incurs, but it will suffice for now to fixate on this objection.[9] Note that being the default option doesn't mean endurantism$_p$ is true—a lot of good philosophy is, after all, about demonstrating that such default positions are false. Perdurantism$_p$ might provide excellent theoretical benefits to outweigh these costs, or there might be some other compelling line of reasoning to think perduranitsm$_p$ is true. Hence the endurantist$_p$'s commonly accepted obligation to undermine such arguments and defray such alleged benefits of perdurantism$_p$. With that in mind, let's turn to motivations perdurantists$_p$ advance in favor of their enterprise.

The analogy with space

The exposition from the section "A Rough (and Misleading) Sketch of Persistence" relied upon analogies with space to explain the position of the caricature perdurantist. Not only is this an illustrative device, but this supposed analogy between space and time has also been a motivation for supporting perdurantism$_p$ (Hofweber, 2009, pp. 305–6; Rea, 1998; Sider, 2001, pp. 87–92; Taylor, 1955, p. 600; Williams, 1951, p. 463). The argument has two premises.

1. If an object exactly occupies (spatial) region R then, for every sub-region of R, the object has a part that exactly occupies that sub-region.
2. Space and time are analogous, in particular the temporal analogue of premise one is true.

So we get this conclusion.

> ∴ *Doctrine of Arbitrary Temporal Parts (DATP)*: If x persists through interval T then x has a temporal part that exists during T.[10]

DATP clearly entails that things have temporal parts, and so we have an argument for perdurantism$_p$. Both premises come under fire. The first premise has problems if *extended simples* can exist, that is, objects that exactly occupy an extended region but have no proper parts. Several subscribe to this possibility (Bigelow, 1995, pp. 21–7; Markosian, 1998; McDaniel, 2007; Simons, 2004). The second premise comes under pressure because of the fear that space and time *aren't* analogous. For instance, that time is disanalogous from space in the sense that things have spatial, but not temporal, parts is *exactly* what the endurantist$_p$ endorses in the first place. So the perdurantist$_p$ has quite a task to motivate the analogy in a way that will be compelling to the unbelieving endurantist$_p$. Nor need the endurantist$_p$ rely solely on a brute intuition that space and time are disanalogous in that manner. They might offer positive reasons for thinking there is such a disanalogy, say by endorsing presentism (the thesis that only the present exists). In that case, the allegation goes, objects could not be extended in time, for there are no times *to be extended over*. Similarly, the endurantist$_p$ might say that they cannot have temporal parts at other times, because nothing exists at other times (so the temporal parts wouldn't exist either).[11]

Properties: The semantic issues

Perdurantism was traditionally part of a package deal, alongside eternalism (the thesis that *every* time exists) and the B-theory of time. B-theory holds that the world is fundamentally tenseless (i.e., the only fundamental temporal relations are tenseless relations such as "earlier than," "later than" and "simultaneous with"). It is to be contrasted with A-theory: that the fundamental temporal properties are tensed (e.g., "is past," "is present," and "is future"). Rightly or wrongly, the debate over which theory is true historically centered on whether tensed statements could be translated into tenseless statements without loss of meaning. Many (again, rightly or wrongly) have taken the answer to this debate about meaning to inform the metaphysical debate about tense: if such translations *can* be offered then the world is fundamentally tenseless, and if not then it is fundamentally tensed.[12]

As part of this enterprise, perdurantism gets conscripted (Parsons, 2005, p. 1; Quine, 1960, pp. 170–6). The general analysis is:

> *Perdurantist Analysis of Temporary Predication (PATP)*: x is F at $t =_{df} x$'s instantaneous temporal part at t is F.

So

> "Right now, the cup of coffee is hot"

can be translated as

> "There is a time t; t is simultaneous with this utterance; and the instantaneous temporal part of the cup of coffee at t is hot."

Clearly PATP entails perdurantism$_p$. However, it looks like PATP is unnecessary to get the desired tenseless translations (Butterfield, 1985; Gallois, 1998, pp. 264–5; Sider, 2001, pp. 76–8). We could just have had

> "There is a time t; t is simultaneous with this utterance; and the cup of coffee is hot at t."

There are no fundamentally *tensed* predicates involved in that sentence either, but also no mention of temporal parts. So the B-theorist can do without perdurantism$_p$ and this line of argument appears to be fruitless.[13] Nonetheless, it is worth mentioning, as many perdurantists$_p$ believe that, once you accept perdurantism$_p$, you should endorse PATP anyhow.

Properties: Sortals and stage theory

This common endorsement of PATP causes further problems. For instance, given mereological universalism (the thesis that for any ys the ys compose a further object) there will be an object composed of all of the temporal parts of Pavarotti until New Year's Eve 1999, as well as the temporal parts of some turnip from that point forth. That weird, gerrymandered object is such that, given PATP, it is (at some time) a tenor and (at another, later, time) a turnip. But no turnip has ever been a famous tenor, so PATP must be false (Braddon-Mitchell and Miller, 2006; Parsons, 2005; Varzi, 2003).[14]

There are a few ways to rescue PATP. One rejoinder is to say that PATP doesn't apply to sortal predicates. Instead, an object falls under a given sortal at a given time *not* by having a temporal part at that time that falls under it, but by the object simply falling under the sortal atemporally. So my temporal parts aren't human, although the object *composed* of my temporal parts (i.e., me) is a human *simpliciter*. It's true that I am a human *at a given time* solely because I am human simpliciter, *pace* PATP. So we can avoid the problem if we build exceptions for sortal predicates into PATP.

However this does give rise to a new problem. In cases of fission, where one cell splits into two, the perdurantist$_p$ will say that before fission occurs the two post-fission cells are sharing temporal parts at those pre-fission times. But if the cells are the four-dimensional objects composed out of the temporal parts then, before fission takes place, there are *two* cells present. Compare to a spatial analogy. Imagine two conjoined twins. At the location where they are conjoined (say, where their conjoined arms are located) there are two people present there. Similarly, when the cells are sharing temporal parts before fission takes place, *both* of them are present. Yet it seems wrong to think that two cells exist before fission takes place, or that the number of objects present at any given time depends on what goes on in the future (for if fission did not occur, there would be but one cell).[15]

It's at this juncture that perdurantism breeds a cousin: stage theory (sometimes called "exdurantism") (Hawley, 2001; Sider, 2001). Stage theorists accept the ontology that perdurantists$_p$ believe in, but identify everyday things with the instantaneous objects, *not* the four-dimensional wholes composed out of them. If everyday objects are the instantaneous things then, in the pre-fission scenario, we are looking at just the one instantaneous thing (which is a cell). Ergo, unlike before, we are looking at just one cell, not two. That's the upside; the downside is that objects now seem to exist only for an instant, which isn't right at all. Here stage theorists make a move analogous to David Lewis's move for talking about objects existing at different possible worlds (Lewis, 1986, pp. 192–263). For Lewis, things only exist at one possible world. But facts about what *could* be the case are true in virtue of those things having (numerically distinct) *counterparts* at other worlds. Similarly, the stage theorist says that while the cell might not exist at other times, it *did* or *will* exist at other times in virtue of standing in counterpart relations to (numerically distinct) cells that exist at those times.

Just as there are problems with defining perdurantism and endurantism, there are problems with defining stage theory. For instance, Katherine Hawley sets up the difference as whether or not the sortal terms apply to the temporal parts (in which case stage theory is true), or to those things composed of them (in which case, standard perdurantism is true). But some perdurantists *do* think the sortal terms apply to the parts (Noonan, 1985; Wasserman, 2003b) and instead opt for some other way out of the problems posed above. So we might instead define stage theory in terms of what it is in virtue of which *de re* temporal predications are made: the perdurantist says it is in virtue of having an instantaneous temporal part at *t* that an object was/will be F at *t*, whereas the stage theorist says it is in virtue of being counterpart-related to an F-thing that exists at *t*.[16] Whatever the merits of stage theory, I shall press on only with standard perdurantism in mind. The reader will be left to her own devices to determine what stage theorists should say about issues raised in the rest of this chapter.

Properties: The metaphysical issues

In addition to the semantic issues concerning properties, there are also metaphysical concerns. There are a few problems in this area (see Wasserman, 2006) but here I'll concentrate just on the problem of temporary intrinsics. Imagine there is a man who is sitting in the morning, while in the afternoon he is standing. So he is sitting, and he is standing—which is a contradiction (Lewis, 1986, pp. 202–4). The challenge then is to give an explanation which dissolves the alleged contradiction.[17] Not everyone takes this challenge seriously, saying it can be solved trivially by merely talking about the man sitting *at one time* and standing *at a totally different time* (Hofweber, 2009; Rychter, 2009).[18] I don't think we should underplay such moves, but as more ink has been spilt on the side of those who do take the problem seriously, I shall press on.

The perdurantist$_p$ endorses a metaphysical analogue of PATP: that an object is F at a certain time in virtue of its instantaneous temporal part at that time being F. So the man sits at one time in virtue of his temporal part at that time sitting, and stands at another time in virtue of his temporal part, at a totally different time, standing. There is no contradiction, any more than there is with one spatial part of me being one way (e.g., my hand having five fingers) and another part being another way (e.g., my head *not* having five fingers). The problem, then, is avoided—although not everyone is happy with this. Some worry that now the objects themselves aren't sitting or standing, only *parts* of them are (Olson, 2007, pp. 102–6 and 122–5; Sider, 2001, pp. 92–8); others are worried that there are similar problems of change that *can't* be answered using temporal parts (Egan, 2004).

Those endurantists[p] who take the problem seriously have a variety of options. One standard move is to say that properties like *sitting* and *standing* are in fact relations (Mellor, 1981; van Inwagen, 1990b). So the man is "sitting related" to one time, and "standing related" to a different time. This is no more a contradiction than, say, the fact that I stand in the "brother of" relation to one man, but not to another. But, so goes one reading of Lewis's rejection of this option, if we know anything we know that properties like *sitting* aren't relations. An alternative reading of Lewis's problem is that this makes sitting, an intrinsic property, into something extrinsic, for it now depends on the existence of other things (i.e., times). Exactly what Lewis's problem was, and whether it does indeed turn out to be problematic, is still an open question (Wasserman, 2003a).[19]

There are alternatives to this relationist approach. We could take properties to be time-indexed (so there is the property of *sitting-at-10am-on-June-16th-2010* rather than *sitting*). Alternatively, just as there are different ways to scream—for example, loudly or ferociously—we might say that there are different "timely" ways to *instantiate* a property. We can instantiate *sitting* in a "10am-ly" way and *standing* in a "11am-ly" way (Haslanger, 1989; Johnston, 1987; Rea, 1998, pp. 240–6). Or there are even stranger variations where we think *objects* are relations between times and properties (or *times* are relations between properties and objects) (MacBride, 2001). These approaches are, for better or worse, riffs on the relationist approach, but there are some quite different moves. We might endorse presentism, for as the present moment moves on the state of affairs of the man sitting ceases to exist, and we then have an explanation of why the proposition that he sits and the proposition that he stands are not both true (Fiocco, 2010; Hinchcliff, 1996; Merricks, 1994; Zimmerman, 1998). Or we might think there are "distributional properties" (Parsons, 2004), or resolve it by invoking momentary tropes (Ehring, 1997). In each case, of course, the perdurantist[p] will make the same move as above, accusing the endurantist[p] of having mangled our commonsense conception of properties in the process, thus incurring a cost that perdurantism[p] manages to avoid (and the endurantist[p] will demur, or alternatively argue that the costs are, on reflection, worth it).[20]

Humean supervenience

Lewis has another argument for perdurantism$_p$ (Lewis, 1983, pp. 76–7; see also Noonan, 2001). It relies on the following principles:

> *Supervenience Thesis*: If two worlds are identical with regards to all local matters of fact then they are identical with regards to all other qualities.[21]

> *Recombination Thesis*: If *x* happens intrinsically at one region and *y* happens intrinsically at another distinct region (where "happens intrinsically" means that its happening doesn't depend upon things that take place outside the region) then there are worlds at which any combination of *x* and *y* occur.

Lewis then says that it is possible for there to exist objects which are qualitatively identical to what would be my temporal part at this instant if I had one. That is, given I exist at *t* and have certain intrinsic properties at *t*, it's possible for there to be someone who pops into existence at *t* and who has exactly the same intrinsic properties I have at *t*, yet exists for but one instant. This possibility applies *mutatis mutandis* to everyone and everything, and given the recombination thesis there is therefore a world, *w*, at which, for every instant at that world, there exist qualitative duplicates of what would be the instantaneous temporal parts of things at this world were such things to exist. Intuitively, even the endurantist can agree with that: there *could* be a world which contained scads of objects being brought into existence and then instantly annihilated by some evil demon, where each object was qualitatively identical to an object at the actual world at the corresponding time at which it existed. But *w* would be identical to our world with regards to the *local* matters of fact, and so given the Supervenience Thesis the actual world and *w* are qualitatively identical in all regards. So temporal parts actually exist.

Pressure has been applied to the principle of supervenience (Wasserman et al. 2004, pp. 309–17), as well as its application, with worries that there is no non-question begging reason to believe that a world of perdurers is qualitatively locally identical to a world of endurers (Gallois, 1998, pp. 265–7; Haslanger, 1994; Rea, 1998, pp. 246–51). The principle of recombination has also come under fire (Noonan, 2003; Wasserman et al. 2004, pp. 303–9), on the understanding that the endurantist is unlikely to endorse it.

Cultural prejudice

The Trobriand islands are full of yams, although the Trobriander people do not believe yams exist. Instead they believe "taytu" and "yowanna" exist. A "taytu" corresponds to what we think of as an unripened yam, whereas a "yowanna" corresponds to what we think of as a ripened yam (Lee, 1950, p. 91). However, where we think a ripened yam is numerically identical to some unripened yam, the Trobriander people believe that the taytu and yowanna are numerically distinct. So our cultures disagree over what objects exist (we say yams do, they say they don't; we say taytu and yowanna don't exist, they say they do).

If there's no principled method to discover which culture is correct, we have a problem, and at first blush that seems to be the case. If we turn to physics, there is no magical "yam particle" which stays with the yam throughout the ripening process, nor some "taytu particle" that departs. If we turn to botany, then while botanists may talk about yams, that's only because they're influenced by Western culture. Had things played out differently and it had been the Trobriander people running universities across the world, we would instead be looking askance at any botanist who didn't know what a taytu or a yowanna was. If this thinking is right then it'd be sheer prejudice to think one culture is correct and the other incorrect. Thus we should—so runs the argument from cultural prejudice—believe that either both are right or both are wrong.

The yam case is just a placeholder for all kinds of examples along these lines.[22] We can imagine more exotic cultures that thought that, for any filled spacetime region, there was an object that exactly occupied that region. The same reasoning holds for these exotic cultures. So either every filled spacetime region is exactly occupied by an object, or none are. As it's weird to say none are so occupied (how can a spacetime region be *filled* if there is no object there to fill it?), we should say they all are. If every filled spacetime region contains an object, clearly any sub-region an object occupies must contain an object, which entails DATP, and *a fortiori* perdurantism$_p$.[23]

Vagueness

Sider (2001, pp. 120–39; 2008, pp. 257–61) extends Lewis's argument from vagueness for mereological universalism (Lewis, 1986, pp. 212–13) into an argument for perdurantism$_p$.[24] Take the following scenario. We make a teddy bear in a factory, and then feed it into a wood chipper. We take snapshots of the process with a camera that captures a picture every billionth of a nanosecond. In some snapshots it is definitely the case that the teddy bear is intact (e.g., a minute before we pass it through the whirling blades of the chipper) and other snapshots definitely depict cases where the teddy bear has ceased to be (e.g., as all of the fluffy body of the bear has passed through the chipper, leaving only a pile of tatters and stuffing). In between there are cases where it is vague whether the teddy bear has been destroyed or not.

Sider thinks this scenario entails perdurantism$_p$ because he accepts a semantic theory of vagueness: that vagueness is a matter of language, not of the world. For instance, a man might be n centimeters in height, where being n centimeters in height qualifies for being "vaguely tall." On this view, that vagueness is a result of our linguistic community failing to have a consensus that being n centimeters in height makes you tall (although we do have a consensus that, say, a man 120 centimeters in height is definitely not tall whereas someone 187 centimeters in height definitely is). So the sentence being vague is because of facts about language, not the world itself. One motivation for thinking this is that it is somewhat reprehensible to think that the world itself could be vague (when it comes to existence, at least), for the vaguely existing objects would have to hover in some shadowy realm between existence and nonexistence. This is, allegedly, conceptually impossible: existing seems to be the kind of thing that an object either does or does not do—either you're in or you're out.

So if vagueness is semantic, then in those situations where we want to say it's vague whether the teddy bear exists this isn't because there are vague objects, but because it is vague *which* objects our words refer to. Perdurantism$_p$ (combined with mereological universalism) allows us to say just that. Given perdurantism$_p$, each snapshot depicts an instantaneous object that exists at some given time. Given mereological universalism, any set of photos we select depicts a set of instantaneous temporal parts that all belong to some object. At some instant t it is vague whether the teddy bear exists, and this vagueness is a result of our linguistic community never having settled whether "the teddy bear" refers to an object composed of temporal parts that *doesn't* include the instantaneous object depicted in the snapshot taken at t, or whether it does. Both those objects definitely exist (so the *world* isn't vague), but we just haven't settled which object "the teddy bear" refers to (so *language* is the source of vagueness). Thus, says Sider, to save the idea of vagueness being a semantic phenomenon, we must endorse perdurantism$_p$ (plus universalism).

As noted above, the vagueness argument for perdurantism$_p$ is very similar to the vagueness argument for universalism, so attacks on the latter often work as attacks on the former. For instance, some deny that vagueness is semantic, saying that the world itself can be vague (Barnes, 2010; van Inwagen, 1990a, pp. 213–27). Others argue that we are too quick to suppose that there are cases of vague composition (Barnes, 2007; Merricks, 2005; Nolan, 2006), and perhaps there are sharp cut-off points in the series of when things compose, so that the teddy bear always goes from definitely composing to definitely not (Cameron, 2007, pp. 115–6; Effingham, 2011b; Hudson, 2000; Markosian, 2004). Other rejoinders specifically target the argument for perdurantism$_p$. For instance, Yuri Balashov (2005b) argues, in a similar vein to the objection from the section "Against Perdurantism$_p$" (Thomson, 1983, p. 213), that the vagueness argument carries a burdensome commitment to objects that appear *ex nihilo*, contrary to the laws of physics. Indeed, there is a small cottage industry of papers arguing against Sider's argument (Gallois, 2004; Varzi, 2005).[25]

One popular approach to avoiding the problem bears mentioning. Some believe that the endurantist can say exactly what the perdurantist says: that there are scads of objects that exist, exactly as many as the perdurantist says exists, but that these objects endure instead of perdure (Haslanger, 1994, pp. 354–6; Koslicki, 2003; Lowe, 2005; Mackie, 2008, pp. 761–2; Miller, 2005c; Steen, 2010).[26] Call this position *promiscuous* endurantism given that it populates our ontology so promiscuously. Promiscuous endurantism is one of the theoretical positions that highlights so vividly the lack of consensus concerning what the terms of art mean. If one is a populationist then promiscuous endurantism makes no sense— to be promiscuous *is what it is* to be a perdurantist$_p$ (see, e.g., Effingham, 2009a, p. 302; Olson, 2006a, pp. 744–5). Sider, an explicit perdurantist$_p$, will therefore be unfazed by promiscuous endurantism—such endurantists simply agree with him and label themselves differently. Equally, though, it works the other way. If one endorses a different set of definitions then the argument from vagueness *won't* turn out to be an argument for a different version of perdurantism (but then it was never meant to be).

Material constitution

Perdurantism$_p$ offers one of the more popular solutions to the problem of material constitution.[27] However, as Stephan Blatti's chapter in this volume is dedicated to material constitution, I shall say no more about it here.

Supersubstantivalism

Supersubstantivalists believe that objects are numerically identical to the regions of spacetime that they exactly occupy—that we are, literally, made of spacetime. Various arguments for supersubstantivalism have been proposed

(Schaffer, 2009).[28] The argument goes that as spacetime has temporal parts, and so perdures$_p$, if supersubstantivalism is true then so too must objects perdure$_p$. There hasn't been much discussion of this argument, for supersubstantivalism isn't overwhelmingly popular, however one response comes from Daniel Nolan. The supersubstantivalist probably won't take *every* region to be an object—instead, certain regions will be objects. So persisting objects will have regions as temporal parts, but might not have regions *which are objects* as temporal parts. Now we have a supersubstantivalist ontology where, although there are scads of instantaneous regions (but surely even the endurantist believes in instantaneous regions?), there aren't scads of instantaneous objects. That, says Nolan, seems to be very against the spirit of perdurance$_p$ (Nolan, forthcoming). Notably, in this ontology things needn't perdure$_p$ but they *are* extended in time and are thus four-dimensional. So it seems that having temporal parts is not intimately tied up with being a four-dimensional object. With that in mind, we move to the next way to define the terms of art.

Dimensionalism

Dimensionalist definitions

The most popular explicit understanding of perdurantism is as a commitment to things being four-dimensional (i.e., extended in time), and endurantism as a commitment to things being three-dimensional (i.e., not extended in time).[29] Call such people dimensionalists:

> Endurantism$_D$: All objects are three-dimensional.
> Perdurantism$_D$: All objects are four-dimensional.

While dimensionalism is the traditional understanding of the theories of persistence, it is somewhat incongruous with the bulk of the debate. Only rarely are arguments advanced *specifically* for objects being three- or four-dimensional, more often aiming instead at the populationist reading of the terms. This isn't to say the two positions are worlds apart. For instance, look back at the analogical argument ("Against Perdurantism$_p$"). That argues for *both* varieties of perdurantism. First, it argues that objects are extended in time (e.g., perdurantism$_D$ is true) and then that DATP is true and they have temporal parts (e.g., perdurantism$_p$ is true). So historically the dimensionalist and populationist readings of the terms have been tightly knit.

Nor is that the only overlap. It's not an uncommon assumption that anything that has temporal parts, in having bits at different times, must be extended over time (and anything that lacks them is three-dimensional). Given such assumptions, any argument for perdurantism$_P$/endurantism$_P$ is an argument for perdurantism$_D$/endurantism$_D$. If we believe the assumption is often an unnoticed suppressed premise, this also explains why people are often unclear whether they are dimensionalists or populationists, for the two positions would then amount to the same thing.

But the assumption isn't mandatory, and they do come apart. We've already seen this with Nolan's theory where objects perdure$_D$ but do not perdure$_P$ (Josh Parsons says the same—see later). Or another case. We could imagine a man (composed of temporal parts) who lives for 72 years, but time travels back in his own life time so he lives out two sets of 36 years concurrently. Imagine another man who is a qualitative duplicate (and so is also composed of temporal parts), but who time travels back three times and lives out three sets of 24 years concurrently. And another who travels back four times and lives out four sets of 18 years concurrently, and so on. Eventually, at the limit, we have a man who only ever exists at a single instant.[30] At the end of every instant, he travels back in time to the instant he just left, living out 72 years of personal time in a single moment of external time. He has temporal parts (so perdures$_P$) but is not extended in time (so endures$_D$). So, again, we have a case where the two positions come apart.

Special relativity

While support for perdurantism$_D$ and endurantism$_D$ is usually parasitic on arguments for perdurantism$_P$ and endurantism$_P$, there are some arguments specifically for the dimensionalist versions (e.g., Lowe, 1998). For the remainder of this section, we shall concentrate on an argument from special relativity that argues specifically for perdurantism$_D$.

The key part of Einstein's theory of special relativity is that simultaneity is relative to what inertial frame you are in. That is, as you change how fast you are going relative to other things, what is simultaneous with you will be different from what is simultaneous with them. As a knock-on effect of this (we shall leave the details aside) the size and shape that objects appear to have from different inertial frames likewise changes. So in one frame of reference an object has one shape (e.g., a pole appears to be quite long if it is at rest relative to you) while in another frame it has a quite different shape (e.g., it appears to be a lot shorter when traveling very fast relative to you). Yuri Balashov (1999) argues that this indicates objects are four-dimensional, and perdurantism$_D$ must be true. His reasoning is to imagine that we are two-dimensional flatlanders observing the passage of a three-dimensional object. The flatlander perspective (at three different instants) is depicted in the top of Figure 1: it appears to be a two-dimensional object changing shape. But it can be explained by the rotation of a three-dimensional object, whereby the flatlander is only seeing cross-sections of it (as depicted in the bottom of the figure). Balashov argues that we are in a similar position, and that the best explanation of the changing shape of objects relative to inertial frames is that they are four-dimensional objects being seen from different three-dimensional perspectives. Obviously, then, the endurantists$_D$ step in and try to offer their own, allegedly superior, explanations (Miller, 2004).[31]

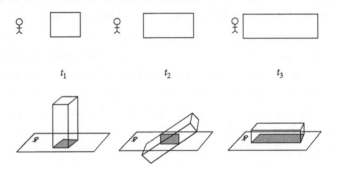

There are other arguments based on special relativity,[32] but this is the one that argues specifically for the four-dimensionality of objects. Interestingly, one of the other arguments from special relativity is concerned with the occupationalist's definitions, to which we now turn.

Occupationalism

Chorology

Rather than concentrating on what parts persisting objects have, as the populationist does, we might concentrate on how objects are located in spacetime. As far as I know, these relations haven't as yet been grouped under an appropriate name, so (for the time being at least) call the relations between an object and a region a *chorological* relation.[33] Chorology has become a recent concern in metaphysics (Gilmore, 2007, p. 179; Hudson, 2005, pp. 97–106; McDaniel, 2007, pp. 132–4; Parsons, 2007; Sattig, 2006). Much attention has been focused on the notion of "exact location" (and whether it can hold between multiple regions).[34] To get a grip on the notion, imagine an instantaneous two-dimensional circle. It *exactly* occupies just one spacetime region, namely a two-dimensional circular shaped region. I've used an instantaneous non-persisting object as an example because what spacetime regions a persisting object exactly occupies is the very bone of contention. Look at Figure 2 depicting a two-dimensional circle, but now persisting through time. Does it exactly occupy *multiple* spacetimes regions? That is, does it exactly occupy each transverse slice of that shaded region (examples are marked on the diagram with dotted lines)? Or does it exactly occupy just one region—namely the entire shaded region?

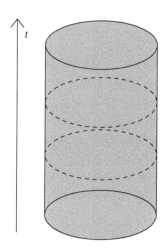

The occupationalist thinks that whether an object perdures or endures depends upon the answer to that question. The endurantist, says the occupationalist, will say the object is multiply located at the infinite number of transverse slices of the shaded region. We can give an explicit definition by introducing some terminology. Take as primitive "path." The path of the object is just that shaded region shown in the diagram—that largest spacetime region where, uncontroversially, the object can be found such that nothing else can be found there without interpenetrating that object. To make the exposition simple, pretend spacetime is Newtonian, and define an instant as follows:

> Region r is an instant $=_{df}$ (i) every part of r is simultaneous with every other part of r and (ii) no region is simultaneous with any part of r that is not itself a part of r.

Then define endurantism as:

> *Endurantism$_O$*: Every object is exactly located at every spacetime region which (i) is a sub-region both of the object's path and some instant *t*; and (ii) has as a sub-region every sub-region of the object's path that only overlaps *t*.

Parsons says that there can be no multi-location (see note 34), but nonetheless calls himself an endurantist. Call his position "pardurantism":

> *Pardurantism$_O$*: Every object is exactly located at just its path, and does not have any temporal parts.[35]

So parduring objects are four-dimensional (thus perdure$_D$) but don't have temporal parts (so endure$_P$). Whereas perdurantism is:

> *Perdurantism$_O$*: Every object is exactly located at just its path and has temporal parts at every instant that it exists at.[36]

Obviously, then, perdurers$_O$ perdure$_P$. Doubtless, some will disagree with Parsons and think pardurantism$_O$ is a form of perdurantism (e.g., Hawthorne, 2006, pp. 103–4), just defining perdurantism as an object being exactly located at just its path. Again, such worries highlight the problem of getting our terms straight, and just as before I don't believe there is any substantive debate to be had here. I will continue to distinguish pardurantism$_O$ from perdurantism$_O$, but nothing hangs on it—treat it as a version of perdurantism if you wish. Just as long as you are clear what *you* mean by the terms I shall not complain.[37]

Arguments for Endurantism$_O$, Pardurantism$_O$, and/or Perdurantism$_O$

The dimensionality of an object sounds like a geometric feature of it, and the geometric features of objects depend upon the geometric features of the regions they are exactly located at (e.g., an instantaneous cube has to be exactly located at a cube-shaped region). Perdurers$_O$ (and pardurers$_O$) are exactly located at temporally extended four-dimensional regions and so will be four-dimensional; endurers$_O$ are exactly located at *lots* of regions, all of which are three-dimensional, and thus will be three-dimensional. So occupationalism might just be a more sophisticated form of dimensionalism, which makes clear what it is to be three- or four-dimensional.[38] Unsurprisingly, then, dimensionalist versions of persistence and occupationalist theories are tightly connected; an argument for one will bear on your position on the other. Because of this, just as many of the arguments for perdurantism$_p$ (from the section "Populationism") entail perdurantism$_D$, many of those arguments will work just as well for perdurantism$_O$ (*mutatis mutandis* for endurantism$_O$).

There aren't many arguments specifically for endurantism$_O$/perdurantism$_O$. Of those that there are, they are—like most arguments concerning persistence—pro-perdurantist. Katherine Hawley (2008) argues that introducing chorological notions, and being a perdurantist$_O$, will help solve problems that perdurantists have with material constitution. Another pro-perdurantist is Cody Gilmore (2006), who offers up an argument from special relativity for perdurantism$_O$. Crudely, the reason there are few endurantists$_O$ is that the above definitions relied upon the notion of an instant, defined in terms of simultaneity. As we move from considering Newtonian spacetimes to the relativistic arena, this makes it a lot harder to say what regions an endurer$_O$ should occupy. From one inertial frame of reference one set of regions will count as instants, so one set of regions will be good candidates for being the regions an endurer$_O$ exactly occupies. But from a different inertial frame, as simultaneity is relative to such frames, different regions will count as instants; *a fortiori* a different set of regions will be the best candidates for being the regions an endurer$_O$ should exactly occupy. So whereas the perdurantist$_O$ just sticks with saying that objects exactly occupy but one region (the path), endurantists$_O$ are going to have a task saying which regions an object should exactly occupy.[39]

Conclusion

Multifarious definitions

As the above discussion demonstrates, there are many different ways of understanding the positions concerning persistence—each very similar, but such that there are circumstances where they can be pried apart in interesting ways. When navigating the literature on persistence it is often important to first settle which definition is being considered (e.g., Wasserman, 2003b, p. 288). However, do note that not every theorist will slot neatly into one of the above categories. Especially in earlier texts, they may be vague over the details of what they mean. Alternatively, they may endorse *multiple* definitions—for instance, saying that perdurantism is the thesis that objects are four-dimensional *and* have temporal parts (which is not, of course, illegitimate, for they may define the terms of art however they want). To compound matters they may concentrate on part of that definition for the rest of their discussion—for instance, solely concentrating on whether or not objects have temporal parts and ignoring whether they are four-dimensional. So do be on your guard when plowing through what has been written on the subject.

Such clarity of definition is not just helpful when it comes to evaluating the arguments for those positions. For instance, some have argued that there isn't *any* difference between the two theories: that perdurantism and endurantism are two ways of talking about the same thing. This is the position of Eli Hirsch (2009).[40] He says that while the perdurantist endorses the existence of temporal parts, and the endurantist does not, this is just the result of a verbal dispute about how to use the word "exist." If we correctly resolve this dispute then we shall see that the perdurantist's use of the word "exist" is such that temporal parts clearly *do* exist, while given the endurantist's use of the word, they clearly do not (in a way that is crudely analogous to an American and an Englishman both being correct about what the shape of a football is).[41] This sort of approach is only applicable to a populationist reading of the debate concerning persistence, for it is only on that reading that we are concerned with what things exist.[42] As soon as we move, say, to the occupationalist definition we still have a live debate (unless one thinks Hirsch can run similar arguments against, not what exists, but what regions existing things exactly occupy). In any case, it is clear that the plausibility of claiming that perdurantism and endurantism are, in fact, two ways of saying the same thing will depend upon what one defines those theories as in the first place. So, again, clarity of definition is paramount.

How do things persist?

The debate over persistence began by asking "How do things persist?" Somewhere along the way, this question seems to have become obscured. Populationism concerns what things there are; dimensionalism, what those things are like; occupationalism, what relations hold between those objects and the regions they occupy. It is not clear that any of this has much at all to do with *how* things persist.

We might think the problem is the question itself—it is difficult to see what one would even *mean* by asking *how* things persist, nor obvious what kind of answer would be appropriate. Perhaps the oddness of the question is what leads metaphysicians to concentrate instead on simpler questions like what things there are, and what those things are like, rather than debating how an object pulls off the simple trick of persisting. There is an alternative: that one thinks there is a specifically metaphysical explanation of certain facts. For instance, an apple is green, and we might think that this has a metaphysical explanation: it is green *in virtue of* instantiating the universal *green* (or having a green trope, etc.). If you buy into such explanations, we could do the same here and look for something to explain how objects exist at multiple times (and thereby persist).

The answers to such a question will likely connect with the above positions. For instance, we might assume perdurantists$_p$ would say that temporal parts are the fundamental things that exist, and persisting wholes exist at different times in virtue of such parts. Notably, though, the perdurantist$_p$ need not accept this claim about fundamentality, believing that the perdurer$_p$ and its temporal parts are on a par (Heller, 1992, p. 700), or even that the former is more fundamental than the latter (Hawthorne, 2006, pp. 99–100).[43] Also, it is not clear to me what the endurantist$_p$ would say (although, if anything, that just looks bad for the endurantist$_p$). Similar moves might work for other answers, for example, that it is in virtue of being exactly located at multiple regions that an enduring$_o$ object persists, or that it is in virtue of being four-dimensional that a perdurer$_D$ persists. So while the above positions ignore the "how" question, some assumptions about metaphysical explanation might restore that feature.

Alternative definitions

The above definitions are the most popular, but not exhaustive. One division thus far ignored is the nature of properties and relations. For instance, one might think that whether an object endures or perdures depends upon one's treatment of parthood (whether it is *simpliciter,* or a relation to a time) (Miller, 2005b; Olson, 2006a); or upon whether objects from different times can be related by the composition relation (Steen, 2010); or the nature of the composition relation (Crisp and Smith, 2005); or whether properties are had intrinsic to a region (Hofweber, 2009); or the manner in which an object is present at a region of spacetime (Fine, 2006).[44] Space prohibits a full discussion of these definitions, which of the above arguments are relevant to such definitions, and whether there are arguments unique to those definitions.[45]

But do bear in mind that nothing crucial could possibly hang on the definitions themselves. It is of little value to debate such terms of art, when the *real* philosophical debate comes about by demarcating two contrary positions, neither of which is obviously true nor obviously false, and offering compelling arguments for/against those positions. The definitions only tell you what the positions are—they don't, in themselves, make for a fruitful avenue of philosophical investigation. Nor should you think that not devoting space to these alternative definitions means they are somehow relegated to being less interesting—it is simply that less has been written on them. Almost certainly, if in ten years time I wrote an article like this we would still discuss divided terminology (although, if we're lucky, each position will have found its own terms by then rather than sharing "perdure" and "endure" between them). But, I would imagine, some of these recent definitions will have more prominence than they are given here.

Notes

1   This position can be found in Wiggins (1980, p. 25) and Oderberg (2004, p. 687).

2   See Gallois (1998, pp. 255–6) for a brief survey of early, and unsuccessful, attempts to define the term.

3   It is used, in this form or a close extension of it, in Caplan and Matheson (2006, p. 60), Crisp and Smith (2005, p. 323), Hawthorne (2006, p. 86), Hudson (2005, p. 8), Miller (2005b, p. 321), McKinnon (2002, p. 291), and Wasserman (2002, p. 207), among others. Note that there are some worries that this definition breaches the mereological principle that an object cannot have a proper part "as big as it itself" at any given time Olson (2006a, pp. 742–4).

4   This is not the only definition of "temporal part." Judith Thomson (1983, p. 207) offers up her own definition. Dean Zimmerman (1996, p. 122) is worried that Sider's definition can't account for gunky spacetimes and offers his own. Parsons and Noonan endorse a definition in chorological terms (Noonan, 2009; Parsons, 2007, p. 216). Effingham (2011c) examines how time travel makes providing a definition of "temporal part" problematic.

5   Interestingly, the first recognized perdurantist—eighteenth century philosopher Jonathan Edwards—seems to have endorsed just this style of definition; see (Helm, 1979).

6   Some demur, thinking that endurantism must make some specific *positive* claims rather than simply a negative denial; see Miller (2005b, p. 314) and Sider (2001, pp. 53–73).

7   There is debate over whether these theses have to be necessarily true. Indeed, there is debate whether there could be mixed worlds where some things endure and others perdure (in which case neither perdurantism$_p$ nor endurantism$_p$ would be true). Because this chapter is merely expository, set aside such quibbles for purposes of argument and let us imagine that the true metaphysics of persistence is necessarily true of all things.

8   Not everyone agrees that temporal parts are counterintuitive (Sider, 2001, p. 218), but certainly your average perdurantist will agree with this (for, after all, if they did not then they are expending an awful lot of effort coming up with arguments for a position that is allegedly true intuitively).

9   For instance, there have been arguments against perdurantism$_p$ on the grounds that you end up with incorrect *de re* modal predications being made of objects (Gallois, 1998, pp. 269–80; Olson, 2006b, pp. 412–14; van Inwagen, 1990b; Wiggins, 1980, p. 168) although that move has to weather a lot of flak (Copeland et al. 2001; Djukic, 2004; Hawley, 2001, ch. 6; Heller, 1993; Noonan, 2001, pp. 130–2; Sider, 2001, pp. 218–24).

10   For more on DATP, see (van Inwagen, 1981, p. 133).

11   For more on the connections between the ontology of time and persistence, see Carter and Hestevold (1994, 2002) and Merricks (1995, 1999). For discussion, see Brogaard (2000), Haslanger (2003, pp. 320–6), Lombard (1999), Lowe (1998), Rea (1998, pp. 236–40), Sider (2001, pp. 68–73), and Vallicella (2002).

12   See Le Poidevin (1998) for an introduction to the history of the debate, and both Markosian (2001) and Dyke (2003) for a discussion of the role of the semantic facts and how they bear on the metaphysical facts.

13   See also Kroon (2001), who replaces the perdurantist semantics with a fictionalist treatment.

14   There are other problems along similar lines. Hud Hudson (2005, pp. 123–36) argues universalist-perdurantism$_p$ commits us to superluminal objects, and Yuri Balashov (2003a, 2003b) agrees but takes it to be a *reductio ad absurdum* of universalism. See also Balashov (2007b). See Sattig (2002, 2003, 2006), Stone (2007), and Gallois (1998, pp. 267–9) for other problems with PATP that don't rely upon universalism.

15   Sattig (2008) offers a quite different problem for fission when combined with perdurantism$_p$ to do with identity across time.

16   See Balashov (2007a, 2008), Hansson Wahlberg (2008), and Moyer (2008) for more problems and discussion concerning stage theory and its definition.

17   See Hansson Wahlberg (2007, 2010) for an argument that there is no contradiction to be dissolved.

18   See Raven (2011) for a response.

19   See also Rodriguez-Pereya (2003) and Stone (2003) for different problems with the relationist view.

20   Sider (2001, pp. 98–109) tries to bolster the argument from temporary intrinsics by discussing what goes on in timeless worlds and cases of time travel; for discussion see Effingham and Melia (2007), Hawley (2006), Markosian (2004), Miller (2006a), Sider (2004), and Simons (2005). Nor is this the only place that time travel is relevant to the metaphysics of persistence. For instance, if we built

an object out of many copies of a single time-traveling atom, this might pose problems for both endurantism$_p$ (Effingham and Robson, 2007; Effingham, 2010; Smith, 2009) and perdurantism$_p$ (Gilmore, 2007); for discussion see Eagle (2010a, 2010b) and Gilmore (2009, 2010).

21 As noted by Wasserman, Hawthorne, and Scala (2004, pp. 314–17), Lewis actually relies on a slightly weaker principle—but for this short exposition we need not worry about such details.

22 See Korman (2010, p. 121, note 6) for a roster.

23 See Sider (2008, pp. 257–61) for one version of the argument; see Effingham, (2011a) and Korman (2010) for discussion.

24 See Heller (1991), Le Poidevin (2000), and Miller (2006b) for discussion of other connections between perdurantism and vagueness.

25 See also Sider (2004) for a response to some of the above.

26 See Varzi (2007) and Correia (2005) for discussion of this position.

27 There is a response to the perdurantist claims about material constitution that is becoming increasingly standard. See Benovsky (2009, pp. 60–2), Eddon (2010), McGrath (2007a), Moyer (2009), Steen (2010), and Wasserman (2002).

28 Effingham (2009b, p. 42) also lists more supporters of supersubstantivalism.

29 Obviously in universes with varying numbers of spatial and/or temporal dimensions "three-dimensional" and "four-dimensional" will be innocuous misnomers.

30 Such a scenario is imagined by Kurt Gödel (1949, p. 561).

31 See Balashov (2009) and Sider (2001, pp. 79–87) for discussion.

32 See Balashov (1998), Hales and Johnson (2003), and Rea (1998, pp. 231–36). See Gilmore (2002) and Balashov (2005a) for discussion of Balashov (1998).

33 From the Greek "khoros" meaning "space" or "site." "Topology" has the superior etymological claim but is, of course, already taken. "Chorology" is also a term in geography, having been first coined by the ancient Greek geographer Strabo in his *Geography* and latter resurrected by Richard Hartshorne (1939). Presumably there won't be any confusion.

34 Josh Parsons (2007, 2008)—see (Hudson, 2008) for discussion—thinks it is conceptually impossible for objects to be multi-located; see also Schaffer (2009, pp. 141–2). Others think it entails a paradox (Barker and Dowe, 2003, 2005); see Beebee and Rush (2003), McDaniel (2003), and Hansson Wahlberg (2009) for discussion. If they are correct then, presumably, the only theories that could be true would be perdurantism$_o$ or pardurantism$_o$ (*q.v.*).

35 See Parsons (2000, 2007).

36 The definitions of pardurantism$_o$ and perdurantism$_o$ are presented here in a somewhat cruder fashion than Parsons himself presents them. But it will suffice for expository purposes to overlook some nuanced details.

37 Indeed, Endurantism$_O$, Pardurantism$_O$, and Perdurantism$_O$ aren't exhaustive of the possible combinations of chorological relations. However, a lot of the alternatives will be deviant theories no one endorses, so I shall deal with these three options as they are the only current extant options.

38 Compare with Merricks (1999, pp. 126–7) who thinks we have to cash occupationalism out in populationist terms.

39 For further discussion, see Balashov (2008) and Gibson and Pooley (2006).

40 See also Miller (2005a), and McCall and Lowe (2003, 2006) for different arguments for the same conclusion.

41 I've taken the example from Manley (2009, p. 8), although he thinks the example itself doesn't get to the heart of the matter. Refer to his article for a (far less crude) discussion of the issues.

42 See Sider (2009) and McGrath (2007b) for discussion of Hirsch's argument.

43 And, of course, if fundamentality and "in virtue of" come apart (e.g., it's not the case that for all true propositions, the Ps, and the collection of fundamental things, the *xs*, that the Ps are true in virtue of the *xs*) then there will be *yet more ways* of distinguishing different varieties of perdurantism and endurantism—some concentrating on what things are fundamental, some on what it is in virtue of which the propositions are true, some concerned with neither, etc.

44 See Simons (2008) for discussion of the final option.

45 Although, notably, Fine (2006) offers one of the few extant arguments specifically *for* endurantism—and that argument is for endurantism as he has defined it.

References

Balashov. Y. (1998), "Enduring and perduring objects in Minkowski space-time." *Philosophical Studies,* 99, 129–66.

—(1999), "Relativistic objects." *Nous,* 33, 644–62.

—(2003a), "Temporal parts and superluminal motion." *Philosophical Papers,* 32, 1–13.

—(2003b), "Restricted diachronic composition, immanent causality and objecthood: a reply to Hudson." *Philosophical Papers,* 32, 23–30.

—(2005a), "Special relativity, coexistence and temporal parts: a reply to Gilmore." *Philosophical Studies,* 124, 1–40.

—(2005b), "On vagueness, 4D and diachronic universalism." *Australasian Journal of Philosophy,* 83, 525–31.

—(2007a), "Defining exdurance." *Philosophical Studies,* 133, 143–9.

—(2007b), "About stage universalism." *The Philosophical Quarterly,* 57, 21–39.

—(2008), "Persistence and multi-location in spacetime," in D. Dieks, ed., *The Ontology of Spacetime II.* London: Elsevier, pp. 59–81.

—(2009), "Pegs, boards, and relativistic persistence." *Pacific Philosophical Quarterly*, 90, 167–75.

Barker, S. and Dowe, P. (2003), "Paradoxes of multi-location." *Analysis*, 63, 106–14.

—(2005), "Endurance is paradoxical." *Analysis*, 65, 69–74.

Barnes, E. (2007), "Vagueness and arbitrariness: Merricks on composition." *Mind*, 116, 105–13.

—(2010), "Ontic vagueness: a guide for the perplexed." *Nous*, 44(4), 601–27.

Beebee, H. and Rush, M. (2003), "Non-paradoxical multi-location." *Analysis*, 63, 311–7.

Benovsky, J. (2009), "Eternalist theories of persistence through time: where the differences really lie." *Axiomathes*, 19, 51–71.

Bigelow, J. (1995), *The Reality of Numbers*. Oxford: Clarendon Press.

Braddon-Mitchell, D. and Miller, K. (2006), "Talking about a universalist world." *Philosophical Studies*, 130, 499–534.

Brogaard, B. (2000), "Presentist four-dimensionalism." *The Monist*, 83, 341–56.

Butterfield, J. (1985), "Spatial and temporal parts." *The Philosophical Quarterly*, 35, 32–44.

Cameron, R. (2007), "The contingency of composition." *Philosophical Studies*, 136, 99–121.

Caplan, B. and Matheson, C. (2006), "Defending musical perdurantism." *British Journal of Aesthetics*, 46, 59–69.

Carrara, M. (2005), "Comments on Hughes." *Dialectica*, 59, 481–4.

Carter, W. and Hestevold, H. (1994), "On passage and persistence." *American Philosophical Quarterly*, 31, 269–83.

—(2002), "On presentism, endurance, and change." *Canadian Journal of Philosophy*, 32, 491–510.

Chisholm, R. (1976), *Person and Object*. London: Allen & Unwin Ltd.

Copeland, J., Dyke, H. and Proudfoot, D. (2001), "Temporal parts and their individuation." *Analysis*, 61, 289–93.

Correia, F. (2005), "Comments on Varzi." *Dialectica*, 59, 499–502.

Crisp, T. and Smith, D. (2005), "'Wholly present' defined." *Philosophy and Phenomenological Research*, 71, 318–44.

Djukic, G. (2004), "Do four-dimensionalists have to be counterpart theorists?" *Australasian Journal of Philosophy*, 82, 292–311.

Dyke, H. (2003), "Temporal language and temporal reality." *The Philosophical Quarterly*, 53, 380–91.

Eagle, A. (2010a), "Location and perdurance." *Oxford Studies in Metaphysics*, 5, 53–94.

—(2010b), "Duration in relativistic spacetime." *Oxford Studies in Metaphysics*, 5, 113–7.

Eddon, M. (2010), "Why four-dimensionalism explains coincidence." *Australasian Journal of Philosophy*, 88, 721–8.

Egan, A. (2004), "Second-order predication and the metaphysics of properties," in F. Jackson and G. Priest, eds, *Lewisian Themes*. Oxford: Clarendon Press, pp. 49–67.

Ehring, D. (1997), "Lewis, temporary intrinsics and momentary tropes." *Analysis*, 57, 254–8.

Effingham, N. and Melia, J. (2007), "Endurantism and timeless worlds." *Analysis, 67*, 140–7.

Effingham, N. and Robson, J. (2007), "A mereological challenge to endurantism." *Australasian Journal of Philosophy, 85*, 633–40.

Effingham, N. (2009a), "Composition, persistence and identity," in R. Le Poidevin, P. Simons, A. McGonigal and R. Cameron, eds, *The Routledge Companion to Metaphysics*. London: Routledge, pp. 296–309.

—(2009b), "Universalism, vagueness and supersubstantivalism." *Australasian Journal of Philosophy, 87*, 35–42.

—(2010), "Mereological explanation and time travel." *Australasian Journal of Philosophy, 88*, 333–45.

—(2011a), "Undermining motivations for universalism." *Nous, 45*(4), 696–713.

—(2011b), "Sider, Hawley, Sider and the vagueness argument." *Philosophical Studies, 154*, 241–50.

—(2011c), "Temporal Parts and Time Travel." *Erkenntnis, 74*, 225–40.

Fine, K. (2006), "In defense of three-dimensionalism." *Journal of Philosophy, 103*, 699–714.

Fiocco, M. (2010), "Temporary intrinsics and relativization." *Pacific Philosophical Quarterly, 91*, 64–77.

Gallois, A. (1998), *Occasions of Identity*. Oxford: Oxford University Press.

—(2004), "Comments on Ted Sider: *Four-Dimensionalism*." *Philosophy and Phenomenological Research, 68*, 648–57.

Geach, P. (1972), *Logic Matters*. Oxford: Blackwell.

Gibson, I. and Pooley, O. (2006), "Relativistic persistence." *Philosophical Perspectives, 20*, 157–98.

Gilmore, C. (2002), "Balashov on special relativity, coexistence, and temporal parts." *Philosophical Studies, 109*, 241–63.

—(2006), "Where in the relativistic world are we?" *Philosophical Perspectives, 20*, 199–236.

—(2007), "Time travel, coinciding objects, and persistence." *Oxford Studies in Metaphysics, 3*, 177–98.

—(2009), "Why parthood might be a four place relation, and how it behaves if it is," in L. Honnefelder, E. Runggaldier and B. Schick, eds, *Unity and Time in Metaphysics*. Berlin: Walter de Gruyter, pp. 83–133.

—(2010), "Coinciding objects and duration properties: reply to Eagle." *Oxford Studies in Metaphysics, 5*, 95–111.

Gödel, K. (1949), "A remark about the relationship between relativity theory and idealistic philosophy," in P. Schlipp, ed., *Albert Einstein: Philosopher-Scientist*. Evanston, IL: Library of Living Philosophers, pp. 557–62.

Hales, S. and Johnson, T. (2003), "Endurantism, perdurantism and special relativity." *Philosophical Quarterly, 53*, 524–39.

Hansson Wahlberg, T. (2007), "The problem(s) of change revisted." *Dialectica, 61*, 265–74.

—(2008), "Can I be an instantaneous stage and yet persist through time?" *Metaphysica, 9*, 235–9.

—(2009), "Endurance per se in B-time." *Metaphysica,* 10, 175–83.

—(2010), "The tenseless copula in temporal predication." *Erkenntnis,* 72, 267–80.

Hartshorne, R. (1939), *The Nature of Geography: A Critical Survey of Current Thought in the Light of the Past.* Lancaster, PA: The Association of American Geographers.

Haslanger, S. (1989), "Endurance and temporary intrinsics." *Analysis,* 49, 119–25.

—(1994), "Humean supervenience and enduring things." *Australasian Journal of Philosophy,* 72, 339–59.

—(2003), "Persistence through time," in M. Loux and D. Zimmerman, eds, *Oxford Handbook of Metaphysics.* Oxford: Oxford University Press, pp. 315–54.

Hawley, K. (2001), *How Things Persist.* Oxford: Oxford University Press.

—(2006), "Review of Theodore Sider's *Four Dimensionalism.*" *Nous,* 40, 380–93.

—(2008), "Persistence and determination." *Philosophy,* 83, 197–212.

Hawthorne, J. (2006), *Metaphysical Essays.* Oxford: Oxford University Press.

Heller, M. (1991), *The Ontology of Physical Objects: Four-Dimensional Hunks of Matter.* Cambridge: Cambridge University Press.

—(1992), "Things change." *Philosophy and Phenomenological Research,* 52, 695–704.

—(1993), "Varieties of four-dimensionalism." *Australasian Journal of Philosophy,* 71, 47–59.

Helm, P. (1979), "Jonathan Edwards and the doctrine of temporal parts." *Archiv Für Geschichte Der Philosophie,* 61, 37–51.

Hinchliff, M. (1996), "The puzzle of change." *Philosophical Perspectives,* 10, 119–36.

Hirsch, E. (2009), "Ontology and alternative languages," in D. Chalmers, D. Manley and R. Wasserman, eds, *Metametaphysics: New Essays on the Foundations of Ontology.* Oxford: Oxford Univesity Press, pp. 231–59.

Hofweber, T. (2009), "The meta-problem of change." *Nous,* 43, 286–314.

Hudson, H. (2000), "Universalism, four-dimensionalism, and vagueness." *Philosophy and Phenomenological Research,* 60, 547–60.

—(2005), *The Metaphysics of Hyperspace.* Oxford: Oxford University Press.

—(2008), "Reply to Parsons, reply to Heller, reply to Rea." *Philosophy and Phenomenological Research,* 76, 452–70.

Hughes, C. (2005), "More fuss about formulation: Sider (and me) on three- and four-dimensionalism." *Dialectica,* 59, 463–80.

Johnston, M. (1987), "Is there a problem about persistence?" *Proceedings of the Aristotelian Society Supplementary Volume,* 61, 107–35.

Korman, D. (2010), "Strange kinds, familiar kinds, and the charge of arbitrariness." *Oxford Studies in Metaphysics,* 5, 119–44.

Koslicki, K. (2003), "The crooked path from vagueness to four-dimensionalism." *Philosophical Studies,* 114, 107–34.

Kroon, F. (2001), "Parts and pretense." *Philosophy and Phenomenological Research,* 63, 543–60.

Lee, D. (1950), "Lineal and non-lineal codification of reality." *Psychosomatic Medicine,* 12, 89–97.

Le Poidevin, R. (1998), "The past, present, and future of the debate about tense," in R. Le Poidevin, ed., *Questions of Time and Tense,* Oxford: Oxford University Press, pp. 13–42.

—(2000), "Continuants and continuity." *The Monist,* 83, 381–98.

Lewis, D. (1983), *Philosophical Papers Volume I.* Oxford: Oxford University Press.

—(1986), *On the Plurality of Worlds.* Oxford: Oxford University Press.

Lombard, L. (1999), "On the alleged incompatibility of presentism and temporal parts." *Philosophia,* 27, 253–60.

Lowe, E. (1998), "Tense and persistence," in R. Le Poidevin, ed., *Questions of Time and Tense,* Oxford: Oxford University Press, pp. 43–59.

—(2005), "Vagueness and endurance." *Analysis,* 65, 104–12.

MacBride, F. (2001), "Four new ways to change your shape." *Australasian Journal of Philosophy,* 79, 81–9.

Mackie, P. (2008), "Material objects and metaphysics." *The Journal of Philosophy,* 105, 756–71.

Manley, D. (2009), "Introduction: a guided tour of metametaphysics," in D. Chalmers, D. Manley and R. Wasserman, eds, *Metametaphysics: New Essays on the Foundations of Ontology.* Oxford: Oxford Univesity Press, pp. 1–37.

Markosian, N. (1998), "Simples." *Australasian Journal of Philosophy,* 76, 213–28.

—(2001), "Critical study of *Questions of Time and Tense.*" *Nous,* 35, 616–29.

—(2004), "Two arguments from Sider's *Four-Dimensionalism.*" *Philosophy and Phenomenological Research,* 68, 665–73.

McCall, S. and Lowe, E. (2003), "3D/4D equivalence, the twins paradox and absolute time." *Analysis,* 63, 114–23.

—(2006), "The 3D/4D controversy: a storm in a teacup." *Nous,* 40, 570–8.

McDaniel, K. (2003), "No paradox of multi-location." *Analysis,* 63, 309–11.

—(2007), "Extended simples." *Philosophical Studies,* 133, 131–41.

McGrath, M. (2007a), "Four-dimensionalism and the puzzles of coincidence." *Oxford Studies in Metaphysics,* 3, 143–76.

McGrath, M. (2007b), "Temporal parts." *Philosophy Compass,* 2, 730–48.

McKinnon, N. (2002), "The endurance/perdurance distinction." *Australasian Journal of Philosophy,* 80, 288–306.

Mellor, H. (1981), *Real Time.* Cambridge: Cambridge University Press.

Merricks, T. (1994), "Endurance and indiscernibility." *Journal of Philosophy,* 91, 165–84.

—(1995), "On the incompatibility of enduring and perduring entities." *Mind,* 104, 523–31.

—(1999), "Persistence, parts and presentism." *Nous,* 33, 421–38.

—(2005), "Composition and vagueness." *Mind,* 114, 615–37.

Miller, K. (2004), "Enduring special relativity." *Southern Journal of Philosophy,* 42, 349–70.

—(2005a), "The metaphysical equivalence of three and four dimensionalism." *Erkenntnis,* 62, 91–117.

—(2005b), "A new definition of endurance." *Theoria,* 71, 309–32.

—(2005c), "Blocking the path from vagueness to four-dimensionalism." *Ratio*, 18, 317–31.

—(2006a), "Travelling in time: how to wholly exist in two places at the same time." *Canadian Journal of Philosophy*, 36, 309–34.

—(2006b), "Vagueness, persistence and indeterminate identity." *Erkenntnis*, 64, 223–30.

Moyer, M. (2008), "Why we shouldn't swallow worm slices: a case study in semantic accommodation." *Nous*, 42, 109–38.

—(2009), "Does four-dimensionalism explain coincidence?" *Australasian Journal of Philosophy*, 87, 479–88.

Nolan, D. (2006), "Vagueness, multiplicity and parts." *Nous*, 40, 716–37.

—(forthcoming), "Balls and all," in S. Kleinschmidt, ed., *Mereology and Location*. Oxford: Oxford University Press.

Noonan, H. (1985), "A note on temporal parts." *Analysis*, 45, 151–2.

—(2001), "The case for perdurance," in G. Preyer and F. Siebelt, eds, *Reality and Humean Supervenience*. Lanham, MD: Rowman and Littlefield, pp. 123–39.

—(2003), "A flawed argument for perdurance." *Analysis*, 63, 213–5.

—(2009), "Perdurance, location, and classical mereology." *Analysis*, 69, 448–52.

Oderberg, D. (2004), "Temporal parts and the possibility of change." *Philosophy and Phenomenological Research*, 69, 686–708.

Olson, E. (2006a), "Temporal parts and timeless parthood." *Nous*, 40, 738–52.

—(2006b), "The paradox of increase." *The Monist*, 89, 390–417.

—(2007), *What Are We? A Study in Personal Ontology*, Oxford: Oxford University Press.

Parsons, J. (2000), "Must a four-dimensionalist believe in temporal parts?" *The Monist*, 83, 399–418.

—(2004), "Distributional properties," in F. Jackson and G. Priest, eds, *Lewisian Themes*. Oxford: Clarendon Press, pp. 173–80.

—(2005), "I have not now, nor have I ever been, a turnip." *Australasian Journal of Philosophy*, 83, 1–14.

—(2007), "Theories of location." *Oxford Studies in Metaphysics*, 3, 201–32.

—(2008), "Hudson on location." *Philosophy and Phenomenological Research*, 76, 427–35.

Quine, W. (1960), *Word and Object*. Cambridge, MA: MIT Press.

Raven, M. (2011), "There is a problem of change." *Philosophical Studies*, 155, 23–35.

Rea, M. (1998), "Temporal parts unmotivated." *The Philosophical Review*, 107, 225–60.

Rodriguez-Pereya, G. (2003), "What is wrong with the relational theory of change?" in H. Lillehammer and G. Rodriguez-Pereya, eds, *Real Metaphysics: Essays in Honour of D. H. Mellor*. London: Routledge, pp. 184–95.

Rychter, P. (2009), "There is no puzzle about change." *Dialectica*, 63, 7–22.

Sattig, T. (2002), "Temporal parts and complex predicates." *Proceedings of the Aristotelian Society*, 102, 329–36.

—(2003), "Temporal predication with temporal parts and temporal counterparts." *Australasian Journal of Philosophy*, 81, 355–68.

—(2006), *The Language and Reality of Time*. Oxford: Oxford University Press.

—(2008), "Identity in 4D." *Philosophical Studies,* 140, 179–95.

Schaffer, J. (2009), "Spacetime the one substance." *Philosophical Studies,* 145, 131–48.

Sider, T. (2001), *Four-Dimensionalism.* Oxford: Oxford University Press.

—(2004), "Replies to Gallois, Hirsch and Sider." *Philosophy and Phenomenological Research,* 68, 674–87.

—(2008), "Temporal parts," in T. Sider, J. Hawthorne and D. Zimmerman, eds, *Contemporary Debates in Metaphysics.* Malden, MA: Blackwell, pp. 241–62.

—(2009), "Ontological Realism," in D. Chalmers, D. Manley and R. Wasserman, eds, *Metametaphysics: New Essays on the Foundations of Ontology.* Oxford: Oxford University Press, pp. 384–423.

Simon, J. (2005), "Is time travel a problem for the three-dimensionalist?" *The Monist,* 88, 353–61.

Simons, P. (2004), "Extended simples: a third way between atoms and gunk." *The Monist,* 87, 371–84.

—(2008), "Modes of extension: comments on Kit Fine's 'In Defence of Three-Dimensionalism'." *Philosophy,* 83, 17–21.

Smith, D. (2009), "Mereology without weak supplementation." *Australasian Journal of Philosophy,* 87, 505–11.

Steen, I. (2010), "Three-dimensionalist's semantic solution to diachronic vagueness." *Philosophical Studies,* 150, 79–96.

Stone, J. (2003), "On staying the same." *Analysis,* 63, 288–91.

—(2007), "Persons are not made of temporal parts." *Analysis,* 67, 7–11.

Taylor, R. (1955), "Spatial and temporal analogies and the concept of identity." *The Journal of Philosophy,* 52, 599–612.

Thomson, J. (1983), "Parthood and identity across time." *The Journal of Philosophy,* 80, 201–20.

Vallicella, W. (2002), "The creation-conservation dilemma and presentist four-dimensionalism." *Religious Studies,* 38, 187–200.

van Inwagen, P. (1981), "The doctrine of arbitrary undetached parts." *Pacific Philosophical Quarterly,* 65, 123–37.

—(1990a), *Material Beings.* Ithaca, NY: Cornell University Press.

—(1990b), "Four-dimensional objects." *Nous,* 24, 245–55.

Varzi, A. (2003), "Perdurantism, universalism, and quantifiers." *Australasian Journal of Philosophy,* 81, 208–15.

—(2005), "Change, temporal parts, and the argument from vagueness." *Dialectica,* 59, 485–98.

—(2007), "Promiscuous endurantism and diachronic vagueness." *American Philosophical Quarterly,* 44, 181–9.

Wasserman, R. (2002), "The standard objection to the standard account." *Philosophical Studies,* 111, 197–216.

—(2003a), "The argument from temporary intrinsics." *Australasian Journal of Philosophy,* 81, 413–19.

—(2003b), "Review of *How Things Persist*." *Australasian Journal of Philosophy*, 81, 286–8.

—(2006), "The problem of change." *Philosophy Compass*, 1, 48–57.

Wasserman, R., Hawthorne, J. and Scala, M. (2004), "Recombination, causal constraints and Humean supervenience: an argument for temporal parts?" *Oxford Studies in Metaphysics*, 1, 301–18.

Wiggins, D. (1980), *Sameness and Substance*. Oxford: Blackwell.

Williams, D. (1951), "The myth of passage." *The Journal of Philosophy*, 48, 457–72.

Zimmerman, D. (1996), "Persistence and presentism." *Philosophical Papers*, 25, 115–26.

—(1998), "Temporary intrinsics and presentism," in P. van Inwagen and D. Zimmerman, eds, *Metaphysics: The Big Questions*. Malden, MA: Blackwell, pp. 206–19.

Personal Identity

David B. Hershenov

Personal Identity is the branch of metaphysics that inquires into what kind of beings we are and what it takes for us to persist from one time to another. One way to approach the topic is to ask what the referent is of the pronoun "I." A *person* is the obvious answer for "I" is a *personal* pronoun. This quick response just serves to elicit more nuanced questions. What traits make someone a person—is it mere consciousness or self-consciousness or something else? Moreover, are human persons *essentially* persons, that is, thinking beings that will cease to exist when they lose a certain mental capacity? And if we are essentially persons, are we material or immaterial thinking things, or a compound of a material body and immaterial mind? Another possibility is that the pronoun picks out individuals that are persons for only a phase of their existence. Perhaps we are not essentially thinking beings but are necessarily living animals that begin our lives as mindless embryos, then become persons with the onset of the appropriate mental activity and might someday end up in a permanent vegetative state.

The latter possibility suggests that the field or problem of Personal Identity has been misnamed, for we may not be fundamentally persons. Our second question about personal identity has also been misnamed as the problem of Diachronic Identity, that is, what makes x at T_1 identical to y at T_2. Identity is a simple, indefinable property, hence there is nothing in virtue of which x and y are identical. As David Lewis notes, "There is never any problem about what makes something identical to itself. Nothing can fail to be. And there is never any problem about what makes two things identical" (Lewis, 1986, pp. 192–3). Consider that if x is identical with y in virtue of, say, the appropriate psychological relations, but y *just is* identical with itself, then x and y would have different properties and hence be distinct rather than identical.[1] According to Harold Noonan, what is really being asked about the misnamed problem of

Diachronic Identity is kind membership—that is, specifying what conditions an object has to satisfy to be a K. This will involve asking what sort of changes an individual of kind K could undergo (Noonan, 2003, pp. 87–9).[2] For instance, could one obtain a different body or survive dramatic psychological changes?

Assuming we know what it takes for a person and an animal to survive, how do we determine whether we are fundamentally one rather than the other? Philosophers have traditionally relied upon thought experiments to draw out our commitments regarding our fundamental metaphysical nature. John Locke distinguished a person from his body as well as his soul with the help of imaginary scenarios in which a person moved from one body or soul to another, in virtue of his consciousness so relocating. Locke's modern heirs usually consider themselves to be providing thought experiments that are scientifically more respectable as they avoid soul talk and instead restrict discussion to transferring brains, or parts crucial to cognition, from body to body (Shoemaker, 1963; Shewmon, 1997; Unger, 1990). They might instruct their readers to imagine themselves as undergoing cerebrum transplants and ask them whether they would consider themselves identical to the post-transplant person with their pre-operation brain or to the individual with their pre-operation body. It is assumed that the individual for which readers phenomenologically experience a prudence-like concern would be the one to which they were identical. The dominant response is that the thought experiments reveal that we have switched bodies and so it is our psychology, not our bodily life processes, that is essential to us.

It would be a mistake to ignore these thought experiments on the grounds that they are too farfetched, perhaps even impossible, to be taken seriously. We are not now epistemically situated to defend such a view of their impossibility. Moreover, philosophically sophisticated neurologists have provided detailed accounts of how they could occur (Shewmon, 1997).[3] Anyway, the technical or physical impossibility turns out to be irrelevant. If we have a strong conviction that we would not remain behind in a mindless state if our cerebrum was removed, that likely indicates that we believe our psychology is essential to us. So if our cerebrum was destroyed rather than transplanted, the former an all too real possibility, the loss of our psychology should mean our destruction. Thus strong reactions to what may be physically impossible can still inform us about more mundane persistence.

However, as often happens in discussions of thought experiments, a more nuanced hypothetical is put forth and interpreted in a manner that undermines the earlier conclusions. Derek Parfit (1983) made this possible through his seminal claim that *identity is not what matters in survival.* What this bit of jargon means is that what we really care about is not that we continue to exist but only that our psychology does. Our concern that there exists a future being with one's psychology is not premised on the fact that we will be the subject of that psychology. He conjectures that someone else coming to possess our psychology would be about as good for us as our continuing to exist as the thinker of our thoughts (Parfit, 1983, p. 279). To persuade us, Parfit begins by pointing out that if only one of our cerebral hemispheres survived the removal procedure, the other destroyed in the process, we would identify with the recipient of that remaining functioning hemisphere, just as we would identify in the absence of any fictional transplant with the maimed possessor of our reduced but still functioning cerebrum after a stroke destroys one of the hemispheres. But that identification can't be maintained if both our cerebral hemispheres are separated and successfully transplanted into distinct bodies. It would be arbitrary to identify ourselves with the person possessing one of the hemispheres realizing our psychology and it would be logically problematic to be identical to both cerebrum recipients if they were considered distinct persons. It thus can't be claimed that personal identity across time consists of just the appropriate continuation of our psychology. It must include a uniqueness stipulation, sometimes labeled a "no-branching" clause. Nevertheless, Parfit suggests that we would care about both of our like-minded successors in much the same manner as we would about our own future self in the absence of fission.[4] Although each has qualitatively the same psychology as we would have had if we had survived with just one functioning cerebral hemisphere, neither is identical to us because of the no-branching clause (Parfit, 1983, pp. 262–3). Yet each cerebrum could have been possessed by a person identical to us in the absence of the other's existence. Since what prevents the original person from being identical to one of its psychologically continuous successors is something extrinsic to its relationship with that successor, he considers the no-branching clause to be trivial and thus concludes that identity can't be what matters to us (Parfit, 1983, p. 263). While identity might consist of the appropriate psychological relations and a no-branching clause, what matters to us just consists of the psychological relations.

As a result of Parfit's novel ideas, a cottage industry arose, some philosophers working to affirm and apply his claim about identity not mattering, others laboring to deny and explain away their appeal. One of the former is Eric Olson, who puts the results of fission to work showing that the earlier discussed *whole* cerebrum transplants have been misinterpreted (Olson, 1997). Our concern for the being that receives our undivided cerebrum should not be understood as providing any more metaphysical insight into our identity than such concern did in the fission scenario. We would stay behind as the mindless animal rather than move with the intact and functioning cerebrum. Practical questions about what matters to us and metaphysical questions regarding our persistence should be separated. The answer to the first will not enlighten us about the latter.

A number of philosophers fail to share Parfit and Olson's intuitions about identity not mattering (Baker, 2000, pp. 129–30; Unger, 1990, pp. 211–94). They insist that they want to survive into the future and find little comfort in a merely qualitatively identical replacement. Identity, as Peter Unger (1990) argues, seems to be a precondition for much of what we value. It is not enough that their psychology continues; they want to be the subject of those future experiences, pleasures and achievements, and so on.[5] Perhaps this attitude to identity mattering is even more evident when contemplating one's young son or daughter splitting because our concern for our children's well-being is more dependent upon their identity than their psychology. Our concern for them won't drop if their psychology changes dramatically as they develop. But I suspect that there would be a drop of concern if one's child fissions. Concern here seems to track identity. Your love and concern grew out of the individual being your child and will remain directed at the future being with whom s/he is identical. It seems more obvious here that identity matters than in cases where we come to know and care for someone in virtue of their personality. However, Robert Nozick and Noonan suggest that even when considering just oneself, there will be a drop in concern if identity is not preserved. Noonan (2003, pp. 169–70) suggests that Parfit's claim can't account for people's different reactions to his examples of simple and branch-line teletransportation.[6] The former consists of our bodies being scanned and destroyed, with the information sent to Mars where a qualitatively similar body is reassembled. Branching teletransportation involves one's earthly organism not being destroyed after scanning, but surviving long enough to talk to one's replica. Nozick suggests that if Parfit is right, then we should have the same concern for the replica on Mars in both cases. But in the branch-line case, our belief that we survive on Earth results in much less concern for the replica than in the first scenario, despite no difference in psychology.

As Katherine Hawley (2005) notes, what also makes the argument about identity not mattering suspect is that it draws upon a dubious explanation of the fission scenario, one that violates the Only x and y rule. That rule states that whether x is identical to y should not depend on anything extrinsic to the relationship between x and y. She tries to explicate the intuition that there is something suspect about positing a no-branching clause where otherwise conditions for identity would have been met. She is quite skeptical of individuals being dependent upon each other for their existence (or nonexistence) in the absence of a causal connection. So if the original (pre-fission) person would be the post-transplant person possessing the left hemisphere of the cerebrum if it wasn't for a psychologically similar competitor person possessing the right cerebral hemisphere, then the person with the right cerebral hemisphere can determine the existence of the person with the left hemisphere without any causal interaction.[7] There would have been a different person with the left hemisphere if not for the existence of the person with the right likewise being psychologically continuous with the original person. So the person with the left hemisphere owes its existence to the presence of the person with the right hemisphere, and vice versa, but there are no causal connections between the person with the left hemisphere and the person with the right, despite the existence of each playing a role in the creation or sustaining of the other. So without any causal support or interference, the possessors of the right and left hemispheres can determine the existence and identity of the other. Moroever, the original pre-division person goes out of existence if two persons possess the transplanted cerebral hemispheres, even though the pre-division person is then physically indistinguishable from scenarios in which it survives with one hemisphere transplanted and the other destroyed.[8]

Philosophers are divided about whether it has been established that identity matters. If it doesn't, and prudence-like concern fails to track identity, thus undermining the ontological significance of the whole cerebrum-transplant thought experiment, then what considerations would provide an answer to whether we are persons or organisms? Hud Hudson (2007, p. 217) appeals to "a big picture, best candidate, general metaphysics defense." He asks how well the metaphysics assumed by an account of personal identity deals with a host of problems—coincidence, vagueness, composition, temporal predication, transworld identity, and so on. Peter van Inwagen (1990) searches for a compositional principle that could make the Xs (particles) compose a (composite) Y and concludes the only plausible account is that the Xs are caught up in the life of an organism.

More than anyone else, Olson transformed the debate by highlighting the problem of too many thinkers, a consequence of the larger puzzle of how there could be spatially coincident objects, two distinct things made of the same matter in the same place at the same time.[9] He argued that if people weren't animals, then there would be two thinkers where we want just one. In fact, making matters worse, besides the animal and the person thinking with the same brain, the brain itself may be an additional thinker. How well a theory does with the problem of too many thinkers is perhaps the closest we have to a criterion for selecting a theory of personal identity. Nothing else strikes at our self-conception as much as having to admit other beings thinking our thoughts. Any reason you had to think you were the person, the animal would also have. Inevitably, one of you would be wrong, undercutting the other's claim to knowledge. And if an animal thought it was the person then it would seem that it couldn't *qua* animal be said to be an autonomous or free agent. The animal would fail to exercise the appropriate control and responsibility if it endorses actions thinking it was someone else.

So unwelcome are these extra thinkers that metaphysicians have gone to incredible lengths to avoid them, accepting views that one suspects they never would have advocated in the absence of pressure from the problem of too many thinkers. This possibility drove Unger from materialism to immaterialism.[10] Others have sought to revive the medieval philosophical and biological views of Aquinas that involve animals coming into and going out of existence merely with the acquisition or loss of rationality (Hershenov, 2008). Olson was compelled to deny the commonsense platitude that there exist such entities as brains and heads. However, Jeffrey McMahan, Ingmar Persson, Hudson, and maybe Thomas Nagel (1971) have instead identified us with roughly brain-sized thinking parts within an organism, parts that neither we nor anyone else has likely ever seen or touched. Lynne Rudder Baker is led to claim that although the person and the animal are not identical, they are so intimately connected that we should say the person and the animal are one and the same person and also one and the same animal. "Sameness" doesn't entail identity. Baker and Lewis claim that recognizing that we count as the same by a relation other than identity takes the sting off non-identical thinkers of the same thoughts. Noonan actually accepts the proliferation of thinking creatures but tries to mitigate the confusion by *pronoun revision*, claiming that while the word "I" is used by however many overlapping thinkers, it always refers to just one of them, that is, the one with the maximal psychological persistence conditions (Noonan, 2003, p. 211). Four-dimensionalists avoid the spatially coincident thinking animal and person by claiming that the thought of the organism and person is produced by a brief stage that they share at any moment. Ted Sider and Hawley actually endorse the claim that we are identical to an instantaneous stage that will only exist for a moment!

So it might seem that if the above sketch exhausts the most plausible views on offer, then there won't be a very intuitive answer to the question what kind of being we are. But that doesn't mean it won't be fruitful for readers to consider these accounts in more detail, weighing the pros and cons, perhaps coming to see one theory, on balance, as superior to the others.

Neo-Lockean theories

"Neo-Lockean" is a label for any theory that understands us to persist across time by having the appropriate links between our mental states. Locke stressed memory, though not by name, writing: "The self is that conscious thinking thing . . . which is concerned for itself as far as that consciousness extends. [It is] only by consciousness whereby it becomes concerned and accountable, and owns and imputes to itself past actions" (Locke, 1975, pp. 341 and 346). His account seems to suffer a problem with backward causation and multiple origins that bears on the too many thinkers problem. Assume you have memories extending back to your early childhood. Then through either the natural process of forgetting, stroke or head trauma, you lose your earliest memory of something that happened to you. Let's say that this memory was of an experience of an event at T_1 (1977). Your earliest memory is now of a later time T_2 (1978). Given that Locke held that "for whatever any substance has thought or done which I cannot recollect and by my consciousness make my own thought and action, it will no [longer] belong to me" (Locke, 1975, p. 345), it would seem that you are not identical to a being that existed in 1977! If the earliest experience you can *now* recall is from 1978, then that means you have changed your origins! Thus an event in the near present, a memory loss, could *cause* your first moment of existing in the past to change. Even if such a relation is not incoherent, it sounds like a very unwelcome sort of backward causation.

It might be thought the backward causation problem can be eliminated by adopting psychological continuity rather than direct psychological connections as the criterion for personal identity. Psychological connections mean that the same memories (desires, beliefs, intentions, etc.) remain across time. Psychological continuity requires just overlapping chains of memory (or other mental states): at T_N (now) one can recall T_2 (1978) and at T_2 one could recall T_1 (1977) even though at T_N one can't recall the events of T_1. Overlapping chains of memory (or intentions, beliefs, desires, etc.) would seem to imply that there would be no loss of a person, no new origins and no present event changing your first moment on the planet.

But it isn't clear that such a move is in the spirit of Locke, for it lacks the intuitive appeal that one goes back in time as far as one's consciousness extends (Schechtman, 1996). The importance of direct psychological connections rather than the overlapping chains of psychological continuity is evidenced in the claims of modern day neo-Lockeans like Parfit (1983, p. 206) and Lewis (1983). They stress psychological connectedness more than continuity. Parfit writes "of these two general relations, connectedness is more important (than continuity) in both theory and practice." He mentions that we have a great regret for loss of memories of a good life, even if psychological continuity is not threatened. The same is true for sustaining desires for those we love (Parfit, 1983, p. 300). We want our life to have an overall unity, not be episodic, though such fluctuations are compatible with psychological continuity (Parfit, 1983, p. 301).[11] Lewis (1983, p. 66) makes a similar point in his account of Methuselah: "It is incumbent on us to make it literally true that he will be a different person after one and one-half centuries or so."

If a psychological identity criterion must involve some appeal to psychological connectedness not captured by psychological continuity, the threat of backward causation can be avoided by admitting a rather embarrassing overpopulation. If one believes there are a lot of temporally overlapping persons, as does Lewis, then a blow to the head eliminates one person whose earliest memory was of 1977, but doesn't introduce a new person or change anyone's origins. The second person already existed connected from now to T_2 (1978). But if there are many embedded thinkers, then we have a severe problem of too many thinkers.

So given the alternatives, it might seem worth accepting the psychological continuity account. However, that still leaves a mystery about the relationship between the person that Locke distinguished from the thinking substance. Persons and thinking substances would both seem to meet Locke's definition of a person as a "thinking intelligent being that has reason and reflection, and that can consider itself as itself, as the same thinking being in different times and places" (Locke, 1975, p. 335). Sydney Shoemaker's solution is to just identify them (Shoemaker, 1963).[12] However, this is not the only source of a too many thinkers problem. Olson has pressed the question that if we are persons that don't come into existence until our brain has developed to where it can support a certain mental life, perhaps this not occurring until after birth, what happened to the fetus or newborn when the person came into existence? Surely the onset of thought couldn't destroy the previously mindless animal. So the person and the animal come to be co-located. But if the person uses its brain to think, why can't the animal do the same? Are there then two thinkers and two thoughts where we thought there was just one? And if the animal can think, isn't it a person as well by Locke's criterion, meaning there would be two persons where we thought there was just one? All of this might leave one hoping for a better way to understand the relationship between persons and animals.

Animalism

Animalism understands the human person and the human animal to be identical. The major appeal of animalism is that it avoids the spatially coincident thinkers discussed earlier. "Person" is just a phase sortal of the organism. "Person" is metaphysically no different from "adolescent" and "student" and "bachelor," terms that pick out individuals by traits that don't have anything to do with their persistence conditions. They can cease to exist as adolescents, teachers, bachelors, and persons without going out of existence. What is essential to an animal's persistence is the continuation of biological processes constitutive of life.

The downside of animalism is that it doesn't recognize any ontological importance to our psychological capacities and fails to capture our intuitions in the transplant scenarios. The transplant can be handled, if at all, by abandoning the claim that identity matters and running afoul of the rationale behind the Only x and y rule.[13] However, Olson's attack on the psychological accounts of our identity is not limited to just offsetting the transplant intuition with the Parfitian approach. He appeals to a function/substance distinction to determine whether we could be persons rather than animals (Olson, 1997, pp. 31–7). He doubts that a *person* is a substantial kind. All the different persons (divine, human, robotic) suggest to Olson that the term "person" functions more like "locomotor" than as a substance sortal. Birds, cars, angels, and motorboats are all locomotors. But what could they have in common that makes them the same substantial kind? Adding an engine to a rowboat doesn't make the rowboat go out of existence, replaced by a locomotor. That sounds right.

However, there is something problematic about the substance/function distinction of Olson's: that organisms are substantial kinds yet persons, like locomotors, are functional kinds. First, organisms strike me as instances of functional kinds—entropy resisters or metabolizers. They just don't display their function in their names as do computers and automobiles. Secondly, if any artifact can be a substance, an automobile seems to be good example. However, if a locomotor is a functional kind rather than substantial kind, then I am afraid that automobiles couldn't be substances. Yet replace the horse pulling a carriage with a motor and substantial change may indeed have occurred, with a new substance, the automobile, replacing its predecessor. Olson's example of adding an engine to a rowboat doesn't invite the same description of substantial change. Since the relationships of the carriage to the automobile and the rowboat to the powerboat seem analogous but elicit different judgments, more work needs to be done on what functional kinds aren't substantial kinds.

Ironically, animalism may also suffer a variation of the too many thinkers problem. However, these are problems shared with many, but not all, of its materialist rivals. They involve the problem of too many thinkers due to the existence of vague boundaries, the problem of thinking parts of the animal like the brain and head (Olson, 2007, p. 216), and bizarre cases of conjoined twins sharing only a cerebrum with which they both think.

Animalists assume that we are composed of physical simples, particles smaller than atoms. Given the vagueness of which simples are those of our outermost boundary, there would be many equally good candidates for us. If we are composed of one set of particles rather than another set including, say, one more or one less atom, the other would also be a perfectly fine candidate for being a thinking creature like ourselves. So overlapping us, completely or partially, would be many entities using our neurological equipment to think (Unger, 2007).

Animalists avoid the too many thinkers problem by claiming that there is only one animal that possesses a vague boundary in reality. The vagueness is not just due to our language being imprecise, that is, our never finding it useful to set down stricter guidelines governing usage. Rather, objects are "smeared" across the world (van Inwagen, 1990, pp. 213–37). There really isn't a fact of the matter about their borders. It is not that there are many precise candidate objects with an exact number of atoms that we haven't bothered giving a name, but that there is only one object without an exact number of constituent atoms. Many other philosophers object to conceiving of the world as being vague. They have difficulty imagining what it could mean for objects to have an indeterminate number of parts. Perhaps even more difficult than comprehending vague borders is making sense of vague temporal beginnings and endings. If things could indeterminately exist, then we would have to make sense of something sort of existing and sort of not existing.[14] Opponents of worldly vagueness instead will often endorse unrestricted composition in which any two or more things have a sum. So there will be many very odd, scattered, gerrymandered objects. But trying to restrict composition will result in a principle of composition infected by vagueness, rendering it indeterminate how many things there are in the world (Lewis, 1986, pp. 212–3; Sider, 2001, pp. 120–39).

Positing vagueness in the world won't enable the animalist to get rid of all of her too many thinker problems. There was an actual case of conjoined fetal twins who shared a cerebrum but not a brainstem, nor any other vital organs involved in the life processes thought to individuate organisms (Metz, 2001, pp. 289–90). Given that animalists tend to individuate animals in terms of life processes controlled by brainstems (Olson, 1997, pp. 132–4 and 140–3; van Inwagen, 1990, pp. 149–207), the just-described conjoined twins would be two organisms sharing a cerebrum. If such twins had lived long enough to think and if animals are considered the subjects of thought, then there could be two thinkers sharing the same cerebrum and thus apparently thinking and feeling the same. Neither would be able to refer to itself or know that it was one rather than the other twin. While such cases of conjoined twins are rare, we can conceive of a possible world in which they are not uncommon. And claims about the nature of human persons and human organisms and their relationship should apply in every metaphysically possible world. We don't want an account of the relationship of organisms and their brains to work just for our actual world.

The brain itself poses a problem of an embedded thinker for the animalist. If the animal thinks in virtue of the brain, the brain would seem to strictly or non-derivatively be the thinker. It would be best to identify oneself with the being strictly thinking one's thoughts. Olson claims the problem of the thinking brain is the most troublesome for his position, but provides little relative advantage to his materialist rivals. His response is to deny the existence of the brain![15] There really aren't any brains, only atoms arranged brain-wise.

Constitution theories

Perhaps the most sophisticated response to animalism is that of Baker.[16] She counters that when the relation between one entity and another that it *constitutes* is understood correctly, there will be no duplication of thinkers or thoughts. Thus there will be no extra thinkers. Nor will there be any worries about whether one is the person or the organism. Her theory is appealing because it saves the widespread intuition about our being essentially thinking creatures and advertises itself as doing so without suffering all of the problems that plague other accounts that posit a spatially coincident person and organism. Her constitution account can also be generalized to explain the objects of the everyday world. The reasoning behind animalism's identification of the person and animal, and the next section's account of persons as just brain-sized parts of animals, cannot explain the relationship of, say, the statue and the clay, a coin and its metal, or a river and its water.

Accounts of constitution frequently begin with the example of the statue and the lump of clay said to constitute it. Despite being physically no different, it is maintained that they are distinct entities. The lump could have existed before the statue came into existence. The statue didn't exist until the sculptor came along and molded the lump into, say, the shape of a famous politician. And the statue will be destroyed if it loses too much of its shape, but the lump would persist through that change. However, if the statue has its hand replaced by a hand composed of a different type of material or just different clay, the statue would survive the "repairs" but the original lump of clay would not. There would then be a different lump constituting the statue. So for such reasons it is argued that the statue and the lump of clay are distinct.

Baker claims that when one entity constitutes or is constituted by another, each can *borrow* properties from the other. The entity which borrows a property has it *derivatively,* the other has it *nonderivatively.* The constituted entity can have properties nonderivatively if the object constituting it couldn't have those same properties without constituting it. For example, the statue is nonderivatively beautiful and valuable while the lump wouldn't possess such properties if it didn't constitute the statue. So the lump is beautiful and valuable derivatively. The constituting entity, on the other hand, could have a property nonderivatively if it could possess that property even when it didn't constitute another object. For example, the lump of clay nonderivatively possesses the property of weighing two thousand pounds. It would have that weight if it had never been shaped by the sculptor. And if the constituted entity (the statue) has a property that the constituting entity (the lump) could have without constituting anything, then the former has it derivatively. The statue's possession of weight is an example of such a derivative property. There are two things, the statue and the lump, but they don't each weigh a separate ton, forcing the scale to register four thousand pounds when the clay statue is placed upon it. The lump and the statue share the same weight. They possess the same token property of weighing two thousand pounds.

Baker believes that the constitution relation between persons and animal bodies is analogous to that of statues and lumps. A person is distinguished by her capacity for self-consciousness, what Baker calls a robust "first-person perspective." Possession of such a perspective entails a consciousness of oneself as a being with beliefs and desires. Baker believes that you and I are essentially persons. The animal that constitutes a person doesn't have the property of personhood essentially (and nonderivatively). It can exist without being self-conscious. When the animal was an embryo it was not a person. Yet in certain circumstances, the animal constitutes a person. When a person emerges, it is not a phase of the organism but a substance in its own right.

Baker maintains that when the animal constitutes the person there do not arise two fully separate thinking beings, each with its own mind and mental properties that are duplicates of the other's. Both the animal and person have the same mind and share the same desire and belief properties. It is just that one of them will have certain of these properties derivatively and the other will have those same properties nonderivatively. She also believes that the human animal is the subject of certain mental states and events independently of its constitution relation (Baker, 2000, pp. 61–2, 68, and 101–5). That is, the animal's undergoing such thoughts doesn't entail that it constitutes a person. These nonderivative moods, feelings, believings, desirings, and so on will be called "first-order" mental states or events. Events such as an animal's fear of the dark, investigation of a curious object, boredom in the absence of certain stimuli, comfort around familiar voices or anxiety in the presence of strange faces are all examples of mental phenomena that an organism could have without self-consciousness. The person, on the other hand, is involved in such first-order mental events derivatively, borrowing the mental properties from the animal.

Baker argues that the animal is also a person when it comes to constitute the person. But this doesn't mean that there are two persons in the same place, one essentially a person and the other contingently. There is only one person. The property of personhood is derivatively possessed by the organism while held nonderivatively of the being which is essentially a person.[17]

Only the entity that is nonderivatively a person can refer to itself by use of first person pronouns. When that entity says or thinks "I," it refers to itself. The spatially coincident animal also refers to the person by the first person pronoun. The organism can't refer to itself *qua* animal by the first person pronoun. It lacks self-consciousness of itself as an organism. It can't think of itself as itself. "I" does not work as an essential indexical for it. The only first-order thoughts it can reflect upon are those that are nonderivatively thought by the person. So when the constituted person thinks "I am essentially a person," the animal doesn't think that thought falsely about itself but thinks it truly of the person. It seems built into the nature of the animal rather than a result of pronoun revision, a mere convention.

Baker's critics maintain she hasn't eliminated the problem of the thinking animal (Olson, 2007, pp. 60–5; Zimmerman, 2002). Why are its capacities less than the person? Its physical microstructure is no different from the person's. One would think if it has the same neurological structures as the person, then it should have the same mental life. Well, perhaps that is too reductionist. Relations are often relevant to something's existence and capabilities. A lump that eroded to look like someone is not a statue but the physically identical intentional production is a sculpture. You and your atom-for-atom duplicate on Twin Earth could have different beliefs because you stand in different relations to the world. However, appealing to history or relations doesn't seem to work since the animal and person could have come into existence at the same time. Why shouldn't the animal be able to refer to itself *qua* animal? How could it lack a capacity of the person when neither composition nor relations seem to distinguish the two? The difference just must be brute, left unexplained. One would think that difference in psychological capacities has to have a neurological or relational difference.

Even if the constitution account avoids the problem of too many thinkers, it still must confront the criticism that it doesn't offer a principled account of when it occurs (Olson, 2007, pp. 65–71). For instance, why doesn't mere sentience bring about a new constituted creature? Why should constitution only occur with the onset of self-consciousness? Is there a third entity, a merely sentient one, constituted by the animal and itself constituting the person? Or perhaps we are essentially sentient and only contingently self-conscious. Baker's condition that a new set of causal powers would arise when a newly constituted entity comes into existence, as opposed to an existing entity merely acquiring a new property, also seems to be met by the onset of mere sentience (Baker, 2000, p. 41). Moreover, thought experiments involving the loss of our personhood and the onset of a condition like that of late-stage Alzheimer's disease often elicit intuitions that we would be the individuals in those unfortunate states. And the modal intuitions in the transplant scenarios also seem to be satisfied since one might think that the transplantation of an infant's brain or Alzheimer's patient's brain, both devoid of the capacity for a robust first-person perspective, would be the transplantation of those very same sentient beings.

Baker has more recently claimed that we *persons* come into existence with the emergence of mere sentience, probably before our birth (Baker, 2007, pp. 75–82). She appeals to a rudimentary sense of self combined with what is normal development for the species. The latter excludes dogs and cats from being persons. But relying upon what is normal for the species is problematic because that could change with mutations. The species could, over time, become "dumbed down." That would mean our origins and whether newborns are persons would be determined by events that occur after our deaths![18]

Persons as spatial parts of animals

There are theories that claim we are not essentially self-conscious persons for some of the reasons just given about transplants and prudential concern. Most advocates of the account claim that we don't cease to exist until the mind is completely extinguished, not merely devoid of higher capabilities. All of this could be maintained by a modified constitution account. What is not compatible with constitution is claiming that we are each roughly a brain-sized part of the animal.[19] There are a number of considerations motivating the brain-sized person view (BSPV). The main reason is that the person is that part of the animal body which *directly produces* thought. The larger, embedding animal thinks merely derivatively in virtue of its person part that strictly thinks. Also motivating the view are problems posed by the spatial coincidence accepted by constitution theorists. If persons were but parts of organisms, then differences in their nature and persistence should be expected.

Also supporting the BSPV are strange cases of conjoined twins that make it difficult to maintain that persons are identical to organisms or even spatially coincident with organisms. One involves a case of twins that appear to be one animal with two heads (McMahan, 2002, pp. 35–9, 60–1, and 87–8; Persson, 1999, pp. 525–7). The thoughts of the two heads seem as distinct as yours and mine. Minds would seem to be unified by some sort of internal causal conditions and access, but the two heads don't have such privileged or direct access to each other. Since there would appear to be two distinct persons, then they can't both be identical to the one animal, subverting the claim of animal–person identity advocated by van Inwagen and Olson.[20]

The animalist has to treat such conjoined (dicephalic) twins as just one thinking individual cut off from itself, half of its thought not accessible to the other.[21] That will strike many readers as an implausible interpretation. They will find it more intuitive to treat each head as belonging to a different person. And as McMahan writes, "because there is no reason to suppose that the dicephalic twins are a different kind of entity from ourselves, or that a different account of personal identity applies to them, we should further conclude that we are not animals either" (McMahan, 2002, p. 39).

Ironically, the conjoined twins scenario provides the animalist with the resources to explain away the initial appeal of such an approach, which is that minds cut off from each other belong to different thinkers. Since the two heads belong to the same animal, then if the animal can think, it can think with both brains. We would describe this thinking animal as one individual whose mind is divided, its thoughts cut off from each other. So, surprisingly, the very scenario which the BSPV provides support of the claim that the person is a substance distinct from the animal guarantees the existence of a creature with a divided mental life. Thus the advocates of the BSPV can't reject the animalist account of the dicephalus on the grounds that its positing a single thinker with a divided mind is implausible. Furthermore, the two-headed animal would appear to meet the self-consciousness criterion of being a person, so advocates of the BSPV seem to have to accept that there can even be divided persons, not just animals with divided minds. Unless supporters of the BSPV have an argument that can deny thought to the human animal, they will have to admit that their theory posits a thinking being cut off from its own thought, thus undercutting the initial appeal of their theory when contrasted with the animalist in its handling of the two-headed animal.

Persson and McMahan contend that the human animal only thinks in a derivative sense. So they might not be bothered by an animal having a divided mind *derivatively*, but draw the line at a being that thinks nonderivatively having a divided mind. To help the reader get a grasp on this idea of a divided thinker, McMahan offers the analogy of the horn and the car of which it is a part. There might be two noisy entities, the horn and the car, but there is really only one noisemaker, the horn. Likewise, there is really only one "thoughtmaker," the small person embedded within the animal.

Olson thinks the real problem with the BSPV is that it is unprincipled (Olson, 2007, pp. 91–8). There is no reason to claim the brain's parts and only its parts are *directly involved* in the production of thinking. If the heart is not directly involved with thought, why are there blood vessels in the brain? One might maintain that thought is really produced by the firing of neurons. But not every part of the neuron is involved in firing messages. Some serve other tasks like maintaining structural integrity or waste removal. Olson compares the difficulty to being directly involved with production of thought to being directly involved with the production of an artifact in a factory involving many workers, suppliers, managers, tools, and materials. But I think there might be an unknowable fact of the matter with individuating artifacts and beliefs. Too simply, if too much of the matter composing the artifact and the brain had been different, the artifact and thought would have been replaced by a numerically distinct but qualitative duplicate.

However, even if Olson's objection could be met, it would seem that BSPV only delays the return of the problem of spatially coincident thinkers.[22] If it is correct to maintain that the human animal could survive being pared down to the size of the brain (Merricks, 2001, pp. 52 and 135; Olson, 1997, pp. 45 and 133; Shewmon, 1997, pp. 48–50; van Inwagen, 1990, pp. 172–81), the animal would then be composed of every part of the brain and nothing else.[23] It is quite odd that the animal would then only be derivatively a thinker. This queerness could be reinforced if it were metaphysically possible for a functioning brain-sized animal to be made first and then head, neck, trunk, and other appendages added later. It is very hard to explain why at the early stage only the brain-sized person would be strictly (nonderivatively) the thinker. It seems that there would be at least two brain-sized entities genuinely thinking the qualitatively same thoughts. If the animal then nonderivatively thinks, it is hard to follow the BSPV and later claim that when the animal becomes larger it no longer is really strictly a thinker but is only a thinker in some derivative sense. But even if that is so, there *once* were two spatially coincident nonderivative thinkers.

Four-dimensionalism

Positing a different kind of thinking part of the animal might avoid the just-canvassed problems. These thinking parts would be temporal parts rather than spatial parts of animals. The idea is that people have parts extended in time as well as space. People would thus be more like events than previously thought. Just as an event like a baseball game that began an hour ago is not now wholly present, but has innings existing in the past and future, only a temporal part of you is present at this moment. Temporal parts are the distinctive component of four-dimensionalism. Informally, a temporal part of an entity will exist only at a time and will then overlap all of the entity's other parts that exist at that time.[24] So your arm at this moment is not your instantaneous temporal part because it doesn't overlap all of your other parts. Once temporal parts are understood, four-dimensionalism (4Dism) can be defined as the view that necessarily, each spatiotemporal object has a temporal part at every moment of its existence (Sider, 2001, p. 59). Three-dimensionalism (3Dism) denies that things persist in virtue of having temporal parts.

The idea of temporally extended four-dimensional objects avoids the spatial coincidence of three-dimensional objects that are "wholly present" at every moment of their existence. The animal came into existence before the person, but they overlap for a good part of their existence, apparently sharing temporal parts. At any moment, only a shared temporal part of the animal and person are present, so "they don't crowd each other out" (Sider, 2001, p. 156). Since the person and animal have different temporal boundaries, they don't share all their parts in common and thus there isn't the mystery of how they could differ in mental, sortal, or modal properties without differing in any parts. The animal and the brain, or the brain and the parts directly involved in the production of thought, would never become spatially coincident in the manner that proved to be problematic in the previous section. Reducing the size of the animal to that of the brain would only come to mean that they share a temporal part.

Since 4Dists tend to accept unrestricted composition to avoid the vagueness of composition, identity, and existence, there would be countless objects with thinking parts for some portion of their existence. The only nonarbitrary sum of parts to deserve the label "person" would be the one with only thinking parts (Hudson, 2001, pp. 122–8). The most common 4Dist version understands persons as sums or "worms" made up of thinking instantaneous temporal parts known as stages. Even if composition was restricted to *natural* objects (Hawley, 2001, pp. 90–4), persons would be embedded within animals. Animals wouldn't be persons since they had many temporal parts that didn't think. The worm composed of thinking parts thus thinks in virtue of its temporal parts thinking. Some of those parts are shared with the animal but there is only one stage thinking at any moment. Noonan-style pronoun revisionism may account for why the "I" applies to the person-worm rather than the animal, a stage, or less than the maximal sum of stages.

However, just as it would be arbitrary to claim that a worm including mindless embryonic and corpse stages is the person, Hudson thinks it likewise arbitrary to claim a stage of the person includes all the parts of any of the animal's concurrent temporal parts. Arms and legs, for instance, are irrelevant to the production of thought. So the person will be "found under the skin" and thus not literally share stages with the animal (Hudson, 2001, p. 143). The person will consist only of those parts of the animal that are directly involved with the production of thought. Hudson writes of persons: "Presumably, then, they are those (spatially and temporally gappy) space-time worms that are certain proper, temporal parts of the brain and central nervous system of the living human organisms" (Hudson, 2001, p. 147). Since the roughly brain-sized person is temporally extended, it avoids the problems of wholly present spatially coincident thinkers that plagued the 3Dist account of brain-sized persons. No larger entity can be pared down to the size of the thinking part and wholly coincide with the parts directly involved in the production of thought. Rather, on the 4Dist account, they would come to share some but not all of their identical temporal parts.

Other metaphysical puzzles such as brain fission and transplants appear, at first, not to be as problematic for the 4Dist. Lewis claims that the worm theory doesn't run afoul of the Only x and y rule, or claim that identity fails to matter because there were two person-worms before and after fission (Lewis, 1983). However, there is a problem of how both worms can use the same pre-fission stage to refer to themselves, since they are thinking with the same stage. Lewis must accept that the reference of "I" is ambiguous as the stage-sharing worms must get by with a "we intention." They have to think prior to fission. "We hope that one of us survives." But how could there be concern for self if one couldn't think about just one's own future? Sider claims that Lewis fails to preserve the platitude that identity matters, for "the goal was to say that identity matters but this requires what happens to another person cannot matter to me" (Sider, 2001, p. 203).

If 4D worms only think in virtue of our stages thinking, then they don't strictly or nonderivatively think our thoughts. There is a strong pull to claim that we are identical to whatever strictly thinks our thoughts. Champions of stage theory like Hawley and Sider claim that their approach better handles the thought experiments. Positing only one person before fission means that discoveries aren't *later* made about how many people were there all along. And since two person-worms aren't using the stage to think, there isn't a problem of a person referring or showing concern for himself.[25] However, since stages are momentary entities, a pre-fission stage is not identical to a post-fission stage, so one might wonder again about prudential concern and preserve the platitude of identity mattering.[26] Hawley's view is that persons don't persist in virtue of identity. Rather, different stages can be the *same person* if they are appropriately connected (Hawley, 2001, p. 62). So I would not be identical to either of the post-fission stages, but I am the *same person* as both. Sameness of person doesn't entail identity.[27] So if we care about identity, then the stage view fails to deliver. But if we care about sameness of the person in the absence of identity, then the stage view can handle fission.[28]

Sider admits that the tenseless statement "I am identical to a post-fission person with my left cerebral hemisphere" is false. However, he claims a statement like "I *will be* the person with my transplanted left cerebral hemisphere" is true, for I really have that property. What makes the above statement true is that there exists a person in the future who bears the temporal-counterpart person relation to me (an analogue of the better known modal counterpart theory). "The temporal counterpart relation is the same relation used by the worm theorist to unite the stages of spacetime worms" (Sider, 2001, p. 194). So I, a stage, literally have the property of surviving fission and transplantation. I am not talking about someone else. The analysis of my having this property involves another object in the future, "but I am the one with the temporal property" (Sider, 2001, p. 195). The counterpart relation, unlike identity, is not transitive, so I can have two counterparts in the post-fission future that are not identical. But I will be both of them.

Even if 4Dists can make better sense of the practical concerns raised by fission and transplants, and can do so without running afoul of the Only x and y rule, they are still confronted with some moral problems, since the animal and person could have conflicting interests. This will be true not only if persons and animals are worms of different durations but if the same stage is both the animal and the person, for their temporal counterparts (and their interests) will diverge. Consider an experimental drug that may prevent the further decline into Alzheimer's disease, but will far more likely kill the users. The person, who goes out of existence anyway with the loss of self-consciousness, might think she has nothing to lose, since either the disease or the drug's unwanted side effects will end her existence. However, it may be in the interest of the animal not to take the drug since it (or its temporal counterparts that are the "same" animal) could survive with the minimal sentience of late stage Alzheimer's disease. One could imagine other scenarios in which the interests diverge. The person of the future may desire a brain transplant to a better body but that would doom the animal to a mindless existence. Or in a slightly less distant future, too many medical prosthetics might mean the preservation of the person but the replacement of the organic animal with a numerically distinct inorganic individual. Or the animal and person may both want to donate their organs at their deaths, or believe dignity demands a quick burial, but the possible different timings of their deaths mean the similar interests of both can't be realized. One dies, or goes out of existence, when it loses its capacity for a first-person perspective, the other with the irreversible cessation of life processes. If someone counters that the animal doesn't care about its identity, a la Parfit, the response should then be "why should the person?" And if neither identity nor being the same person (in Hawley's sense) matters, 4Dism loses much of its appeal with handling transplants and fission.

Of course, there will only be moral conflicts if stages and worms can think. But it is not obvious that they can. Worms are attributed thoughts in virtue of their stages. Stages are often construed as being as finely grained as change (Hawley, 2001, p. 51). It is hard to conceive of how they could be the subjects of thought because they are too short-lived (Schechtman, 1996, p. 23–30). Stage theorists are well aware that they have to explain how such short-lived creatures could think. Hawley and Sider's answer is that the brief stage has the appropriate causal connections to other stages (Hawley, 2001, p. 55; Sider, 2001, pp. 196–7). The claim is that such "lingering properties" as having conscious feelings, thinking of Vienna, digesting, or growing are possessed in virtue of a stage being appropriately causally related to other stages (Hawley, 2001, pp. 53–7; Sider, 2001, pp. 188–208). So being conscious will be a relational property of a stage. But it is really a property of the stage and not just of the collection of causally related stages. In that way it is like being a parent. One can't be a parent without a child, but the property is not possessed by the pair of individuals—the parent and the child—but by the parent alone. The idea, then, is that as long as a stage is appropriately related to later and earlier stages, a thought can be ascribed to that stage.

3Dists and 4Dists will both accept that having beliefs may depend upon causal connections to the past. So the stage theorist will insist that thought is just more relational than previously recognized. A stage can think if it is appropriately related to other stages. Moreover, *it* truly has the beliefs, not the collection of stages. Some 3Dists will retort that they do not understand how the momentary stage could possess thoughts with content even if causally linked to other stages. They might claim to understand how something could come into existence and immediately have contents if it borrowed them from something that existed long enough to have thoughts. Or they might accept that swamp chemicals could coalesce and an individual pop into existence with immediate beliefs if it has dispositions to manifest those beliefs. Even if such a creature were to be destroyed a moment after beginning to exist, it would not be *essentially* a momentary being like the stage. Our 3Dist will be reluctant to attribute dispositions to beings that *necessarily* can't manifest them. Likewise for the 3D aggregate of atoms that compose you at any moment, only to be somewhat scattered with your next breath. Such an aggregate seems to be arranged person-wise for too short of a time to think, even though it is causally connected to its successor aggregate. However, even if one is willing to extend beliefs to momentary objects, it is much harder to say they really feel pain. A momentary thing doesn't exist long enough to feel even a twinge. And it seems too far from our conception of enduring pain to claim that an instantaneous stage is in pain if it is appropriately related to other stages. Pain doesn't seem relational in the way belief possession might be. It seems that only a longer lasting object could actually feel the pain.

Perhaps readers will find it a dialectical stalemate, there not being a causal or momentary disposition analogy that satisfies the 3Dist, nor a large enough disanalogy to bother the 4Dist. So let's try a different tack. Since 4Dists are fond of analogies between space and time,[29] a spatial example will be put forth to suggest that causal connections in the production of thought are insufficient to make something the subject of thought. Imagine some of your very small spatial parts, which must include some in the brain, that when causally interacting in the appropriate manner give rise to thought. It seems safe to say that if certain neurons weren't causally connected to others, there wouldn't be thought. But it doesn't follow that any of the particular neurons (or their parts) are thinking. They causally contribute to thought but none are themselves thoughts or, more importantly, the subject of thought. They are too small to be the thinker. To think otherwise is to be guilty of a fallacy of division. Likewise, appropriately causally connected temporal stages may give rise to thought but such relations don't justify ascribing thought to any of the momentary stages. At best it suggests a longer temporal part consisting of the briefer stages doing the thinking. But that admission would be the downfall of any claim that identified us with a momentary stage, for it is hard to believe that we are not thinkers. If it is correct to claim that stages cannot think, then if we were identical to such stages, we would be thoughtless creatures. Whatever its merits at solving other metaphysical problems, it is hard to take such an account seriously.

If stages don't last long enough to think, 4Dists might just respond that the thinking parts should have a longer duration than stages.[30] Moreover, this would bring an additional problem of individuating thoughts and experiences. But even if stages can think, there will still be a version of the Unger problem of the thinking many for stages. Any stage will have a vague spatial boundary. Since the indeterminacy will be due to the limits of our language or knowledge and not due to worldly vagueness, there will be many plausible stage candidates. If one can think, so will the others.

Needed research

Can stages think and feel? More work needs to be done explaining how having pains and beliefs could consist of being related to a series of short-lived entities. And if stages can't think, will worms be able to think? Perhaps a case can be made that they think derivatively in virtue of thinking segments that are longer than stages. The stage theory's account of persistence without identity also calls for more exploration. Can it do justice to the platitude that identity matters? Will substituting concern for the same person suffice, when sameness of person allows many nonidentical stages to be the same person if appropriately related? And can either worm theory or the stage theorist's account of temporal counterparts handle the moral conflicts that will arise given their abundant ontology?

The animalist's identification of the person and the animal might seem better suited to handle the moral and other dilemmas. But to defend it, more work must be brought to bear on the animalist's distinctions between function and substantial kinds. The literature on natural kinds will perhaps offer some help here. And can the animalists with their restricted principle of composition avoid the world being vague or find a way to make that claim palatable? Could worldly vagueness be made attractive enough that it solves the problem of the thinking many? Assuming animalists can escape the quicksand of vagueness, or sink no faster than anyone else, could an animalist account be put forth that avoids relying upon the Parfitian thesis that identity doesn't matter? Can any 3Dist materialist account avoid running afoul of the Only x and y rule when dealing with fission?

This is another area of research that is calling out for investigation. It may be that Baker's account of the first-person perspective can. Perhaps her account of nonderivative properties and derivatively borrowing properties will be the best we can do, for it may be that without spatially coincident objects we can't have the objects of the ordinary world—chairs, money, mountains, and persons—and avoid the gerrymandered explosion of objects that the 4Dist delivers. Pronoun revision also needs more exploration. It may be able to make the overlap of thinkers more acceptable. Or further research might reveal it to be one more instance of a too-quick linguistic fix to a substantial metaphysical problem. More research also needs to be done on individuating thoughts if the BSPV is going to be able to defend the intuition that the person is the entity whose parts directly produce thought. Perhaps the BSPV can borrow (somewhat) the constitution account of derivative properties to avoid too many thinkers.

On the other hand, it might be that all the difficulties of materialist accounts with solving the too many thinkers problem should lead us to take a second look at soul theories. Perhaps future metaphysical research will force those in the philosophy of mind to reconsider a theory they thought discredited. In fact, recent work has suggested that soul theories may not have been mortally wounded by the problems of mind–body interaction and the neurological dependence of thought (Plantinga, 2007).

Notes

1   I owe this reductio to Nathan Salmon.

2   See also Sider (2001, p. 149).

3   D. Alan Shewmon also reports on brains removed from human fetuses aborted live by hysteronomy and sustained for over 90 minutes. And monkeys have undergone brain and head transplants with some success (Shewmon, 1997, p. 49).

4   The phenomenology of concern seems to be the same as that of prudential concern.

5   Baker adds that "our practices of apologizing, promise keeping and intending become incoherent if we suppose our interest in identity is really only in psychological continuity" (Baker, 2000, p. 129).

6   See also Unger's account of "century fission" (Unger, 1990, p. 268) and a critique in Hershenov (2004b).

7   Richard Swinburne lampooned this position, suggesting that the original person should bribe a nurse before undergoing the procedure to ensure that one of the

hemispheres didn't survive removal, thus ensuring his survival (Swinburne, 1973–4, p. 237).

8 See also Noonan (2003, p. 136).

9 Sydney Shoemaker called this "the problem of too many minds" (Shoemaker, 1999, p. 291).

10 See Unger (1990) for the materialist conception of persons. He moves to a defense of dualism in Unger (2007, pp. 362–465).

11 Parfit adds that connections which are distinctive between people should be given more weight.

12 Noonan (2003, p. 63) suggests pronoun revision to rescue Locke from Shoemaker's challenge, one made earlier by Thomas Reid and Joseph Butler.

13 It is worth mentioning that there is another form of animalism, the hylomorphism of Aristotle and Aquinas that offers a way to capture the belief that we are rational animals and yet that we go with our transplanted brain. I explore how it construes transplants and the metaphysical costs of doing so in my (Hershenov, 2008).

14 But see Baker (2007, pp. 123–7) for a defense of the contrary view based on the claim that things come in and go out of existence gradually.

15 Independent support for this approach is provided by van Inwagen's compositional principle that the Xs compose a Y if and only if they are caught up in a life. This is not as arbitrary (and disjunctive) a compositional principle as there would have to be to include cerebra, heads, and hand complements.

16 See also the constitution account of Shoemaker (1999). He argues that animals can't think at all because they have the wrong persistence conditions.

17 Baker protests that those who think that there are two persons are conceiving of the two beings in the constitution relation as if they were fully separate entities that just happen to be in the same place at the same time. Such a perspective overlooks the unity relation that a constituted object has to that which constitutes it. There is more to constitution than just spatial coincidence. While constitution is not identity, it is not full separateness either. Baker insists that the constitution relation makes it possible for two things to be the same F without being identical. To claim that x and y are the same F should be understood as stating that *either* x and y stand in a constitution relation to each other or they are identical to each other.

18 The modern species concept that emphasizes reproductive community could also lead to an individual animal's species membership being determined by events that occur after its demise.

19 McMahan and Persson (discussed in the next section), and perhaps Thomas Nagel and Roderick Chisholm. Parfit (1983, pp. 273 and 469) claims this about

Nagel. Chisholm (1978, p. 33) is also motivated by considerations of mereological essentialism.

20 The second case explored in the animalist section involves what appears to be two organisms sharing only a single cerebrum and thus sharing a mind. That might mean too many thinkers for the animalist but not for the BSPV, which just posits one thinker attached to a pair of bodies.

21 The animalist could try to support his treatment of the dicephalus as the same thinker cut off from himself, by pointing out that few of us would accept the seeming analogous claim of Locke that Sleeping Socrates and Waking Socrates are distinct persons (Locke, 1975, p. 342). The advocate of BSPV might respond that, unlike Sleeping Socrates and Waking Socrates, the dicephalic minds have different locations, or think at the same time, or one can be destroyed without the other, or they could each learn separately and acquire concepts differently. I offer an animalist response in Hershenov (2004a).

22 Persson and McMahan's accounts may fall prey to informal fallacies of composition and division for it is not clear that they can have the person and the organism derivatively possess each other's properties. The problem of too many thinkers may reemerge with the person thinking "I am *essentially* a person" and the organism thinking the same thought derivatively. The organism will be thinking something false since it is not essentially a person. So Noonan-style pronoun revisionism is needed.

23 Incidentally, if readers believe that the minimal thinking being is just part of the brain and thus smaller than the smallest, maimed brain-sized animal, the problem can still be reproduced with the brain and its minimal thinking part, rather than the animal and the brain. Brains can change their size.

24 Something is a temporal part of x during interval T if and only if (i) the object exists at, but only at, times in T, (ii) it is part of x at every time during T, and (iii) at every moment during T it overlaps everything that is part of x at that moment (Sider, 2001, p. 59).

25 How do we refer to a momentary object? Hawley (2001, pp. 56–60) points out that the stage theorist doesn't suffer here any difficulty that the 3Dist can avoid when predicating properties of an object at any moment.

26 And it might have animal counterparts whose interests are opposed to its person counterparts.

27 There will actually be continuum many people prior and post fission. Hawley and Sider admit that this diachronic counting is a problem of their view, just one outweighed by its merits.

28 For other advantages of the stage view in dealing with the standard thought experiments see Hawley (2001, pp. 130–1 and 206–7).

29 "The more the analogy holds, the more entitled we are to expect it to hold in new areas. We thereby should expect the part–whole relation to behave with respect to time as it does with respect to space" (Sider, 2001, p. 87).

30 If persons are such extended thinking segments, that will mean that stage theory loses one of its advantages over worm theory in that it allows continuants (the ordinary objects that we have named) to have their temporary intrinsic properties *simpliciter*. This problem of temporary intrinsics, due to Lewis (1986), is that such properties as shape would have to be construed as disguised relations to time on the 3Dist approach to avoid enduring entities having the contradictory properties of being bent and straight. But the 4D worm would have intrinsic properties and avoid contradiction and relations to times in virtue of its temporal parts having such properties. Yet this doesn't give the worm intrinsic properties *simpliciter*. However, if we are stages, then we would have such properties *simpliciter*, not in virtue of anything else having them. But if the person segment that thinks has smaller stages as parts, then the person will have other temporary intrinsics derivatively in virtue of his component stages having them *simpliciter*.

References

Baker, L. R. (2000), *Persons and Bodies: A Constitution View*. Cambridge: Cambridge University Press.

—(2007), *The Metaphysics of Everyday Life: An Essay in Practical Realism*. Cambridge: Cambridge University Press.

Chisholm, R. (1978), "Is there a mind-body problem?" *The Philosophic Exchange*, 2(4), 25–34.

Hawley, K. (2001), *How Things Persist*. Oxford: Clarendon Press.

—(2005), "Fission, fusion and intrinsic facts." *Philosophy and Phenomenological Research*, 71(3), 602–21.

Hershenov, D. (2004a), "Countering the appeal of the psychological approach to personal identity." *Philosophy*, 79, 445–72.

—(2008), "A hylomorphic account of thought experiments concerning personal identity." *American Catholic Philosophical Quarterly*, 82(2), 481–502.

Hudson, H. (2001), *A Materialist Metaphysics of the Human Person*. Ithaca, NY: Cornell University Press.

—(2007), "I am not an animal!," in D. Zimmerman and P. van Inwagen, eds, *Persons: Human and Divine*. Oxford: Oxford University Press, pp. 216–34.

Lewis, D. (1983), "Survival and identity," in *Philosophical Papers I*. Oxford: Oxford University Press, pp. 55–72.

—(1986), *The Plurality of Worlds*. Oxford: Blackwell Press.

Locke, J. (1975), *An Essay Concerning Human Understanding,* ed. P. Nidditch. Oxford: Oxford University Press.

McMahan, J. (2002), *The Ethics of Killing: Problems at the Margins of Life.* Oxford: Oxford University Press.

Merricks, T. (2001), *Objects and Persons.* Oxford: Oxford University Press.

Metz, E. (2001), *Ultrasound in Obstetrics and Gynecology.* New York: Thieme Medical Publishers.

Nagel, T. (1971), "Brain bisection and the unity of consciousness." *Synthese,* 22, 396–413.

Noonan, H. (2003), *Personal Identity* (revised edn). London: Routledge.

Olson, E. (1997), *The Human Animal: Identity without Psychology.* Oxford: Oxford University Press.

—(2007), *What Are We? A Study in Personal Ontology.* Oxford: Oxford University Press.

Parfit, D. (1983), *Reasons and Persons.* Oxford: Oxford University Press.

Plantinga, A. (2007), "Materialism and Christian belief," in D. Zimmerman and P. van Inwagen, eds, *Persons: Human and Divine.* Oxford: Oxford University Press, pp. 99–141.

Persson, I. (1999), "Our identity and the separability of persons and organisms." *Dialogue,* 38, 521–33.

Schechtman, M. (1996), *The Constitution of Selves.* Ithaca, NY: Cornell University Press.

Shewmon, D. A. (1997), "Recovery from 'brain death': a neurologist's apologia." *Linacre Quarterly,* 64, 30–96.

Shoemaker, S. (1963), *Self-Knowledge and Self-Identity.* Ithaca, NY: Cornell University Press.

—(1999), "Self, body and coincidence." *The Proceedings of the Aristotelian Society: Special Volume,* 73, 287–306.

Sider, T. (2001), *Four Dimensionalism: An Ontology of Persistence and Time.* Oxford: Clarendon Press.

Swinburne, R. (1973–4), "Personal identity." *Proceedings of the Aristotelian Society,* 74, 231–48.

Unger, P. (1990), *Identity, Consciousness, and Value.* Oxford: Oxford University Press.

—(2007), *All the Power in the World.* Oxford: Oxford University Press.

van Inwagen, P. (1990), *Material Beings.* Ithaca, NY: Cornell University Press.

Zimmerman, D. (2002) "The constitution of persons by bodies: a critique of Lynne Rudder Baker's theory of material constitution." *Philosophical Topics,* 30(1), 295–339.

Free Will

Kevin Timpe

It is sometimes said that Augustine discovered the faculty of the will and as a result inaugurated philosophy's fascination with issues related to free will (Scanlon, 2005, p. 160).[1] While philosophers prior to Augustine clearly discussed related issues of, for example, voluntariness and agency, one finds in Augustine a focus on a faculty distinct from reason which is necessary for praise and blame that one would be hard-pressed to find in earlier thinkers. Augustine addressed the importance of free will in many of his works, including the *Confessions*, *City of God*, and of course *On Free Choice of the Will*. But he never seems to question whether or not humans have free will. That is, the following question is one that Augustine never seems to raise because he thought the answer was an obvious yes:

The Existence Question: Do humans have free will?[2]

In recent years, the existence question has come to be at the forefront of many of the debates concerning free will as an increasing number of scholars are skeptical about the existence of free will. My aim in this chapter is not so much to answer the existence question, but to provide a framework for understanding how the question should be answered. I also provide a taxonomical overview of aspects of the contemporary literature in order to show how one's answer to the existence question depends on other issues pertaining to the nature of free will.

Do we have free will? Preliminaries to approaching the question

Before we can turn to addressing how we should address the existence question, much less answer it, we must first get clear on some terminological issues. The terminology surrounding the free will question is dicey because many of the terms get used in multiple ways. For instance, Peter van Inwagen, one of the most influential figures in contemporary free will debates, argues that free will should be defined in terms of the ability to do otherwise. According to van Inwagen, free will involves,

> hav[ing] both the following abilities: the ability to perform that act and the ability to refrain from performing that act. (This entails that we *have been* in the following position: for something we did do, we were at some point prior to our doing it able to refrain from doing it, able not to do it.)[3] (van Inwagen, 2008)

Others, however, take the line that Augustine seems to take and define free will in terms of its being the control condition on moral responsibility; that is, they think that having free will just is controlling your actions in the way required for you to be properly held morally responsible for those actions (McKenna, 2008, p. 30; Timpe, 2008, p. 10; Vargas, 2007, p. 218). And while some take these two understandings of free will to be coextensive (Kane, 2002a, p. 17), there are others for whom the two can come apart (Fischer and Ravizza, 1998).[4] For purposes of this chapter, I'm going to stipulate the following definition of free will:

> *Free will* = $_{df}$ the control condition on moral responsibility; that is, the capacity or set of capacities governing an agent's actions, the exercise of which are necessary for the agent to be morally responsible for those actions.

With this stipulation made, we are now in a position to define the two major families of views with respect to free will. The differentia between these two families of views is how they answer the following question, which has received a preponderance of attention in contemporary discussions:

> *The Compatibility Question*: Is the existence of free will compatible with the truth of causal determinism?[5]

Compatibilists answer the compatibility question in the affirmative, holding that it is possible for agents to have free will even if causal determinism (hereafter, simply determinism) is true, while incompatibilists hold that the truth of determinism and the existence of free will are mutually exclusive. Neither answer to the compatibility question by itself takes a stand on either the existence question or the truth or falsity of causal determinism. While the majority of contemporary compatibilists think that free will does exist, there is at least one exception (Levy, 2009); furthermore, few compatibilists are committed to the truth of determinism. Similarly, incompatibilism per se takes no stand on either the truth of determinism or the proper answer to the existence question; all that incompatibilism commits one to is the claim that it is not possible for the thesis of determinism to be true and for there to be free will. However, many incompatibilists answer the existence question in the affirmative, and thus think that the thesis of determinism is false; such incompatibilists are called libertarians. (We will return to species of incompatibilism which answer the existence question negatively below.)

Because libertarians and many compatibilists agree that there is such a thing as free will but disagree on at least one important feature of it (viz. its relationship to determinism), many authors use the terms "libertarian free will" and "compatibilist free will" to differentiate these two understandings of freedom. However, Peter van Inwagen argues that one ought not use the phrases "libertarian free will" and "compatibilist free will." For van Inwagen, these phrases are problematic because their use suggests that the debate between libertarians and compatibilists regarding free will is a debate about different purported existants, when really both libertarians and those compatibilists who believe in free will actually believe in the same existing thing, disagreeing instead over its relationship to the truth of determinism. Van Inwagen writes:

> All compatibilists I know of believe in free will. Many incompatibilists (just exactly the libertarians: that's how "libertarian" is defined) believe in free will. And it's one and the same thing they believe in. Compatibilists say that the existence of this thing (whose conceptual identity is determined by the meaning of the English word "able," or of some more-or-less-equivalent word or phrase in some other language) is compatible with determinism; incompatibilists say that the existence of this thing is incompatible with determinism. If Alice used to be an incompatibilist and has been converted by some philosophical argument to compatibilism, she should describe her intellectual history this way: "I used to think that free will was incompatible with determinism. I was blind but now I see: Now I see that *it* is compatible with determinism." And her use of "it" does not have to be apologized for: this very thing she used to think was incompatible with determinism, she now thinks is compatible with determinism. (Compare: I used to think that knowledge was incompatible with the logical possibility of a Universal Deceiver. Now I see that *it* is compatible with the logical possibility of such a being.) What Alice should *not* say is this:
>
> I used to think that free will was one thing, a thing incompatible with determinism. Now I think it's another thing, a thing compatible with

determinism. The thing I used, incorrectly, to call "free will" *is* incompatible with determinism; I was right to think it was incompatible with determinism. But it doesn't exist (I mean no agent has it), and it couldn't exist, and if it did exist, it wouldn't be right to call it "free will."

Talk of "libertarian free will" is therefore at best useless. . . . [L]ibertarians who become compatibilists shouldn't say, "I see now that there is no such thing as what I called 'free will.'" They should say, "I see now that free will doesn't have some of the properties I thought it had; for one thing, it isn't incompatible with determinism." (van Inwagen, 2008)

While van Inwagen is correct that both incompatibilists and those compatibilists who believe in free will believe in the same existant,[6] there is still reason to think the phrases that van Inwagen finds "at best useless" have an acceptable usage. Responding to this terminological restriction by van Inwagen, Lynne Rudder Baker argues that there *is* a legitimate use of the phrase "libertarian free will" and, by the same set of reasons, "compatibilist free will":

"Libertarian free will" is shorthand for "a libertarian conception of free will," just as "Newtonian simultaneity" is shorthand for "a Newtonian conception of simultaneity." Peter van Inwagen has complained vehemently about my use of a term like "libertarian free will"; so, I am stipulating what "libertarian free will" is to denote. Since "free will" is a term of philosophical art, it does not (*pace* van Inwagen) have an unambiguous pre-theoretical meaning. "Libertarian free will" and "compatibilist free will" are as innocent as "Newtonian simultaneity" and "Einsteinian simultaneity." All these terms are clear and unambiguous. (Baker, 2009, p. 173, note 44)

In what follows, I will follow Baker in thinking there is an acceptable use of the terms "libertarian free will" and "compatibilist free will," despite agreeing with van Inwagen that both sides of this debate are agreeing on the existence of a single thing.

General positions with respect to the nature of free will

In addition to the debate between compatibilists and incompatibilists regarding the compatibility question, there are other crucial questions regarding the nature of free will. Setting aside the compatibility question, how should we understand this thing called "free will"? Answering this question is difficult, at least in part because there are "many varieties of free will," only some of which are "worth wanting" (Dennett, 1984, pp. 72 and 153–72). As Manuel Vargas notes,

> As numerous incompatibilists have long acknowledged, there are plenty of senses of freedom, and perhaps of responsibility, that are compatible with determinism. What is at stake, at least in the mainstream of philosophical work on free will, is the kind of freedom that is the distinctive mark of responsible agency and attendant judgments of deservingness of moralized praise and blame.[7] (Vargas, 2009, p. 49)

As indicated earlier, I'm going to stipulate that "free will" and "freedom" refer to the kind of freedom or control over one's actions that is required for moral responsibility.[8] While this isn't the only (or perhaps even the most important) kind of freedom, this is the freedom that is central to the majority of the contemporary philosophical debates about free will.

But even with this restriction about the kind of free will made, there is still a further important issue regarding the nature of free will that needs to be addressed. As I've argued elsewhere (Timpe, 2008, ch. 1), the contemporary free will literature contains two dominant general conceptions of the nature of free will. According to the first of these, which has received the majority of the attention in the literature, free will is primarily a function of being able to do otherwise than one in fact does. For example, I have free will with respect to drinking too much espresso if I could have exercised temperance and stopped after three shots. According to the second approach, free will is primarily a function of an agent being the source of her actions. On this approach, I drink the espresso of my own free will if nothing outside of me is causally sufficient for my action or choice. Both of these notions can be seen in the following passage taken from Robert Kane:

> We believe we have free will when we view ourselves as agents capable of influencing the world in various ways. Open alternatives, or alternative possibilities, seem to lie before us. We reason and deliberate among them and choose. We feel (1) it is "up to us" what we choose and how we act; and this means we could have chosen or acted otherwise. As Aristotle noted: when acting is "up to us," so is not acting. This "up-to-us-ness" also suggests (2) the ultimate control of our actions lies in us and not outside us in factors beyond our control.[9] (Kane, 2005, p. 6)

The vast majority of the contemporary free will literature focuses on the first of these two approaches, so much so that John Martin Fischer (1999, p. 99) refers to it as the traditional view: "Traditionally the most influential view about the sort of freedom necessary and sufficient for moral responsibility posits that this sort of freedom involves the availability of genuinely open alternative possibilities at certain key points in one's life." In contrast, a smaller, but growing, percentage of the extant literature focuses primarily on the issues of "sourcehood" and "origination" that are at the heart of the second approach to free will. I will call the first of these conceptions—the conception that free will is primarily a matter of having alternative possibilities—the "alternative possibilities conception." Similarly, I will call the second of these conceptions—that free will is primarily a matter of our being the source of our choices in a way that cannot be traced to sufficient causal antecedents outside of us—the "sourcehood conception."

The distinction between the alternative possibilities conception and the sourcehood conception, on the one hand, and the debate between compatibilists and incompatibilists over the correct answer to the compatibility question, on the other hand, are orthogonal to each other. There are compatibilists and incompatibilists who embrace the alternative possibilities conception,[10] just as there are compatibilists and incompatibilists who prefer the sourcehood conception.[11] Therefore, how one attempts to address the existence question will depend not only on one's answer to the compatibility question, but also on which of these two conceptions of the nature of free will one endorses. Rather than settle these issues here, in what follows I will simply assume that one is able to give an account of what free will is that specifies these issues as one prefers.

Positive answers to the existence question

Let us turn now to ways in which one could attempt to answer the existence question. I first consider ways in which one could attempt to justify a positive answer to the existence question; I will then show ways one could approach giving a negative answer to the same question. There are at least two general ways one could attempt to argue for the existence of free will, which I will call "indirect" and "direct."

Indirect proofs

I begin with indirect proofs for the existence of free will. These proofs proceed by showing that free will is a necessary condition on something else that is itself actual; they are indirect in the sense that they go "through" this other existant. Peter van Inwagen provides one such argument as follows:

> There are, moreover, seemingly unanswerable arguments that, if they are correct, demonstrate that the existence of moral responsibility entails the existence of free will, and, therefore, if free will does not exist, moral responsibility does not exist either. It is, however, evident that moral responsibility does exist: if there were no such thing as moral responsibility nothing would be anyone's fault, and it is evident that there are states of affairs to which one can point and say, correctly, to certain people: That's *your* fault.[12] (van Inwagen, 2008, p. 328)

Other indirect proofs could be offered that free will is necessary for basic desert, justified deliberation, agency, rationality, the autonomy and dignity of persons, creativity, cooperation, self-expression, artistic creativity, or the value of friendship and love.[13] Whatever form an indirect proof takes, two steps will be needed for such a proof to be successful:

i. the proof will have to succeed in showing that free will is necessary for this further object, *x*; and
ii. it will have to be the case that the actuality of *x* is evident or established by a further argument.

So by their very nature, indirect proofs for the existence of free will involve two steps, both of which will be open to dispute. Consider van Inwagen's indirect proof based around moral responsibility described earlier. For him, it is "evident" that there is moral responsibility; but a number of philosophers—moral responsibility skeptics, a few of which we'll consider below—deny the existence of free will, thereby taking issue with step (ii) of van Inwagen's indirect proof. Or consider, for example, an indirect proof based on justified deliberation. According to van Inwagen, deliberating about performing a particular activity presupposes that one believes that it is possible to perform it:

> If someone deliberates about whether to do A or to do B, it follows that his behavior manifests a belief that it is *possible* for him to do A—that he *can* do A, that he has it within his power to do A—and a belief that it is possible for him to do B. Someone's trying to decide which of two books to buy manifests a belief with respect to each of these books that it is possible for him to buy *it* just as surely as would his holding it aloft and crying, "I can buy this book."[14] (van Inwagen, 1983, p. 155)

Van Inwagen considers Baron Holbach, who denied the existence of free will. Van Inwagen thinks it obvious that Holbach deliberated. ("Does he deliberate? Well, of course he did" [van Inwagen, 1983, p. 157].) Van Inwagen concludes not only that free will exists, but that either Holbach really believed in it as well or had inconsistent beliefs:

> There is at least some reason to suspect that he [Holbach] did not believe that *he* lacked free will. I have given arguments above for the conclusion that no one could deliberate about whether to perform an act that he does not believe it is possible for him to perform. Even if these arguments are wrong, their *conclusion* has been accepted by everyone I know of who has thought about deliberation.[15] (van Inwagen, 1983, p. 156)

And lest the reader think that only van Inwagen (or libertarians in general) give indirect arguments of this sort, similar arguments are advanced by a number of leading compatibilists.[16]

Given their structure, there are two ways to resist indirect arguments for the existence of free will, each taking aim at one of the steps in the general form that indirect arguments take above. One could, for instance, deny the existence of the "further thing" that the indirect argument claims requires free will. This is exactly what Saul Smilansky does, for example, with respect to van Inwagen's indirect argument based on moral responsibility:

> Van Inwagen seems to think that the reality of libertarian moral responsibility *can* be proved in a way that he himself admits fails in the case of libertarian free will: the existence of libertarian moral responsibility is, in some unclarified way, immediately obvious, while this is not so with libertarian free will. As he puts it, "surely we cannot doubt the reality of moral responsibility?" (p. 206). . . . We all just know, it is claimed, that we are sometimes morally responsible in the libertarian sense. This of course would seem to contradict what many philosophers have claimed. . . . The existence of libertarian moral responsibility is far from being obvious: many people have doubted this and still doubt it. Since libertarian moral responsibility depends on the at best problematic notion of libertarian free will, it is highly implausible to see the existence of libertarian moral responsibility as obvious; and this is even more implausible if the existence of libertarian moral responsibility is thought to be obvious independently of the case for libertarian free will. (Smilansky, 1982, pp. 30 and 32)

As Smilansky here shows, in order for an indirect argument for the existence of free will to be successful, it must proceed via something which both requires free will and which itself has been successfully established to exist.

A second way to resist indirect arguments for an affirmative answer to the existence question would be to attack the other step in the general schema of indirect arguments. On this tack, one calls into question free will's purported necessity for the further thing which is taken to exist. Derk Pereboom, for instance, argues that van Inwagen's indirect argument on the basis of rational deliberation fails insofar as it is false that one must believe (and thus false that one must *truly* believe) that one has the metaphysical ability to pursue either of two courses of action (which is what van Inwagen thinks free will is) in order to rationally deliberate (Pereboom, 2008a).

It should be noted that there are no proofs for a negative answer to the existence question that are clearly indirect.[17] Even if one showed (i) that free will was necessary for some further thing and (ii) that the further thing did not exist, that would be insufficient to prove that there was no free will. For while on this approach the existence of free will is necessary for the existence of the further thing, the existence of the further thing is not necessary for the existence of free will.

Direct proofs

I turn then to direct proofs. First, I'll consider how direct proofs for an affirmative answer to the existence question go, and then discuss direct proofs for the denial of free will. Unlike indirect proofs, direct proofs don't try to establish that free will exists by showing how it is a necessary condition for some further thing (like moral responsibility or rational deliberation). Direct proofs work as follows. First, one specifies an account of what exactly free will is (e.g., free will is *xyz*) and then one attempts to show that that thing exists (e.g., "Hey look, there's *xyz* in the world").[18] One can take the direct approach to show the existence of compatibilist free will, or to show the existence of libertarian free will. (As we'll see later, one can also take a direct approach to show that free will does not exist.)

Consider first a direct proof for the existence of compatibilist free will. John Martin Fischer's particular version of compatibilism is the most influential compatibilist view in the contemporary free will and moral responsibility literature.[19] Even William Rowe, an incompatibilist, refers to Fischer's view as "the most plausible compatibilist account of freedom" (Rowe, 2006, p. 298).[20] According to Fischer's specific brand of compatibilism, which he calls "semi-compatibilism," the truth of causal determinism is *compatible* with moral responsibility even if causal determinism ends up being *incompatible* with a certain kind of freedom. Fischer differentiates between two kinds of control (or what he sometimes calls two kinds of free will): guidance control and regulative control. Regulative control involves having control over which of a number of genuinely open possibilities becomes actual. And while semicompatibilism is officially agnostic about whether regulative control is compatible with the truth of causal determinism, Fischer himself finds it "highly plausible" that regulative control is incompatible with causal determinism (Fischer, 2007, p. 56).[21] But, for reasons I do not have time to explore here,[22] Fischer thinks that regulative control is not required for moral responsibility. The freedom-relevant condition necessary for moral responsibility (what I earlier gave as the working definition of free will for this chapter) is guidance control, and such control is compatible with determinism. Fischer's discussion of guidance control is extensive. Here, let me simply give a brief overview that is hopefully sufficient for the task at hand. According to Fischer, "guidance control of one's behaviors has two components: the behavior must issue from one's own mechanism, and this mechanism must be appropriately responsive to reasons" (Fischer, 2002, p. 307). The responsiveness that Fischer takes to be required here, which he calls moderate reasons-responsiveness, requires that the agent "act on a mechanism that is regularly receptive to reasons, some of which are moral reasons" (Fischer and Ravizza, 1998, p. 82). This means that the volitional structure that results in the agent's choices manifests an understandable pattern of recognizing moral reasons for choosing in various ways. Such an agent "recognizes how reasons fit together, sees why one reason is stronger than another, and understands how the acceptance of one reason as sufficient implies that a stronger reason must also be sufficient" (Fischer and Ravizza, 1998, p. 71). Furthermore, the agent's volitional structure must also be reactive to those reasons in the right kind of way:

> In the case of reactivity to reasons, the agent (when acting from the relevant mechanism) must simply display *some* reactivity, in order to render it plausible that his mechanism has the "executive power" to react to the actual incentive to do otherwise. (Fischer and Ravizza, 1998, p. 75)

The second requirement for guidance control is that the agent takes responsibility for the reasons-responsive mechanism that results in her choices; that is, that the mechanism is *her own,* or one for which she has taken responsibility. This feature of Fischer's view marks an important difference from purely structural or hierarchical compatibilist accounts (such as Harry Frankfurt's). For Fischer, "the *mere existence* of [the right kind of volitional] mesh is *not* sufficient for moral responsibility; the *history* behind the mesh is also relevant" (Fischer and Ravizza, 1998, p. 196). So in order for an agent to be morally responsible, he needs to have taken responsibility for his volitional structure. This involves three related elements:

> First, the agent must see that his choices have certain effects in the world—that is, he must see himself as the source of consequences in the world (in certain circumstances). Second, the individual must see that he is a fair target for the reactive attitudes as a result of how he affects the world. Third, the views specified in the first two conditions—that the individual can affect the external world in certain characteristic ways through his choices, and that he can be fairly praised and/or blamed for so exercising his agency—must be based on his evidence in an appropriate way. (Fischer, 2006, p. 224)

Putting these various elements together, we can summarize Fischer's view as follows:

> *Fischer's Condition*: a person chooses freely only if he chooses as he does (i) because of an appropriately reasons-responsive mechanism and (ii) because that individual has taken responsibility for his mechanism in an appropriate way.

We might think of these two aspects as respectively insisting on the agent having the right kind of mesh and the right history behind that mesh. (Taken together, these two aspects clearly mark this view as a sourcehood approach—or as Fischer often puts it, an "actual-sequence" approach to free will and moral responsibility [Fischer, 2006, p. 224]—rather than an alternative possibilities approach.)

While Fischer is never explicit about the following, it's pretty clear from his discussions of guidance control that he thinks that at least some individuals at some times meet the requirements laid out in Fischer's Condition.[23] At least some rational agents have moderately reasons-responsive mechanisms such that they are capable of appropriately responding to moral reasons. Furthermore, some of these agents are such that they have taken responsibility for their moderately reasons-responsive mechanisms. Thus, given the nature of free will as construed by Fischer, there are at least some agents who have free will, and the existence question is answered in the affirmative.

Robert Kane is the libertarian who has done the most to prove via a direct route the existence of free will. Kane writes of the "two pronged modern attack on free will":

> The first prong of the modern attack on libertarian free will comes from *compatibilists,* who argue that, despite appearances to the contrary, determinism does not really conflict with free will at all. . . . The second prong of the modern attack on libertarian free will goes a step further, . . . arguing that libertarian free will itself is *impossible* or *unintelligible* and has no place in the modern scientific picture of the world. Such an ultimate freedom is not something we could have anyway, says its critics. (Kane, 2007, pp. 8–9)

In response to the first prong, Kane endorses a number of arguments which aim to show that free will is incompatible with the truth of causal determinism. Kane endorses a version of van Inwagen's influential Consequence Argument (Kane, 2007, pp. 10–13),[24] but as we'll see later his account of what free will is entails another argument for incompatibilism.

For present purposes, I'll focus on Kane's response to the second prong of the attack, insofar as it is more related to Kane's attempt to prove the existence of free will. Kane writes:

> I think libertarians must accept the empirical challenge of determinism (that it might turn out to be true), if libertarians are going to be serious about finding a place for free will *in the natural order* where we exist and exercise our freedom. This is the "Existence Question" for free will, and . . . it cannot be finally settled by armchair speculation, but only by future empirical inquiry. (Kane, 1996, p. 184)

Kane wants to avoid appeal to "extra factor strategies" such as immaterial souls, noumenal selves, agent-causation, and so on, if at all possible. He thinks it is possible to avoid extra factors because the conditions required for free will are (i) indeterminism, (ii) alternative possibilities (or "the ability to do otherwise"), and (iii) ultimate responsibility. Since Kane is an incompatibilist, it is easy to see why he thinks free will requires indeterminism. Furthermore, not all indeterminism is relevant for free will; the indeterminism must be related to what the agent is able to do. Shortly, we'll see later that the need for alternative possibilities is also entailed by the third condition, which Kane thinks is more fundamental for the existence of free will. The basic idea behind ultimate responsibility is as follows:

> to be *ultimately responsible* for an action, an agent must be responsible for anything that is a sufficient reason, cause, or motive for the action's

occurring. . . . [This] tells us that free will is only possible if *some* voluntary choices or actions in our life histories did *not* have sufficient causes or motives that would have required us to have formed them by still earlier choices. (Kane, 2005, pp. 121–2).[25]

Kane doesn't think that every free and voluntary choice needs to lack sufficient causes or motives; he allows for the fact that some of an agent's actions can be necessitated by her character—that is, by her will, motives, purposes, and so on. In these cases, the necessitated action will be free only if the agent freely formed her character which necessitated the later action:

If agents are to be ultimately responsible for their own wills, then if their wills are already set one way when they act, *they* must be responsible for their wills having been set that way—not God . . . or fate or society or behavioral engineers or nature or upbringing. And this means that some of their past voluntary choices or actions must have played an indispensable role in the formation of their present purposes and motives.[26] (Kane, 2002b, p. 412)

On these will-setting occasions, the agent will satisfy what Kane calls the plurality condition, for on these occasions the agent is choosing between two competing options that are each such that she could have done them voluntarily, intentionally, and rationally (Kane, 2002b, p. 411). (This is why ultimate responsibility entails alternative possibilities, at least at some point in the causal history of an agent's actions.) Kane's classic example of a will-setting occasion is the story of a business woman, Anne:[27]

Consider a business-woman who faces a conflict of this kind [as described in will-setting actions]. She is on the way to a meeting important to her career when she observes an assault taking place in an alley. An inner struggle ensues between her moral conscience, to stop and call for help, and her career ambitions that tell her she cannot miss the meeting. She has to make an effort of will to overcome the temptation to go on to her meeting. If she overcomes this temptation, it will be the result of her effort, but if she fails, it will be because she did not *allow* her effort to succeed. And this is due to the fact that, while she wanted to overcome temptation, she also wanted to fail, for quite different reasons.[28] (Kane, 2002b, p. 417)

When properly elaborated, Kane contends that this case shows the various conditions that must be met in order for an agent, such as Anne, to have free will.

So far, this establishes what Kane thinks is *required for* free will. But it does not establish that we *have* free will. In order to do the latter step, Kane appeals to recent work in the philosophy of mind which can help explain how human agents can have free will:

> Imagine in cases of conflict characteristic of self-forming actions . . . like the businesswoman's, that the indeterministic noise which is providing an obstacle to her overcoming temptation is not coming from an external source, but has its source in her own will, since she also deeply desires to do the opposite. To understand how this could be, imagine that two crossing recurrent neural networks are involved in the brain, each influencing the other, and representing her conflicting motivations. . . . The input of one of these neural networks consists in the woman's reasons for acting morally and stopping to help the victim; the input of the other network comprises her ambitious motives for going on to her meeting.
>
> The two networks are connected so that the indeterminism that is an obstacle to her making one of the choices is present because of her simultaneous conflicting desire to make the other choice—the indeterminism thus arising from a tension-creating conflict in the will, as we said. This conflict . . . would be reflected in appropriate regions of the brain by movement away from thermodynamic equilibrium. The result would be a stirring up of chaos in the neural networks involved. (Kane, 2007, p. 28)

According to Kane, whichever of these two networks wins out, it will be the case that the agent has willed the outcome in the sense required for free will. Kane then cites the work of neurobiologists Gordon Globus, Francis Crick, and Christof Kock, and philosopher of mind Owen Flanagan as providing some empirical support for this account of competing neural networks (Kane, 1996, pp. 39 and 130). While Kane doesn't think that this empirical support is conclusive, he does think that it gives "tentative" support to the existence of libertarian free will (Kane, 1996, p. 197).

Negative answers to the existence question

As stated earlier, there are no clearly indirect arguments for the nonexistence of free will, for arguing that free will is necessary for some further thing x, but then showing that x isn't actual would not establish that free will does not exist. If one could instead argue that free will were sufficient for some further thing x and then show that x wasn't actual, that would entail that free will doesn't exist; but there are no such arguments in the literature. So, the attempts to answer the existence question in the negative that I will examine here will be direct attempts. But here there are two different ways one could develop a direct denial for the existence of free will, which I shall refer to as contingent denials and categorical denials. A contingent denial will be a view which holds that while it is possible that free will exists, it is a contingent fact that free will does not exist. Categorical denials will be stronger: free will does not exist because it is impossible for it to exist.[29]

Contingent denials

Derk Pereboom's "hard incompatibilism" is an example of contingent denial. Pereboom's case for hard incompatibilism has a number of steps. First, he argues against compatibilist accounts of free will. He offers a manipulation-based argument against compatibilism, which aims to show that,

> an action's being produced by a deterministic process that traces back to factors beyond the agent's control, even when she satisfies all the conditions on moral responsibility specified by the prominent compatibilist theories, presents in principle no less of a threat to moral responsibility than does deterministic manipulation. (Pereboom, 2008b, p. 93)[30]

The second step in Pereboom's argument is to argue that any satisfactory incompatibilist view which affirms the existence of free will must be of a certain sort. One way of classifying varieties of incompatibilism is in terms of what kind of indeterminism is required for free will. Some forms of incompatibilism hold that the indeterminism is (or needs to be) found in ordinary causation between events, while others postulate an additional kind of causation—agent-causation—to account for the indeterminism.[31] According to agent-causal views, the indeterminism involved in event-causation provides the opportunity for free will, but doesn't by itself provide for the kind of control needed. As Pereboom says in an early paper,

> According to one libertarian view, what makes actions free is just their being constituted (partially) of indeterministic natural events. . . . But natural indeterminacies of these types cannot, by themselves, account for freedom of the sort required for moral responsibility. As has often been pointed out, such random physical events are no more within our control than are causally determined physical events, and thus, we can no more be morally responsible for them than, in the indeterminist opinion, we can be for events that are causally determined. (Pereboom, 1997, p. 253)

Insofar as he thinks that event-causal libertarian views are unable to secure any more control than are compatibilist accounts, if there is to be libertarian free will, we would have to be agent-causes. However, Pereboom thinks it unlikely that we are agent-causes.

> Although our being undetermined agent causes has not been ruled out as a coherent possibility, it is not credible given our best physical theories. Thus we need to take seriously the prospect that we are not free in the sense required for moral responsibility. (Pereboom, 2008c)

Why think that we are not agent-causes, given our best physical theories?

> If agent-causes are to be capable of such free decisions, they would require the power to produce deviations from the physical laws—deviations from what these laws would predict and from what we would expect given these laws. But such agent-causes would be embodied in a world that, by the evidence that supports our current theories in physics, is nevertheless wholly governed by the laws of physics. (Pereboom, 2001, p. 79)

Therefore, according to Pereboom's hard incompatibilism, unless future investigation warrants a substantive rethinking of our view of the world in which we live, we ought to conclude that we lack the kind of free will required for moral responsibility. Given that we *could* have such freedom if the world were different (i.e., if we were agent-causes), his view is only a contingent denial of free will.

Categorical denials

In contrast, Saul Smilansky and Galen Strawson both advocate categorical denial. Unlike a number of individuals who deny the existence of libertarian free will, Smilansky sees the attraction it presents:

> The various things that free will could make possible, if it did exist, such as deep sense of desert, worth, and justification *are* worth wanting. They remain worth wanting even if something that would be necessary in order to have them is not worth wanting because it cannot be coherently conceived. It is just this, the impossibility of the conditions for things that are so deeply worth wanting, which makes the realization of the absence of free will so significant. (Smilansky, 2002, p. 504, note 3)

But the existence of free will is impossible because "the conditions required by an ethically satisfying sense of libertarian free will, which would give us anything beyond sophisticated formulations of compatibilism, are self-contradictory and hence cannot be met" (Smilansky, 2002, pp. 490–1).[32] In rejecting the possibility of free will at this step, Smilansky draws on the influential work of Galen Strawson. Strawson is probably the most influential categorical denier of the existence of free will. Strawson's categorical denial is the conclusion of his Basic Argument, which comes in a variety of expressions. Here are two of them:

1. Nothing can be *causa sui*—nothing can be the cause of itself.
2. In order to be truly morally responsible for one's actions, one would have to be *causa sui,* at least in certain crucial mental aspects.
3. Therefore nothing can be truly morally responsible. (Strawson, 1994, p. 5)

A more elaborate version of the Basic Argument is as follows:

> (1) It is undeniable that one is the way one is, initially, as a result of heredity and early experience, and it is undeniable that these are things for which one cannot be in any [way] responsible (morally or otherwise). (2) One cannot at any later state of life hope to accede to true moral responsibility for the way one is by trying to change the way one already is as a result of heredity and previous experience. For (3) both the particular way in which one is moved to try to change oneself, and the degree of one's success in one's attempt to change, will be determined by how one already is as a result of heredity and previous experience. And (4) any further changes that one can bring about only after one has brought about certain initial changes will in turn be determined, via the initial changes, by heredity and previous experience. (5) This may not be the whole story, for it may be that some changes in the way one is are traceable not to heredity and experience but to the influence of indeterministic or random factors. But it is absurd to suppose that indeterministic or random factors, for which one is *ex hypothesi* in no way responsible, can in themselves contribute in any way to one's being truly morally responsible for how one is. (Strawson, 1994, p. 7)

Although both versions of the Basic Argument given here are expressed in terms of moral responsibility, it should be clear from the context that at issue here is the kind of control required for moral responsibility—that is, free will as defined earlier.[33] And if it is true, as Strawson claims, that such free will requires control over things that it is impossible for us to control, then it will be the case that free will is not only nonexistent, but necessarily so. The existence of free will is categorically denied.

Conclusion

While contemporary free will debates have focused on a number of issues—Is free will compatible with determinism? Is free will compatible with indeterminism? Does free will require agent-causal powers?—a central question in recent years has been the existence question—do humans have free will? Above, I've canvassed the major ways that philosophers have set out to answer the existence question, both in the affirmative and in the negative. And while I haven't tried to provide an answer to the existence question, the complexities of the issues involved in doing so should now be clear. In particular, I've shown how one's approach to providing an answer to the existence question depends on how one thinks about other issues pertaining to the nature of free will. It remains for future work to continue to refine these various positions and arguments, with the aim of getting us closer to the truth of the matter.[34]

Notes

1   A more cautious claim is made by Copleston (1993, vol. II, p. 82).

2   This question is not the same as the more general existence question "does free will exist?," for it is possible there exist agents which have free will but are not human. While little if anything that I say in what follows hangs on whether or not humans in particular have free will, I will continue to frame the Existence Question in terms of humans both for ease of explication and because most metaphysicians working on free will think that humans are as good a candidate for having free will as any other.

3   Actually, it is not quite correct to say this is how van Inwagen defines free will. What van Inwagen defines is not free will but the "free will thesis." Van Inwagen advises that one "define sentences, not terms" (van Inwagen, 2008). In what follows, I danger not to take van Inwagen's advice. For more on this definition of free will, see van Inwagen (1975, p. 188) and Clarke (2003, p. 3).

4   The relationship between these two definitions of free will is all the more confusing because van Inwagen also says that free will, on his preferred definition, is required for moral responsibility: "Without free will there is no moral responsibility: if moral responsibility exists, then someone is morally responsible for something he has done or for something he has left undone. . . . Therefore, if moral responsibility exists, someone has free will. Therefore, if no one has free will, moral responsibility doesn't exist" (van Inwagen, 1983, p. 162).

For van Inwagen, this is because moral responsibility requires the ability to do otherwise, which for him, as seen above, just is free will.

5 Causal determinism is the thesis that a proposition, call it *P*, which completely describes the way that the entire world was at some point in the distant past, excluding all the temporally relational facts about the world, together with a proposition, call it *L*, which expresses the conjunction of all the laws of nature, entails a further proposition describing a unique future. That is, given *P* and *L*, there is only one possible way for the future to be. See Timpe (2008, pp. 12–14) and van Inwagen (1983, ch. III).

6 As Matt Talbert rightly points out in a personal correspondence, while incompatibilists and those compatibilists who believe in free will are referring to whatever capacity or set of capacities satisfies the control condition on moral responsibility, they disagree about the nature of this existant, and likely also the role that it plays.

7 Vargas (2010) comments as follows:

> I've been told that in the good old days of the 1970s, when Quine's desert landscapes were regarded as ideal real estate and David Lewis and John Rawls had not yet left a legion of influential students rewriting the terrain of metaphysics and ethics respectively, compatibilism was still compatibilism about free will. And, of course, incompatibilism was still incompatibilism about free will. That is, compatibilism was the view that free will was compatible with determinism. Incompatibilism was the view that free will was incompatible with determinism. What philosophers argued about was whether free will was compatible with determinism. Mostly, this was an argument about how to understand claims that one could do otherwise. You needn't have bothered to talk about moral responsibility, because it was just obvious that you couldn't have moral responsibility without free will. The literature was a temple of clarity. Then, somehow, things began to go horribly wrong. To be sure, there had been some activity in the 1960s that would have struck some observers as ominous. Still, it was not until the 1980s that those first warning signs gave way to the first boulders careening towards the pillars of the temple. It was then that the meanings of terms twisted. Hybrid positions appeared. By the late 1980s a landslide had begun, giving way to a veritable avalanche of work in the mid-1990s that continues up to now. Now, self-described compatibilists and incompatibilists make frequent concessions to each other, concessions that made little sense in the framework of the older literature. New positions and strange terminology appear in every journal publication. The temple of clarity is no more.

8 In response to the question "What is at the heart of the traditional concept to free will?," Daniel Dennett responds as follows: "Here's a suggestion: *Free will*

is whatever it is that gives us moral responsibility" (Dennett, 2008, p. 254).
While Dennett is right to relate free will with moral responsibility, the former
is not sufficient for the latter, as there are other necessary conditions on moral
responsibility; see Timpe (2008, pp. 9–10).

9 See also Kane (2002a, p. 10) for a similar discussion.

10 Alternative possibilities compatibilists include David Lewis, Kadri Vihvelin, and
Joseph Campbell. The most notable alternative possibilities incompatibilist is
Peter van Inwagen. For a further discussion of these positions, see Timpe (2008),
particularly chapters 1 and 2.

11 Sourcehood compatibilists include Harry Frankfurt and John Martin Fischer;
source-hood incompatibilists include Robert Kane, Eleonore Stump, Derk
Pereboom, and Kevin Timpe. For further discussion, see Timpe (2008),
particularly chapters 5, 6, and 7. Furthermore, it might be that one is agnostic
between the alternative possibilities and sourcehood conceptions of free will;
Al Mele and Manuel Vargas are two such examples.

12 Later in the same essay, van Inwagen says the following about moral responsibility:
"Since "moral responsibility" figures prominently in my statement of the free-will
problem, one might expect that at this point I should define this term, or at least
define some sentence or sentences in which it occurs—"*x* is morally responsible
for *y*," perhaps. I won't do this. If I *did* offer a definition in this general area, it
would be something like this:

   x is morally responsible for the fact that $p =_{df}$ It is *x*'s fault that *p*.

But so much confusion attends the phrase "moral responsibility" (the confusion
is of our own making; as Berkeley said," . . . we have first raised a dust, and then
complain we cannot see") that I despair of straightening it all out in a paper that is
not devoted to that topic alone."

13 See, among others: Kane (1996), Ekstrom (1998), Fischer (2006, pp. 21–4 and
ch. 5), and Dennett (1984, ch. 7).

14 Van Inwagen's argument takes as its starting point Richard Taylor's position
(Taylor, 1963, ch. 5), but differs from Taylor's in a number of important ways.
For related discussions, see Coffman and Warfield (2005), Nelkin (2004a, 2004b),
and Pereboom (2008).

15 Van Inwagen goes on in the same passage to say that the conclusion that
deliberation requires free will is "as near to being uncontroversial as any
philosophically interesting proposition can be." As we'll see in a minute, this
conclusion is the subject of considerable controversy; whether this tells against van
Inwagen's account or against the state of philosophically interesting propositions,
I'll leave for the reader to decide.

16 An example here would be Peter Strawson's influential article "Freedom and Resentment" (Strawson, 1962). Fischer often talks as if he supports an indirect argument for the existence of free will; see Fischer (2006), particularly chapters 2, 3, and 5. However, as shown later, Fischer also advances a direct answer to the existence question as well.

17 Manuel Vargas suggests, in personal correspondence, that Nietzsche may offer an indirect proof for the nonexistence of free will. Vargas suggests that Nietzsche "thinks that free will might be sufficient for moralized blaming, but he's independently skeptical about moralized blaming (e.g. on an interpretation where he's an error-theorist about morality in general), so there is good reason to be dubious that free will in the "superlative metaphysical sense" can be had. Of course, he goes on to attack that notion on independent reason, but I wonder if he isn't at least implicitly committed . . . to an argument of the [indirect] sort." For a related discussion, see Leiter (2010).

18 In personal correspondence, Manuel Vargas suggests that there is another way direct arguments for the existence of free will could go, which he calls "arguments from paradigm cases." On such an approach, one says that a particular case is obviously an instance of moral responsibility (and thus, on the definition of free will adopted above, a case of free will), and then works out an error theory about why others would ever doubt the existence of moral responsibility and free will. Peter Strawson's work would be one example of such an approach.

19 A number of the works in which Fischer develops and defends his compatibilist view of free will are co-authored with Mark Ravizza. Given that this view is further refined by Fischer in more recent single-authored work, in what follows I will refer to the view primarily as Fischer's account.

20 Similarly, Michael McKenna writes: "I believe that theirs is the best case for compatibilism to date" (McKenna, 2005, p. 132).

21 In particular, Fischer is inclined to accept the soundness of van Inwagen's Consequence Argument which argues that if determinism is true, then no one ever has the freedom to choose otherwise.

22 See, for instance, Fischer (2006, chs 2 and 6).

23 In Fischer et al. (2007, p. 4) there is a chart attributing belief in the existence of free will to Fischer.

24 The Consequence Argument is presented in van Inwagen (1983, ch. III). For further discussions of the Consequence Argument, see Huemer (2000), Baker (2008), and van Inwagen (2004). The latter also has the distinction of perhaps being the most entertaining read in the free will literature.

25 For an extended elaboration and defense of this argument, see Kane (1996), especially chapter 7.

26   For a related discussion of the connection between free will and moral character, see Pawl and Timpe (2009).

27   The name "Anne" is given to the business woman by Pereboom (2008b, p. 102).

28   For a criticism of Kane's business-woman example, see (Pereboom, 2008b, pp. 101–5).

29   Positions which engage in Categorical Denials are often referred to as Free Will Impossiblilism.

30   For a further discussion of Pereboom's manipulation argument, see Pereboom (2001), particularly chapter 4.

31   A third view holds that the required indeterminism is of neither of these sorts of causation, instead holding that free will requires no positive causal contribution at all. On some such views, exercising the kind of control at issue in free will need not be understood causally at all. For a recent defense of such a noncausal view, see Goetz (2009). A very worthwhile discussion of these species of libertarian views is found in Clarke (2005).

32   Smilansky's view is more complex than is indicated here, in part due to his denial that there is just one kind of free will: "compatibilism and incompatibilism are indeed logically inconsistent, but it is possible to hold a mixed, intermediate position that is not fully consistent with either" (Smilansky, 2002, p. 491). For a full description and defense of his view, see Smilansky (2000).

33   More specifically, Strawson has in mind what he calls "true ultimate responsibility": "responsibility and desert of such a kind that it can exist if and only if punishment and reward can be fair or just without having any pragmatic justification, or indeed any justification that appeals to the notion of distributive justice" (Strawson, 2002, p. 452). Strawson also defines true moral responsibility as "responsibility of such a kind that, if we have it, then it makes sense, at least, to suppose that it could be just to punish some of us with (eternal) torment in hell and reward others with (eternal) bliss in heaven" (Strawson, 1994, p. 9). Strawson appears to think these two definitions are equivalent; however, see Clarke (2005, p. 20) for an argument that they are not.

34   I would like to thank Matt Talbert and Manuel Vargas for helpful comments on an earlier draft of this chapter.

References

Baker, L. R. (2008), "The irrelevance of the consequence argument." *Analysis*, 297, 13–22.

—(2009), "The second-person account of the problem of evil," in K. Timpe, ed., *Metaphysics and God: Essays in Honor of Eleonore Stump*. New York: Routledge, pp. 157–74.

Clarke, R. (2003), *Libertarian Accounts of Free Will.* New York: Oxford University Press.

—(2005), "On an argument for the impossibility of moral responsibility." *Midwest Studies in Philosophy,* 29, 13–24.

Coffman, E. J. and Warfield, T. (2005), "Deliberation and metaphysical freedom." *Midwest Studies in Philosophy,* 29, 25–44.

Copleston, F. (1993), *A History of Philosophy.* New York: Doubleday.

Dennett, D. (1984), *Elbow Room: The Varieties of Free Will Worth Wanting.* Cambridge, MA: Bradford Books.

—(2008), "Some observations on the psychology of thinking about free will," in J. Baer, J. C. Kaufman and R. F. Baumeister, eds, *Are We Free? Psychology and Free Will.* New York: Oxford University Press, pp. 248–59.

Ekstrom, L. W. (1998), "Protecting incompatibilist freedom." *American Philosophical Quarterly,* 35, 281–91.

Fischer, J. M. (1999), "Recent work on moral responsibility." *Ethics,* 110, 93–139.

—(2002), "Frankfurt-type examples and semi-compatibilism," in R. Kane, ed., *The Oxford Handbook of Free Will.* Oxford: Oxford University Press, pp. 281–308.

—(2006), *My Way: Essays on Moral Responsibility.* New York: Oxford University Press.

—(2007), "Compatibilism," in J. M.Fischer, R. Kane, D. Pereboom and M. Vargas, eds, *Four Views on Free Will.* Malden, MA: Blackwell, pp. 44–84.

Fischer, J. M. and Ravizza, M. (1998), *Responsibility and Control: A Theory of Moral Responsibility.* Cambridge: Cambridge University Press.

Goetz, S. (2009), *Freedom, Teleology, and Evil.* London: Continuum.

Huemer, M. (2000), "Van Inwagen's consequence argument." *Philosophical Review,* 109, 525–44.

Kane, R. (1996), *The Significance of Free Will.* Oxford: Oxford University Press.

—(2002a), "Introduction: the contours of contemporary free will debates," in R. Kane, ed., *The Oxford Handbook of Free Will.* Oxford: Oxford University Press, pp. 3–41.

—(2002b), "Some neglected pathways in the free will labyrinth," in R. Kane, ed., *The Oxford Handbook of Free Will.* Oxford: Oxford University Press, pp. 406–37.

—(2005), *A Contemporary Introduction to Free Will.* New York: Oxford University Press.

—(2007), "Libertarianism," in J. M. Fischer, R. Kane, D. Pereboom and M. Vargas, eds, *Four Views on Free Will.* Malden, MA: Blackwell, pp. 5–43.

Leiter, B. (2010), "Nietzsche," in T. O'Connor and C. Sandis, eds, *The Blackwell Companion to Philosophy of Action.* Malden, MA: Blackwell.

Levy, N. (2009), "Luck and history-sensitive compatibilism." *Philosophical Quarterly,* 59, 237–51.

McKenna, M. (2005), "Reasons reactivity and incompatibilist intuitions." *Philosophical Explorations,* 8, 131–43.

—(2008), "Putting the lie on the control condition for moral responsibility." *Philosophical Studies,* 139, 29–37.

Nelkin, D. (2004a), "Deliberative alternatives." *Philosophical Topics,* 32, 215–40.

—(2004b), "The sense of freedom," in J. K. Campbell, M.O'Rourke and D. Shier, eds, *Freedom and Determinism*. Cambridge, MA: MIT Press, pp. 105–34.

Pawl, T. and Timpe, K. (2009), "Incompatibilism, sin, and free will in heaven." *Faith and Philosophy*, 26, 396–417.

Pereboom, D. (1997), "Determinism *al dente*," in D. Pereboom, ed., *Free Will*. Indianapolis: Hackett, pp. 242–72.

—(2001), *Living without Free Will*. Cambridge: Cambridge University Press.

—(2008a), "A compatibilist account of the epistemic conditions on rational deliberation." *The Journal of Ethics*, 12, 287–307.

—(2008b), "Hard incompatibilism," in J. M. Fischer, R. Kane, D. Pereboom and M. Vargas, eds, *Four Views on Free Will*. Malden, MA: Blackwell, pp. 85–125.

—(2008c), "Defending hard incompatibilism again," in N. Trakakis and D. Cohen, eds, *Essays on Free Will and Moral Responsibility*. Newcastle upon Tyne: Cambridge Scholars Press.

Rowe, W. (2006), "Free will, moral responsibility, and the problem of 'oomph.'" *The Journal of Ethics*, 10, 295–313.

Scanlon, M. J. (2005), "Arendt's Augustine," in J. D. Caputo and M. J. Scanlon, eds, *Augustine and Postmodernism: Confessions and Circumfession*. Bloomington: Indiana University Press, pp. 159–72.

Smilansky, S. (1982), "Van Inwagen on the 'obviousness' of libertarian moral responsibility." *Analysis*, 42, 29–33.

—(2000), *Free Will and Illusion*. Oxford: Clarendon Press.

—(2002), "Free will, fundamental dualism, and the centrality of illusion," in R. Kane, ed., *The Oxford Handbook of Free Will*. Oxford: Oxford University Press, pp. 489–505.

Strawson, G. (1994), "The impossibility of moral responsibility." *Philosophical Studies*, 75, 5–24.

—(2002), "The bounds of freedom," in R. Kane, ed., *The Oxford Handbook of Free Will*. Oxford: Oxford University Press, pp. 441–60.

Strawson, P. (1962), "Freedom and resentment." *Proceedings of the British Academy*, 48, 187–211.

Taylor, R. (1963), *Metaphysics*. Englewood Cliffs, NJ: Prentice-Hall.

Timpe, K. (2008), *Free Will: Sourcehood and its Alternatives*. London: Continuum.

van Inwagen, P. (1983), *An Essay on Free Will*. Oxford: Clarendon Press.

—(1975), "The incompatibility of free will and determinism." *Philosophical Studies*, 27, 185–99.

—(2004), "Van Inwagen on free will," in J. K. Campbell, M. O'Rourke and D. Shier, eds, *Freedom and Determinism*. Cambridge, MA: MIT Press, pp. 213–30.

—(2008), "How to think about the problem of free will." *The Journal of Ethics*, 12, 327–41.

Vargas, M. (2007), "Response to Kane, Fischer, and Pereboom," in J. M. Fischer, R. Kane, D. Pereboom and M. Vargas, eds, *Four Views on Free Will*. Malden, MA: Blackwell, pp. 204–19.

—(2009), "Revisionism about free will: a statement and defense." *Philosophical Studies*, 144, 45–62.

—(2010), "The revisionist turn: a brief history of recent work on free will," in J. Aguilar, A. Buckareff, and K. Frankish, eds, *New Waves in the Philosophy of Action*. London: Palgrave-Macmillan.

10

God

Graham Oppy

There are at least two different kinds of significant metaphysical questions about God. At any rate, there are two different kinds of significant metaphysical questions about God that I propose to take up in this chapter. These metaphysical questions are related to two importantly different kinds of arguments about the existence of God: those that argue against the existence of God on the basis of claimed inconsistency in the notion of God—or claimed incompatibility between the claim that God exists and other claims plausibly supposed to be true—and those that argue for the existence of God on the basis of inference to the best explanation from claims plausibly supposed to be true.

One kind of significant metaphysical question about God arises in connection with the following schema:

(A) It is doxastically possible that X is at least partly explained by the existence of God, an aspect of God, an action of God or the like.

The significant metaphysical question about God that arises in connection with this schema is this: Are there false instances of it? That is, are there Xs for which it is the case that it is not even doxastically possible that those Xs are at least partly explained by the existence of God, an aspect of God, an action of God or the like? Are there Xs for which it is logically inconsistent, logically incoherent or broadly logically impossible to suppose that those Xs are at least partly explained by the existence of God, an aspect of God, an action of God, or the like?

Another kind of significant metaphysical question about God arises in connection with the following schema:

(B) X is best explained by the existence of God, an aspect of God, an action of God, or the like.

The significant metaphysical question about God that arises in connection with this schema is this: Are there true instances of it? That is, are there Xs for which it is the case that the best explanation for those Xs lies in the existence of God, aspects of God, actions of God, or the like?

Since there are many different conceptions of God, there are many different sets of significant metaphysical questions that are generated by our schemas. As our conception of God is allowed to vary, we may get different answers to the question whether there are Xs for which it is logically inconsistent, logically incoherent, or broadly logically impossible to suppose that those Xs are at least partly explained by the existence of God, an aspect of God, an action of God, or the like. As our conception of God is allowed to vary, we may get different answers to the question of whether there are Xs for which it is the case that the best explanation for those Xs lies in the existence of God, aspects of God, actions of God, or the like.

We begin, then, with a discussion of conceptions of God, with uses of the words "god" and "God." After that preliminary discussion, we shall return to the metaphysical questions that arise in connection with Schema A and Schema B.

Conceptions of God

A natural proposal about the word "god" is that it connotes something like "a supernatural being or force that has and exercises power over the natural world but that is not, in turn, under the power of any higher-ranking or more powerful category of supernatural beings or forces," where supernatural beings and forces include (i) persons and forces that do not have spatiotemporal locations while nonetheless being causally responsible for and/or having causal effects on things that do have spatiotemporal locations, and (ii) spatiotemporally located persons that bring about causal effects at spatiotemporally remote locations in the absence of spatiotemporally continuous causal processes connecting their actions to these effects (unless somehow making use of quantum entanglement or the like). Given this account of the word "god," a natural proposal about the word "God" is that it connotes "the god." That is, the word "God" refers to the one and only god, on the assumption that there is just one god; else, it fails to refer.[1]

As I have already noted, there is considerable divergence of opinion, among those who suppose that the word "God" does refer, concerning the properties and attributes of the referent of that term. Before we can proceed with our investigation, we need to make a brief overview of the range of this opinion.[2]

Many theists—that is, many of those who suppose that the word "God," or its cognate in some language other than English, refers[3]—claim that God is "perfect," "maximal," "infinite," "greatest," "supreme," "ultimate," or the like. Often, these modifiers are paired with the very general descriptor "being" in the construction of definite descriptions that God is supposed uniquely to satisfy: "the perfect being," "the maximal being," "the infinite being," "the greatest (possible) being," "the supreme being," "the ultimate being," and the like. Other times, these modifiers are taken to apply to a base set of properties or attributes, recording respects or ways in which God is "perfect," "maximal," "infinite," "greatest," "supreme," "ultimate," or the like. Perhaps, for instance, God is "perfectly good," or "maximally powerful," or "infinitely compassionate," or "supremely wise," and so forth. Either way, this kind of talk yields a first class of divine attributes which, for want of a better term, I shall call "extensive modifiers": attributes such as perfection, maximality, infinity, greatness, supremacy, ultimacy, and the like.

Many theists claim that there is a range of nonrelational "metaphysical" attributes that are properly attributed to God. These nonrelational "metaphysical" attributes divide into two classes: those that are not typically ascribed to God's creation, and those that are at least sometimes supposed to be shared by parts of God's creation. In the former camp are such attributes as "simplicity," "indestructibility," "impassibility," "eternity," and the like. In the latter camp are such attributes as "personality," "agency," "consciousness," "freedom," and so forth. Among theists who claim that there are nonrelational "metaphysical" attributes that are properly attributed to God, there is division of opinion about the extent to which it is *literally* true that God possesses the properties that are thus attributed. Some theists suppose that it is only analogically, metaphorically, or figuratively true that God possesses attributes that are literally possessed by parts of God's creation; it is only analogically, metaphorically, or figuratively true that God is a person, an agent, conscious, free, and so forth. Others extend this stricture even to properties that are supposed uniquely possessed by God; it is only analogically, metaphorically, or figuratively true that God is simple, eternal, impassible, indestructible, or the like. Yet others suppose that it is literally true that God possesses properties from both of the classes identified earlier; it is literally true that God is a person, an agent, conscious, free, and so forth, and it is literally true that God is simple, indestructible, eternal, impassible, and so forth.

Many theists claim that there is a range of general relational "metaphysical" attributes that are properly attributed to God. These general relational "metaphysical" attributes are typically generated from something like the claim that God is the "creator," "ground," or "source" of things other than God. Thus, for example, many theists suppose that God is the creator—and sustainer—of the physical universe, responsible for bringing about and sustaining the existence of the physical universe, and for bringing about and sustaining the laws that govern the evolution of the physical universe. Beyond this, many theists suppose that God is the creator and sustainer of much—or even all—else besides. Some theists suppose that God is the maker (or ground, or source) of logic and logical truth, of mathematics and mathematical truth, of modality and modal truth, of values and truths about value, of morality and moral truth, and so on.[4]

Many theists claim that there is a range of "evaluative" attributes that are properly attributed to God. Thus, for example, many theists claim that God is good, just, beautiful, rational, wise, worthy of worship, and so forth. Perhaps correlatively, many theists suppose that there is a range of "reactive attitude" attributes that are properly attributed to God. Thus, for example, many theists claim that God is loving, caring, sympathetic, benevolent, provident, jealous, angry, and so on. In both of these cases, again, there is division of opinion about the extent to which it is *literally* true that God possesses the properties that are thus attributed. Some theists suppose that it is only analogically, metaphorically, or figuratively true that God possesses "evaluative" or "reactive attitude" attributes that are also possessed by human beings; it is only analogically, metaphorically, or figuratively true that God is good, just, beautiful, rational, wise, worthy of worship, loving, caring, sympathetic, benevolent, provident, jealous, angry, and so forth. Other theists suppose that it is literally true that God possesses "evaluative" and "reactive attitude" attributes that are also possessed by human beings; it is literally true that God is good, just, beautiful, rational, wise, worthy of worship, loving, caring, sympathetic, benevolent, provident, jealous, angry, and so forth.

The properties and attributes that we have considered to this point might all be properly viewed as *generic* properties and attributes of God. Most theists agree that God is properly—though perhaps only analogically, metaphorically, or figuratively—described using *some* extensive modifiers, nonrelational "metaphysical" attributes, general relational "metaphysical" attributes, "evaluative" attributes, and "reactive attitude" attributes. However, there are at least two further classes of properties and attributes that lead to much greater division of opinion among theists.

Many theists suppose that, apart from the general relational "metaphysical" attributes mentioned earlier, there are also specific relational "metaphysical" attributes that are properly attributed to God. These specific relational "metaphysical" attributes divide into two kinds. On the one hand, there are God's particular interventions in the course of mundane events: God's bringing about of miracles, granting of religious experiences, answering of petitionary prayers, and so forth. On the other hand, there is God's overall planning for and guidance of human history: God's provision of an eschatological frame for human existence and activity, provision of a soteriological frame for human existence and activity, and so forth. While many theists may agree that there are these two kinds of specific relational "metaphysical" attributes that are properly attributed to God, they may well disagree about further details. For instance, theists often disagree about which events are genuine miracles, which experiences are genuine religious experiences, which events are truly answers to petitionary prayers, what is the true destiny of humanity, wherein salvation really lies and so forth. Consider, for example, the peculiarly Christian doctrines of the trinity, incarnation, atonement, and resurrection. There are many theists who do not accept any of these doctrines, and hence who do not accept the imputation of properties and attributes to God that are made on the basis of these doctrines. Or, for another example, consider the peculiarly Catholic doctrine that a plenary indulgence can be gained on any day by recitation of the rosary or pious exercise of the stations of the cross. There are many Christian theists who do not accept this doctrine, and hence who do not accept the imputation of properties and attributes to God that is made on the basis of this doctrine.

As I noted at the outset, there is widespread disagreement among theists about the attributes of God. On the one hand, there is disagreement among theists about which of the categories of attributes that I have distinguished have literal application to God. On the other hand, for each—or, at any rate, almost all—of the categories of attributes that I have distinguished, there is disagreement about which of the attributes in those categories have any kind of proper application—literal, analogical, metaphorical, or figurative—to God. However, we need only a quite minimal conception of God in order to generate interesting questions in connection with the two schemas identified at the beginning of this chapter. In particular, if we suppose that it is literally true that, if God exists, God is the maker of the physical universe—where it is understood that only an agent can be a maker—then we have all we need to establish a launching pad for interesting metaphysical inquiry. Since almost all contemporary metaphysical speculation about God assumes at least this much, there is no danger that, given only this minimal initial assumption, our subsequent investigation will fail to engage with widespread concerns in contemporary metaphysical speculation about God.

Schema A (The doxastic possibility that God exists)

It is clear that, if there are true instances of Schema A—that is, if there are true instances of the claim that it is doxastically possible that X is at least partly explained by the existence of God, an aspect of God, an action of God, or the like—then it is doxastically possible that God exists.

There are various grounds on which it has been denied that it is doxastically possible that God exists. Some have claimed that the sentence "God exists" is meaningless; whence, plausibly, it follows that the sentence "It is doxastically possible that God exists" fails even to express a meaningful claim. Others have claimed that the sentence "God exists" expresses a claim that is logically contradictory, logically incoherent, or broadly logically impossible; whence, plausibly, it follows that the sentence "It is doxastically possible that God exists" expresses a falsehood.

Grounds for supposing that the sentence "God exists" is meaningless are diverse. Some have supposed that the sentence "God exists" is meaningless because it is neither empirically verifiable nor true in virtue of meaning.[5] Some have supposed that the sentence "God exists" is meaningless because it has no proper use in those religious language games that give meaning to the name "God."[6] Some have supposed that the sentence "God exists" is meaningless because it entails other sentences that are meaningless, for example, "There is a person without a body who acts in the world."[7] It is beyond the compass of this chapter to investigate these claims; I propose to proceed on the—arguably commonsensical—assumption that the sentence "God exists" is at least meaningful.[8]

Grounds for supposing that the sentence "God exists" expresses a claim that is logically contradictory, logically incoherent, or broadly logically impossible are also quite diverse. It is clear that we can select, from the range of properties and attributes mentioned in our earlier discussion, sets of properties and attributes that are jointly logically inconsistent. Thus, for example, it is simply incoherent to suppose that it is both literally true that God is impassible and literally true that God possesses certain kinds of reactive attitudes, for example, that God is literally jealous, angry, moved by our suffering, or the like. It is also clear that we can choose to interpret properties that belong to the range of properties and attributes mentioned in our earlier discussion in ways that are logically inconsistent or incoherent. In particular, this point is made vivid by some recent discussions of, say, omnipotence or omniscience.[9] However, it seems prima facie implausible—not to mention downright uncharitable—to suppose that there is no logically coherent conception of God possessed by at least some theists. Since it is plainly beyond the compass of this chapter to investigate these issues further, I propose to proceed on the—arguably commonsensical—assumption that it is doxastically possible that God exists.[10]

Given the assumption that it is doxastically possible that God exists, then it is surely plausible to suppose that there are true instances of schema A—that there are true instances of the claim that it is doxastically possible that X is at least partly explained by the existence of God, an aspect of God, an action of God, or the like. Perhaps, for example, it is doxastically possible that the existence of the physical universe is at least partly explained in terms of God's creative activity. However, the most interesting question that arises in connection with schema A concerns not the existence of true instances of the schema, but rather the existence of false instances *given* that there are true instances. Some theists have said that everything else—and they mean literally everything else—arises from God. God doesn't just make the physical universe and the physical laws. God also makes logic and logical law, mathematics and mathematical law, morality and moral law, value and axiological law, modality, meaning, and so on. Can all—or, indeed, any—of this be so?

In order to think about this question, it seems to me that we should start by considering things from the standpoint of the causal order. Making is a causal activity; to make something so is to cause it to be so. Moreover, to make something so is to effect a change in the causal order. At one point in the causal order, something is not so, and then, as a result of causal activity, that thing comes to be so.[11] The creation of the physical universe can be taken to be a paradigm here. Initially, in the causal order, God exists and the physical universe does not. Then, in the causal order, God causes the physical universe to come into existence, and to operate according to physical laws that God also causes to come into effect. Generalizing from this paradigm case, we have something like the following causal principle:

(C) When God makes something, there is a point in the causal order where that thing is absent, and then God's activity makes it the case that that thing is present at (some) subsequent points in the causal order.

(C) imposes clear in-principle constraints on God's creative activities. God cannot make—cannot bring about—anything that is true at all points in the causal order, nor can God make—bring about—anything that must already be true in order to make it possible for God to bring things about. If we suppose—as we should—that no point in the causal order can be either logically contradictory or logically incomplete, then it seems to me that we cannot also coherently suppose that God makes logic and logical law. If we suppose that God is always *one,* then we must be supposing that there is no point in the causal order at which mathematics and mathematical law fails to obtain— whence it surely follows that we cannot coherently suppose that God makes mathematics and mathematical law. If we suppose that there are things that are always necessarily true of God,[12] then we must be supposing that there is no point in the causal order at which modality and modal distinction has not yet been instantiated—whence it surely follows that we cannot coherently suppose that God makes modality and modal distinction. If we suppose that God is always good, beautiful, and supremely valuable, then we must be supposing that there is no point in the causal order at which value and axiological law, morality and moral law, and beauty and aesthetic law have not yet been instantiated— whence it surely follows that we cannot coherently suppose that God makes value and axiological law, morality and moral law, and beauty and aesthetic law. If we suppose that God is always conscious and capable of agency, then we must be supposing that there is no point in the causal order in which consciousness and capacity for agency are uninstantiated—whence it surely follows that we cannot plausibly suppose that God makes it the case that there are conscious agents (though, of course, for all that has been argued to this point, we can plausibly suppose that God makes it the case that there are conscious agents other than God).[13] And so on.

In the face of this argument, some theists might be tempted to say that these problematic things—logic and logical law, mathematics and mathematical law, morality and moral law, value and axiological law, beauty and aesthetic law, modality, meaning and so forth—are all just ideas in the mind of God, and hence in that way dependent upon God for their existence. But that suggestion is surely no help. For we can ask: have these ideas always been in the mind of God, or not?[14] If they have not always been in the mind of God, then exactly the same difficulties arise again. Was God not one before God had the ideas of mathematics and mathematical law? Did God have logically contradictory properties before God had the ideas of logic and logical law? Was nothing in

God necessary before God had the ideas of modality and modal distinction? Was God neither good nor beautiful before God had the ideas of value and axiological law, morality and moral law, and beauty and aesthetic law? Was God neither conscious nor capable of agency before God had the ideas of agency and consciousness? And so forth. On the other hand, if these ideas have always been in the mind of God, then we need to ask: Could they have been otherwise? That is, could there have been different mathematical, logical, modal, axiological, moral, and aesthetic ideas in the mind of God? (Could it have been, for example, the God was given to quussing rather than plussing?[15]) If so, then, *ex hypothesi*, it is merely a brute fact that the mind of God contains the mathematical, logical, modal, axiological, moral, and aesthetic ideas that it happens to contain. Even if we suppose that God exists of necessity, and that, of necessity, there are mathematical, logical, modal, axiological, moral, and aesthetic ideas in the mind of God, it remains the case that, on the view presently under consideration, the *content* of the particular mathematical, logical, modal, axiological, moral, and aesthetic ideas that are in the mind of God is not in any way dependent upon God. On the other hand, if not—that is, if there could not have been different mathematical, logical, modal, axiological, moral, and aesthetic ideas in the mind of God—then, even if we suppose that God exists of necessity, and that, of necessity, there are mathematical, logical, modal, axiological, moral, and aesthetic ideas in the mind of God, it remains no less the case that the *content* of those ideas is not in any way dependent upon God. After all, on the suppositions now in play, there is *nothing* that God could or can do, no way that God could or can be, that would change the content of those ideas. In short, if we suppose that mathematical, logical, modal, axiological, moral, and aesthetic ideas have always been in the mind of God, then whether we think that the presence of those particular ideas in the mind of God is necessary or contingent, we are driven to the conclusion that the *contents* of those ideas are ontic surds, not in any way dependent upon God's existence, properties, actions or the like.

In the face of this further argument, some theists may be tempted to say that we can defeat the idea that the contents of ideas in the mind of God are ontic surds by appealing to further esoteric doctrines about the properties and attributes of God. One thought—pursued, for example, in Kretzmann (1983)— is that the doctrine of divine simplicity might be invoked to save the day. If we suppose that God is absolutely simple in the sense that God is identical to each of his attributes, then we can suppose, for example, that God just is perfect goodness, perfect beauty, perfect wisdom, and so on. Moreover, we can then go on to embrace pairs of theses like the following, which seem sufficient to license the idea that God does indeed make morality and moral law.

(D) God conceived of as a moral judge identical with perfect goodness itself approves of right actions just because they are right and disapproves of wrong actions just because they are wrong.

(E) Right actions are right just because God conceived of as a moral judge identical with perfect goodness itself approves of them and wrong actions are wrong just because God conceived of as a moral judge identical with perfect goodness itself disapproves of them.

There are at least three problems here. First, it is unclear how this idea could extend to cover mathematics, modality, meaning, and other problematic categories. Second, the doctrine of divine simplicity, in the form that Kretzmann gives it, seems to be incoherent in more than one way: it identifies attributes that are plainly different, and it assumes that there can be instantiated attributes that are not instantiated in a bearer of attributes.[16] Third, and most important, any theory that yields both (D) and (E) just has to be wrong, at least on the assumption that "because" is univocal, irreflexive, and transitive. Given univocity and transitivity, (D) and (E) entail, for example, that right actions are right just because right actions are right. But that contradicts irreflexivity. The underlying problem here, I think, is that even if you grant that God is "perfect goodness itself," it is simply incoherent to suppose that one thing is both the measure of goodness and also that which makes it the case that it is (itself) the measure of goodness. If you think that "perfect goodness itself" is the measure of goodness, then I think you have no choice but to say that it is then simply a brute given that "perfect goodness itself" is the measure of goodness.

Even if the above argument provides good reason for supposing that it cannot be that God makes (all of) logic and logical law, mathematics and mathematical law, morality and moral law, value and axiological law, modality, meaning, and so on, it leaves open the question of exactly what can be coherently supposed to be made by God.[17] However, to pursue that further question would take us beyond the compass of the present chapter. Instead, we now turn our attention to the second of the two schemas that I suggested give rise to significant metaphysical questions about God.

Schema B (Causal order and the cosmological argument)

There are various people who will suppose that there are no true instances of Schema B, that is, of the claim that X is best explained by the existence of God, an aspect of God, an action of God, or the like. In particular, those who suppose that it is meaningless to suppose that God exists, and those who suppose that it is logically inconsistent to suppose, or logically incoherent to suppose, or logically impossible that God exists, will naturally suppose that there are no true instances of Schema B. Following the lead established in the preceding discussion of Schema A, I propose simply to suppose—without argument, or at least for the sake of argument—that it is doxastically possible that God exists.

Once we grant that it is doxastically possible that God exists, it is plausible to suppose that we grant that it is doxastically possible that there are some true instances of Schema B. For instance, if it is doxastically possible that God exists, then it seems plausible to suppose that it is doxastically possible that the best explanation of the existence of God is the necessary existence of God. For the purposes of the subsequent discussion, I wish to rule out "trivial" cases like this. What is of interest to me are instances of Schema B in which X is not something that is in dispute between theists and nontheists. The paradigm case—the one that I shall explore in detail later—is the existence of the domain of natural causes. Could it be that the existence of the domain of natural causes is best explained by the creative activities of God? Or, at any rate, could it be that the existence of the domain of natural causes is better explained by the creative activities of God than by any competing putative explanation?

Some people may suppose that this question is not particularly interesting. According to these people, when it comes to questions about what the best explanation is, what one ought to do is to consider total theory in the light of total evidence. The best theory—the theory that one ought to accept—is the theory that gives the best overall explanation of the total evidence that one has. Moreover, questions about best explanation concerning matters of detail are always simply "spoils to the victor": the best overall explanation of the total evidence is, *ipso facto*, the best explanation concerning any matter of detail. If we suppose—as nontheists must—that our best overall explanation of the total evidence is one that makes no mention of God's existence, attributes or activities, then, on the account currently under consideration, we must also suppose that there is no X that is best explained by God's existence, attributes, activities, or the like.

It is not clear that a view of this kind is defensible. After all, one might think, one can only work out which is the best overall explanation of the total evidence by considering how competing putative explanations fare on all of the particular pieces of evidence that one has to hand. And, one might also think, it is implausible to suppose that we ever really do arrive at best overall explanations of total evidence; for a range of reasons, we simply don't have the capacity to compare total theories on total evidence. At any rate, for the purposes of subsequent discussion, I am going to assume that we can make sensible comparisons of the explanatory virtues of different theories with respect to particular pieces of evidence. In particular, I am going to assume that we can make sensible comparisons of the explanatory virtues of naturalism and theism when it comes to the explanation of the existence of the domain of natural causes. This discussion is meant to illustrate the way in which Schema B can be used to raise and address interesting metaphysical questions.

We begin, then, with the assumption that there is a domain of natural causes. For the purposes of discussion, it might ease exposition to suppose that the domain of natural causes can just be identified with the physical universe that we inhabit. It might ease exposition even further to suppose that the physical universe that we inhabit is a standard Friedmann-Robertson-Walker (FRW) universe.[18] However, it is a substantive hypothesis that the domain of natural causes does not extend beyond the spatiotemporal manifold within which we are embedded, and it is an even more substantive—indeed, I think, almost certainly false—hypothesis that our universe is a standard FRW universe. Of course, we do suppose that the physical universe that we inhabit is at least a part of the domain of natural causes; what is left open is whether the physical universe is a proper part of the domain of natural causes. In order not to beg any questions, we do not suppose that the domain of natural causes is a domain in which there are none but natural causes; rather, we suppose that the domain of natural causes is the smallest domain beyond which there are no natural causes.

The hypotheses to be compared are (a) the naturalist hypothesis that there are none but natural causes and (b) the theistic hypothesis that there are none but natural and divine causes.[19] The method is to consider the theoretical— and, in particular, explanatory—virtues of these two hypotheses when they are paired with hypotheses about the global shape of causal reality, that is, the global shape of the domain of causes.

A *first* hypothesis about the global shape of the domain of causes is that it involves an infinite regress under the causal relation. If there is an infinite regress under the causal relation, then, under the naturalistic hypothesis, there is an infinite regress of natural causes. However, under the theistic hypothesis there are several at least prima facie possibilities. First, there might be a finite series of natural causes preceded by an infinite regress of divine causes. Second, there might be both an infinite regress of natural causes and an infinite regress of divine causes. Third, there might be an infinite regress of natural causes preceded by a finite series of divine causes.

It is incoherent to suppose that there is an infinite regress of natural causes preceded by a finite series of divine causes, since, *ex hypothesi*, there is no natural cause that uniquely succeeds the last of the finite series of divine causes (hence, no natural cause that is the one that is caused by that last divine cause). So we can set this case aside.[20]

If we compare the hypothesis that there is an infinite regress of natural causes with the hypothesis that there is a finite series of natural causes preceded by an infinite regress of divine causes, then it seems clear that the former hypothesis is more explanatorily virtuous, since it invokes only one kind of cause (as against two), and since, otherwise, the two hypotheses are explanatorily on a par (since each involves an infinite regress of causes).

If we compare the hypothesis that there is an infinite regress of natural causes with the hypothesis that there is both an infinite regress of natural causes and an infinite regress of divine causes then, again, it seems clear that the former hypothesis is more explanatorily virtuous, since it invokes only one kind of cause (as against two), since it invokes only one infinite regress (as against two), and since, otherwise, the two hypotheses are explanatorily on a par. (Might the theistic hypothesis have an explanatory advantage here if it says that each of the natural causes also has a theistic cause? No. Even under this further assumption, the divine causes in the theistic hypothesis would have exactly the same explanatory standing as the natural causes under the naturalistic hypothesis.)

Collecting the various threads together: under the hypothesis that there is an infinite regress under the causal relation, the hypothesis that there are none but natural causes is more explanatorily virtuous than the hypothesis that there are both divine and natural causes, insofar as we are merely concerned with explaining the fact that there is a domain of natural causes.

A *second* hypothesis about the global shape of the domain of causes is that it involves an initial contingent cause. This hypothesis admits of further elaboration: it might be that the initial contingent cause involves a contingent state of a necessarily existent being; or it could be that the initial contingent cause involves a contingent state of a contingently existing being.

Suppose, first, that there is an initial contingent cause involving a contingent state of a contingently existing being. Under the naturalistic hypothesis, there is a finite series of natural causes beginning with an initial contingent cause involving a contingent state of a contingently existing natural entity. Under the theistic hypothesis, there is a finite series of natural causes preceded by a finite series of divine causes, beginning with an initial contingent state involving a contingently existing divine being. If we compare these two hypotheses, then it is clear that the former is more explanatorily virtuous, since it invokes only one kind of cause (as against two), and one category of being (as against two), and since the two hypotheses are otherwise explanatorily on a par.

Suppose, second, that there is an initial contingent cause involving a contingent state of a necessarily existing being. Under the naturalistic hypothesis, there is a finite series of natural causes beginning with an initial contingent cause involving a contingent state of a necessarily existing natural entity. Under the theistic hypothesis, there is a finite series of natural causes preceded by a finite series of divine causes, beginning with an initial contingent state involving a necessarily existent divine being. If we compare these two hypotheses, then it is clear that the former is more explanatorily virtuous, since it invokes only one kind of cause (as against two), and one category of being (as against two), and since the two hypotheses are otherwise explanatorily on a par.[21]

Perhaps it might be objected here that it is a mistake to suppose that the postulation of a metaphysically necessarily existent natural entity is no less explanatorily virtuous than the postulation of a metaphysically necessarily existent divine entity. Certainly, it must be conceded that many naturalists have rejected the suggestion that there are any necessarily existent entities. However, it seems to me that it is nonetheless a mistake to suppose that naturalists cannot countenance metaphysically necessarily existent natural entities. If naturalists are going to take metaphysical necessity seriously, then, given the assumption that there is an initial state of the actual world, there is much to recommend *to them* the view that says that all metaphysically possible worlds have initial states that involve the same entities that are present in the initial state of the actual world. But, on that theory of metaphysical possibility, if there is an initial natural causal state involving an initial natural entity, then the existence of that initial natural entity does turn out to be metaphysically necessary.

A *third* hypothesis about the global shape of the domain of causes is that it involves an initial necessary cause. Under the naturalistic hypothesis, there is a finite series of natural causes beginning with an initial necessary cause (a necessary state of a necessarily existent natural being). Under the theistic hypothesis, there is a finite series of natural causes preceded by a finite series of divine causes, beginning with an initial necessary cause (a necessary state of a necessarily existent divine being). If we compare these two hypotheses then, again, it is clear that the former is more explanatorily virtuous, since it invokes only one kind of cause (as against two), and only one category of being (as against two), and since the two hypotheses are otherwise explanatorily on a par. (Again, I anticipate that some may object that necessary states of necessarily existent entities are not naturalistically kosher. But I demur. Naturalists can countenance metaphysically necessary states of metaphysically necessarily existent entities; and, if they do, they do best to adopt the view that says that all metaphysically possible worlds overlap with some initial segment of the actual world.)

Collecting together the various strands of the argument, we have the following conclusion: no matter what hypothesis we make about the global shape of the domain of causes, the relevant naturalistic hypothesis is more explanatorily virtuous than the relevant theistic hypothesis, insofar as we are merely concerned with explaining the fact that there is a domain of natural causes.

Perhaps some may be tempted to object to this conclusion in the following way. If we compare the view of a theist who holds that there is a finite series of natural causes preceded by a finite series of divine causes, beginning with an initial contingent cause (a contingent state of a necessarily existent divine being), and a naturalist who holds that there is an infinite regress of natural causes, we have been given no reason at all to suppose that the view of that naturalist is more explanatorily virtuous than the view of that theist. Indeed, isn't it plausible to claim that, in this particular case, the view of the theist is actually more explanatorily virtuous than the view of the naturalist, at least insofar as we are merely concerned with explaining the fact that there is a domain of natural causes?

I can certainly grant—at least for the sake of argument—that, in this particular case, the view of the theist is more explanatorily virtuous than the view of the naturalist, at least insofar as we are merely concerned with explaining the fact that there is a domain of natural causes; there is simply no inconsistency between this concession and the conclusion of the argument that I set out earlier. Schematically, my argument has a conclusion that looks like this: N_1 is preferable to T_1; N_2 is preferable to T_2; N_3 is preferable to T_3. It is perfectly consistent with this conclusion that, say, T_3 is preferable to N_1. However, if we suppose that the choice between N and T is either a choice between N_1 and T_1, or N_2 and T_2, or N_3 and T_3, then it still follows from my argument that N should be chosen ahead of T. But, if we set all other considerations aside, and concern ourselves solely with explanation of the fact that there is a domain of natural causes, then it is perfectly proper to suppose that the choice between N and T is either a choice between N_1 and T_1, N_2 and T_2, or N_3 and T_3. (Alternatively, we might argue the case as follows. Suppose that it is true that T_3 is preferable to N_1. It is still true that N_3 is preferable to T_3. And if, further, T_2 is preferable to N_3, it is still true that N_2 is preferable to T_2. Assuming that we cannot have violation of transitivity, it is guaranteed that there is a naturalistic hypothesis that is preferable to all of the theistic hypotheses.)

No doubt others will be tempted to object that the above argument is vitiated by the use that it makes of controversial theories of metaphysical necessity and metaphysical possibility. How could these appeals to controversial theories of metaphysical necessity and metaphysical possibility be justified given the aims of the argument?

Perhaps it might be said that judgments about naturalist invocations of metaphysical necessity and metaphysical possibility are to be assessed by naturalist lights, that is, in terms of what naturalists judge to be the best available interpretations of metaphysical necessity and metaphysical possibility. However, that response seems to undermine the idea that we are undertaking a neutral cost-benefit analysis of rival metaphysical hypotheses: for, it might be said, there is no reason to suppose that theists will be satisfied with naturalist interpretations of metaphysical necessity and metaphysical possibility.

A better response is to observe that theists who countenance metaphysical necessity and metaphysical possibility typically accept the same *kind* of theory that has here been offered to naturalists. For, on the assumption that God exists necessarily and that God's existence cannot be causally posterior to anything else, it follows that, if God's causally initial state is metaphysically necessary, then all possible worlds overlap with some initial segment of the actual world; and it also follows that, if God's causally initial state is metaphysically contingent, then all possible worlds have initial states that involve the same entities that are present in the initial state of the actual world. Insofar as we are merely concerned with explaining the fact that there is a domain of natural causes, the *extent* of the domain of metaphysical possibility is plainly irrelevant. Disagreement between theists and naturalists about what is metaphysically necessary and metaphysically possible has no implications for the cost-benefit analysis of competing explanations of the fact that there is a domain of natural causes.

Given all of the preceding discussion, I conclude that, if we focus merely on explanation of the fact that there is a domain of natural causes, naturalism trumps theism. In light of recent literature—and, in particular, in light of recent enthusiasm for causal cosmological arguments[22]—this may seem to be a surprising conclusion. As that literature makes clear, there are many people who suppose that it is possible to develop cosmological proofs of the existence of God based on considerations concerning the explanation of the fact that there is a domain of natural causes without so much as asking about the comparative explanatory virtues of naturalistic theories. The main moral that I draw from the preceding discussion is that you are very likely to go wrong if you try to develop arguments for a preferred view using only resources available from within that view and without considering the resources available from competing standpoints.

Schema B (Fine-tuning and the argument for design)

Even if it were conceded that, if we focus merely on explanation of the fact that there is a domain of natural causes, naturalism trumps theism, it might still be argued that this shows neither that there is no useful purpose that might be served by causal cosmological arguments nor that we need look very far in order to find further data that will reverse the explanatory ranking. For example, it might be suggested that considerations about the alleged fine-tuning of the universe for life, and considerations about the presence of consciousness in the universe, immediately give the explanatory edge to theism.

Consider, first, the alleged fine-tuning of the universe for life. The allegation that the universe is fine-tuned for life is typically based in some version of the claim that, if the values of various physical parameters had been slightly different, then life would not—and could not—have arisen in the universe. The question that is then posed is this: What explanation is there of the fact that these parameters take life-permitting values—that is, that they take values that fall within the narrow ranges that characterize life-permitting universes? Setting aside any scruples that one might have about the claim that the universe is fine-tuned for life—that is, supposing without any further critical discussion that it is simply true that the universe is fine-tuned for life[23]—we ask: does one of theism and naturalism provide a better explanation than the other does of the fine-tuning of the universe for life?

In order to think about this question, it seems to me to be fruitful to consider hypotheses about where in the causal order the fine-tuning for life of our universe first makes its appearance. But, in order to think about where in the causal order the fine-tuning for life of our universe first makes its appearance, we need first to consider hypotheses about where in the causal order our universe initially makes its appearance. On the one hand, it could be that there is no part of the natural causal order that precedes our universe; on the other hand, it could be that there is some part of the natural causal order that precedes our universe. Furthermore, it could be that all parts of the natural causal order are fine-tuned for life, or it could be that there is some initial part of the natural causal order that is not fine-tuned for life. Finally, if there is a divine causal order that is antecedent to the natural causal order, then it could be that there is an initial part of the divine causal order in which it has not yet been determined that our universe is fine-tuned for life, or it could be that, at all points in the divine causal order, it is determined that our universe is fine-tuned for life.

Suppose we say that the global causal order is fine-tuned for life at any point at which it is determined that our part of the natural order is fine-tuned for life. Then we have two major hypotheses: either the global causal order is everywhere fine-tuned for life, or else there is an initial part of the global causal order that is not fine-tuned for life.

First, we consider the suggestion that the global causal order is everywhere fine-tuned for life. Following our earlier discussion, we consider four hypotheses about the shape of the global causal order: infinite regress, necessary origin, contingent origin (but involving necessary existents), and contingent origin (involving only contingent existents). We compare the explanatory merits of naturalism and theism on each of these four hypotheses in turn.

If the global causal order is an infinite regress that is everywhere fine-tuned for life, then naturalism says that there is an infinite regress of natural causes, and that each point in that regress is fine-tuned for life. Whatever theism says—that there is an infinite regress of divine causes preceding a finite series of natural causes, all of which are fine-tuned for life, or that there are infinite regresses of both divine and natural causes, each of which is fine-tuned for life—it is clear that naturalism is more explanatorily virtuous.

If the global causal order has a necessary origin and is everywhere fine-tuned for life, then naturalism says that there is a necessary initial natural state that is necessarily fine-tuned for life, whereas theism says that there is a necessary initial divine state that is necessarily fine-tuned for life (i.e., there is a necessary initial divine state at which it is already determined that our part of the natural order is fine-tuned for life). Again, it is obvious that, in this case, naturalism is more explanatorily virtuous.

If the global causal order has a contingent origin involving necessary existents, then there are two possibilities for fine-tuning: either it is necessary or it is contingent. If it is necessary, then the argument goes the same way as the previous case. If the fine-tuning is contingent, then, in order to compare naturalism and theism, we need to compare ranges of possibilities. On the present hypothesis, naturalism says something like this: it is a matter of brute contingency that the universe is fine-tuned for life; there is no explanation of why the relevant values fall in the life-permitting range. And theism says something like this: it is a matter of brute contingency that God makes a universe that is fine-tuned for life; there is no explanation of why God has the preferences, intentions, beliefs, desires, and so forth that lead to the making of a universe that is fine-tuned for life rather than some other kind of universe. While, as always, the cost of naturalism is less, we cannot immediately conclude that it is more virtuous in this case. For it might be that, if we imagine uniform sampling applied to the two cases, we judge that it is much more likely that we should end up with fine-tuning on the theistic hypothesis than on the naturalistic hypothesis. However, if we suppose—as I think we should—that God could make any universe that is possible on the naturalist hypothesis, then we are surely entitled to the conclusion that the range of possibilities is no narrower on the theistic hypothesis than it is on the naturalistic hypothesis.[24] And, if that is so, then we can conclude that naturalism is also more explanatorily virtuous than theism if the global causal order has a contingent origin involving necessary existents and in which the fine-tuning of the global causal order is contingent.

If the global causal order has a contingent origin involving only contingent existents, then, I think, the argument goes the same way as the case in which the global causal order has a contingent origin involving necessary existents and in which the fine-tuning of the global causal order is contingent.

Collecting together the various parts of the argument, we can conclude that, if the global causal order is everywhere fine-tuned for life, then naturalism trumps theism insofar as we are concerned merely with explanation of the fact that the universe is fine-tuned for life.

Second, we consider the suggestion that there is an initial part of the global order that is not fine-tuned for life. Here, things get even messier, because we need to consider a range of hypotheses about where fine-tuning is introduced into the causal order. Fine-tuning might be introduced into our universe after some initial segment of the universe. Or it might be introduced at the origin of our universe, after some initial segment of the natural causal order. Or it might be introduced at some earlier point in the natural causal order, after some initial segment of the natural causal order. Or it might be introduced at some point in the divine causal order that precedes the natural order, after some initial segment of the divine causal order.

On the supposition that fine-tuning is introduced into the causal order in any of the first three ways just mentioned—that is, if it is introduced into our universe after some initial segment of the universe, or if it is introduced at the origin of our universe, after some initial segment of the natural causal order, or if it is introduced at some earlier point in the natural causal order, after some initial segment of the natural causal order—naturalists are driven to the conclusion that fine-tuning arises as the result of an objectively chancy process. However, on the supposition that fine-tuning is introduced into the causal order in the fourth of the ways mentioned earlier—that is, if it is introduced at some point in the divine causal order that precedes the natural order, after some initial segment of the divine causal order—theists are also driven to the conclusion that fine-tuning arises as the result of an objectively chancy process. Hence, we can conclude that, on any version of the suggestion that there is an initial part of the global order that is not fine-tuned for life, it turns out that fine-tuning arises as the result of an objectively chancy process. Consequently, given the assumption that God *could* have preferences, intentions, beliefs, desires, and so forth that lead to the making of any of the universes that the naturalist supposes are possible, it seems that we quickly arrive at the conclusion that, if there is an initial part of the global order that is not fine-tuned for life, naturalism trumps theism insofar as we are concerned merely with explanation of the fact that the universe is fine-tuned for life.

And so, collecting together the threads of the overall argument, we can indeed conclude that, insofar as we are concerned merely with the explanation of two facts—the fact that there is a domain of natural causes and the fact that our universe is fine-tuned for life—naturalism trumps theism. Surprising as it might seem, theism has no explanatory advantage over naturalism when it comes to the explanation of either of these two facts; theism is always more theoretically expensive than naturalism, and it never gives a more satisfying explanation of that which is to be explained.

Coda

Even if it is accepted that the fact that there is a domain of natural causes and the fact that our universe is fine-tuned for life are not—separately or collectively—better explained by theism than by naturalism, it may still be thought that we shall not need to go much further afield in order to find facts that are much better explained by theism than by naturalism. As foreshadowed above, it might be said—for example—that the fact that there are *conscious* agents in our universe is much better explained by theism than by naturalism.[25] Or it might be said—perhaps relatedly—that the fact that there are *rational* agents in our universe is much better explained by theism than by naturalism.[26]

Does the explanatory advantage swing back from naturalism to theism when these further facts—that there are conscious agents in our universe and that there are rational agents in our universe—are thrown onto the scales? Unlike the cases that we have examined so far—weighing the virtues of theist and naturalist explanations of the fact that there is a domain of natural causes and the fact that our universe is fine-tuned for life—these new cases do not allow a straightforward comparison in the light of hypotheses about the global shape of the causal order. According to theism, consciousness and reason are initial and universal properties of the causal order; there is no point in the causal order at which there fails to be a conscious, rational agent. However, according to naturalism, consciousness and reason are neither initial nor universal properties of the causal order; for any points in the causal order at which there are conscious, rational agents in particular locations, there are earlier points in the causal order at which there are no conscious, rational agents at those same locations. How, then, shall we set about evaluating the comparative explanatory merits of theism and naturalism when it comes to the existence of conscious, rational agents in our universe?

Many people suppose that it is a mystery how consciousness and reason could be found *in* a purely natural world: how could mere aggregations of molecules possibly be sites of consciousness and reason? Many other people suppose that it is a mystery how consciousness and reason could be found *beyond* a purely natural world: how could unembodied entities possibly be sites of consciousness and reason? As things stand, we clearly don't have sufficient reason to say that the explanatory advantage swings back from naturalism to theism when these further facts—that there are conscious agents in our universe, and that there are rational agents in our universe—are thrown onto the scales. (At the very least, we could only have sufficient reason to say this if we had some adequate way of evaluating the comparative mysteries.)

Moreover, the ground on which we might seek further facts that would deliver such a swing in explanatory advantage is plausibly not very broad. On the one hand, there are the limitations that are imposed by the kinds of arguments that we developed in connection with Schema A: we cannot expect that considerations about logic, meaning, mathematics, value, modality, morality, aesthetics, or anything else of a normative kind will suffice to make the pendulum swing. And, on the other hand, it is surely implausible to suppose that considerations about miracles, religious experience, and divine intervention in the mundane world can provide sufficient impetus; if naturalism trumps theism in all other explanatory domains, then we surely have very good reason to think that there are no miracles, veridical religious experiences, divine interventions in the mundane order and the like.

If all of this is even roughly right, then it suggests that theists need to be quite heavily invested in the idea that there really is a mystery how consciousness and reason could be found in a purely natural world. If we follow Dennett (1991)—and others—in supposing that allegations of mystery are seriously misplaced, then, I think, we must come very close to thinking that naturalism defeats theism; there simply is no domain in which theistic explanation is better than naturalistic explanation.

Notes

1 See Oppy (2009) for an extended discussion and justification of this account of the meaning of the word "God."

2 For more detailed discussions, see, for example, Hoffmann and Rosenkrantz (2002), Morris (1992), Swinburne (1977), and Wierenga (1989).

3 Here I *stipulate* a meaning for the term "theist." Some may say that I would do better to use the term "monotheist," arguing that all polytheists—including those who do not suppose that there is a supreme god—are, *ipso facto*, theists. However, it is now standard to use the term "theist" in the way that I have here stipulated.

4 See, for example: Adams (1999) and Leftow (forthcoming).

5 Notoriously, see Ayer (1936).

6 Perhaps no less notoriously, see, for example, Phillips (1976).

7 This view is at least suggested by remarks in Rundle (2004).

8 This claim has been little contested, even by nontheists, since Mackie (1982, pp. 1–3). There are, of course, notable exceptions, for example, Nielsen (1985) and Martin (1990).

9   See, for example, Everitt (2004, chs 13 and 15) and Martin (1990).

10 Again, this follows the standard practice even of most nontheists who have written about God since Mackie (1982). Perhaps Sobel (2004) might be thought to be an exception. However, I take it that he can allow that it is doxastically possible that there is something that is objectively worthy of worship, even though he supposes that it is metaphysically impossible for there to be any such thing.

11 In order to ward off possible misunderstanding, I emphasize that "then" has no temporal connotations in this discussion (and likewise for "next," "thereafter," and so forth). There are various views that one might have about the connections that hold between time and causation, and between the direction of time and the direction of causation. Perhaps time and causation necessarily coincide. Perhaps there can be time without causation. Perhaps there can be causation without time. My discussion is meant to be neutral between these kinds of hypotheses.

12 Remember: "always" here means "at every point in the causal order"!

13 In connection with agency we can also make the following point. It is obviously incoherent to suppose that God first acts in order to then bring it about that there is agency and the capacity for agency in the world. God must already have the capacity to act if God is to act.

14 Again, remember: "always" here means "at every point in the causal order"!

15 For an explanation of what it is to quus, see Kripke (1982).

16 There are other versions of the doctrine of divine simplicity that have been the subject of recent discussion and defense. See, for example, Brower (2008) and references therein. I do not think that "truth-maker" versions of the doctrine of divine simplicity have the capacity to provide substantive support for the claim that God makes all of logic and logical law, mathematics and mathematical law, morality and moral law, value and axiological law, modality, meaning, and so on.

17 Of course, like any philosophical argument, the foregoing is both contestable and susceptible of improvement. At the very least, it marks a first attempt at addressing views that have been vehemently defended by some contemporary theists. For an instance of such defense, see Plantinga (2007).

18 FRW models are the Standard Models of modern cosmology. Almost all cosmologists agree that slightly modified FRW models fit very well with the observable universe, that is, with the post-inflationary universe. For further discussion, see, for example, Oppy (2006).

19 Some theists may suppose that there are other categories of causes: perhaps, for example, there are other kinds of supernatural causes—angelic, demonic, Satanic, and the like. However, in the interest of easing exposition, I simply ignore this consideration.

20 Neil Manson asked me: What about Leibniz's hypothesis that there is an infinite regress of natural causes, each sustained or made to be by a single act of God? Am I deeming that hypothesis simply incoherent? I reply: I am not deeming

incoherent the suggestion that each natural cause is preceded by both a divine (sustaining) cause and a natural (efficient) cause. However, on the coherent version of this suggestion there is no action of the divine (sustaining) cause that is prior to all natural causes; and so this proposal is properly regarded as falling to the same kind of objection that I make against the proposal that there are two infinite regresses, one of natural causes and one of divine causes.

21   Neil Manson asked me: Does it make sense to suppose that there might be initial contingent states of a necessarily existing being? I answer: For my purposes, it would not matter if the answer to this question were negative. All I am concerned to argue is that, if we are prepared to countenance initial contingent states of a necessarily existing being, then we should prefer the naturalistic version of this hypothesis to its theistic alternative. (However, I should add that I cannot see any decisive objection to the thought that there are things that must be even though there is no particular *way* that they must be.)

22   See, for example, Craig and Sinclair (2010), Gale and Pruss (1999), Koons (2000), O'Connor (2008), Pruss (2006), and Rasmussen (unpublished).

23   For discussion pro and con, see the essays in Manson (2003).

24   Could it reasonably be denied that God *could* have preferences, intentions, beliefs, desires, and so forth that lead to the making of some of the universes that the naturalist supposes are possible? I don't think so; but there is doubtless room for further debate on this point. (Note that, if the relevant values do not fall in the life-permitting range, then what we get is a universe in which life does not arise. Consequently, it is not here relevant whether God's moral perfection rules out creation of universes with unfavourable balances of pain over pleasure and bad over good. The issue is whether it can be coherently supposed that God *could* choose to make a universe in which life will never arise. As I indicated above, I can't see why not.)

25   See, for example, Taliaferro (1994) and Moreland (2010).

26   See, for example, Reppert (2010).

References

Adams, R. (1999), *Finite and Infinite Goods: A Framework for Ethics.* Oxford: Oxford University Press.

Ayer, A. (1936), *Language, Truth and Logic.* London: Victor Gollancz.

Brower, J. (2008), "Making sense of divine simplicity." *Faith and Philosophy,* 25, 3–30.

Craig, W. and Sinclair, D. (2010), "The Kalam cosmological argument," in W. L. Craig and J. P. Moreland, eds, *Blackwell Companion to Natural Theology.* Oxford: Blackwell, pp. 101–201.

Dennett, D. (1991), *Consciousness Explained.* Harmondsworth, England: Penguin.

Everitt, N. (2004), *The Non-Existence of God*. London: Routledge.

Gale, R. and Pruss, A. (1999), "A new cosmological argument." *Religious Studies,* 35, 461–76.

Hoffmann, J. and Rosenkrantz, G. (2002), *The Divine Attributes*. Oxford: Blackwell.

Koons, R. (2000), *Realism Regained*. New York: Oxford University Press.

Kretzmann, N. (1983), "Abraham, Isaac and Euthyphro: God and the basis of morality," in D. Stump, ed., *Harmartia: The Concept of Error in the Western Tradition*. Lewiston, New York: Edwin Mellen Press, pp. 35–46.

Kripke, S. (1982), *Wittgenstein on Rules and Private Language*. Oxford: Blackwell.

Leftow, B. (forthcoming), *Divine Ideas*. Ithaca, NY: Cornell University Press.

Mackie, J. (1982), *The Miracle of Theism*. Oxford: Clarendon.

Manson, N., ed. (2003), *God and Design: The Teleological Argument and Modern Science*. London: Routledge.

Martin, M. (1990), *Atheism: A Philosophical Justification*. Philadelphia: Temple University Press.

Moreland, J. P. (2010), "The argument from consciousness," in W. L. Craig and J. P. Moreland, eds, *Blackwell Companion to Natural Theology*. Oxford: Blackwell, pp. 282–343.

Morris, T. (1992), *Our Idea of God*. Notre Dame, IN: University of Notre Dame Press.

Nielsen, K. (1985), *Philosophy and Atheism*. Buffalo, NY: Prometheus Books.

O'Connor, T. (2008), *Theism and Ultimate Explanation: The Necessary Shape of Contingency*. Oxford: Blackwell.

Oppy, G. (2006), *Philosophical Perspectives on Infinity*. Cambridge: Cambridge University Press.

Oppy, G. (2009), "Gods," in J. Kvanvig, ed., *Oxford Studies in Philosophy of Religion, Volume 2*. Oxford: Oxford University Press, pp. 231–50.

Phillips, D. (1976), *Religion without Explanation*. Oxford: Blackwell.

Plantinga, A. (2007), "Two dozen (or so) theistic arguments," in D. Baker, ed., *Alvin Plantinga*. Cambridge: Cambridge University Press, pp. 203–27.

Pruss, A. (2006), *The Principle of Sufficient Reason*. Cambridge: Cambridge University Press.

Rasmussen, J. (unpublished), "A New Argument for a Necessary Being." Available at: www.nd.edu/~jrasmus1/docs/philrel/NewNecBeing.pdf.

Reppert, V. (2010), "The argument from reason," in W. Craig and J. P. Moreland, eds, *Blackwell Companion to Natural Theology*. Oxford: Blackwell, pp. 344–90.

Rundle, B. (2004), *Why there is Something rather than Nothing*. Oxford: Oxford University Press.

Sobel, H. (2004), *Logic and Theism: Arguments for and against the Existence of God*. Cambridge: Cambridge University Press.

Swinburne, R. (1977), *The Coherence of Theism*. Oxford: Clarendon.

Taliaferro, C. (1994), *Consciousness and the Mind of God*. Cambridge: Cambridge University Press.

Wierenga, E. (1989), *The Nature of God: An Inquiry into Divine Attributes*. Ithaca, NY: Cornell University Press.

New Directions in Metaphysics

Tony Roy and Matthew Davidson

This book is mostly a companion to topics in object-level metaphysics. Questions are raised about properties and possibilities, physical and spiritual objects, and the like. Philosophers propose various theories in reply. But such theorizing leads to abstract properties and possible worlds, and to concrete incars which exist while inside of the garage but not out. What is worse, there certainly seems to be significant disagreement between very capable philosophers about all sorts of issues in metaphysics. Some disputes can be traced all the way back to disagreements between Plato and Aristotle. Thus one might seek a new direction for metaphysics. In this chapter we examine two such approaches. The first, "deflationary" approach interprets apparently controversial cases so that they do no harm. According to this approach, there *really* isn't the disagreement between metaphysicians there appears to be. The second, "experimental metaphysics," attempts to investigate the sources of intuitions that undergird object-level metaphysical theorizing. Perhaps the reason why there is significant disagreement between metaphysicians is that the intuitions on which metaphysical views rest are faulty epistemically.

In this chapter, we begin with an account of the standard approach to metaphysical questions as crystallized in Quine (1980a). We then turn to an examination of the revisionary experimental and deflationary approaches. In so short a space we shall not be able to give anything like a complete account or evaluation of these strategies. However we do suggest that as new directions for metaphysics they miss the mark. The initial concern about disagreement over bizarre results is real, but is adequately addressed without disconnecting from the world or standard method.

Quine's method for metaphysics

Quine's method for metaphysics and his "criterion of ontological commitment" are part of the background against which contemporary metaphysics is conducted. But, perhaps for this reason, the method is often left unstated, and so understood and either adopted or resisted in different versions. We characterize the method, and apply it in some cases to illustrate contested results.

Though Quine himself may not have been content to start this way, let us suppose there is a world and that ordinary claims and theories are true and false by virtue of the way it is. Then we get at what there is by saying what in the world makes our claims and theories true—since, by hypothesis, if the claims and theories are true, something in the world makes them true.[1] Faced with some claim or theory, the conditions under which it is true may be less than obvious. But we may offer an account of that in the world which makes it true. So the ordinary claims and theories are data with metaphysical results. Quine imagines that we offer accounts of truth conditions in an "extensional" language along the lines of that from Frege and Russell. This language is characterized by quantifiers and variables in the usual way. Given this, his approach to ontological commitments is characterized by a pair of key theses.

Quine is notorious for having stated multiple, not entirely equivalent, formulations of his first thesis. However, for our purposes, it is clear enough what he has in mind. In his essay "On what there is" (1980a), he says in slogan form, "to be is to be the value of a variable" (p. 15) and more explicitly,

Q1   A theory is committed to those and only those entities to which the bound
       variables of the theory must be capable of referring in order that the
       affirmations made in the theory be true. (pp. 13–14)

This thesis has both a positive and a negative side. In the same article (1980a), Quine begins by emphasizing the negative side. He thinks he is not automatically committed to objects of reference by the use of proper names (for they can be done away with via the Theory of Descriptions), and not committed to meanings, properties or the like, by the use of predicates. We need not pause here, as there are problems enough from the positive part. We are positively committed to whatever things must be in the range of variables for our affirmations to be true. So, to take an example from Quine, perhaps we accept an ordinary claim or theory according to which "some zoölogical species are cross-fertile." If its truth condition is,

∃x∃y(x is a zoölogical species ∧ y is a zoölogical species ∧ x ≠ y ∧ x is cross-fertile with y)

then we are committed to zoölogical species as such. But if we are able to offer some other account which does not require species in the range of the variables, say,

∃x∃y(x is an animal ∧ y is an animal ∧ x ≠ y ∧ x is not of the same species as y ∧ x is cross-fertile with y)

then so long as the account is adequate in other respects, we might be committed just to the animals required for its truth. Quine speaks of "paraphrasing the statement as to show that the seeming reference to species on the part of our bound variable was an avoidable manner of speaking" (p. 13). But, whatever "paraphrase" may come to, we have at least competing theories of the conditions under which the original claim is true, with divergent commitments. Observe that arguments are *valid* when there is no (possible) case that makes the premises true and conclusion not. So a test for this project of regimenting truth conditions is that it should preserve logical consequence—for if validity hinges on nothing more than truth conditions, and truth conditions are properly preserved, then logical consequence should be preserved as well.

We thus employ Quine's method when we move from data including theories or claims regarded as true, to accounts of the conditions under which they are true, and from such accounts to ontological commitments. We have suggested that Quine supposes accounts of truth are given in something like the extensional (canonical) notation of Frege and Russell. But this suggests a second thesis.

Q2 The truth condition for any expression (which has a truth value) may be expressed in some extensional language.

Suppose this is false, that there are true expressions whose truth condition has no expression in an extensional language. Then the situation is as follows:

Expressions with extensional truth conditions are a subset of all expressions with a truth condition. But then Q1 itself would seem to be problematic insofar as there is room for true theories whose commitments are not those to which bound variables must be assigned. Faced with some recalcitrant or problematic bit of data, one might "opt out" of the method, on the ground that data fall into the range to which the method does not apply. But Q2 closes this gap. Given this, in Russell's apt phrase, opting out might seem to have "many advantages; [but] they are the same as the advantages of theft over honest toil" (1985, p. 71).

Q2 is particularly significant when data seems non-extensional. Extensional expressions are characterized by stability of truth value under certain substitutions. Let us say singular terms are *co-referential* when they pick out the same object, (possibly relational) predicates are *co-referential* when they apply to the same objects, and sentences are *co-referential* when they have the same truth value. Then,

> ES A sentence is *extensional* iff switching a singular term, predicate or sentential part for one with the same reference cannot alter the truth value of the whole sentence.

For a stock example, suppose "is a creature with a heart" and "is a creature with a kidney" apply to the same individuals—where Lois believes that Superman has a heart, but being unaware of Kryptonite biology, does not believe that he has a kidney. And compare "Lois believes Superman is a creature with a kidney" with "It is not the case that Superman is a creature with a kidney." Under our assumptions, both are false. But switching the co-referential "Superman" with "Clark" flips the first to true, and leaves the second unchanged; switching the co-referential "is a creature with a heart" for "is a creature with a kidney" again changes the first to true and leaves the second unchanged; and either switch has the effect of changing the sentential part, "Superman is a creature with a kidney," for one with the same truth value. So the first fails each of the conditions for extensionality, and the other none. Expressions from the canonical notation all satisfy ES. But other languages might do so as well. Certain fragments of ordinary language are extensional, as might be a language with infinitely long expressions.

Quine might justify Q2 as a theoretical or experimental result: as a matter of fact, when we set out to give truth conditions for the sentences of science or whatever, we find that expressions of the canonical notation or of some (maybe extended) extensional language suffice. But there may be other reasons to accept Q2. Quine begins (1980c) linking sameness of truth value on substitution of singular terms to the indiscernibility of identicals. By the indiscernibility of identicals, if $a = b$, the properties of a are the same as the properties of b. So, given a picture of language as picking out things and saying that they have whatever features they do, from $a = b$ and Fa we expect Fb. We have assumed that there is a world and that sentences are true or false by virtue of the way it is. Without prejudicing the question of what sorts of things there are, and of the nature of their properties or relations, one might think that this assumption amounts to saying that there are things with properties and relations, and that it is the things with their properties and relations that make sentences true and false. Say this is right. Then all we need to describe the world is the ability to pick out things and to say that they have whatever properties and relations they do. It may be that the truth condition for some sentence is that things or the world satisfy some complex condition; but so long as we are able to state this condition, there is nothing more to be said about the world. This seems to be just the sort of thing extensional languages are fitted to do. And it motivates Q2.

Now consider what happens when extensionality seems to fail. Quine (1980c) opens with the point about the indiscernibility of identicals, and then moves to an example where substitution seems problematic. Based on the true identity, "Cicero = Tully," we might substitute into

"Cicero" contains six letters

to obtain, "'Tully' contains six letters." But the former is true and the latter is false. However, this is held not to be a failure of substitutivity, insofar as nothing in the displayed sentence names Cicero. Rather, what is named is a word that contains six letters. A proper substitution is based on,

"Cicero" = Tully's other name that begins with "C"

to get the perfectly true, "Tully's other name that begins with 'C' contains six letters." By requiring extensionality, we thus require clarity about what things are said to have what properties—in this case, it is the *name* with the property of having six letters, where substitution works as one would expect for designators of it. And this clarity is just right when we are concerned about questions of ontology.[2]

More substantively, suppose we let a language have an operator $\langle F \rangle$ for "at some future time" and that, as it happens, "is Bob's brother" and "is Bob's sibling" are co-extensional, although Bob has a sister on the way. In this case, $\langle F \rangle \exists x (x$ is

Bob's sibling ∧ x is female) is true, while ⟨F⟩∃x(x is Bob's brother ∧ x is female) is false. So extensionality fails. A response, like the one above, is that we have not gotten the objects and properties right. Thus, ∃t∃x(t is a time after now ∧ x is Bob's sibling at t ∧ x is female at t) is true, while ∃t∃x(t is a time after now ∧ x is Bob's brother at t ∧ x is female at t) is false. But there is no failure of extensionality insofar as there is a sister and time to which "x is Bob's sibling at t" applies but "x is Bob's brother at t" does not; so the relations are not co-extensional, even though they apply to the same persons now. Of course, among the objects over which the quantifiers range are times.

Little changes if we consider an operator ◊ for what is possibly the case, where ◊∃x(x is Bob's sibling ∧ x is female) is true, while ◊∃x(x is Bob's brother ∧ x is female) is false. Where "x is Bob's sibling" and "x is Bob's brother" actually apply to the same individuals, extensionality fails. One response is to let the quantifiers range over *worlds*. Thus ∃w∃x(w is a way the world could be ∧ x is Bob's sibling at w ∧ x is female at w) is true, while ∃w∃x(w is a way the world could be ∧ x is Bob's brother at w ∧ x is female at w) is false. But there is no failure of extensionality, insofar as there is a sister and world to which "x is Bob's sibling at w" applies but "x is Bob's brother at w" does not; so the relations are not co-extensional, even though they actually apply to the same persons. And we quantify over ways the world can be.

Of course, these are not the only responses. Quine is satisfied enough with the response for times, and with corresponding ontological commitments. But he is not at all happy with the appeal to worlds.[3] At any rate, within the method, one is pressed to (i) accept the commitments, (ii) reject the data, or (iii) offer an alternative account of the truth conditions. In the ordinary case original data is secure—more secure than philosophical theories proposed to account for it. So we are engaged in the project of offering theories to account for truth, and so to identify corresponding ontological commitments.

To see in a different way how such results may be troubling, consider a case from van Inwagen (2004), where he applies Quine's method, backed by entailment considerations, for the result that there are abstract properties. Van Inwagen takes as his example,

Spiders share some of the anatomical features of insects.

This has the apparent form, ∃x(x is an anatomical feature ∧ insects have x ∧ spiders have x), which is true only if something in the range of the variables is an anatomical feature. But features, qualities, characteristics, properties, and the like may seem to be just the same thing. (And if there are distinctions to be made between any of these, it is likely that one will be no more palatable than another to those of nominalist leanings.) So by Q1 there is an apparent commitment to properties—unless of course we are willing to reject the data, or there is an acceptable way to account for the data that avoids the consequence.

In this case, the data seems secure—there is no denying that spiders share some of the anatomical features of insects. It is impossible to survey all the attempts to account for the data. But the difficulty of providing alternatives is highlighted by the requirement that an account of truth conditions should preserve logical consequence. Consider a (reasonably traditional) response along the following lines: spiders share some of the anatomical features of insects just in case spiders are like insects in some anatomically relevant ways. We require a resemblance between spiders and insects. But van Inwagen observes that this seems to require quantification over "ways one thing can be like another," something like $\exists x (x$ is a way one thing can be like another $\land$ x is anatomically relevant $\land$ spiders are like insects in x); thus there is commitment to ways one thing can be like another. But this may seem to be a perversion of the resemblance strategy. Perhaps the idea is merely to observe that there is an unstructured relation between the class of spiders and the class of insects, so that spiders stand in the "share-some-of-the-anatomical-features-of" relation to insects, or to emphasize its primitive nature, say, the class of spiders *blaphs* the class of insects. So far, so good. But consider the argument,

1. If two female spiders are of the same species, then one is like the other in all anatomically relevant ways.
2. If a is like b in some anatomically relevant way, and b is like c in the same way, then a is like c in that way.

---

3. An insect that is like a female spider in some anatomically relevant ways is like any female spider of the same species in some anatomically relevant ways.

The argument is valid. And if the premises and conclusion are given a structured account then the conclusion follows by the usual methods. (Challenge: try it!) But it is hardly clear how the conclusion results where the premise and conclusion are unstructured. Van Inwagen thinks that accounts which preserve consequence will have a quantificantional structure not much simpler than the apparent quantificational structure of the "original" (cf., van Inwagen, 2001).

When it comes to saying what these things are like, van Inwagen offers a theory which, he says, is "nearly vacuous" (2004, p. 131). If we set out to describe the intrinsic nature of a pen or the like, we will have a great many things to say—about the nature of the ink, the working of the ball, or whatever. But not so for abstract objects in general, and properties in particular. Van Inwagen does, however, lay out a certain *role* which is at least inconsistent with some things others have had to say about properties. His idea is to identify the property role with the role, "thing that can be said of something." This lets him reach some interesting results about properties. Even so, he remains concerned about the lack of content about their intrinsic nature: "the fact that this theory is inconsistent with various interesting and important theses about properties shows that, although it may be very close to being vacuous, it does not manage to be entirely vacuous" (p. 138). So his application of the method leaves us with the result that there is a role to be played, and that something plays the role, but not much to say about the role players.[4] And similarly in other cases.[5]

But this may seem to be a crucial failure. Against all Quine intended, the result of his method may seem to be shadowy realms that are a "bloated universe" with a "rank luxuriance" that "offend the aesthetic sense of us who have a taste for desert landscapes" (compare Quine, 1980a, pp. 3–4). Perhaps, then, if there are problems about the things, there are problems about the method according to which there are the things. And this may lead us to seek alternatives to the standard approach.

Deflationary metaphysics

While fights about ontology rage, as Thomasson observes, "there's long been a suspicion . . . that some of the fights aren't real" (2009, p. 444). Many of these suspicions have a source in Carnap (1950).[6] We discuss a couple of recent versions as developed by Amie Thomasson and Eli Hirsch.

Verbal disputes

Suppose, as children will do, Hannah and Christina adopt new names, Hannah calling herself "Harry" and Christina "George," and Christina calling herself "Harry" and Hannah "George." Hannah declares that Harry is an astronaut and George a scientist, Christina that Harry is a scientist and George an astronaut.

When the dispute finally boils over into recriminations and tears, it is easily mediated, for it is *merely verbal*.

In Hannah's language (LH), "Harry is an astronaut" is true just in case "George is an astronaut" is true in Christina's language (LC); both sentences express the proposition that Hannah is an astronaut. And "George is a scientist" is true in LH just in case "Harry is a scientist" is true in LC; these sentences express the proposition that Christina is a scientist. So Hannah and Christina express the same propositions in their own languages—which is to say (on an account Hirsch accepts) that their sentences hold true in the same possible worlds.

Hirsch argues that something similar applies to typical debates about rocks, trees, tables, and the like—about "moderate-sized dry goods." Consider an argument between a mereological essentialist (RC, Roderick Chisholm) and a four-dimensionalist (DL, David Lewis). According to the mereological essentialist, objects cannot gain or lose parts. But the four-dimensionalist allows that things may have different parts at different places and times. Suppose that before us are a pencil and a soccer ball (Hirsch, 2005, p. 75ff). Members of the DL community allow that some one thing is first pencilish and then soccerballish, having the pencil as a part at the one time, and the ball as a part at the other; members of the RC community deny that there is any thing of the sort. All the same, restricting quantifiers (and simplifying a bit), members of the DL community allow that nothing composed by a single mass is first pencilish and then soccerballish; where this, according to the mereological essentialist, is necessarily equivalent to the claim that nothing is first pencilish and then soccerballish. And members of the RC community allow that there is at the earlier time a pencil and at the later a ball; and this, according to the four-dimensionalist, is necessarily equivalent to the claim that there is the pencilish and soccerballish thing. So the situation is as follows.

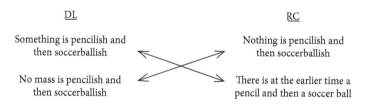

According to the DL community necessarily, something is pencilish and then soccerballish if and only if there is at the earlier time a pencil and then a soccer ball; and according to the RC community necessarily, nothing is pencilish and then soccerballish if and only if nothing composed by a single mass is pencilish and then soccerballish. And Hirsch accepts a view according to which, if "sentences (as uttered in certain contexts) are necessarily equivalent, they express (in those contexts) the same condition or state of the world, the same way the world is" (1993, p. 20; compare 2011, p. xi)—with the result that the necessarily equivalent sentences express the same propositions. So each community expresses in its own way what is agreed upon by the other, and our dispute is, again, merely verbal.

But this is not obviously right.[7] Consider again sentences accepted by the DL community—including the claim that nothing composed by a single mass is pencilish and then soccerballish. Their claims are true on a class of worlds populated by four-dimensional objects. So what is allowed by the DL community is that nothing in such a world composed by a single mass is pencilish and then soccerballish. But sentences accepted by the RC community are true on worlds where objects do not change parts; so for the result that nothing in one of their worlds is pencilish and then soccerballish, they require that nothing composed by a single mass in one of *those* worlds is pencilish and then soccerballish. But this is not what is given by the DL community. Similarly sentences accepted by the RC community, including the claim that there is at the earlier time a ball and then a pencil, are true on worlds that respect mereological essentialism. So what is allowed by the RC community is that the pencil and ball are included in such worlds. But sentences of the DL community are true on a different class of worlds; so for the result that something is pencilish and then soccerballish, they require that there is a pencil and a ball in one of *those* worlds. So we have the same sentences, but different worlds and so different propositions (compare Hawthorne, 2009; McGrath, 2008).

The situation is complicated since (as Hirsch assumes) the different views are supposed to be *necessarily* true. So there are not *possible* worlds of the different sorts. Still, in the spirit of Hirsch (2009, p. 237, note 24) let us suppose "vaguely and ignorantly" that in the manner of relevance logics not all worlds are possible worlds. Then there is room to distinguish the different views on the class of worlds.

Hirsch has a reply that structured propositions, which are fine-grained enough to distinguish four-dimensional from mereological objects, do the serious ontologist no good. A single possible world may be sufficient to make different but equivalent structured propositions true in its own way. Similarly, on his view, it does no good to jump to structured worlds, with objects that match up to one metaphysical view or another. On a charitable interpretation, sentences from any camp may come out true at worlds of the one sort. He agrees it is "doubtful" that each side can express the structured facts it interprets the other side to be expressing. However, Hirsch thinks a requirement of this sort is implausible. "Each side has sufficiently adequate grasp of what the other side's assertions amount to as long as it understands what [unstructured] facts are being asserted by the other side" (2008, p. 512). However the point is not that each side does not *grasp* what the other side's admissions come to, but rather that given the assumed necessity of structure in worlds, there is no neutral ground for the expression of supposed unstructured facts. Again, Hirsch allows there is a problem if there are *different* structured worlds corresponding to different sentences. Then he is inclined to agree that, once we accept a view which allows for his "quantifier variance,"

> There is no point in trying to hold onto language-shaped facts that are in the world independent of language. However, we can retain the notion of an unstructured fact. I think this is indeed our most basic notion of "reality," "the world," "the way it is," and this notion can remain invariant through any changes in our concept of "the things that exist." (2002b, p. 59)

But this is question-begging against the point from above according to which sentences from the different camps are true at *different worlds*. His unstructured facts build in that there can be no differences among views that differ about certain necessary facts. If we start with the view that there can be nothing to disagree about, it is no surprise that debates are merely verbal (compare Hirsch, 2011, p. xii). Observe also that even Hirsch apparently starts out with a sort of serious metaphysical perspective: a view which competes with ones on which worlds are necessarily structured.

In his essay "Ontological realism" (2009), Theodore Sider suggests that reality has an objective nature, where EXISTENCE is a property expressed by the existential quantifier which tracks that nature. EXISTENCE is a property of properties had by property P if and only if something has P. "Serious metaphysicians" who argue about the ball and pencil (or whatever) thus argue about the extension of EXISTENCE. We need not take a stand on this now. At least what we seem to have are different theories which describe the world in different ways. Certain of these theories are incompatible insofar as they are true on different ranges of worlds. And perhaps certain languages apply across objects in different ranges of worlds.

In this case, as Hirsch suggests, there is no reason to deny that claims from the different languages may be true at the same time (see below for discussion of ordinary language). Debate is more than merely verbal when, in some sense, the languages are true on incompatible classes of worlds.

Ordinary ontology

Amie Thomasson suggests that, while demonstrating intertranslability of disputant's claims would be sufficient to demonstrate that a debate is merely apparent, it is not necessary (2007, p. 197). She does not argue that claims in typical metaphysical debates are intertranslatable. Still, her idea is that apparently controversial metaphysical questions either are not interestingly controversial—or else do not have answers at all. Either way, supposed controversies are a chimera. Thomasson begins with an account of reference and quantification. From this she derives her consequences for ontology, modality, and then metaphysical method.[8]

Thomasson's view

The account of reference is developed against the background of debates in philosophy of language. It may seem natural to associate certain *contents* with both descriptions and ordinary names. On Russell's familiar account, "The present king of France is bald" is true just in case there is a present king of France, there is at most one present king of France, and whatever is a present king of France is bald; just in case, $\exists x(\text{PKF}x \land \forall y(\text{PKF}y \to x = y) \land \text{B}x)$. Since there is no present king of France, the first conjunct fails, and this sentence is false. Similarly, "Aristotle was a philosopher" might come to "The student of Plato and teacher of Alexander was a philosopher" and be given an analysis along the same lines.

But such accounts of the semantics of names have been subject to sustained criticism from Kripke (1980) and others. Thus, for example, many of us have, at best, only the vaguest idea of Empedocles. Perhaps you have never heard of him. Perhaps you think of him only vaguely as "an ancient Greek" or "an ancient Greek philosopher." Of course, you may be an authority on Empedocles and his philosophy. Plausibly, however, even those of us who do not know much about Empedocles can sensibly refer to him and ask, say, how many elements he thought there were. But if we are not sure how many elements he thought there were, it is unlikely that our idea of him is sufficient to distinguish him from various other Greek philosophers including, say, Anaximenes. So our idea of him is not sufficient for reference to him on a Russell-style account.[9] Thus *causal* and *direct reference* theories postulate causal chains which reach from the use of ordinary names, to "baptisms" at which the names are attached to objects, and so from uses to objects named, with the result that ordinary names contribute objects, not contents, to propositions; so a use of "Empedocles" contributes Empedocles, not some shadowy content which may be insufficient to identify him.

Thomasson thinks neither of these views is correct. Grant that Empedocles is not uniquely identified by a content associated with "Empedocles." So there is space for causal chains. But neither is causation sufficient. Consider a certain statue, together with the lump of clay, and atoms of which it is composed. Suppose you point and say, "Let this object be called 'Wazam'." With others, Thomasson holds that some content is required to disambiguate the *kind* of thing you mean to name—whether the statue, lump, or atoms.[10] Perhaps it makes a difference if your ceremony occurs in a museum, a pottery class, or chem lab. But her point remains: explicitly or implicitly, a kind or category is required to identify the object named. Then the contents with the causal chains are sufficient to identify the objects. Thus names are associated with the kind or category as content. One reply is that, even though categories are part of the semantic story by which names contribute objects to propositions, names do not retain an association with those categories as contents (see Schaffer, 2009, pp. 144–5). But there may be reasons to resist this suggestion. To borrow a story from Roy (2000, p. 73), suppose someone overhears in a market, "Quine is very good" and takes it as an evaluation of some Australian wine; upon remarking to his wife at a later time that he would "try to pick up some Quine" he will surely not have succeeded in referring to Quine—despite his intention to use the word the way it was used by those from whom he heard it. The case is hardly decisive, but suggests at least constraints on contents associated with use of the term for successful reference (see also Thomasson, 2007, pp. 42–3).

According to Thomasson, these categorical concepts establish "frame-level" application and coapplication conditions for terms (2007, pp. 38–44). So, for example, application conditions may fail in an attempt to designate a statue or lump in the presence of a hologram or mirage just insofar as there is no lump or statue to be named. And coapplication conditions under which terms are reapplied to a thing may diverge, say for the statue and the lump—as when the statue is smashed into a ball, and the lump continues to exist but the statue does not. In the ordinary case, application and coapplication conditions are fulfilled when things and their parts have the right properties. However, at some fundamental level, such conditions need not depend on *things,* but may be fulfilled just by the *way the world is*; so a condition *F* may be fulfilled when "it is *F*(ing)"—as "it is raining" is true without any object as the referent of "it" (Thomasson, 2007, p. 41; 2008, pp. 69–70; compare O'Leary-Hawthorne and Cortens, 1993).

In Thomasson's hands, these considerations have far-reaching consequences. Consider negative existence claims. A direct reference theory faces a standard difficulty with "Sherlock Holmes" in "Sherlock Holmes does not exist" insofar as there is no Holmes to contribute to the proposition that he does not exist. A natural proposal is that "Sherlock Holmes does not exist" is true when the causal chain reaching from "Sherlock Holmes" ends in a "block" (e.g., Donnellan, 1974). But Thomasson observes that this notion of a "block" is not entirely clear. One can imagine encouraging a child, who wonders if Holmes still exists after going over the Reichenbach falls in "The final problem," not to despair, as he is not gone and returns in the next story. On Thomasson's view, we properly say an object does not exist when a chain does not terminate in an object *of the appropriate kind.* So there is no *person* Holmes but there is the fictional character. And we are left with a corresponding condition for things there are: if application and coapplication conditions for terms are satisfied, then there are the corresponding objects, whether Holmes, the Eiffel Tower, or Quine. And the existential quantifier has a natural substitutional interpretation: $\exists x(\Phi)$ is true just in case Φ is true in some substitution instance given application and coapplication conditions for some (possible) term (2007, pp. 45–8, 110–25). Thomasson is especially concerned to distance this view from an antirealism on which objects exist only given our language, conventions, or concepts. There are objects corresponding to satisfied application and coapplication conditions— but such conditions might be satisfied (to the extent that they are not conditions on humans) even where there are no humans at all.

There are also modal consequences. Thomasson argues, against Quine (1980c), for analytic entailment. So, for a simple case, anything that is a house is a building. And, more importantly, there may be analytic entailment from and to contents associated with application and coapplication conditions. So, van Inwagen (1990) notoriously argues that there may be "simples arranged table-wise" without tables (for discussion, see Blatti in this volume). But Thomasson holds that satisfaction of application and coapplication conditions for simples arranged tablewise analytically entails satisfaction of application and coapplication conditions for tables. So necessarily, if there are simples are arranged tablewise, there is a table.[11,12] Thus the analytic entailments have modal consequences. Perhaps, then, it follows from coapplication conditions that a certain statue is not possibly smashed into a ball. On this account then, the modal property of the statue has no "substantive" truth-maker in the world—it is rather an artifact of the conditions under which the object is identified and reidentified. Thus Thomasson has an easy answer to the "grounding" problem. The worry is that the statue and lump, say, are composed of all the same atoms yet differ in modal properties—where the lump is possibly smashed into a ball, but the statue not. But the problem goes away, if it is not the world but rather differing conditions of application and reapplication that are the source of the properties.

Given this much background, consider a metaphysical debate about whether there is some object, say, a table. Your friend (a commonsensical chap) says it exists, and you (a mereological nihilist) say that there are simples arranged tablewise but no table. If "table" is used in different senses, there is no disagreement. So suppose you both use the term under the same application conditions. But, says Thomasson, given application conditions for "table," if there are simples arranged tablewise, it is immediate that there is a table. So your nihilist position is unstable. Your natural reply is that there may be simples arranged tablewise without a unified *thing* or *object* they compose. But Thomasson does not think this generic claim about "things" can revive the question; and explores three attempts to make sense of the generic "thing" or "object." First, "thing" and "object" may be used against the background of implied sorts or categories. In this case, questions about things or objects are answerable, but return us to a situation like the one before. If tables are among the sorts that are things, it is immediate that simples arranged tablewise are things. But if there are (as Dr. Seuss would say) things1 and things2 associated with different sorts and so different application conditions—where you say there are no things1 and your friend that there are things2—there is nothing about which you disagree. Second, "thing" and "object" have a covering use. In this case, "object" or "thing" is used as a placeholder for a sortal term, and apply in case some sortal term does (this has an effect like the substitutional quantification described above). But this leaves no room to deny that there is a table on the ground that nothing is composed by the simples—for, again, if simples are arranged table-wise then there is a table and therefore a thing. So far, then, you have not denied that there is a table.

Thomasson thinks hope for metaphysical debate depends on a third, purely neutral use of "thing" or "object." This use should not collapse into a covering or sortal usage; rather, it is to be sortally neutral. But this, she thinks, is a dead end.

> The method [we have seen] for understanding the truth-conditions for existence claims gives us reason to think that existence questions stated using such a "neutral" use of "thing" or "object" are defective and unanswerable questions. For on that view, existence claims of the form "there is a P" or "P(s) exist" are true just in case the frame-level application conditions for the term "P" are fulfilled in the grounding situation(s). But "thing" and "object" on the neutral use are not supposed to have application conditions . . . If "thing" and "object" do not have application conditions, we cannot evaluate the truth of simple existence claims stated using these terms (such as "there is an object" or "some thing exists") by considering whether or not these application conditions are fulfilled. (2009, p. 461)

The problem is not merely epistemological, but apparently rather that things themselves answer to application and coapplication conditions—so that an attempt to identify or quantify over objects apart from such conditions is essentially incomplete.

Thus we are left with the "easy" answer to metaphysical questions: as long as the application conditions for "table" are met (and they are, at least in many cases) there are tables! And the nihilist position does not even get off the ground—its apparently controversial questions either fail to be controversial or remain unanswerable because they are ill formed.

Sider again

Return to Sider's (2009) view that EXISTENCE is a property that tracks the structure of the world. "Serious metaphysicians" who argue about tables and simples arranged tablewise thus argue about the extension of EXISTENCE. But this debate may rush to the answer before the question.

Suppose we require as a necessary condition on EXISTENCE,

> EX Things contribute to EXISTENCE only if they, together with other relevant aspects of the world, are truth makers for Thomasson-style application and coapplication conditions (including modal conditions) for terms that designate them.

From the above discussion of Hirsch, something like this seems to match what many serious metaphysicians have in mind. Suppose *being a table* has EXISTENCE; then some object satisfies application and coapplication conditions, including modal conditions, for "table"; so $\exists x(x$ is a table) on a sortal or substitutional account of the quantifier uncontested by Thomasson. But according to Thomasson, tables are not truth-makers for modal properties; so on her view it is not the case that *being a table* has EXISTENCE; so according to Thomasson, $\sim\exists x(x$ is a table). Thomasson thus combines a "serious nihilism" on which no things are truth-makers for modal properties, with "ordinary" (or "lightweight") universalism on which there are things to meet arbitrary satisfied application and coapplication conditions, and modal features are an artifact of those conditions. Suppose $\exists xs$(the xs are simples arranged tablewise). Then, conditions for the ordinary claim that there are simples arranged tablewise are satisfied; and (let us agree) it follows that there is a table. But it does not follow that $\exists x(x$ is a table). On Thomasson's account, analysis of ordinary claims does not extend to quantified ones, insofar as such analyses do not extend to the required truth-makers for EXISTENCE. And modal features of the simples do not imply modal features of the table—for this is just a version of the grounding problem. So there is room for a philosopher to accept one of $\exists xs$(the xs are simples arranged table-wise) or $\exists x(x$ is a table) but not the other.

We come neither to praise some serious ontological view nor to bury it. Rather, the point is that one may have such views and disagree about them. Indeed in doing metaphysics, as for Hirsch and Thomasson, it is difficult to avoid staking out serious metaphysical positions. Roughly, for the views we have considered in this section, deflationism is motivated when differences about necessary features of the world get "washed out" by language. To the extent that such disagreements are recovered, disagreement about serious ontological claims arises in just the way one might expect. So, if Thomasson is right, we may take it as data that there are simples arranged tablewise and tables in the ordinary sense, but need a theory about whether to accept $\exists x(x$ is a table). At this stage, we are thrown back on considerations of the sort Quine and Sider raise about the nature of the world. (Observe also that we have so far been able to make sense of metaphysical debate on the basis of Thomasson-style sortally based quantification. But, on the face of it, it seems natural for us to think that the serious metaphysician is equipped to understand a neutral sort as well, insofar as objects have their properties apart from application and coapplication conditions.)

Experimental metaphysics

If metaphysicians can't reach an agreement on many of the most important issues in metaphysics, perhaps there is something wrong with the intuitions that under-gird our belief in those things. In the last decade or so, a number of philosophers have attempted to test experimentally philosophical intuitions, mainly those of laypeople (see in particular the papers in DePaul and Ramsey, 1999; Knobe and Nichols, 2008; along with Appiah, 2008). The methods used by these philosophers are most commonly associated with those of empirical disciplines like psychology and sociology. Many of these experiments have been in epistemology and ethics, though some have come in the realm of metaphysics. This movement has come to be known as "experimental philosophy," and we'll call the application of its methods to metaphysical topics "experimental metaphysics."

Experimental results

Experimental metaphysics has yielded a number of interesting findings. Here are four.

There are framing effects in subjects' intuitions concerning compatibilism and incompatibilism (Knobe and Nichols, 2007)

In an experiment run by Knobe and Nichols, subjects are given a description of a universe in which determinism holds. This is designated "Universe A" in the experiment. The subjects then are presented with one of the following two questions:

1. In Universe A, a man named Bill has become attracted to his secretary, and he decides that the only way to be with her is to kill his wife and 3 children. He knows that it is impossible to escape from his house in the event of a fire. Before he leaves on a business trip, he sets up a device in his basement that burns down the house and kills his family. Is Bill fully morally responsible for killing his wife and children?
2. In Universe A, is it possible for a person to be fully morally responsible for their actions?

The first question involves much more in the way of concrete detail designed to elicit an emotional response than the second question does. In response to the first question, 72% of subjects said Bill was responsible for killing his family. In response to the second question, 86% of people answered "no." Knobe and Nichols give further experimental evidence that indicates the different responses are caused by different cognitive processes associated with each question: the first question gives rise to emotions that the second, more theoretical, question doesn't. It is the presence of these emotions that explains the ascription of responsibility and the acceptance of compatibilism in the first case; and it is the absence of these emotions that explains the negative answer given to the second question, and the acceptance of incompatibilism in the second case.

Again, there are framing effects in subjects' intuitions concerning compatibilism and incompatibilism (Nahmias et al. 2007)

Nahmias et al. (2007) gave their subjects one of two hypotheses. Either they were given the scenario stated below with psychologically "non-reductionist language" (in brackets) or in "reductionist language" (without brackets).

> Most respected neuroscientists [psychologists] are convinced that eventually we will figure out exactly how all of our decisions and actions are entirely caused. For instance, they think that whenever we are trying to decide what to do, the decision we end up making is completely caused by the specific chemical reactions and neural processes [thoughts, desires, and plans] occurring in our brains [minds]. The neuroscientists [psychologists] are also convinced that these chemical reactions and neural processes [thoughts, desires, and plans] are completely caused by our current situation and the earlier events in our lives, and that these earlier events were also completely caused by even earlier events, eventually going all the way back to events that occurred before we were born.
>
> So, if these neuroscientists [psychologists] are right, then once specific earlier events have occurred in a person's life, these events will definitely cause specific later events to occur. For instance, once specific chemical reactions and neural processes [thoughts, desires, and plans] occur in the person's brain [mind], they will definitely cause the person to make the specific decision he or she makes.

The subjects then were asked if individuals in the situation described were free or responsible for their actions. Roughly 40% of the subjects given the "reductionist" scenario said that individuals in the situation described were free/responsible for their actions, while roughly 85% of those given "psychological" language said that individuals in the situation described were free/responsible for their actions (p. 227).

There are framing effects in subjects' intuitions concerning personal identity. (Nichols and Bruno, 2010)

Bernard Williams (1970) argues that our intuitions concerning personal identity are affected by the way different thought experiments are framed. Nichols and Bruno take Williams' article as a starting point for their own investigation of the effects of framing on subjects' intuitions about personal identity. They are able to show that one can elicit either intuitions that favor psychological continuity as necessary for personal identity or bodily continuity as sufficient for personal identity, depending on the sorts of scenarios one gives subjects. They are also able to show that intuitions that personal identity requires psychological continuity are more robust than intuitions that personal identity involves bodily continuity.

Personality traits predict one's intuitions with respect to incompatibilism and compatibilism

Feltz and Cokely (2009) have shown that extraversion in personality type predicts compatibilist intuitions. To demonstrate this, they gave subjects a scenario nearly identical to the psychologically non-reductionistic scenario in Nahmias et al. (2007). Subjects who tested as high on extraversion on the Big 5 personality inventory were more likely to be compatibilists. Those who tested low on extraversion were more likely to be incompatibilists.

Experimental consequences

All of these results might be thought to lead to a sort of skepticism about the intuitions that provide justification for philosophers' metaphysical beliefs. These results seem to show intuitions shot-through with irrationality. However, we don't think the traditional metaphysician has any significant cause to worry. First, it's not at all clear to us how much epistemic force the intuitions and views of the *hoi polloi* should have on the confidence with which philosophers' hold their own philosophical views. Philosophers have spent a great deal of time thinking carefully about issues in metaphysics (among other areas).[13] The presence of irrational metaphysical belief in non-philosophers is a sociologically and psychologically interesting fact. But any inference to irrationality in philosophers' metaphysical beliefs is illicit. This isn't to say that philosophers aren't or can't be irrational in the way they hold their metaphysical positions. Of course they can be.

Second, it is worth noting that in each of our cases above, it is the philosopher *qua philosopher* who determines what is and isn't an appropriate way to form metaphysical beliefs.[14] It is the philosopher who notes that the way questions are framed shouldn't affect our judgments concerning personal identity or the truth of compatibilism or incompatibilism. It's the philosopher who notes that if a personality type is causing one's philosophical belief, an epistemically defective belief-producing process is operative. It's not true a priori that philosophers are rational. But any sort of argument from results in experimental philosophy to a thorough-going skepticism about the epistemic value of our intuitions risks self-defeat.

Third, suppose that all of the above-mentioned results had been shown to hold in philosophers, rather than in ordinary non-philosophers. It's not at all clear that these results would give us any more reason for skepticism in metaphysics than we already had. We already knew that there is deep and widespread disagreement among those very well-situated epistemically (or so it would seem) regarding such diverse issues as the nature and existence of properties, relations, numbers, and possible worlds; the existence of God; the nature of composition; the nature of the mind; the nature of time; and the nature of ordinary material objects. We knew that many people persist in their metaphysical views in spite of the fact that they acknowledge there are people better-situated epistemically than they with respect to many of their views (witness, e.g., the esteem in which David Lewis is held and the number of philosophers who have adopted his views on the nature of possible worlds). We knew that the views a philosopher winds up holding are influenced greatly by the views of one's teachers (in a way not dissimilar from the way geography plays a significant role in the religious views a person winds up holding). We don't think that these factors from within the discipline of metaphysics (and philosophy more broadly) should incline one toward skepticism about one's metaphysical beliefs. Yet they seem to us a much more powerful reason for skepticism than results in experimental metaphysics are.

Finally, while such considerations may induce a sort of philosophical caution, it is not clear what significance they have for *method* as such. Observe that much metaphysical discussion is driven by data of the sort, "spiders share some of the anatomical features of insects" and "there is a table"—neither controversial, nor called into question by experimental results. Further, on the standard account, a metaphysic does not result directly from intuition, but rather from *theories* to account for data. There may, of course, be divergent intuitions about which theories best account for data or even what data must be accounted for. However, the overall picture moves philosophical metaphysics from direct dependence on intuition about what there is, to a potential for reasoned debates about explanatory power.

A modest proposal[15]

If we are correct, some proposed new directions for metaphysics are wrong turns. Even so, we are left with the original concern that ordinary metaphysics leads only to a messy pileup or dead end. We are left with deep and widespread metaphysical disagreement. We have argued that one shouldn't think that central metaphysical disputes are chimerical, at least not in the way Hirsch and Thomasson propose. We also have argued that experimental metaphysics at best doesn't pose a problem for traditional metaphysics, and at worst poses no worse problem than the traditional metaphysician already had. How should one think of the state of metaphysics, then?

We think that contrary to the views of some, a great deal of progress has been made in metaphysics. It is true that as metaphysics has progressed, metaphysicians haven't come to consensus in the way scientists have come to consensus on many of the central questions in science. But we have a much better view of logical space than we had a hundred years ago (with Russell's seminal work in analytic metaphysics), or three hundred years ago (at the height of the flowering of modern metaphysics), or in the time of Plato and Aristotle. Consider, for instance, philosophical debate around the nature of abstracta. As a result of the work of philosophers such as David Lewis (1986, 1999a), David Armstrong (1978, 1989, 1997), Alvin Plantinga (1974), Peter van Inwagen (2001, 2004), and Roderick Chisholm (1976, 1989), we have a much more robust idea of what properties, relations, propositions, and possible worlds might be like. It is true that we have no consensus as to what any of these things are. But as a result of the work of these philosophers, we are able to see more clearly the layout of logical space. This is real philosophical progress, we submit. This sort of progress has been made in many areas of metaphysics: compatibilism and incompatiblism, realism and anti-realism, the nature of space and time, and the nature of ordinary material objects.

It would be naïve to expect or hope for anything like the sort of consensus one sees in science. But we do hope and expect that metaphysicians will continue to illuminate options for possible answers to longstanding metaphysical problems.[16]

Notes

1   Here we mean to commit ourselves only to the thesis that truth supervenes on being. In particular, truth supervenes on what things there are and the properties and relations they instantiate. (See Bigelow, 1988, p. 133; Lewis, 1999a, pp. 206–7; 2001; and Merricks, 2007 for discussion).

2   Indeed, Quine thought the confusion of use and mention was the source of many ontological sins, particularly in the work of Russell.

3   That is, he rejects possible worlds as most philosophers think of them. In Quine (1969, pp. 147ff.) he suggests (if one really wants to countenance the existence of possible worlds) that one might take possible worlds to be sets of quadruples of real numbers representing objects' occupying regions of spacetime.

4   To be fair, van Inwagen does think that various (controversial) things follow from the fact that properties are things that can be said-of an object: They can exist when not instantiated, they exist necessarily, they can't be parts of physical objects, they can't be sensed, physical objects aren't bundles of them, existence is a property, and there are haecceities.

5   For further discussion see also Thomasson's excellent discussion of Quine's method in this volume, van Inwagen (2009) and Cameron (2008).

6   Though it's worth noting that many of the important ideas in Carnap (1950) may be found in Quine (1980a).

7   There are different replies to reasoning of this sort. A direct response is that one side in a metaphysical debate does not always have equivalents to offer the other. Hirsch considers a response of this sort for platonism and nominalism (2009, pp. 252–6 and other places).

8   Arguments of this sort appear in Hirsch as well–though he does not argue from reference. See, for example, Hirsch (2002a).

9   Though see Loar (1976) and Jackson (1998) for dissenting views.

10 Compare to Wiggins' (1967) discussion of reference under a sortal.

11 Thomasson finds in such considerations reason to reject the 'only' part of the constraint from Quine's criterion Q1. For, 'Quine's test for ontological commitment ignores the fact that there are often implicit commitments to certain kinds of entities even where we are not yet quantifying over them' (2007, p. 167). But either we accept the analytic entailments or not. If not, as Thomasson acknowledges, the threat to Q1 goes away. But if we accept the entailments, surely they should be part of our best theories–so that if a theory is committed to simples arranged tablewise, and from this there must be a table, our theory is thereby committed to the existence of the table. So the threat to Q1 is not clear.

12 Compare to the two-tier theory of the necessary a posteriori in places like Davies and Humberstone (1980), Tichy (1983) and Sidelle (1989).

13 The claim that philosophers are expert intuiters of matters epistemic and metaphysical is more fully explored in Williamson (2007).

14 The same goes for results in experimental ethics and experimental epistemology.

15 We suspect that however much disagreement there might be about the nature of our proposal, there will be widespread agreement that our proposal is quite a bit more modest than that of Jonathan Swift.

16 We'd like to thank Gordon Barnes and Tom Crisp for discussion of these issues.

References

Appiah, A. (2008), *Experiments in Ethics.* Cambridge: Harvard University Press.

Armstrong, D. (1978), *A Theory of Universals.* Cambridge: Cambridge University Press.

—(1989), *Universals: An Opinionated Introduction.* Boulder, CO: Westview Press.

—(1997), *A World of States of Affairs.* Cambridge: Cambridge University Press.

Bigelow, J. (1988), *The Reality of Numbers: A Physicalist's Philosophy of Mathematics.* Oxford: Oxford University Press.

Blatti, S. (2012), "Material constitution." This volume.

Cameron, R. (2008), "Truthmakers and ontological commitment: or how to deal with complex objects and mathematical ontology without getting into trouble." *Philosophical Studies,* 140, 1–18.

Carnap, R. (1950), "Empiricism, semantics and ontology." *Revue Internationale de Philosophie,* 4, 20–40. Reprinted in many places, including Carnap (1956), *Meaning and Necessity.* Chicago: University of Chicago Press, pp. 205–21.

Chisholm, R. (1976), *Person and Object.* London: George Allen and Unwin.

—(1989), *On Metaphysics.* Minneapolis: University of Minnesota Press.

Davies, M. and Humberstone L. (1980), "Two notions of necessity." *Philosophical Studies,* 38, 1–31.

DePaul, M. and Ramsey, W. (1999), *Rethinking Intuition.* Lanham, MD: Rowman and Littlefield.

Donnellan, K. (1974), "Speaking of nothing." *Philosophical Review,* 81, 3–31.

Feltz, A. and Cokely, E. (2009), "Do judgments about freedom and responsibility depend on who you are? Personality differences in intuitions about compatibilism and incompatibilism." *Consciousness and Cognition,* 18, 342–50.

Hawthorne, J. (2009), "Superficialism in ontology," in Chalmers, D. , Manley, D. and Wasserman, R., eds, *Metametaphysics: New Essays on the Foundations of Ontology.* Oxford: Clarendon Press, pp. 213 –30.

Hirsch, E. (1993), *Dividing Reality.* Oxford: Oxford University Press.

—(2002a), "Against revisionary ontology." *Philosophical Topics,* 30, 103–27.

—(2002b), "Quantifier variance and realism." *Philosophical Issues,* 12, 51–73.

—(2005), "Physical-object ontology, verbal disputes, and common sense." *Philosophy and Phenomenological Research,* 70, 67–97.

—(2008), "Langauage, ontology, and structure." *Noûs,* 42, 509–28.

—(2009), "Ontology and alternative languages," in Chalmers, D., Manley, D., and Wasserman, R., eds, *Metametaphysics: New Essays on the Foundations of Ontology.* Oxford: Clarendon Press, pp. 231–59.

—(2011), "Introduction," in E. Hirsch, *Quantifier Variance and Realism: Essays in Metaontology.* Oxford: Oxford University Press.

Jackson, F. (1998), "Reference and description revisited," in J. Tomberlin, ed., *Philosophical Perspectives 12: Language, Mind, and Ontology.* Oxford: Blackwell, pp. 201–18.

Knobe, J. and Nichols, S. (2007), "Moral responsibility and determinism: the cognitive science of folk intuitions." *Noûs,* 41, 663–85. Reprinted in Knobe, J. and Nichols, S. (2008).

—(2008), *Experimental Philosophy.* New York: Oxford University Press.

Kripke, S. (1980), *Naming and Necessity.* Cambridge, MA: Harvard University Press.

Lewis, D. (1986), *On the Plurality of Worlds.* Oxford: Blackwell.

—(1999a), *Papers on Metaphysics and Epistemology.* Cambridge: Cambridge University Press.

—(1999b), "Armstrong on combinatorial possibility," in Lewis (1999a). Originally published in *Australasian Journal of Philosophy,* 70, 211–24.

—(2001), "Truthmaking and difference making." *Noûs,* 35, 602–15.

Loar, B. (1976), "The semantics of singular terms." *Philosophical Studies,* 30, 353–77.

McGrath, M. (2008), "Conciliatory metaontology and the vindication of common sense." *Noûs,* 42, 482–508.

Merricks, T. (2007), *Truth and Ontology.* Oxford: Oxford University Press.

Nahmias, E., Coates, J., and Karvan, T. (2007), "Free will, moral responsibility, and mechanism: experiments on folk intuitions." *Midwest Studies in Philosophy* 31, 1, 214–42.

Nichols, S. and Bruno, M. (2010), "Intuitions about personal identity: an empirical study." *Philosophical Psychology,* 23, 293–312.

O'Leary-Hawthorne, J. and Cortens, A. (1995), "Towards ontological nihilism." *Philosophical Studies,* 79, 143–65.

Plantinga, A. (1974), *The Nature of Necessity.* Oxford: Oxford University Press.

Quine, W. V. O. (1969), *Ontological Relativity and Other Essays.* New York: Columbia University Press.

—(1980a), "On what there is," in W. V. O. Quine, ed., *From a Logical Point of View.* Cambridge, MA: Harvard University Press, pp. 1–19.

—(1980b), "Two dogmas of empiricism," in W. V. O. Quine, *From a Logical Point of View.* Cambridge, MA: Harvard University Press, pp. 20–46.

—(1980c), "Reference and modality," in W. V. O. Quine, *From a Logical Point of View.* Cambridge, MA: Harvard University Press, pp. 139–59.

Roy, T. (2000), "Things and *de re* modality." *Noûs*, 34, 56–84.

Russell, B. (1985), "The philosophy of logical atomism," in D. Pears, ed., *The Philosophy of Logical Atomism*. Lasalle: Open Court, pp. 35–156.

Schaffer, J. (2009), "The deflationary metaontology of Thomasson's *Ordinary Objects*." *Philosophical Books*, 50, 142–57.

Sidelle, A. (1989), *Necessity, Essence, and Individuation*. Ithaca, NY: Cornell University Press.

Sider, T. (2009), "Ontological realism," in Chalmers, R., Manley, D., and Wasserman, R., eds, *Metametaphysics: New Essays on the Foundations of Ontology*. Oxford: Clarendon Press, pp. 384–423.

Thomasson, A. (2007), *Ordinary Objects*. Oxford: Oxford University Press.

—(2008), "Existence questions." *Philosophical Studies*, 141, 63–78.

—(2009), "Answerable and unanswerable questions," in Chalmers, R., Manley, D. and Wasserman, R. eds, *Metametaphysics: New Essays on the Foundations of Ontology*. Oxford: Clarendon Press, pp. 444–71.

—(2012), "Research problems and methods in metaphysics." This volume.

Tichy, P. (1983), "Kripke on necessity a posteriori." *Philosophical Studies*, 43, 225–41.

van Inwagen, P. (1990), *Material Beings*. Ithaca, NY: Cornell University Press.

—(2001), *Ontology, Identity, and Modality*. Cambridge: Cambridge University Press.

—(2004), "A theory of properties," in D. Zimmerman, ed., *Oxford Studies in Metaphysics, vol I*. New York: Oxford University Press, pp. 107–38.

—(2009), "Being, existence, and ontological commitment," in Chalmers, D., Manley, D., and Wasserman, R., eds, *Metametaphysics: New Essays on the Foundations of Ontology*. Oxford: Clarendon Press, pp. 472–506.

Wiggins, D. (1967), *Identity and Spatiotemporal Continuity*. Oxford: Blackwell.

Williams, B. (1970), "The self and the future." *The Philosophical Review*, 79, 161–80.

Williamson, T. (2007), *The Philosophy of Philosophy*. Oxford: Blackwell.

Annotated Bibliography

Chapter 1 Research problems and methods

Ayer, A. J. (1946/1952), *Language, Truth and Logic,* New York: Dover. After visiting the Vienna Circle, Ayer wrote this book to promote the logical positivist ideas of the circle to a broader philosophical audience. It provides an accessible classic statement of the logical positivist view. In it, one can find criticisms of metaphysics (considered as anything other than analysis), a vision of the proper function of philosophy as engaged only in analysis, and an articulation of the conventionalist approach to modality, as well as much else.

Chalmers, D. J., Manley, D., and Wasserman, R., eds (2009), *Metametaphysics: New Essays on the Foundations of Ontology.* Oxford: Oxford University Press. This collection has set the stage for the reemergence of metametaphysics as a core topic of debate. It includes an excellent introduction by David Manley surveying the origins of the debate and the different positions available, along with 16 original essays. The essays are by many of the leading contributors to contemporary debates in metaphysics, and include defenders of serious metaphysics (such as Peter van Inwagen and Theodore Sider) as well as those of a more skeptical or deflationary bent (such as David Chalmers, Eli Hirsch, Huw Price, and Stephen Yablo).

Evnine, S. (2008), "Modal epistemology: our knowledge of necessity and possibility." *Philosophy Compass,* 3(4), 664–84. An excellent survey of views about how we can acquire modal knowledge, including the conventionalist approach, and the idea (developed in very different ways by Yablo and Chalmers) that conceivability provides some kind of guide to possibility.

Gendler, T. and Hawthorne, J., eds (2002), *Conceivability and Possibility.* Oxford: Oxford University Press. This anthology begins with a helpful and substantive introduction to issues surrounding the relation between conceivability and possibility. It includes 13 original essays on conceivability, possibility, and the relation between them, by George Bealer, Kit Fine, Alan Sidelle, Ernest Sosa, Crispin Wright, and others, including the seminal essays by David Chalmers and Stephen Yablo.

Kripke, S. (1972/1980), *Naming and Necessity.* Cambridge, MA: Harvard University Press. Kripke's landmark lectures arguing that there are necessary a posteriori and (perhaps) contingent a priori truths. These lectures were thought to put the final nail in the coffin of the idea that necessary truths were analytic statements knowable a priori and to reinvigorate the idea that discoverable modal facts form part of reality.

Quine, W. V. O. (1953/2001), *From a Logical Point of View* (second edition). Cambridge, MA: Harvard University Press. Includes reprints of nine of Quine's papers. "On What There Is" lays out Quine's criterion of ontological commitment, setting the stage for the Quinean approach to ontology. "Two Dogmas of Empiricism" includes influential arguments against the tenability of a distinction between analytic and synthetic statements, and in favor of the view that ontological questions are "on a par with questions of natural science" (p. 45).

Schiffer, S. (2003), *The Things We Mean*. Oxford: Oxford University Press. One of the most important developments and defenses of a kind of deflationary metaphysical view. Schiffer argues that many disputed entities in metaphysics, including fictional characters, properties, events, and (the main case under discussion here) propositions are "pleonastic" entities. A pleonastic entity, on Schiffer's view, is one whose existence supervenes on the premises of "something from nothing" transformations from true sentences we accept that contain no mention of such things. Thus on this view existence questions about such pleonastic entities may be trivially answered by any competent users of the relevant concepts; they are not "deep" questions for metaphysical debate.

Sidelle, A. (1989), *Necessity, Essence and Individuation: A Defense of Conventionalism*. Ithaca, NY: Cornell University Press. This book provides the best-developed contemporary defense of a conventionalist view of modality. Sidelle shows how we can retain the idea that the most basic modal truths are analytic, while still accounting for the fact that some necessary truths (Kripkean a posteriori necessities) require empirical discovery. Thus, he argues, Kripke's influential arguments in fact give us no reason to hold a deeply realist view of modality.

Sider, T. (2012), *Writing the Book of the World*. Oxford: Oxford University Press. This book develops the most important recent defense of metaphysics as engaged in deep and serious disputes (not mere verbal disputes or disputes that can be resolved trivially or via conceptual analysis). Sider argues that the world has structure and that the job of metaphysics is to discern the fundamental structure of reality. Ontological debates, he argues, are substantive provided their crucial expressions "carve nature at the joints." This provides the basis for him to argue that many metaphysical debates are substantive, as against various forms of ontological deflationism.

Soames, S. (2003), *Philosophical Analysis in the Twentieth Century, Volume 2: The Age of Meaning*. Princeton, NJ: Princeton University Press. An excellent and comprehensive history of analytic philosophy. It includes (*inter alia*) detailed discussions of the rise and fall of logical positivism, of Wittgensteinian and ordinary language approaches to philosophy, and of Quine's and Kripke's key contributions.

Chapter 2 Modality

Armstrong, D. (1989), *A Combinatorial Theory of Possibility*. Cambridge: Cambridge University Press. Possibilities as combinations of actual elements. A proposal to regard worlds as fictions is profitably compared with Gideon Rosen (1990), "Modal fictionalism." *Mind*, 99, 327–54.

Divers, J. (2002), *Possible Worlds*. London: Routledge. Comprehensive and scholarly discussion of worlds, including Lewis's modal realism, and alternatives on which worlds are actual entities of a type different from the world in which we live.

Jubien, M. (2009), *Possibility*. Oxford: Oxford University Press. The attack on possible worlds, and positive theory as described in "Modality" above. Corresponding positive theories of physical things and designation contrast with prevailing theories as represented in, say, Kripke (1980).

Kripke, S. (1980), *Naming and Necessity*. Cambridge, MA: Harvard University Press. Readable and influential 1972 lectures. Against theories of Bertrand Russell and others on which proper names work like descriptions, names are rigid designators. Results for modality, against Quine and more generally.

Lewis, D. (1986), *On the Plurality of Worlds*. New York: Basil Blackwell. Forceful presentation of modal realism. Develops the theory, shows what it can do, and objects to alternatives.

Linsky, L., ed. (1971), *Reference and Modality*. Oxford: Oxford University Press. Anthology focusing on Quine's worries and responses. Includes Quine (an early edition of 1980), Arthur Smullyan (1948), and Kripke (1963b) mentioned in "Modality" above. Some articles are technical.

Loux, M., ed. (1979), *The Possible and the Actual: Readings in the Metaphysics of Modality*. Ithaca, NY: Cornell University Press. Another excellent anthology. Nice introduction by Loux, and papers developing both theories of possible worlds, and objections. Includes Robert Adams (1974), Plantinga (1976), Fabrizio Mondadori and Adam Morton (1976), and William Lycan (1979) all mentioned in "Modality" above.

Melia, J. (2003), *Modality*. Montreal: McGill-Queen's University Press. A short and readable introduction to issues in the metaphysics of modality.

Plantinga, A. (1974), *The Nature of Necessity*. Oxford: Oxford University Press. A pioneering theory of modality and possible worlds. Some of his related papers, including (1976), are collected in Plantinga (2003), *Essays in the Metaphysics of Modality*, ed. M. Davidson, Oxford: Oxford University Press.

Roy, T. (1993), "Worlds and modality." *Philosophical Review*, 102, 335–62. Somewhat different, but more detailed exposition of themes from "Modality" above, along with Roy (1995), "In defense of linguistic ersatzism." *Philosophical Studies*, 80, 217–42; and Roy (2000), "Things and *de re* modality." *Noûs*, 34, 56–84.

Chapter 3 Universals and abstract objects

Armstrong, D. (1989), *Universals: An Opinionated Introduction*. Boulder, CO: Westview Press. Armstrong carefully explicates, compares, and assesses a number of different views regarding the nature of universals. As the title indicates, this overview serves a dual role—to evaluate and assess the major historical and contemporary views on this topic, and to set the stage for Armstrong's defense of a particular version of realism regarding universals.

Burgess, J. and Rosen, G. (1997), *A Subject with No Object*. Oxford: Oxford University Press. Burgess and Rosen, who both have admittedly anti-nominalist views on the metaphysics of abstract objects, provide a sustained examination and critique of various ways to develop nominalist accounts of mathematics and related areas, providing a valuable (and novel) framework within which to carry out comparative evaluations of different nominalist strategies. Their discussion is surprisingly even-handed and sympathetic, and in addition benefits from being focused by their own concerns—that is, those of the realist—and not by the concerns more typically emphasized by proponents of the views they discuss.

Field, H. (1980), *Science Without Numbers: A Defence of Nominalism*. Princeton, NJ: Princeton University Press. This is Field's celebrated attempt to defend a version of nominalism in the face of Quine's indispensability argument. Field, in essence, argues here that we can explain indispensability in terms of conservativeness instead of in terms of truth, and develops a technically sophisticated framework for defending such a view.

—(1989), *Realism, Mathematics, and Modality*. New York: Basil Blackwell. This volume collects Hartry Field's important papers on the topics listed in the title, with a clear emphasis on those works that serve, in one way or another, his attempt to defend nominalism by developing a fictionalist account of mathematics. The papers not only address issues in the metaphysics of mathematics and the existence of abstract objects, but also, as a result of a clear focus on applications of mathematics, involve wider themes and concerns including the nature and structure of space-time and the proper understanding of modality.

Frege, G. (1980), *Die Grundlagen der Arithmetik*, trans. J. Austin. Evanston, IL: Northwestern University Press. The Grundlagen is one of Frege's three great works, and the one that is most philosophically oriented. Frege here develops his logicist project of reducing mathematics to logic, and, of particular interest to the metaphysician, of reducing the ontology of mathematics to the ontology of logic. Among the main tools mobilized by Frege in this project are second-order abstraction principles.

Hale, R. (1988), *Abstract Objects*. Oxford: Blackwell. Hale here develops and defends a version of Fregean neo-logicism that provides an account of abstract objects. He pays particular attention to arguments – epistemological, semantic, and metaphysical—that purport to show that abstract objects either cannot exist, or cannot do the work we desire them to do even if they do exist, and outlines how a Fregean version of Platonism can answer these objections.

Lewis, D. (1983), "New work for a theory of universals." *Australasian Journal of Philosophy*, 61, 343–77. In this paper Lewis attempts to distinguish between properties, which are abundant and either are or correspond to sets, and universals, which are sparse, metaphysically more robust, and in some sense or another more "natural." Lewis argues that while properties, on this understanding, are appropriate to some philosophical tasks, such as explaining the semantic values of predicates, universals are required in order to handle other important philosophical problems, such as explaining the nature of causation and the nature of laws.

Quine, W. V. O. (1948), "On what there is." *Review of Metaphysics*, 2, 21–38. In this article Quine formulates his famous existence test—"To be is to be the value of a variable"—and fleshes out an account of the role of quantifiers in theorizing in order to flesh out the test itself. In addition, he here formulates two objections to universals (and hence, indirectly, to higher order logic): first, such entities, if they existed, would be metaphysically bizarre in a manner in which particulars are not, and second, we do not need to quantify over such entities in order to explain facts about quantitative similarity and dissimilarity anyway.

Chapter 4 Naturalism and physicalism

Chalmers, D. J. (1996), *The Conscious Mind: In Search of a Fundamental Theory*. Oxford: Oxford University Press. An insightful and influential work, much of which is devoted to an extended argument against physicalism on the grounds that consciousness cannot plausibly be taken to be nothing over and above the physical. The book is especially useful for its articulation of the physicalist commitment to supervenience and its development of an approach to modality that vindicates the appeal to conceivability as a way of establishing metaphysical conclusions.

Craig, W. L. and Moreland, J. P., eds (2000), *Naturalism: A Critical Analysis*. New York: Routledge. Ten papers attack naturalism in a wide variety of ways. Naturalism is argued to be incompatible with several phenomena most of us will acknowledge—knowledge itself, ordinary material objects, the mind, moral demands. More contentious claims alleged to be incompatible with naturalism include scientific realism, libertarianism about free will, realism about properties, theism and the detectability of intelligent design in nature. An especially useful aspect of the anthology is its illustration of the variety of construals of "naturalism."

Gillett, C. and Loewer, B., eds (2001), *Physicalism and its Discontents*. Cambridge: Cambridge University Press. Seventeen papers on central questions about physicalism, divided into three sections: defenses and articulations of the doctrine, worries about it, and a set of papers focusing specifically on the controversy over the hopes for a physicalist accommodation of consciousness. The initial paper by David Papineau ("The Rise of Physicalism") is especially useful as a presentation of a positive case for the doctrine, including an historical overview of relevant scientific developments. Papers on formulation touch on the notion of realization, the relevant kinds of super-venience, different ways of understanding necessity and the literature on "reduction." A significant number of the papers critical of physicalism are not based on familiar topics from the mind–body problem but present more original concerns about the doctrine as a global view of the world.

Heckmann, H. D. and Walter, S., eds (2003), *Physicalism and Mental Causation: The Metaphysics of Mind and Action.* Charlottesville, VA: Imprint Academic. Fourteen papers on the intersection of the two topics in the title. The anthology includes several helpful papers on how physicalism might best be formulated, including how this interacts with questions about multiple realizability and "downward causation." Several papers touch on important arguments advanced by Jaegwon Kim as part of his long campaign to cast doubt on popular "nonreductive" forms of physicalism. There are some very useful papers on the causal completeness (a.k.a. "causal closure") of physics and how this may or may not be used in arguing for physicalism, and several papers are devoted to the prospects for physicalist treatments of mental causation, including some attention to action theory.

Jackson, F. (1998), *From Metaphysics to Ethics: A Defence of Conceptual Analysis.* New York: Oxford University Press. Developed from his 1995 John Locke Lectures at Oxford, Frank Jackson argues here for a pair of important claims. First, he argues that when doing "serious" metaphysics, the main problem we face is that of a "location problem": locating a given phenomenon in a comprehensive picture of the world to which we are otherwise committed. Physicalism is such a picture, though other doctrines illustrate the same point. Second, he argues that conceptual analysis is required if we want to tackle such a location project; indeed, he argues specifically that the physicalist is committed to the a priori derivability of all the facts from the physical facts, a commitment that many will find too implausible to accept. The last half of the book is devoted to illustrating his claims about metaphysics and analysis in the case of meta-ethics and the metaphysics of color.

Kim, J. (1993), *Supervenience and Mind: Selected Philosophical Essays.* Cambridge: Cambridge University Press. A collection of several influential papers on supervenience and its use in formulating physicalism and other positions, as well as papers on the metaphysics of events, causal connections and the mind–body problem. Many of these papers form critical parts of Kim's long-lasting attempt to argue that the hope for a "nonreductive" materialism is bound to fail, so that one must either be a dualist, an eliminativist or an outright reductive physicalist.

—(1998), *Mind in a Physical World: An Essay on the Mind-Body Problem and Mental Causation.* Cambridge, MA: MIT Press. A short book presenting a concentrated argument for insisting on a reductive form of physicalism. Kim argues that appealing to supervenience can neither provide an adequate formulation of physicalism nor provide an account of mental causation; the only way for the physicalist to account for such is by means of "functional reduction." The book is especially noteworthy for his argument for thinking that the physicalist must appeal to realization and for his critique of Nagelian intertheoretic reduction with the proposed new account of "functional reduction."

Ladyman, J. and Ross, D. (2007), *Every Thing Must Go: Metaphysics Naturalized.* New York: Oxford University Press. A vigorous and challenging book that aims both to set out a view about how metaphysics ought to proceed so that it is properly disciplined by scientific discoveries and to illustrate the procedure by using it to argue for a metaphysical view dubbed "ontic structural realism." The proposed method for doing metaphysics in a naturalistic fashion is articulated in the "Principle of Naturalistic Closure," which prescribes that we only endorse metaphysical claims that help unify two or more specific scientific hypotheses that are already taken seriously by current scientific institutions. Ontic Structural Realism (OSR) is the view, roughly, that there are no "self-subsistent" objects, where the objects that are allowed to exist by OSR are "purged of their intrinsic natures, identity, and individuality, and they are not metaphysically fundamental" (p. 131). A distinctive book illustrating how epistemic naturalism might look when thoroughly pursued.

Melnyk, A. (2003), *A Physicalist Manifesto: Thoroughly Modern Materialism.* A full-scale, comprehensive development and defense of physicalism. Melnyk proposes a formulation of physicalism according to which all causal or contingent particulars (including particular instantiations of properties) are either physical or physically realized, defends a careful account of realization, defends this formulation against other approaches, argues that physicalism is committed to reductionism in the "core" sense of reduction (while spelling out how this is not a commitment that should worry proponents), develops a theory of causation meant to vindicate the causal status of nonphysical but physically realized properties, and provides an extensive review of empirical evidence for and against the doctrine. Melnyk's book stands as a must-read for both proponents and opponents of physicalism.

Papineau, D. (1993), *Philosophical Naturalism.* Oxford: Blackwell. A systematic yet concise study of three central topics for the philosophical naturalist: physicalism, the nature of the mind and the nature of knowledge. In the first third, Papineau argues for physicalism on the grounds of a causal argument, including a "manifestability" argument for supervenience that differs somewhat from the usual causal interaction arguments. An original and interesting account of the significance of multiple realizability for "reduction" is included as the second chapter. The discussion of the mind includes a clear presentation of a teleological theory of mental representation and a proposed diagnosis of why consciousness can so persistently seem to be something nonphysical.

Poland, J. (1994), *Physicalism: The Philosophical Foundations.* New York: Oxford University Press. A systematic study that focuses very much on the question of how physicalism should be formulated and what presuppositions may be guiding one's choice of formulation. In general, Poland takes physicalism to be a "research programme" of "non-eliminative, structural unification that accords a certain sort of privilege to physics" (p. 13). In articulating the substantive theses to which this programme is committed he emphasizes the explanatory goals of physicalism; for instance, thesis T4 is that "[a]ll instantiations of non-physical objects and attributes are vertically explainable in terms of physical or physically-based objects and attributes" (p. 208). The book is especially useful for its careful discussion of how physicalism need *not* be committed to certain contentious claims often associated with it, even while it develops a position that is far from easily established.

Robinson, H., ed. (1993), *Objections to Physicalism*. New York: Oxford University Press. Thirteen papers critical of physicalism, many from very impressive contemporary metaphysicians and logicians. An important variety of arguments are presented, from familiar objections based on the phenomenon of consciousness to arguments from the existence of mathematics and logics and John Foster's "succinct case for idealism."

Savellos, E. E. and Yalçin, Ü. D., eds (1995), *Supervenience: New Essays*. New York: Cambridge University Press. Seventeen papers focusing on the different ways in which the notion of supervenience may be made precise and what use it may have in philosophical argument. Several of the papers directly address physicalism and the ways in which it may be committed to a supervenience claim, including the relations between supervenience, reduction, and ontological dependence. The very long first essay by Brian McLaughlin, "Varieties of Supervenience," is very valuable as providing an overview of the relevant parameters of supervenience claims and what logical relations hold between different kinds of supervenience.

Shoemaker, S. (2007), *Physical Realization*. New York: Oxford University Press. A short but dense book setting out a comprehensive way of thinking about "realization" and its utility as a metaphysician's tool. Shoemaker's account is an elaboration of the "subset view" of realization according to which, roughly, a property F is realized by a property R when the set of the causal powers individuative of F is a proper subset of those individuative of R. Shoemaker refines this account and shows how to extend it to a variety of complex cases; he also uses the developed framework to offer an account of "emergent" properties, a notion that both physicalists and their opponents should want clarified.

Chapter 5 Mind

Block, N. (1978), "Troubles with functionalism," in C. W. Savage, ed., *Minnesota Studies in the Philosophy of Science, Vol. IX*. Minneapolis: University of Minnesota Press, pp. 261–325. Reprinted in Block (1980), pp. 268–305. This is Block's classic summary and assessment of functionalist theories of mind, circa 1980. It contains a reasonable explication of the history and motivation for functionalism, along with some of the technical apparatus used to develop the theory. Perhaps more importantly, it contains a series of very clearly stated objections to functionalism, including the problem of inputs and outputs, the problems of inverted and absent qualia, and the nation of China example.

Chalmers, D. (1996), *The Conscious Mind: In Search of a Fundamental Theory* New York: Oxford University Press. David Chalmers' first book contains his most extensive and detailed arguments for recognizing phenomenal properties (i.e., qualia) as fundamental constituents in our ontology—a version of property dualism. The book contains, in its middle portion, his well-known developments of the zombie and absent qualia arguments. The opening part of the book sets out the semantic and meta-philosophical framework against which the direct arguments are developed, and which should not be skipped despite the author's suggestions to the contrary. The final portion of the book contains a speculative and epiphenomenalist account of qualia in terms of information, which has been much less influential than the first two parts of the book.

Fodor, J. (1974), "Special sciences, or the disunity of science as a working hypothesis," *Synthese,* 28, 97–115. Reprinted in N. Block (1980), pp. 120–33. Fodor's "Special Sciences" paper is the canonical position paper for the anti-reductive approach. Fodor argues that the laws of the special sciences (those other than physics) are not reducible to those of physics if they relate kinds that are functionally individuated, and therefore multiply realizable. The reason is that multiple realization is supposed to be incompatible with the biconditional bridge laws that are required for classical Nagelian reduction. Then Fodor tries to convince us that psychology is in just such a position, through a combination of argument, urging and example.

Kim, J. (1998), *Mind in a Physical World: An Essay on the Mind–Body Problem and Mental Causation* Cambridge, MA: MIT Press. This summarizes Kim's position in the late 1990s, and does so by laying out simply and concisely almost all of the main metaphysical issues about minds that dominated the literature. [Kim doesn't take property dualism seriously in this book, but does in subsequent work.] In particular, Kim explains the problems with supervenience and the central importance of mental causation, and he deploys versions of his influential disjunction and exclusion arguments.

Kripke, S. (1971), "Identity and necessity," in M. Munitz, ed., *Identity and Individuation.* New York: New York University Press, pp. 135–64. This contains a brief version of Kripke's arguments for the necessity of identity and against physicalism about the mind. The versions of the arguments offered here contain the central elements that he developed in *Naming and Necessity,* in an article length form.

Lewis, D. (1972), "Psychophysical and theoretical identifications," *Australasian Journal of Philosophy,* 50, 249–58. This paper contains Lewis' second direct argument for the mind–brain identity theory. In his earlier work, the main argument involved the transitivity of identity. In this article, Lewis appeals to his well-known model for defining theoretical terms and a semantic thesis about the meanings of mentalistic terms. There is no straightforward answer to whether the argument in this paper supports the identity theory or functionalism, as Lewis himself later recognized.

McLaughlin, B. (1992), "The rise and fall of British emergentism," in A. Beckermann, H. Flohr and J. Kim, eds, *Emergence or Reduction?* Berlin: Walter de Gruyter, pp. 49–93. McLaughlin's scholarly summary of historical emergentist views is the standard resource on that version of property dualism, even though it is not an advocacy piece. Moreover, in explicating emergentism, McLaughlin essentially lays out the requirements for any non-emergentist theory that is not reductive, as functionalism purports to be.

Putnam, H. (1967/1975), "The nature of mental states," in H. Putnam, *Mind, Language and Reality: Philosophical Papers, Volume* 2. New York: Cambridge University Press, pp. 429–40. Originally titled "Psychological Predicates" and subsequently reprinted with its current and more metaphysical title, this paper is the definitive statement of Putnam's early functionalism. Here Putnam explains the idea of a probabilistic automaton in terms of Turing machines, first deploys the multiple realization argument (although he does not call it that), and puts forward functionalism as an empirical hypothesis. Putnam also anticipates some objections to the view, including some whose popularity he underestimated such as the kind-splitting and disjunctive-kind replies.

Smart, J. J. C. (1959), "Sensations and brain processes," *Philosophical Review,* 68, 141–56. Smart's article is the canonical statement and defense of the mind–brain identity theory, containing all the elements of its contemporary version except for the necessity of identity. The central portion of the article is a detailed series of objections and replies, in which Smart successfully defuses an array of semantic and epistemic reasons on account of which the identity theory was purported to be inconsistent. Among these is the famous Objection 5, which he attributes to Max Black. In response to it, Smart introduces the notion of "topic neutral" expressions, which was subsequently influential in metaphysics of mind and science.

Chapter 6 Material constitution

Baker, L. R. (2007), *The Metaphysics of Everyday Life: An Essay in Practical Realism.* Cambridge: Cambridge University Press. In *Persons and Bodies: A Constitution View* (2000), Baker concentrated primarily on a defense of her view that persons are nonidentically constituted by the human animals with which they coincide. Here she broadens her defense of this view (and modifies it slightly) to encompass artifacts of all kinds. Baker is led by a pragmatic worldview that she calls "practical realism," according to which metaphysical inquiry should be responsive to serious reflection on all of our successful cognitive practices, be they scientifically vindicated or not. Her discussion ranges widely beyond the problem of material constitution to such topics as causation, ontological vagueness, and the three-dimensionalism vs four-dimensionalism debate.

Bennett, K. (2009), "Constitution, composition, and metaontology," in D. Chalmers,
D. Manley, and R. Wasserman, eds, *Metametaphysics: New Essays on the Foundations
of Ontology*. Oxford: Oxford University Press, pp. 38–76. In this paper, Bennett
considers the merits of various versions of what she calls "dismissivism" about
metaphysical questions, and she does so by examining whether they offer plausible
accounts of two current disputes: the problems of composition and material
constitution. She concludes that, while not merely verbal, these disputes have
reached a stalemate: all theoretical options have been exhausted, and decisive new
evidence is not forthcoming.

Hawthorne, J. (2003), "Identity," in M. Loux and D. Zimmerman, eds, *The Oxford
Handbook of Metaphysics*. Oxford: Oxford University Press, pp. 99–130. For a highly
sophisticated, contemporary, and yet relatively brief inquiry into the metaphysics
of identity, one would be hard-pressed to do better than this article. Topics
covered include Leibniz's Law, the identity of indiscernibles and the three deviant
identity views discussed in "Material Constitution" above (relative, temporal, and
contingent).

Johnston, M. (1992), "Constitution is not identity," *Mind,* 101, pp. 89–105. In this
paper, Johnston gives one of the most forceful and encompassing defenses of the
orthodox, constitutionalist position. Interestingly, his case culminates in the view
that constitution is a vague relation and that, for this reason, it could not possibly be
captured by the identity relation, since identity is not vague.

Rea, M. (1995), "The problem of material constitution." *Philosophical Review,* 104,
525–52. In this seminal paper, Rea argues that, despite their differences, the four
most familiar puzzles of material constitution—the "growing argument," the "ship of
Theseus puzzle," the "body-minus argument," and the "clay statue puzzle"—underlie
one general problem, the "problem of material constitution," in the sense that "every
solution to the problem of material constitution is equally a solution to each of these
four puzzles, though not vice versa" (p. 525).

Rea, M., ed. (1997), *Material Constitution*. Lanham, MD: Rowman and Littlefield. This
collection of previously published articles on the topic of material constitution is
the canonical resource on this topic. Anyone interested in getting up to speed on
the contemporary scholarship would be advised to start here. In addition to the
essays themselves, Rea's masterful introduction, formal presentation of the problem
(Appendix), and scholarly bibliography make this an indispensible volume for
anyone who works on this topic.

Sider, T. (2001), *Four-Dimensionalism: An Ontology of Persistence and Time*. Oxford:
Oxford University Press. In this, the most rigorous and synoptic defense of four-
dimensionalism to date, Sider dedicates an entire chapter (ch. 5) to the application of
his preferred stage view to the problem of material constitution. He argues there that
his view can handle the key cases of coincident objects better than any of the other
competing accounts.

Thomasson, A. (2007), *Ordinary Objects.* New York: Oxford University Press. At heart, an extended defense of commonsense ontology against the eliminativist and nihilist barbarians at the gate, this recent book also incorporates discussions of vagueness, anti-realism, and issues concerning the place and methods of metaphysics.

Van Inwagen, P. (1990), *Material Beings.* Ithaca, NY: Cornell University Press. In this highly influential work, van Inwagen defends the startling claim that only mereological simples and living organisms exist. This is essential reading.

Wiggins, D. (2001), *Sameness and Substance Renewed.* Cambridge: Cambridge University Press. In this overhaul of his 1980 monograph, *Sameness and Substance,* Wiggins makes compelling, neo-Aristotelian cases against Geach's relative identity view and for the constitutionalist position. This is a rich and difficult work that requires, but also repays, careful reading.

Chapter 7 Endurantism and perdurantism

Crisp, T. and Smith, D. (2005), "'Wholly present' defined." *Philosophy and Phenomenological Research,* 71, 318–44. An excellent piece laying out an alternative definition of what it is for enduring objects to be "wholly present." Not only is it interesting in and of itself, but its extensive discussion introduces the reader to the variety of ways that other philosophers have treated defining terms in the philosophy of persistence.

Haslanger, S. (2003), "Persistence through time," in M. Loux and D. Zimmerman, eds, *Oxford Handbook of Metaphysics.* Oxford: Oxford University Press, pp. 315–54. State-of-the-art survey of the problem of temporary intrinsics, and the positions held by those who take the problem seriously.

Hawley, K. (2001), *How Things Persist.* Oxford: Oxford University Press. Monograph arguing for a stage theoretic version spin on perdurantism, covering issues including material constitution and vagueness.

Heller, M. (1991), *The Ontology of Physical Objects: Four-Dimensional Hunks of Matter.* Cambridge: Cambridge University Press. An older monograph arguing for perdurantism. Oft referred to, and many people have a Heller-style perdurantism in mind when they talk about the topic.

Hofweber, T. (2009), "The meta-problem of change." *Nous,* 43, 286–314. An excellent article detailing the reasons for not taking the problem of temporary intrinsics seriously. It also highlights how crucial it is to be clear about what we are doing in metaphysics in order to avoid "Deep Thought" scenarios where, after much discussion, we realize the debate has gone nowhere as we weren't clear enough on what the question was in the first place.

McGrath, M. (2007), "Temporal parts." *Philosophy Compass,* 2, 730–48. Another introduction to the issues involved in persistence. Covers many of the arguments covered in this chapter.

Parsons, J. (2007), "Theories of location." *Oxford Studies in Metaphysics*, 3, 201–32. Extensive introduction to chorology (although Parsons doesn't use that term). Combines this with introducing a set of definitions for terms in the philosophy of persistence.

Sider, T. (2001), *Four-Dimensionalism*. Oxford: Oxford University Press. Required reading for anyone serious about the philosophy of persistence. Sider's book covers just about every argument in the area, with an extensive treatment of issues in material constitution. While Sider himself argues for stage theory, the vast bulk of the book concentrates mainly on perdurantism.

Varzi, A. (2003), "Perdurantism, universalism, and quantifiers." *Australasian Journal of Philosophy*, 81, 208–15. A good introduction to the "tenor-turnip" problem that perdurantists face, along with a suggested solution.

Chapter 8 Personal identity

Baker, L. R. (2000), *Persons and Bodies: A Constitution Approach*. Cambridge: Cambridge University Press. The most sophisticated defense of the constitution approach to persons. Baker defends the thesis that we are essentially self-conscious persons, constituted by bodies. We are ontologically distinct from other animals in virtue of our possessing a rich inner life, a first-person perspective. She offers an account in which the constituted person and constituting animal borrow properties from each. The same property token will be nonderivatively held by one entity and derivatively possessed by the other. She argues that such an account of property sharing can meet the criticisms put forth by opponents of spatially coincident entities such as the too many minds objection.

—(2007), *The Metaphysics of Everyday Life: An Essay in Practical Realism*. Cambridge: Cambridge University Press. Baker extends her constitution account to explain the metaphysics of the everyday world. She argues that only the constitution account can do justice to the features of the objects of folk ontology—in particular, artifacts and people. She takes up Jaegwon Kim's challenge to show how the non-reductive materialist can make sense of mental causation by providing a constitution approach to properties. She defends the existence of vagueness in the world on the grounds that entities gradually come into and go out of existence. While arguing that vagueness is not just linguistic, Baker insists that she can avoid a commitment to vague identity. She defends 3Dism against Sider's argument that considerations of vagueness favor 4Dism. She ends with discussions of ontological novelty and emergence, hallmarks of the constitution view.

Evans, G. (1978), "Can there be vague objects?" *Analysis*, 38(4), 208. A brief, profound, cryptic and famous paper that claims objects cannot be indeterminately identical to each other. So any vagueness in identity must be linguistic, it being indeterminate whether the names pick out the same objects. But objects themselves cannot be indeterminately identical. The argument is roughly that if x has the property of being determinately identical to itself, but y is indeterminately identical to x, then there would be properties determinately distinguishing them, hence they are not indeterminately identical.

Hawley, K. (2001), *How Things Persist*. Oxford: Clarendon Press. Hawley's book is a very clever defense of the stage approach to persistence. Her powerful arguments make an initially counterintuitive position, that you and the other ordinary objects of the world are actually momentary stages, appear more plausible. She offers an account of how "lingering" and historical predicates ("thinking of Vienna" or "having once lived in Vienna") could be applied to momentary objects. She shows that referring to momentary stages is no more problematic than 3D predication of a thing's properties at any instant. She defends an account of persistence that doesn't involve identity, arguing that distinct stages can be the same person. She offers a nuanced account of vagueness, showing how different theories of vagueness can or cannot fit well with different accounts of persistence.

—(2005), "Fission, fusion and intrinsic facts." *Philosophy and Phenomenological Research*, 71(3), 602–21. Hawley aims to explain what philosophical principle is being violated by accounts that run afoul of the Only x and y rule, such as Nozick's closest continuer approach and Shoemaker and Parfit's no-branching clause. She argues that such theories leave the existence and non-existence of entities unexplained, for they lack a causal story accounting for the dependencies of one object upon another.

Hershenov, D. (2004), "Countering the appeal of the psychological approach to personal identity." *Philosophy*, 79, 445–72. Provides an animalist response to McMahan and Persson's claim that a single animal with two heads (dicephalus) reveals people to be but proper parts of animals rather than identical to them. If people accept, *pace* Locke, the intuitive claim that Sleeping Socrates and Waking Socrates are one and the same person, just not psychologically unified, then an analogous argument can be made about the conjoined twins. It is also claimed that McMahan and Persson's use of the dicephalus commits them to accepting that such an animal is itself a self-conscious thinking being with a divided mind, thus undermining the motivating intuition that minds cut off from each other must belong to different persons.

—(2008), "A hylomorphic account of thought experiments concerning personal identity." *American Catholic Philosophical Quarterly*, 82(2), 481–502. Hylomorphism is put forth as a third position between animalist and psychological accounts of personal identity. Although the author doesn't endorse the hylomorphic view, he shows how it can avoid the problem of too many thinkers and at the same time capture the transplant intuition without violating the Only x and y principle. The odd biological consequences of the theory are mitigated somewhat by claiming that the religious, at least, have reasons to believe that human animals are distinct from all other animals and so will have unique persistence conditions.

Hudson, H. (2001), *A Materialist Conception of the Human Person.* Ithaca, NY: Cornell University Press. This book defends a 4Dist account of the person. It introduces the *partist solution* to the problem of the many. Hudson argues that a person can be composed of different fusions of particles at the same time. This is his solution to Unger's problem of the many. There aren't many overlapping thinking beings, rather the same thinker is composed of different sums at slightly different regions of space. What also distinguishes Hudson's 4Dist account is his concern with moral and religious issues. Although Hudson provides a powerful argument for unrestricted composition, he argues that this doesn't lead to an explosion of entities with moral status. He provides an account of which of the many objects with thinking stages is the person. The human animal turns out not to be a person, though it shares parts with persons.

—(2007), "I am not an animal!," in D. Zimmerman and P. van Inwagen, eds, *Persons: Human and Divine.* Oxford: Oxford University Press. Hudson shows the costs of identifying human persons with animals. He claims that one will have to be a 3Dist, hold a restricted theory of composition in which there are no such things as brains and heads, take constitution to be identity and deny the religious doctrine of resurrection.

Lewis, D. (1983), "Survival and identity," in *Collected Papers II.* Oxford: Oxford University Press, 55–72. Lewis responds to Parfit's claim that fission reveals that identity doesn't matter. He claims that no one goes out of existence upon fissioning. Rather, the 4Dist approach reveals that there were two people there all along. So fission, *pace* Parfit, doesn't involve anyone ceasing to exist but what matters to them continuing. Lewis's postscript clarifies his account of stages and takes up the issue of how two worms can think with the same stage.

—(1986), *The Plurality of Worlds.* Oxford: Blackwell Press. The relevance of this famous book to personal identity is its claim that the problem of temporary intrinsics offers a reductio of 3Dist approaches. Moreover, Lewis argues for unrestricted composition on the grounds that otherwise composition will be vague and it will be indeterminate how many things exist. Once unrestricted composition is accepted, the temporal parts account of persons becomes the most attractive of the materialist approaches.

Locke, J. (1975), *An Essay Concerning Human Understanding,* ed. P. Nidditch. Oxford: Oxford University Press. On the topic of personal identity, it has been said that all subsequent writing has consisted merely of footnotes to Locke. Psychological approaches to personal identity are mostly reforms of the memory criterion of identity that is traced back to Locke's claim that one extends as far back in time as one's consciousness. Locke introduced the notion of the person switching bodies which spawned the personal identity thought-experiment industry. The problem of too many thinkers has its roots in Locke since he distinguishes immaterial thinking substances (souls) and persons. The most quoted definition of "person" is Locke's.

He is also responsible for the notion that "person" is a forensic term, thus linking the
metaphysics of personal identity to practical concern.

McMahan, J. (2002), *The Ethics of Killing: Problems at the Margins of Life*. Oxford:
Oxford University Press. The first part of McMahan's book provides the metaphysical
basis for the bioethical views that follow. McMahan defends the view that we are
roughly brain-sized parts of the human animal. His embodied mind account is, in
part, motivated by the idea that whichever parts of the body are directly involved
in the production of thought are the parts that compose us. Arms and legs, for
example, are irrelevant to the production of thought. Other support for the idea
that people are just spatial parts of animals comes from a case of conjoined twins
which appear to be one living animal with two heads and distinct minds. McMahan
argues that since people are merely proper parts of animals, the puzzles of spatially
coincident thinkers are avoided. The animal embedding the person just thinks in a
metaphysically harmless, derivative manner because it has a part that really thinks.

Merricks, T. (2001), *Objects and Persons*. Oxford, Oxford University Press. Merricks
defends the view that the human person and human animal are one and the same
entity. In fact, thinking animals are the only composite entities in Merricks's sparse
ontology. Merricks's novel defense of a sparse ontology is based on a claim that
real objects have macro-level causal powers that are not redundant. Baseballs and
mountains don't exist because if they did they would not cause anything not already
caused by their constituent atoms. Conscious entities, Merricks claims, have causally
efficacious mental powers that do not supervene on the causal properties of their
component atoms. Merricks offers a somewhat different account than van Inwagen's
for paraphrasing our ordinary talk of everyday objects.

Nagel, T. (1971), "Brain bisection and the unity of consciousness." *Synthese*, 22,
396–413. Nagel introduces the split-brain phenomenon to philosophers. The
possibility of minds being divided made Parfit's fission scenarios and their lessons
more plausible. The split-brain phenomenon is also interpreted as providing a
problem for non-reductionist and dualist accounts of the person.

Noonan, H. (2003), *Personal Identity* (revised edition). London: Routledge. No other
book will provide readers with as good a discussion of the historical development
of the personal identity debates. Noonan's book presses more effectively than any
other a defense of the Only *x* and *y* rule against Nozick's closest continuer account
of identity. He also provides a powerful critique of Parfit's famous claim that
identity doesn't matter, for the success of Parfit's claim depends upon the falsehood
of the Only *x* and *y* rule. Noonan's (2003) revised edition includes chapters on the
animalism popularized recently by Olson and also takes into account the latest
debates about vagueness. While favoring a 4Dist worm account, Noonan offers
charitable and nuanced readings of other approaches, even suggesting how the case
for them can be made stronger. His account of pronoun revision may be the most
promising direction for those metaphysicians whose accounts of personal identity
will have to tolerate overlapping thinkers.

Olson, E. T. (1997), *The Human Animal: Identity without Psychology.* Oxford, Oxford University Press. This book changed the debate from which psychological criterion of personal identity was correct to whether psychology had any role to play in the debate about our nature. Olson defends the thesis that biological continuity fully accounts for our identity and persistence. His book-length defense of the animalist view brought the too many minds problem to the forefront of the debate. Olson challenged those who held that we are essentially persons to account for why the spatially coincident human animal could not also think and thus qualify as a person. Olson drew on Parfit's work about identity not mattering to explain away the popular reactions that the cerebrum transplants indicate we switch bodies. Olson argues that what matters to us provides no insight into our metaphysical nature.

—(2002), "Thinking animals and the reference of 'I.'" *Philosophical Topics,* 30(1), 189–207. Olson considers the various metaphysical, psychological, and linguistic moves that theorists can make to deal with the problem of the thinking animal. He offers a sustained discussion of the merits of Noonan-style pronoun revision. This is the idea that while more than one thinking being can think or utter the first-person pronoun, it refers just to the entity with the maximal psychological persistence conditions.

—(2007), *What Are We? An Essay in Personal Ontology.* Oxford: Oxford University Press. Readers of this book will be immediately brought up to date about the major competitors in the contemporary personal identity debate—constitution, soul theories, temporal parts, brain views, animalism, nihilism, and bundle theories. Olson provides chapters on each of the major views. His most persistent criticism is that they can't handle the problem of the thinking animal. His critiques are fair, nuanced, and at times very original and profound. He even makes the nihilist account that there are no persons appear far more respectable than I would have thought. He also provides an illuminating discussion of the drawbacks of his own favored animalist account.

Parfit, D. (1971), "Personal identity." *The Philosophical Review,* 80(1), 3–29. This article made Parfit famous and changed the debate. It foreshadows two of the major themes of his magnum opus, *Reasons and Persons*: that identity is not what matters to us and that there may be no fact of the matter about whether someone survives in certain puzzle cases. This article is a very good place to start for those who don't want to immediately tackle the lengthy *Reasons and Persons.*

—(1983), *Reasons and Persons.* Oxford: Oxford University Press. Perhaps the most influential work in the twentieth century on the topic of personal identity. The book is famous for the novel claim that identity is not what matters to us. Parfit relies upon imaginative thought experiments to make the case that it doesn't matter if you are identical to any future person as long as there is an individual who would be psychologically related to you in the appropriate manner. And what does matter to us, certain psychological relations, admits of degrees. Parfit explores the startling practical implications of these views. He suggests that it isn't irrational to favor one's near future over the distant future. He also claims that utilitarianism can be supported by the view that the unity of each life, and hence the differences between lives, is less deep than previously recognized. His book is unrivaled among contemporary metaphysical works for its impact on ethical theorizing.

Persson, I. (1999), "Our identity and the separability of persons and organisms." *Dialogue*, 38, 519–33. Persson puts forth similar views as McMahan about the possibility of people being parts of animals. He argues that this will meet the animalist charge that those who assert the spatial coincidence of animals and persons will as a result have to tolerate there either being two streams of consciousness or two thinkers sharing the same thoughts. He is slightly more skeptical of the success of the project than McMahan.

Plantinga, A. (2007), "Materialism and christian belief," in D. Zimmerman and P. van Inwagen, eds, *Persons: Human and Divine.* Oxford: Oxford University Press, pp. 99–141. Plantinga presents two modal arguments in favor of the view that material beings are just the wrong type of entities to be thinkers. Perhaps the more important contribution of the article is showing that there is much less than is usually thought to the standard objections to dualism. Plantinga argues against the objections that dualism can't account for the interaction of material and immaterial things, that it fails to explain the neurological dependence of thought, that it is without an answer to Kim's pairing problem, and that it is at odds with the deliverances of modern physics.

Schechtman, M. (1996), *The Constitution of Selves.* Ithaca, NY: Cornell University Press. Schechtman argues that our practical concerns don't match up well with the logical requirements of reidentification accounts of identity that concern most theorists of personal identity. She develops a narrative account of identity that can do justice to our practical concerns, for it admits of degrees and indeterminacy, unlike the reidentification sense of identity. The narrative question of identity is represented by the adolescent asking "Who am I?" The reidentification question is expressed by the same words in the mouth of the amnesiac. The questions expressed by the same sentences are different and so must be their answers.

Shewmon, D. A. (1997), "Recovery from 'brain death': a neurologist's apologia." *Linacre Quarterly*, 64, 30–96. Shewmon is a philosophically informed neuroscientist who combines the hylomorphic doctrine of Aquinas with modern physiology. His medical training allows him to construct thought experiments that are biologically more plausible than those of most metaphysicians. He is one of the world leaders on the definition and criteria of death, perhaps the foremost critic of brain death. He held each of the three criteria for death at one time or another and so is especially well situated to explain their attractions and flaws. The upper-brain criterion coheres with psychological accounts of personal identity while the whole-brain and the traditional circulatory-respiratory criteria fit better with animalist conceptions. Shewmon defends a hybrid account of the person: we survive as long as the appropriate biological integration is present, but we are essentially psychological creatures. Our capacity for psychology is rooted in our organism, and is therein presently.

Shoemaker, S. (1963), *Self-Knowledge and Self-Identity.* Ithaca, NY: Cornell University Press. Introduced the brain transplant thought experiment with his famous case of Brown's brain being put in Robinson's body. This updating of Locke's famous thought experiments unleashed the modern discussion of persons switching bodies. As a result, many philosophers consider the human person to be nonidentical to the human animal.

—(1999), "Self, body and coincidence," in *Proceedings of the Aristotelian Society Supplement,* 73, 287–306. Shoemaker believes that persons are constituted by bodies. His account of constitution differs from Baker's because he insists that human animals can't think at all, not even derivatively. The different persistence conditions of animals and persons ensure that the person has mental properties that the animal lacks.

Shoemaker, S. and Swinburne, R. (1984), *Personal Identity: A Materialist Account.* New York: Blackwell Press. A very clear and accessible introduction to the debate between materialist and dualist accounts of the person by two of the giants in the field. Shoemaker, the materialist, alternates with his co-author, Swinburne, who is a dualist. They both respond briefly to the other's arguments.

Sider, T. (2001), *Four-Dimensionalism: An Ontology of Persistence and Time.* Oxford: Clarendon Press. Perhaps the most impressive defense of 4Dism on offer. Sider provides rigorous statements of the doctrine and reveals that his 3Dist opponents actually have trouble clearly stating their view, contrary to what is often alleged. He presents powerful arguments in favor of 4Dism, maintaining that the most effective is the argument from vagueness. Well-versed in the philosophy of time and its semantics, he criticizes presentist accounts of time to forestall the 3Dist from finding an ally in that theory of time. Sider defends the stage view against the more traditional worm view, arguing it does better with counting objects, the possession of temporary intrinsic properties, and fission. He claims we are momentary stages but can truly be said to have existed at other times in virtue of our having temporal counterparts.

Unger, P. (1990), *Identity, Consciousness, and Value.* Oxford: Oxford University Press. One of the most imaginative defenses of personal identity. No one has put thought experiments to use as much as Unger, nor has anyone thought as deeply about hidden assumptions and flaws in our presentations and reactions to thought experiments. His book is in many ways a response to Parfit's. He defends the position that identity matters and that we survive as long as our psychology is physically realized in the appropriate manner. He provides a very nuanced account of the assimilation of new physical and psychological properties.

—(2006), *All the Power in the World.* Oxford: Oxford University Press. Unger is not afraid to let his arguments lead him to some very unpopular views. He abandons his earlier materialist account of the person. He claims that the problem of the many, which he developed years earlier, means there will be too many thinking beings overlapping us and also that they won't have (libertarian) free will. His solution is to adopt a dualist account of the person.

van Inwagen, P. (1990), *Material Beings*. Ithaca, NY: Cornell University Press. Van Inwagen shows that personal identity cannot be addressed apart from many traditional debates in mereology. He raises the special composition question: when do the Xs compose a Y? His answer is only when they are caught up in a life. So organisms are the only composite objects in van Inwagen's ontology. Restricting composition leads him to defend the notion that there is vagueness in the world. He offers lengthy and provocative defenses of vague existence and vague identity. Despite offering a sparse ontology, he provides a semantics in which ordinary talk comes out mostly as true. There aren't chairs, but there are simples arranged chairwise.

Wiggins, D. (2001), *Sameness and Substance Renewed*. Cambridge: Harvard University Press. The revised edition has a rewritten chapter on personal identity and a new chapter on identity and vagueness. Wiggins's work on sortals popularized the distinction between substance and phase sortals. He defends a classical account of identity against the relative identity challenge of Peter Geach. He is one of the few 3Dists to champion the Only *x* and *y* rule.

Williams. B. (1973), *Problems of the Self*. Cambridge: Cambridge University Press. A collection of Williams's very influential articles on personal identity. He was one of the first defenders of the bodily criterion for personal identity. His seminal article "Personal identity and individuation" critiqued psychological approaches to personal identity by imagining two modern mental duplicates of Guy Fawkes. This led to theorists invoking no-branching rules to deal with duplication, running afoul of the Only *x* and *y* rule. His essay "Self and the future" has led many philosophers to become skeptical of the cases methodology that involves fanciful thought experiments.

Zimmerman, D. (2002), "The constitution of persons by bodies: a critique of Lynne Rudder Baker's theory of material constitution." *Philosophical Topics*, 30(1), 295–337. Zimmerman is one of Baker's more trenchant and charitable critics. He claims that while Baker does a good job explicating the modal aspect of constitution, she fails to provide an adequate account of the mereological side to constitution. He also argues that she can't satisfactorily handle the problem of too many minds that confronts those who maintain there are spatially coincident objects. He doesn't think she can adequately account for how nonidentical entities composed of the same parts standing in the same relations to the environment can have different psychological profiles.

—(2003), "Material people," in M. Loux and D. Zimmerman, eds, *The Oxford Handbook of Metaphysics*. Oxford: Oxford University Press, pp. 492–526. Zimmerman claims that if you are a material being that gains or loses parts, such as a brain or a body, then there is another thing, a mass of matter distinct from you, but having the same intrinsic characteristics, including mental states. But he then claims it is false that wherever you are, there is something else there that has the same intrinsic mental states like feeling sad. Thus he concludes that you are neither a brain nor a human organism nor any other thing that changes its parts – and therefore no version of sensible materialism is true. He concludes that dualism begins to look better given the faults of most materialisms.

Chapter 9 Free will

Fischer, J. M. (2006), *My Way: Essays on Moral Responsibility.* New York: Oxford University Press. John Fischer, whose earlier work on freedom and responsibility was co-authored with Mark Ravizza, defends a view called semicompatibilism. According to this view, one kind of freedom (regulative control) is incompatible with the truth of causal determinism, while the kind of freedom required for moral responsibility (guidance control) is compatible with the truth of causal determinism. This volume brings together many of Fischer's central papers on free will and moral responsibility.

Kane, R. (1996), *The Significance of Free Will.* Oxford: Oxford University Press. Kane offers the most sophisticated extant event-causal libertarian view, and his influence among contemporary incompatibilists is second only to van Inwagen's. Kane argues that free will is grounded in "ultimate responsibility," which requires the falsity of determinism and entails the presence of alternative possibilities during "self-forming actions."

Kane, R., ed. (2002), *The Oxford Handbook of Free Will.* Oxford: Oxford University Press. This is the most valuable and wide-ranging single-volume collection of original papers currently available on the topic, and an updated and expanded second edition is now available. Kane's introduction to the collection offers a fairly comprehensive survey of the recent free will debates, with sections devoted to: (1) Theology and Fatalism; (2) Physics, Determinism, and Indeterminism; (3) The Modal or Consequence Argument for Incompatibilism; (4) Compatibilist Perspectives on Freedom and Responsibility; (5) Moral Responsibility, Alternative Possibilities, and Frankfurt-Style Examples; (6) Libertarian Perspectives on Free Agency and Free Will; (7) Nonstandard Views; and (8) Neuroscience and Free Will. While the volume introduces all of the central issues, the level of sophistication makes this volume less than ideal for the introductory reader.

—(2005), *A Contemporary Introduction to Free Will.* New York: Oxford University Press. This is the best existing introductory textbook on free will. In it, Kane—a leading libertarian—provides an excellent and balanced treatment of most aspects of contemporary debates about free will, while also arguing for Kane's own influential form of libertarianism, which is developed more fully in his *The Significance of Free Will.*

Levy, N. and McKenna, M. (2009), "Recent work on free will and moral responsibility." *Philosophy Compass*, 4, 96–133. This overview article is perhaps the most up-to-date general overview of various central issues in the free will debates. It contains a thorough and even-handed discussion of six central contemporary debates in the free will literature: (1) Frankfurt's argument that moral responsibility does not require the freedom to do otherwise; (2) the heightened focus upon the source of free actions; (3) the debate over whether moral responsibility is an essentially historical concept; (4) recent compatibilist views which endorse the thesis that moral responsibility requires the freedom to do otherwise; (5) the role of the control condition in free will and moral responsibility; and (6) the debate concerning luck. Though an excellent source for surveying information on recent work on free will and moral responsibility, it will best serve those who already have some general knowledge of the extant literature.

Pereboom, D. (2001), *Living without Free Will*. Cambridge: Cambridge University Press. Pereboom's book is influential on a number of accounts. He presents a manipulation-based argument, which he calls the "four-case argument," against contemporary compatibilist accounts of free will. After arguing for incompatibilism, he argues that the only viable version of libertarianism will be agent-causal in nature. Insofar as we have evidence to reject the existence of agent-causation, Pereboom defends a negative answer to the Existence Question. He ends by describing how many of our social practices (e.g., punishment) need to be modified as a result.

Smilansky, S. (2000), *Free Will and Illusion*. Oxford: Clarendon Press. Like Pereboom, Smilanksy also denies the existence of free will, though for different reasons. Here, he argues that compatibilist accounts of free will are insufficient, that libertarian views are too demanding to be sustained, and that hard determinism is unconvincing. Smilansky argues that the illusory beliefs we currently have about the existence of free will play an important role both personally and socially.

Strawson, G. (2010), *Freedom and Belief* (revised edition). Oxford: Oxford University Press. This book contains Strawson's widely known argument for the impossibility of moral responsibility based on the impossibility of being *causa sui*. It also addresses implications of our not having free will, as well as examines the reasons why belief that we do have it is so persistent.

van Inwagen, P. (1983), *An Essay on Free Will*. Oxford: Clarendon Press. Though a little dated, and though he has since changed his view on a number of issues, van Inwagen's book plays a central role in contemporary incompatibilism. Middle chapters contain van Inwagen's influential Consequence Argument, the conclusion of which is that free will is incompatible with the truth of determinism. Van Inwagen also stands as a model of clarity and rigor.

Vargas, M. (2010), "The revisionist turn: a brief history of recent work on free will," in J. Aguilar, A. Buckareff, and K. Frankish, eds, *New Waves in the Philosophy of Action*. London: Palgrave-Macmillan. This interesting discussion by Vargas focuses on methodological issues and how distinct conceptions of the philosophical project generate the peculiar structure of the free will debate. It gives a good sense of the ways in which the contemporary discussions have developed over the past 30 years, while also advancing a defense of Vargas' own view, which he call "revisionism."

Chapter 10 God

Craig, W. L. and Moreland, J. P., eds (2010), *Blackwell Companion to Natural Theology.* Oxford: Blackwell. This volume collects together state-of-the-art surveys of the major arguments for the existence of God—and the argument from evil against the existence of God—by notable contemporary theistic philosophers (including Charles Taliaferro, Alexander Pruss, Robin Collins, Victor Reppert, Stewart Goetz, Timothy McGrew, Lydia McGrew, and the editors of the volume). More than half of its pages are taken up with discussion of cosmological arguments and arguments for design.

Hoffmann, J. and Rosenkrantz, G. (2002), *The Divine Attributes.* Oxford: Blackwell. This book belongs to Blackwell's *Exploring the Philosophy of Religion* series, edited by Michael Peterson. The series aims to occupy the middle ground between elementary text and pioneering monograph. The book has chapters on the idea of God, substantiality, incorporeality, necessary existence, eternality, omniscience, perfect goodness and omnipotence. In most chapters, Hoffmann and Rosenkrantz defend controversial philosophical analyses justified against the background of contemporary debate.

Mackie, J. L. (1982), *The Miracle of Theism.* Oxford: Clarendon. Mackie's book is the gold standard for recent discussions of arguments about the existence of God. Mackie provides clear and concise analyses of a wide range of arguments for and against the existence of God, including ontological arguments, cosmological arguments, arguments for design, arguments from consciousness, moral arguments, Pascal's wager, arguments from evil, arguments from the diversity of religious experience and so forth.

Manson, N., ed. (2003), *God and Design: The Teleological Argument and Modern Science.* London: Routledge. Manson's book is a collection of new and recent essays on arguments for design. Apart from Manson's own excellent introduction, the collection includes papers by Elliott Sober, John Leslie, Richard Swinburne, Paul Davies, William Lane Craig, Robin Collins, Martin Rees, William Dembski, Michael Behe, Michael Ruse and others. The collection provides an excellent introduction to recent debates about arguments for design. [Graham Oppy gives a more detailed review of Manson's book in *Sophia* 43(1), (2004), pp. 127–31.]

Martin, M. (1990), *Atheism: A Philosophical Justification.* Philadelphia: Temple University Press. Martin's book is a comprehensive treatment of arguments about the existence of God. Martin argues that there are no good arguments in favor of belief in God, and that there are many good arguments in favor of failure to believe in God (and, indeed, in favor of believing that God does not exist). [For a detailed critical study of Martin's book, see Oppy, G. (2007), "Atheism: a retrospective." *Philo* 10(1), 72–84.]

O'Connor, T. (2008), *Theism and Ultimate Explanation: The Necessary Shape of Contingency.* Oxford: Blackwell. O'Connor's book provides an interesting defense of a cosmological argument from contingency. The first half of the book is concerned with the development of a general metaphysics and epistemology of modality; the second half applies this framework in the defense of a combined cosmological-cum-design argument for the existence of God. [Graham Oppy reviews O'Connor's book in *Notre Dame Philosophical Reviews* (ndpr.nd.edu), and Graham Oppy analyzes O'Connor's argument in J. Kvanvig, ed. (2011), *Oxford Studies in Philosophy of Religion, Volume 3*. Oxford: Oxford University Press.]

Oppy, G. (2006), *Philosophical Perspectives on Infinity.* Cambridge: Cambridge University Press. This book aims to discuss general philosophical questions about infinity that bear on central issues in philosophy of religion. In particular, this book supplies necessary background for proper understanding of debates about cosmological arguments, arguments for design, Pascal's wager, analyses of omniscience, no-best-world responses to arguments from evil, and much else besides.

—(2009), "Gods," in J. Kvanvig, ed., *Oxford Studies in Philosophy of Religion, Volume 2*. Oxford: Oxford University Press, pp. 231–50. This paper defends the view that to be God is to be the one and only God, where to be a God is to be a supernatural being or force that has and exercises power over the natural world but that is not, in turn, under the power of any higher ranking or more powerful category of beings or forces. The paper considers various alternative views about the meaning of the word "God," and argues against them.

Pruss, A. (2006), *The Principle of Sufficient Reason.* Cambridge: Cambridge University Press. Pruss's excellent book is an extended—book-length!—discussion of the principle of sufficient reason, that is, roughly, of the claim that nothing happens without a reason, cause, sufficient explanation or the like. Pruss defends the principle of sufficient reason with a diverse range of arguments, responds to objections to the principle (including well-known objections from David Hume and Peter van Inwagen) and indicates the various philosophical benefits that—in his view—would flow from acceptance of the principle.

Sobel, J. H. (2004), *Logic and Theism: Arguments for and against the Existence of God.* Cambridge: Cambridge University Press. Sobel's book is the only more recent book to come close to Mackie (1982). Sobel provides detailed and intricate analyses of ontological arguments, cosmological arguments, arguments for design, arguments from miracles, paradoxes of omnipotence and omniscience, logical and evidential arguments from evil, and Pascal's wager. [Graham Oppy gives a lengthy review of Sobel's book in *Philo,* 9(1) (2006), 73–91].

Swinburne, R. (1977), *The Coherence of Theism*. Oxford: Clarendon. This book is the first of a trilogy; the other two volumes are *The Existence of God* (1979) and *Faith and Reason* (1981). The book is concerned with the meaning and coherence of the claim that God exists. After an initial discussion of religious language, there are chapters on many of the attributes that are standardly ascribed to God: freedom, creativity, omnipotence, omniscience, perfect goodness, eternity, immutability, necessity, holiness, and worship-worthiness.

Chapter 11 New directions in metaphysics

Chalmers, D., Manley, D., and Wasserman, R., eds (2009), *Metametaphysics: New Essays on the Foundations of Modality*. Oxford: Clarendon Press. Anthology of original essays. Includes Hirsch (2009), Hawthorne (2009), Sider (2009), Thomasson (2009), and van Inwagen (2009) mentioned in "New Directions in Metaphysics" above.

Hirsch, E. (2011), *Quantifier Variance and Realism: Essays in Metaontology*. Oxford: Oxford University Press. Introduction and collection of published essays including Hirsch (2002a), (2002b), (2005), (2008), (2009), and (2011) mentioned in "New Directions in Metaphysics" above.

Knobe, J. and Nichols, S., eds (2008), *Experimental Philosophy*. New York: Oxford University press. A collection with some of the most important and influential papers in experimental philosophy. Includes Knobe and Nichols (2007) mentioned in "New Directions in Metaphysics" above.

Quine, W. V. O. (1980), *From a Logical Point of View*. Cambridge MA: Harvard University Press. Classic collection of his work. Includes Quine (1980a, 1980b, and 1980c) mentioned in "New Directions in Metaphysics" above. Compare van Inwagen (2009) and Cameron (2008).

Thomasson, A. (2007), *Ordinary Objects*. Oxford: Oxford University Press. The view discussed in "New Directions in Metaphysics" above greatly fleshed out, with replies to many objections. See also Thomasson (2008) and (2009), along with Thomasson (2007), "Modal normativism and the methods of metaphysics." *Philosophical Topics*, 35, 135–60.

Research Guide

Getting started as a researcher in metaphysics can be daunting, both because of the large volume of literature and because so many non-academic writers label their work as "metaphysics." Luckily, a number of high quality research resources exist in print and online. Some offer general overviews of the subject and others are more specialized or topic-specific. This guide is intended to serve as an entry point for research in metaphysics. This list tends to focus on general research resources. The annotated bibliographies connected with each chapter are good starting points for topic-specific research.

Online resources

Not all search engine results are equal. At the time this is being written, the top result in multiple search engines is the Wikipedia entry on "Metaphysics," but in the top-five results we also find references to religion, parapsychology, mysticism, yoga, ESP, crystals, dream interpretation, psychoanalysis, astrology, meditation, life after death, and reincarnation. The editors recommend the following online resources as reliable starting points for research.

Online encylopediae

Internet Encyclopedia of Philosophy
www.iep.utm.edu
A peer-reviewed online encyclopedia based at the University of Tennessee at Martin.

Routledge Encyclopedia of Philosophy Online
www.rep.routledge.com
Requires subscription for full access.

Stanford Encyclopedia of Philosophy
http://plato.stanford.edu

A peer-reviewed online encyclopedia based in Stanford University's Metaphysics Research Lab and Center for the Study of Language and Information.

Online databases, research, and papers

Oxford Bibliographies Online
http://oxfordbibliographiesonline.com
A set of high-quality library subject guides. Requires subscription for full access.

Philosopher's Index
http://philindex.org
Indexes and abstracts almost every philosophy article since 1940. May require library access.

Philosophy Compass
http://philosophy-compass.com
Publishes high-quality invited and peer-reviewed articles that often provide excellent overviews of current and important philosophical topics and problems. Requires subscription for full access.

Philpapers: Online Research in Philosophy
http://philpapers.org/browse/metaphysics
Collects online philosophy papers in various areas. There are extensive collections in both metaphysics and philosophy of mind.

Academic research centers focusing on metaphysics

These sites are good sources to get a sense of where research in metaphysics might be headed next. These sites often contain links to further resources or to publications by participants.

Arché: Philosophical Research Centre for Logic, Language, Metaphysics and Epistemology
www.st-andrews.ac.uk/arche

Buffalo Ontology Site
http://ontology.buffalo.edu

Northern Institute of Philosophy (NIP)
www.abdn.ac.uk/philosophy/nip/index.php

Stanford Metaphysics Research Lab
http://mally.stanford.edu

Blogs

These blogs often highlight work in progress and upcoming conferences and meetings.

Matters of Substance: A group blog devoted to metaphysics
http://substantialmatters.blogspot.com/
The contributor list here includes many notable researchers in contemporary metaphysics.

Metaphysical Values: A blog on the nature of things
http://metaphysicalvalues.wordpress.com/metaphysicalvalues/
Created by the Centre for Metaphysics and Mind, Leeds, UK

Print resources

Encyclopediae and reference works

Sometimes we all need to consult a dictionary when we do not recognize or understand a word. Sometimes we need a reminder of who an historical person was, or we need help distinguishing one philosophical concept or position from another. These resources are intended to meet such needs.

Beebee, H., N. Effingham, and P. Geoff (2011), *Metaphysics: The Key Concepts* (Routledge Key Guides), London: Routledge.

Borcert, D. M. (ed.) (2006), *Encyclopedia of Philosophy* (2nd edn), New York: Macmillan Reference USA. The second edition supplements the original edition and omits or replaces some of the original articles. The original edition is P. Edwards (ed.) (1972), *Encyclopedia of Philosophy*, New York: Macmillan Publishing and Free Press.

Kim, J., E. Sosa, and G. S. Rosenkrantz (eds) (2009), *A Companion to Metaphysics* (2nd edn), Oxford: Blackwell.

Le Poidevin, R., P. Simons, A. McGonigal, and R. Cameron (eds) (2009), *The Routledge Companion to Metaphysics*, London: Routledge.

Introductory volumes and textbooks

When we are looking for a systematic presentation of problems and positions in metaphysics we need volumes like these.

Conee, E. and T. Sider (2007), *Riddles of Existence: A Guided Tour of Metaphysics,* Oxford: Oxford University Press.

Garrett, B. (2001), *What Is This Thing Called Metaphysics?,* London: Routledge.

Hamlyn, D. W. (1984), *Metaphysics,* Cambridge: Cambridge University Press.

Loux, M. J. (2006), *Metaphysics: A Contemporary Introduction* (Routledge Contemporary Introductions to Philosophy), London: Routledge.

Lowe, E. J. (2002), *A Survey of Metaphysics,* Oxford: Oxford University Press.

Taylor, R. (1994), *Metaphysics* (4th edn), New York: Prentice Hall.

van Inwagen, P. (2002), *Metaphysics* (2nd edn), Boulder, CO: Westview Press.

Anthologies

One of the best ways to discover what the widely accepted positions in metaphysics look like or to catch up with the state of the art is to examine a few of these useful anthologies. Some collect classic readings, others solicit and collect special exegetical essays, and still others try to help define the discipline by framing the questions that need to be asked.

Beebee, H. and J. Dodd (eds) (2006), *Reading Metaphysics: Selected Texts with Interactive Commentary,* Oxford: Blackwell.

Chalmers, D., D. Manley, and R. Wasserman (2009), *Metametaphysics: New Essays on the Foundations of Ontology,* Oxford: Oxford University Press.

Crane, T. and K. Farkas (eds) (2004), *Metaphysics: A Guide and Anthology,* Oxford: Oxford University Press.

Gale, R. (ed.) (2002), *Blackwell Guide to Metaphysics,* Oxford: Blackwell.

Kim, J., E. Sosa, and D. Corman (eds) (2011), *Metaphysics: An Anthology* (2nd edn), Oxford: Blackwell.

Le Poidevin, R. (ed.) (2008), *Being: Developments in Contemporary Metaphysics: Royal Institute of Philosophy Supplements Volume 62,* Cambridge: Cambridge University Press.

Loux, M. J. (ed.) (2008), *Metaphysics: Contemporary Readings,* London: Routledge.

Loux, M. J. and D. Zimmerman (eds) (2003), *The Oxford Handbook of Metaphysics*, Oxford: Oxford University Press.

Sider, T., J. Hawthorne, and D. Zimmerman (eds) (2007), *Contemporary Debates in Metaphysics*, Oxford: Blackwell.

Van Inwagen, P. and D. W. Zimmerman (eds) (1998), *Metaphysics: The Big Questions*, Oxford, Blackwell.

A–Z Index of Key Terms and Concepts

Abstract Objects
A type of particular object, distinguished from concrete objects in terms of being some or all of the following: (a) causally inert; (b) mind independent; (c) necessary; (d) nonspatial; (e) nontemporal; (f) nonphysical; and (g) unchanging.

Agent Causation
Causation whereby a metaphysical agent (e.g., a person with free will) causes its own actions, or initiates the series of events leading to some action, without the causing or initiating being causally determined by something other than the agent.

Alexander's Dictum
A metaphysical principle that states: "To be real is to have causal powers."

Alternative Possibilities (Principle of)
The principle that free will requires that agents choose from more than one possible course of action.

Analytic–Synthetic Distinction
A distinction between two kinds of truth. A synthetic truth affirms some substantive claim about how the world is. Its truth does not depend solely upon facts about our language and its use. An analytic truth is made true solely by facts about our language and its use. Analytic truths are often claimed to be true necessarily. Though versions of this distinction are common in the history of philosophy, the existence of this distinction is a matter of dispute in contemporary metaphysics. This distinction is often linked to the epistemic distinction between *a priori* (nonempirical) and *a posteriori* (empirical) knowledge.

Animalism (about Personal Identity)
The view that (a) the human person and the human animal are identical, and (b) the survival of the human animal explains the persistence of an individual person through time.

Anomalous Monism
A nonreductive physicalist account of the mind–body relation such that there are no physical-to-mental bridge laws. Individual mental events are identical with physical events, but the absence of bridge laws means that we cannot fully explain mental events in purely physical terms.

Behaviorism
A materialist theory about the mind and the meaning of mental terms, such that (a) there are no real internal mental states, events, or properties, and (b) when we employ language about internal mental states, events, or properties our talk is really about an organism's observable patterns of behavior and dispositions to behave.

Cantor's Theorem
A mathematical result stating that the cardinality of the set of all subsets of any set is greater than the cardinality of the original set.

Causal Closure
A thesis about the nature of physical domains. The causal closure of the physical maintains that every event can be completely explained by reference to prior physical events and the laws of physics.

Chorology
The philosophy of location or place.

Coincident Objects
Two distinct objects that share the same spatial location and composition at the same time.

Compatibilism
The view that free will is compatible with determinism, that human action can be free even in a deterministic universe.

Conceivability
To be conceivable is to be thinkable, imaginable, or understandable. Conceivability is often invoked in relation to a modal questions about possibility: if humans are capable of conceiving that P, does that mean P is possible?

Conceptualism (or Psychologism)
An approach to the metaphysical status of universals and mathematical objects. It holds that these entities exist, but they are neither abstract nor material (and thus they are not mind-independent). Instead, universals and mathematical objects are mental entities of some sort—ideas, thoughts, mental constructions, etc.

Concrete Objects
Objects that are not abstract. Typically these are thought to be material objects, although if gods and immaterial minds exist, they would also be classified as concrete objects.

Constitution

The asymmetric relation between a thing and what it is made of. X constitutes Y just in case Y is made from X. The constitution relation is usefully compared with the composition relation between a thing and its parts.

Content (Wide vs Narrow)

Roughly, "content" is the object or meaning of a mental event or thought. Wide content theories hold that the content of mental events depends both on an individual's mental states and on the individual's environment. Narrow content theories hold that the content of mental events is determined by an individual's mental states alone.

Contingent Identity

X and Y are contingently identical when X and Y are actually identical, but it is possible that they might not be.

Conventionalism

The view that so-called "necessary truths" are really analytic truths that "illustrate" or "convey" the conventions or the rules of use for our terms or concepts.

Cosmological Argument

A strategy for arguing for the existence of God. Cosmological arguments begin by observing features of existence (e.g., that there is motion, dependent existence, or causality) and arguing that these features are best explained by positing a being capable of causing or grounding these observable features (e.g., an unmoved mover, necessary being, or first cause). Such a being is identified with God.

Counterpart Theory

An account of modality involving a realist conception of possible worlds. For each object A in the actual world (W_0) there might be the "same" object (A*) in another possible world (W_n) where A* is the counterpart of A. A and A* are not numerically identical; rather, A* is the object A would be, if W_n were the actual world. Crudely, if Tom is a lawyer in the actual world, then there is a Tom* who is still Tom (but in W_n) but who is not a lawyer. We can use counterpart theory to explain other modal notions. The claim that it is possible that Tom is a doctor is made true by Tom having a counterpart who is a doctor. Likewise, a necessary property of Tom would be a property that all of Tom's counterparts have.

***De Dicto* Modality**

De dicto (of what is said) possibility and necessity apply to what is the case in a particular possible world. *De dicto* modality does not track objects across possible worlds.

De Re (Modality)
De re (of the thing) possibility and necessity track objects across possible worlds.

Deflationism
In general, a deflationary account of X claims that X is a dispensable or metaphysically insubstantial concept.

Descriptive Metaphysics
The metaphysical programme of attempting to describe the most general features of our actual conceptual structure without judging that conceptual structure as correct or incorrect; this programme is typically associated with the belief that description, rather than revision, is the only proper task of the metaphysician, and so descriptive metaphysics is typically opposed to "revisionary metaphysics."

Design Argument (Teleological Argument)
A strategy for arguing for the existence of God that maintains that the apparent order and directedness of the universe is evidence of the universe having been designed by some designer for some purpose. The designer is understood to be God.

Determinism
The view that all human action is fixed by the past and the laws of nature.

Diachronic Identity
The identity relation between an individual at $time_1$ and at some subsequent $time_2$.

Divine Simplicity
The thesis that God is absolutely simple in the sense that God is identical to each of God's attributes.

Doctrine of Arbitrary Undetached Parts
The claim that for any given sub-region of an area occupied by a material object, a smaller object exists that occupies just that sub-region.

Dualism
The metaphysical thesis that there are exactly two kinds of being. The term is usually used to denote the specific thesis in philosophy of mind that mind and body are distinct substances (so-called Cartesian dualism).

Eliminativism
A materialist theory about the mind–body problem that denies the reality of minds. According to prominent versions of this view, references to minds, mental states, and mental properties can be eliminated from our discourse without any loss in our ability to fully and accurately describe a given situation.

Emergentism

A nonreductive materialist view about the mental. In general terms, emergentism is the view that collections or combinations of basic entities (e.g., bits of matter) can come to exhibit properties and causal powers (e.g., mental states) that go beyond those explainable solely in terms of the more basic entities.

Empiricism

The epistemological thesis that all of our knowledge of reality ultimately derives from sense experience.

Endurantism

A view on the persistence of objects through time. Endurantism denies that things have temporal parts but affirms that things are wholly present whenever they exist. It is the denial of perdurantism.

Essential Properties

A property of a person, artifact, work of art, etc. such that if the property were lost the thing would no longer exist. Views differ with respect to whether essential properties are knowable on the basis of conceptual analysis alone or may be empirically discovered.

Eternalism

The thesis that every time exists.

Event

Events are things that happen in time, for example, "Obama's winning the election."

Existential Quantifier

A logical device that can be used to express the existence of entities, properties, classes, and relations. It is often used to capture the notion of ontological commitment in the practice of ontological paraphrase. We are said to "quantify over" those entities to which we have ontological commitment.

Experimental Metaphysics

A branch of experimental philosophy, this methodological approach employs the empirical analysis of folk intuitions regarding metaphysical issues (typically gathered using standard social scientific survey methods) to inform metaphysical theory construction.

External Question

Questions about the existence or reality of the entities of a theoretical system as a whole, that is, whether there are such things as numbers.

Extreme Nihilism
A mereological view that insists that the only objects that exist are those without proper parts—mereological simples.

Fact
That which is picked out by a true proposition; that which makes a corresponding proposition true.

Fine-Tuning Argument
A version of the design argument. According to this strategy, the universe is said to be fine-tuned for life—that is, if the values of various physical parameters had been slightly different, then life could not have arisen in the universe—and the best explanation for this apparent fine-tuning for life is that the universe was created by God.

Fission
A case in which one thing divides into two or more things, for example, cellular division.

Forms (Platonic Theory of)
Abstract objects posited by Plato that populate an ontologically and epistemically distinct realm from the objects of ordinary experience and that serve to explain any common characteristic shared by two or more ordinary objects. Hence, a red house and a red chair are red because they participate in the form RED. According to Plato, only forms could be genuine objects of knowledge.

Four-Dimensionalism
The position that people and objects have temporal parts as well as spatial parts.

Free Will
According to libertarians and hard determinists, free will is the capacity of agents to choose among alternate possibilities. According to compatibilists, people exercise free will when they are the cause or source of their own actions.

Functionalism
A family of theories about the nature of mental states. Commonly, functionalism is understood to hold that mental states are abstract states of abstract systems that are "realized" by, but not identical to, brain states in human beings.

God (Philosophical Conception of)
A necessary being usually characterized by the possession of various perfections (omnipotence, omnipresence, omniscience, omnibenevolence, etc.) and other special attributes, for example, atemporality.

Hume's Principle

Abstraction principle employed by Frege to define when two classes are equinumerous (i.e., have the same cardinality). The principle states that two classes are equinumerous just in case there is a one-to-one mapping from the members of the first class to the members of the second class. Abstraction principles of this type play an important role in Neo-Fregean accounts of mathematical objects and relations.

Hylomorphism

Generally, the metaphysical view that entities are composed of both a form and matter. Specifically, in discussions of personal identity, a position between animalist and psychological accounts of personal identity.

Identity

Generally: a relation of equivalence or sameness. Metaphysical identity is employed to help identify and differentiate entities. The so-called "Law of Identity" (A=A) expresses the fact that everything is identical to itself. Identity is often understood in terms of two principles: (a) the indiscernibility of identicals, which holds that if two (or more) objects are identical then they possess all the same properties; and (b) identity of indiscernibles (Leibniz's Law), which holds that if two (or more) objects possess all the same properties, then they are identical.

Identity Theory

Account of the relationship between mental states and brain states. Identity theory holds that mental states are identical to brain states. Usually this is understood at the level of types, such that a type of mental state (e.g., pain) is said to be identical with a type of brain state (e.g., C-fiber firings).

Imaginability

To be imaginable is to be thinkable or understandable. Often imaginability is simply a variant of conceivability, but it may require that one be capable of forming a mental image. Like conceivability, imaginability is invoked in relation to modal questions about possibility, that is, whether the ability of humans to imagine P means that P is possible.

Immanent Realism

An account of the metaphysical status of universals and mathematical objects. It affirms that universals, or mathematical objects, exist, and are mind-independent, but denies that they are abstract. Universals (including mathematical objects) are understood to be part of the material world.

Incompatibilism

The view that free will is incompatible with determinism.

Infinite Regress

When a philosophical theory postulates a series or chain of causes or dependencies, the problem arises of how the series began. If the series has no beginning, then the regress is infinite and it is difficult to explain why the series in question exists. If a starting point or foundation is postulated, then the theory must account for why this point in the series is different. Several arguments for the existence of God appeal to the role God could play in avoiding infinite regresses of cause, motion, dependent being, etc.

Interactionism

An account of the apparent interaction of mind and body that holds there is real interaction between mind and body despite their being distinct substances.

Internal Question

Questions about the existence or reality of various entities relative to a theory or linguistic framework—for example, whether, given that one already accepts that there are numbers, there is an even number that is not the sum of two prime numbers.

Lagadonian Language

A hypothetical language where each object or property serves as the name for itself. Such a language lacks ambiguity and can be useful for describing various modal situations. The reference is to the fictional land of Lagoda in Jonathan Swift's *Gulliver's Travels*. The residents of Lagoda communicate by exchanging physical objects rather than words.

Leibniz's Law

The principle that states that two (or more) objects are identical if they possess all the same properties. This principle is sometimes referred to as the identity of indiscernibles.

Libertarianism

The doctrine that humans have free will and that their actions are not determined by the past and the laws of nature.

Linguistic Ersatzism

The account of possible worlds as collections of sentences. An ordinary sentence is true in a world just in case it is a member of the world. A thing is possible if and only if it is true in some world, and necessary if and only if it is true in all.

Logical Positivism

A philosophical movement that emerged in central Europe and dates to the period preceding the Second World War. It is characterized by its strong affinity for applying empirical scientific methods to philosophical problems, the rejection of classical metaphysics, and verificationism.

Material Constitution
The issue of what criteria govern the rules for making up ("constituting") physical objects.

Materialism
The metaphysical thesis that everything real is made of matter.

Memory Criterion of Identity
A type of psychological account of personal identity such that one is identical to the person one remembers being or the person who had the experiences one remembers having.

Mereological Nihilism
The position that nothing is ever a part of anything else. It is the denial of all mereological relations.

Mereological Universalism
The position that any combination of objects makes a new object.

Mereology
The subdiscipline of metaphysics concerning questions regarding the nature of parts, wholes, and their relations, for example, composition, constitution, etc.

Mind–Body Problem
The philosophical problem of explaining the relationship between the mind and the body (or brain).

Minimal Physical Duplicate
Possible world A is a minimal physical duplicate of possible world B just in case they do not differ with respect to the physical facts (i.e., A and B are physically identical).

Modal Realism
The view that other possible worlds exist in addition to the actual world. These possible worlds differ in content but not in kind from the actual world and are spatiotemporally and causally isolated from one another.

Modality
Refers to the philosophical domain that examines the nature of, and relations between, concepts such as necessity, possibility, impossibility, contingency, and actuality.

Monism
The metaphysical thesis there is only one kind of substance in the world, for example, Materialism.

Multiple Realization
The phenomenon where the same properties (e.g., being in pain) are realized (or instantiated) in different places or times in virtue of different physical features. The possibility that mental states could be multiply realized is a traditional objection to early forms of identity theory. The ability of functionalist theories of mental states to account for multiple realization is often seen as a virtue of the functionalist approach.

Naturalism
Broadly, the thesis that all phenomena are part of the natural order. More technically, naturalism can variously represent (singly or in combination) a metaphysical, an epistemic, or a methodological position. Metaphysical naturalism is often employed as an alternative term for physicalism, or as a slightly broader notion constrained by the denial of supernatural entities (i.e., no God and no ghosts). Epistemological naturalism is jointly committed to broadly empirical modes of knowing and the complementary claim that all possible objects of knowledge are known empirically. Methodological naturalism is the thesis that philosophical enquiry should be conducted in a manner that employs or emulates the methods of the natural sciences.

Neo-Fregeanism ("Abstractionism" or "Neo-Logicism")
The view that mathematical objects and relations (and by extension other kinds of objects, e.g., propositions or properties) are metaphysically explained in virtue of their falling under the extension of concepts defined in logical terms alone. See also "Hume's Principle."

Nominalism
Generally it is the denial of the existence of abstract objects or universals (either globally or in specific domains). Nominalism accepts that instances of, for example, colors, relations, numbers, etc. obtain but denies that the color green, the successor relation, or the number three exist. The term is derived from the view that these instances are unified by their falling under the same general term or name—that they exist in name only.

Occasionalism
An account of the apparent interaction of mind and body that holds (a) there is no real interaction between mind and body, and (b) events in the mind and events in the body are altered regularly by means of divine intervention, creating the impression of interaction.

Only X and Y Rule
This rule expresses a constraint on our conception of identity between two objects (X and Y): the issue of whether X and Y are identical must be settled by appealing only to X, Y, and the relations that obtain between them. Nothing extrinsic is allowed to play a role.

Ontological Commitment
For any statement or set of statements, the ontological commitments of the statement(s) are what must exist in order to make the statement(s) true. Some distinguish between apparent and actual commitments of statements, for example, "Two is a prime number" is apparently committed to numbers, but this commitment can be eliminated in favor of, for example, sets, through paraphrase (see "Paraphrase").

Ontology
The subdiscipline of metaphysics concerning questions regarding what exists; views about what does (and does not) exist (or, alternatively, about what there is).

Parallelism
An account of the apparent interaction of mind and body that holds (a) there is no real interaction between mind and body, (b) events in the mind and events in the body unfold in time in parallel, creating the impression of interaction, and (usually) (c) the mind and body come into existence in a state of preestablished harmony that ensures the parallel development of each.

Paraphrase (Ontological)
Method of translating the statements of a theory into first-order quantified logic in order to make ontological commitment explicit. Often we may aim to paraphrase the statements of the theory in a way that will minimize our ontological commitments.

Pardurantism
An account of objects persisting in time such that every object is exactly located at just its path through time, and does not have any temporal parts.

Particulars
Individual objects.

Perdurantism
A view on the persistence of objects through time. Perdurantism affirms that objects have temporal parts. The object is comprised of the sum of its temporal parts. It is the denial of Endurantism.

Personal Identity
The branch of metaphysics that inquires into what kind of beings we are and what it takes for us to persist from one time to another.

Physicalism
The metaphysical thesis that everything real is physical or that the world can be completely described in physical terms.

Platonism
As a technical term, Platonism affirms the existence of abstract objects. Platonism is usually associated with realism about universals or mathematical objects. The term also refers historically to the views of Plato.

Presentism
The thesis that only the present exists.

Principle of Sufficient Reason
A philosophical principle according to which nothing happens without a complete reason or cause. Every question of the form "Why is A the case rather than not?" has a definite answer.

Proper Names
As a technical term, the use of proper names to refer to the same things even in contexts that express possibility and necessity, that is, across possible worlds. See also "Rigid Designators."

Property Dualism
A position on the mind–body problem usually formulated by affirming that a materialist/physicalist ontology is sufficient to explain the world, except that the explanation of consciousness requires the addition of mental properties to the ontology.

Psychological Criterion of Personal Identity
A person is held to be identical over time just in case there is some specifiable psychological continuity for the person, for example, the person inherits various mental features from prior selves.

Rationalism
The epistemological thesis that some of our knowledge of reality is innate or derived from rational reflection.

Realization
A set of properties A is realized by some other set of properties B just in case the obtaining of B is sufficient for A to obtain or be instantiated. In discussions of physicalism, realization is a central notion, as the thesis of physicalism can be expressed as the claim that all properties are physical or realized physically. Physicalist accounts of the mind likewise employ this notion. See also "Multiple Realization."

Reductionism
Reduction is a relation between theories such that a (reduced) theory is entirely explained by or translated into the vocabulary of a second (reducing) theory. Reductionism is

commonly employed in efforts to explain various phenomena (e.g., mental states) in materialistic or physicalist terms. A successful reduction effectively eliminates the commitments of the reduced theory.

Relative Identity

The view that identity is not an absolute relation, but rather that identity claims are always implicitly relative to some sortal concept.

Revisionary Metaphysics

The metaphysical programme of attempting to revise or improve our conceptual scheme in order to improve its ability to interpret phenomena. It is often opposed to "Descriptive Metaphysics."

Rigid Designators

Terms that refer to the same thing even in contexts that express possibility and necessity. Proper names and natural kind terms are understood to designate rigidly.

Serious Metaphysics

A metaphysical approach that aims to provide knowledge of deep features of reality, without its methods being simply those of conceptual or linguistic analysis (nor even these combined with the empirical results from the natural sciences).

Sortal

Broadly, a sortal is a concept (or property) that serves to individuate or distinguish kinds of objects or entities. A sortal answers the question "What is it?"

Sortal Essentialism

The thesis that objects can be sorted into kinds and that an object's kind determines its essence.

Special Composition Question

In mereology, the question of what the necessary and sufficient conditions are under which objects of one sort compose an object of a second sort.

Stage Theory (Exdurantism)

A view accepting the basic ontology of perdurantism, but identifying everyday objects with instantaneous objects rather than four-dimensional wholes composed out of them.

Superdupervenience

Terence Horgan's technical term for supervenience that is explainable in a physicalistically acceptable fashion. See "Supervenience."

Supervenience
A relation of necessary covariation. One family of properties supervenes on another family just in case there can be no difference in the former without some difference in the latter.

Supervenience Thesis
If two worlds are identical with regards to all local matters of fact then they are identical with regards to all other qualities, that is, A-type properties are said to supervene on B-type properties if no two possible worlds differ in their A-type properties without differing in their B-type properties.

Temporal Part
If objects persist though time, then a division of an object that results from dividing the object in time is a temporal part.

Temporary Identity
A type of numerical identity according to which X and Y can be identical at one time and nonidentical at another time.

Temporary Intrinsics (Problem of)
How can one object possess inconsistent or incompatible intrinsic properties over time, without absurdity?

Three-Dimensionalism
The view that objects or people have spatial but not temporal parts.

Time (A Theory vs B Theory)
Recent philosophical treatments of time often divide between what J. M. E. McTaggart called A-theory (or tensed) approaches and B-theory (or ordered) approaches. According to B-Theory the objective order of events exhausts the nature of time such that apparently unanalyzable A-Theory properties such as "in the present" or "three days past" are not really properties at all. A-Theory proponents maintain that tense is primitive and un-analyzable.

Tropes (Property Instances)
Individual instances of a property, for example, the redness of this apple, the flexibility of this rubber band, and the coldness of this snowball. Trope theory is used to offer an account of universals that is not committed to special abstract objects like Platonic forms.

Truthmaker
The truthmaker for a given proposition is that part of reality in virtue of which a particular proposition is true.

Universals
Entities which ground similarities and dissimilarities between objects and their properties by being (in one sense or another) jointly present in the particulars (or individuals) that share the relevant similarity and being absent in one or both of the objects that share the relevant dissimilarity.

Vagueness
Vagueness is a general term for phenomena that either lack clear boundaries or exhibit borderline cases. A putative vague object would either fail to have well-defined boundaries or lack clear identity conditions. According to various semantic theories of vagueness, there are no vague objects; vagueness is always a matter of language or concepts, not a feature of the world.

Verifiability Criterion of Meaning (Verification Principle)
The claim that a statement is meaningful just in case its truth or falsity can be empirically verified.

Index